RESIDENTIAL MORTGAGE LENDING

Fourth Edition

RESIDENTIAL MORTGAGE LENDING

Fourth Edition

Marshall W. Dennis
and
Michael J. Robertson

Prentice Hall
Englewood Cliffs, New Jersey 07632

Library of Congress Cataloging-in-Publication Data

Dennis, Marshall W.
   Residential mortgage lending / Marshall W. Dennis and Michael J.
Robertson. — 4th ed.
     p. cm.
   Includes index.
   ISBN 0-13-183815-6
    1. Mortgage loans—United States.   I. Robertson, Michael J.
II. Title.
   HG2040.5.U5D46   1995
332.7′22′0973—dc20   94-28986
                                               CIP

Acquisitions editor: Catherine Rossbach
Editorial/production supervision and
   interior design: Tally Morgan, WordCrafters Editorial Services, Inc.
Cover design: Mike Fender
Prepress/manufacturing buyer: Ilene Sanford

 © 1995 by Prentice-Hall Inc.
A Simon & Schuster Company
Englewood Cliffs, NJ 07632

Printed in the United States of America
10 9 8 7 6 5 4 3 2 1

ISBN 0-13-183815-6

Prentice-Hall International (UK) Limited, *London*
Prentice-Hall of Australia Pty, Limited, *Sydney*
Prentice-Hall Canada Inc., *Toronto*
Prentice-Hall Hispanoamericana, S.A., *Mexico*
Prentice-Hall of India Private Limited, *New Delhi*
Prentice-Hall of Japan, Inc., *Tokyo*
Simon & Schuster Asia Pte. Ltd., *Singapore*
Editora Prentice-Hall do Brasil, Ltda., *Rio de Janeiro*

CONTENTS

Chapter 6   **PROCESSING THE RESIDENTIAL MORTGAGE LOAN, 89**

Chapter 7   **UNDERWRITING THE RESIDENTIAL MORTGAGE LOAN, 115**

Chapter 8   **MORTGAGE INSURANCE, 131**

Chapter 9   **MARKETING RESIDENTIAL MORTGAGE LOANS, 153**

LIST OF FIGURES

PREFACE

The first book in what has become a series, *Fundamentals of Mortgage Lending*, was published in June 1978. During 1977, while I was writing that book, it was my expectation that revisions would be necessary every three or four years. I was completely wrong. More change has occurred in residential mortgage lending since that first book was written than had occurred during all the years since the Great Depression. This is the seventh revision of that first book in 16 years: strong evidence of the magnitude of change.

The first book and its successor, *Mortgage Lending, Fundamentals and Practices* (first and second editions), were primarily concerned with residential mortgage lending but not exclusively. Two chapters in those earlier books were devoted to the basics of income-property lending. Because of the importance and extent of recent changes in residential mortgage lending, I decided to concentrate on residential mortgage lending in the four editions of the current book.

The basic purpose of this book remains the same as prior editions: to communicate and explain the fundamentals of residential mortgage lending in as simple and concise a manner as possible. It is designed for either a new employee of a mortgage lender or a college student studying real estate finance who wants to supplement that study with practical residential mortgage lending fundamentals.

A new employee of any mortgage lender will probably need at least the first six months to understand both the specific job requirements and some of the fundamentals of residential mortgage lending. This book is for that individual, whether the employing mortgage lender is a mortgage banker, commercial bank, savings and loan institution, credit union, or savings bank.

The backgrounds of those entering the mortgage lending field today range from those with solid real estate finance training to those with no formal academic training. Whatever the background, all of these students can and will succeed if they have the ability to learn and apply what they have learned. No prior knowledge of finance or of any part of mortgage lending is assumed in this book. The reader is assumed to possess only the ability and willingness to learn.

This book discusses each topic beginning with the fundamentals and develops it to the point where the reader will have a basic understanding of that topic. Not all topics are applicable to every mortgage lender, nor are even of interest at the time to all readers, but to understand the basics of modern residential mortgage lending each subject included needs to be comprehensively understood. Changes occur so rapidly in this segment of the economy that an area in which a particular mortgage lender is not involved today may be where the growth and profit potential are tomorrow. All mortgage lenders should prepare for this growth and change by either employing suitably educated personnel or providing that education.

While explaining the fundamentals of residential mortgage lending, this book also examines the similarities and differences that exist among mortgage lenders. Basically, therefore, this text is designed to fulfill the need all mortgage lenders have for a basic text to prepare new employees for the important job of helping finance the growing housing needs of this country.

Finally, as this fourth edition is published, I am pleased to introduce Michael J. Robertson as co-author. Mike is an accomplished third-party underwriter for many mortgage lenders and is also a certified residential appraiser. Mike worked on the chapters covering processing, underwriting, appraisal, and mortgage insurance. He also prepared the conventional loan case study. I'm honored to have Mike as co-author.

ACKNOWLEDGMENTS

I am deeply indebted to a number of experts for their valuable advice and assistance in preparing this book. These individuals were most generous with their time and their experiences in mortgage lending. Some of those named assisted in the preparation of the preceding book, *Mortgage Lending, Fundamentals and Practices*, but I would like to acknowledge them again.

Kathleen J. Brace, President, Brace Financial Group, Agoura Hills, California
John P. Brady, Executive Vice President, Staten Island Savings Bank, Staten Island, New York
Jeffrey L. Briggs, Senior Vice President, Centerbank, Waterbury, Connecticut
David L. Chapman II, Executive Vice President, Lomas & Nettleton, Dallas, Texas
John D. Fitzmaurice, President, General Electric Mortgage Insurance Companies, Raleigh, North Carolina
Edwin R. Goodwin, Senior Vice President, Mortgage and Trust, Inc., Houston, Texas

Gary Hammond, Vice President, First Federal Savings and Loan of Arizona, Phoenix, Arizona

Stuart M. Lopes, Senior Vice President, General Electric Mortgage Insurance Companies, Raleigh, North Carolina

Robert F. McSwain, Consultant, Boston, Massachusetts

Brian L. McDonnell, Director, Mortgage Department, Navy Federal Credit Union, Vienna, Virginia

Ted A. Miller, Vice President, General Electric Mortgage Insurance Companies, Raleigh, North Carolina

Donna J. Pillard, Senior Vice President, Thomson-McKinnion Mortgage Securities, Inc., Memphis, Tennessee

Paul M. Sallarulo, Senior Vice President, Meridan Capital Markets, Fort Lauderdale, Florida

A special thanks to Systems and Forms, Chicago, Illinois, for supplying many of the mortgage forms.

For any possible errors, omissions, or faulty analysis, the author assumes full and sole responsibility.

Finally, a special thank you to my wife, Marilyn, for her many hours of tedious reading of the proofs.

Marshall W. Dennis
Monroe, Connecticut

RESIDENTIAL MORTGAGE LENDING

Fourth Edition

HISTORY OF
MORTGAGE LENDING ——— *1*

Today's student or practitioner of residential mortgage lending may be hard-pressed to keep pace with this rapidly changing business. This is a segment of our society and economy that indeed changes from year to year, if not month to month. The extent of the recent changes in residential mortgage lending is major and is reflected in the following topics:

- first trillion-dollar year in first mortgage originations,
- lowest interest rates in decades,
- rapid deregulation of financial institutions,
- dramatic growth in the use of mortgage-backed securities,
- evolution in alternative types of mortgage instruments,
- failure of many mortgage lending institutions,
- rise and fall of no-verification mortgages,
- reemergence of inequities in mortgage lending.

These developments could lead one to assume that all meaningful changes have occurred in the past couple of years or so. That assumption would be wrong. Mortgage lending is, and always has been, a constantly changing part of our economic life and history. The basic concepts of mortgage lending have developed over centuries, and the use of mortgages can be traced to the beginning of recorded history.

This chapter is divided into two parts. Part One describes the historical development of mortgage lending from its beginning in Babylonia until the Great Depression of the 1930s. Part Two begins with the federal government's intervention in real estate and mortgage lending activity in the 1930s. This decade is often identified as the beginning of the modern period of residential mortgage lending. The chapter ends with an examination of the issues facing residential mortgage lending today.

Many of the complexities of today's residential mortgage lending are the result of problems that existed not only half a century ago but hundreds of years ago as well. To truly understand how and why residential mortgage lending works today, an understanding of this history is essential.

PART ONE: MORTGAGE LENDING, A DEVELOPING CONCEPT

_____ *THE BEGINNING*

The underlying product in all real estate activities is land. Some sociologists claim that the use of land, the desire to acquire it, and the need to regulate its transfer were among the fundamental reasons for the development of governments and laws. As government units developed, laws were formulated to govern the ownership and use of land. Because of the importance of land in an agrarian society, it was soon being used as security for the performance of such obligations as debt repayment and the fulfillment of military service.

Evidence of transactions involving land as security has been uncovered in such ancient civilizations as Babylonia and Egypt. Many of the basic principles of mortgage lending—including the essential elements of naming the borrower, naming the lender, and describing the property—were developed in these early civilizations. For example, there is evidence that the Egyptians were the first to use surveys to describe mortgaged land. This practice was undoubtedly necessitated by the annual flooding of the Nile River, which often obliterated property markers.

During the period when Greek civilization was at its peak, temple leaders often loaned money with real estate as security. In fact, throughout history organized religion has taken a strong interest in real estate and related activities.

_____ *ROMAN LAW*

The Roman Empire developed mortgage lending to a high level of sophistication, beginning with the *fiducia*. This transaction was an actual transfer of possession and title to land. It was subject to an additional agreement that stated that if the borrower fulfilled the obligation a reconveyance would occur. As Roman government became stronger and the law more clearly defined, a new concept of security called the *pignus* was developed. No title transfer occurred. Instead, the land was "pawned." According to this concept, title and possession remained with the borrower, but the lender could take possession of the property at any time if it was deemed that a possibility of default existed.

The most important Roman development regarding mortgages, however, was the *hypotheca*, which was a pledge. The hypotheca is similar to the lien theory (described later) that exists in most states in this country today. The title remained with the borrower, who was also allowed to retain possession of the property. Only if an actual default occurred (a failure on the part of the borrower to perform) was the lender entitled to take possession of and title to the land.

As the Roman Empire receded throughout Europe during the Dark Ages, a Germanic law introduced a new concept. A borrower was given the choice of fulfilling an obligation or losing the security. If the mortgagor defaulted, the mortgagee had to look exclusively to the property itself. This security system was called a *gage* in Germanic law: something was deposited for the performance of an agreement. As the Dark Ages continued and the governmental authority of Rome weakened to such a degree that lenders were not sure they would have support from the central authorities in securing their debts, the hypotheca system decayed and died, and the more primitive concept of the fiducia returned.

ENGLISH DEVELOPMENTS

Later, in Europe, a new system of government and social structure, the feudal system, became widespread. The essential characteristic of the feudal system was the totality of the king's control. He was the owner of all lands and granted their use to certain lords in return for their military fealty. Lords given the use of the land were permitted to continue on the land as long as they fulfilled a military obligation to the king. If this obligation was not fulfilled, or if the lord died, the use of the land was revoked and given to others. In this situation, land served as a security for the performance of an obligation—military service.

Along with the feudal system of land tenure, the Germanic system of the gage was introduced into early English law by William of Normandy in 1066 following the successful invasion of England. The word *mortgage* was not found in English literature until after the Norman invasion. It derives from the French words *mort,* meaning *dead* (the land was *dead* since the mortgagor could not use or derive income from it), and *gage,* meaning *pledge*. During the years after the Norman invasion, the Catholic Church established civil law in England. The Church's policy at this time was that the charging of any interest for money loaned was usury.

As the common law evolved in England, there occurred a gradual shift from a concept of favoritism or protection of the mortgagee to favoritism or protection of the mortgagor. Finally, the common law reached a more balanced position. The initial concept of mortgagee favoritism was dictated by the realities of the economic and legal systems that existed at this early stage of mortgage development.

Mortgage lending was not a common occurrence during this period for two reasons: first, there was very little need for it; and second, no incentive to lend existed without the ability to collect interest. The mortgage lending that did occur was not for the purpose of providing funds to purchase real estate but was usually provided to finance large purchases (such as a new mill or livestock) or perhaps to prepare a dowry for a daughter. Since lenders could not collect interest on these loans, they would take both title and possession of a designated portion of the borrower's land and thus be entitled to all rents and profits. When the obligation was fulfilled, title was reconveyed to the mortgagor. If the mortgagor defaulted, the mortgagee would permanently retain title and possession of the mortgaged land. The mortgagee was also still entitled to expect performance of the underlying obligation.

During the fifteenth century, courts of equity allowed the mortgagor to perform the obligation, even after the required date, and redeem the property. This concept was expanded, and by 1625 nearly all existing mortgage lending practices had ended because a mortgagee never knew when a mortgagor might perform and thus redeem the property. To alleviate this problem, mortgagees would petition the court for a decree requiring the mortgagor to redeem the property within six months or lose the right to do so.

AMERICAN DEVELOPMENTS

Westward expansion in America following the Revolutionary War was financed by land development banks that borrowed primarily in Europe to finance their land purchases in the developing West. Much of this land acquisition was speculative and eventually culminated in the bankruptcy of nearly all these land development banks. Thereafter little, if any, real estate financing was done on an organized basis until after the Civil War.

During the first 75 years of this country's history, most of the population lived on small farms whose ownership was passed down through families. Little need existed for mortgage lending in this society except for an occasional purchase of new land or for seed money. The small amount of mortgage lending that did occur during this period was provided primarily by family and friends. It is important to realize that until the 1920s, the largest category of mortgage lenders in the United States was composed of individuals, not financial institutions.

Thrift Institutions

The birth of various thrift institutions provided an opportunity for change in mortgage lending. The first thrift institution formed was a mutual savings bank, the Philadelphia Savings Fund Society, which was established in 1816. Of greater long-term importance to mortgage lending was the organization of the first building society in the United States. Modeled after societies that had existed in England and Scotland for 50 years, the Oxford

Provident Building Association was organized in 1831 in Frankfort, Pennsylvania. This association, like the ones that soon followed, was intended to exist only long enough for all the organizers to obtain funds to purchase homes. Ironically, the first loan made by this association became delinquent and another member of the association assumed the debt and took possession of the house. Later, other associations were formed, providing a popular means of financing home purchases across the United States.

Even with these new financial institutions, mortgage lending was still not an important part of the economy in the first half of the nineteenth century. Most families still lived on farms, which met basically all their requirements. No urgent need for savings existed. Away from the farm there were few employment opportunities where excess cash could be accumulated for savings. The concept of saving was still new, and the number of active savers was very small. Then, as now, the impetus for mortgage lending was the inflow of savings to the institutions that would lend funds.

Mortgage Companies

After the Civil War, the nation's expansion continued and developments in mortgage lending resumed. Starting with a new westward expansion, which opened virgin lands for farming, a regular farm mortgage business developed in the predominantly rural Midwest. The Midwest is an area where many mortgage companies began, and it still has one of the heaviest concentrations of mortgage companies.

These companies did not originate mortgage loans for their own portfolios, as did the thrift institutions. Rather, these loans were for direct sale to wealthy individuals or to institutional investors such as life insurance companies. Most of these individual and institutional investors were located on the East Coast and needed local mortgage companies to originate loans for them. This need developed into the mortgage loan correspondent system.

The bulk of the mortgage business consisted of financing farms, usually with a prevailing loan-to-value ratio of 40 percent. An occasional 50 percent loan might be made on a farm in a well-developed area. The term of the loan was short (less than five years), with interest payable semiannually and the principal paid at the end of the term. By 1900, outstanding farm mortgages originated by these mortgage companies totaled more than $4 billion.

During this period of time, the population movement to urban areas began to increase, swelled by the ever-mounting numbers of immigrants. In 1892, the United States League of Savings Associations, a trade organization, was founded in response to the expanding savings and loan industry. These institutions provided urban residents a place to save money and a source of funds to use in purchasing homes. Some of these mortgages made by savings and loan associations were repaid on an installment basis and not at the expiration of the term, as were mortgages from other types of lenders.

Commercial Banks

Commercial banks made few real estate loans until the Civil War, when a sudden demand for loans to finance new farmsteads encouraged state-chartered commercial banks to make low-ratio farm mortgages. Except for a brief period of time, federally chartered commercial banks could not make real estate loans.

This competition from state-chartered banks eventually forced a change in federal banking law. In 1913 the Federal Reserve Act authorized federally chartered banks to lend money on real estate. This initial authorization limited mortgage loans to improved farms for a five-year term with the loan-to-value ratio of 50 percent. This authorization was extended in 1916 to include one-year loans on urban real estate.

Many changes have occurred in both state and federal laws relating to the types and terms of mortgage loans made by commercial banks. These changes have tended to lag behind advances made by other mortgage lenders. However, the contribution made by commercial banks to mortgage lending has been meaningful, especially in those areas of the country where they function as the principal mortgage lender.

Turn of the Century

During the period from 1870 to the early 1900s, a few mortgage companies in or near urban areas began to make loans on single-family houses. Initially, such loans constituted a very small percentage of their business, but they gradually grew to account for more and more total origination volume. The Farm Mortgage Bankers Association, a trade organization formed in 1914, changed its name in 1923 to the Mortgage Bankers Association to reflect the increasing emphasis on residential lending.

In the first two decades of this century the typical loan made by a mortgage company on a single-family dwelling called for no more than a 50 percent loan-to-value ratio, with a three- to five-year mortgage term. There were no provisions for amortization of the loan, and interest was generally payable semiannually. The majority of these mortgages were renewed upon maturity, since few families had the money to retire the debt. The mortgage companies originating these mortgages charged the borrower from 1 to 3 percent of the amount of the loan as a fee. Upon renewal, an additional 1 percent fee would be charged.

As the twentieth century progressed, thrift institutions—especially savings and loan associations—continued to expand. Savings banks, which had their greatest growth after the Civil War, remained principally in the New England states, but savings and loan institutions continued to grow and spread across the country. During this time, thrift institutions were originating short-term mortgage loans for their own portfolios.

All mortgage lenders participated in the real estate boom years of the 1920s. This was a period of unrestrained optimism. Most Americans believed growth and prosperity would continue forever. Real estate prices appreciated as much as 25 to 50 percent per year during the first half of the decade. Many lenders forgot their underwriting standards, believing that inflating prices would bail out any bad loan. As with any speculative period, the end came, and along with it, many personal fortunes were dissipated.

Depression Era

The real estate boom of the 1920s began to show signs of weakening long before the stock market crash. By 1927, real estate values that had appreciated excessively in the early 1920s began to decline dramatically. Following the disastrous dive of the stock market in 1929, the entire economy of the United States was in danger of collapse. Real estate values plunged to less than half the level of the year before. The ability of both the individual borrower and the income-property mortgagor to meet quarterly or semiannual interest payments was reduced by the large-scale unemployment that followed the collapse of the stock market and the loss of economic vitality throughout the nation.

Because periodic amortization of mortgages was not common, a six-month lag often occurred before an institutional investor realized a mortgage was in trouble. In addition, the various financial institutions were faced with a severe liquidity crisis, which required them to sell vast real estate and mortgage holdings under very unfavorable conditions. This need to sell real estate holdings to obtain cash, coupled with a rise in foreclosures and tax sales, severely depressed an already crumbling real estate market. Many individual homeowners were threatened with property loss even if they retained their jobs because when their five-year mortgages expired, many were unable to refinance their mortgages: lenders were caught in the liquidity crisis and did not have the funds to lend.

Thrift institutions also experienced problems during this period even though some of their mortgagors had installment-type mortgages. As many workers lost their jobs and unemployment reached 25 percent, the savings inflow to thrifts diminished drastically. All types of financial institutions began to fail, and as a result savers withdrew funds and the liquidity crisis worsened for all lenders. In the early 1930s, many commercial banks and savings and loan institutions failed due to massive withdrawals of savings and the high foreclosure rate. By 1935, 20 percent of all mortgage assets were in the "real estate owned" category.

The vast majority of all foreclosures during the 1930s were made by second and third mortgagees who needed to foreclose immediately in order to protect what little security they had. The highest number of foreclosures occurred from 1931–35, averaging 250,000 each year. The increasing number of foreclosures, especially on family farms in the Midwest, forced the beginning of compulsory moratoria. In the Midwest, where economic deterioration was aggravated by the dust bowl storms, the cry for a moratorium reached the stage of near rebellion, and some violence occurred. Reacting to the hysteria sweeping the farm belt and some of the larger cities, many mortgagees voluntarily instituted forbearance, some for as long as two years. The first law requiring a mortgage moratorium became effective in Iowa in February 1933. Over the next 18 months, 27 states enacted legislation suspending nearly all foreclosures. Most of the moratorium laws enacted during this period were intended to last for two years or less, although many were reenacted and allowed to continue as law until the early 1940s.

It is important to note that during the period when these laws were in effect, some foreclosures did occur. The determining factor on whether to grant relief was the soundness of a debtor's fundamental economic position. If it were determined that a debtor would eventually lose the land anyway, postponing the foreclosure or granting a moratorium was considered a waste of time and an injustice to the creditor. The moratoria of the early 1930s did not provide a solution to the underlying economic problems, but they did provide a respite during which public unrest could be soothed and the federal government could introduce some economic remedies.

PART TWO: GOVERNMENT INTERVENTION

In the early 1930s, the federal government realized that the drop in real estate values would continue to add to the growing depression of the entire economy, preventing its revitalization. Therefore, the government instituted a series of programs designed to help stabilize real estate values and, it was hoped, the entire economy. This marked the beginning of a drastic reversal in previous governmental political philosophy, which had been generally laissez-faire.

FEDERAL LEGISLATION

Beginning in the last year of the Hoover administration, federal legislation usurped, in large measure, control over real estate and mortgage lending activities, which previously had been left to the states.

The first legislation designed to meet the threat of the Depression created the Reconstruction Finance Corporation (RFC) in 1932, which, among other things, provided liquidity to commercial banks. Shortly thereafter, the Federal Home Loan Bank (FHLB) was created to provide a central credit facility to home finance institutions, primarily savings and loan institutions. The next major legislation was the Home Owners Loan Act (HOLA) in 1933. This act provided for federal charters for savings and loan institutions and created the Home Owners Loan Corporation (HOLC), which was designed to provide emergency relief to homeowners by refinancing or purchasing defaulted mortgages. This program kept many tens of thousands of families from losing their homes in the 1930s.

One of the most far-reaching enactments of this period was the National Housing Act (1934), which created the Federal Housing Administration (FHA) and the Federal Savings and Loan Insurance Corporation (FSLIC). FSLIC and the Federal Deposit Insurance Corporation (FDIC) were instrumental in encouraging depositors to return desperately needed deposits to financial institutions. The FHA has provided the framework and the impetus necessary for the development of a true national mortgage market. The FHA has also been credited with either initiating or making popular many innovations in mortgage lending, such as mortgage insurance and the long-term, self-amortizing mortgage.

THE GROWTH ERA

A minimal amount of single-family housing construction occurred from 1926 to 1946 as a result of the Depression and World War II. At the end of the war, however, five million servicemen returned home, and a tremendous demand for housing was created. The government, as part of its responsibility to returning veterans, as well as a way of stimulating housing, passed the Servicemen's Readjustment Act (1944). One of the major features of this act was a guaranty program that provided a desirable way of financing homes for veterans. The most distinguishing characteristic of this guaranty program (then and now) is the lack of a down payment requirement for eligible veterans. Under this program no mortgage insurance premiums are collected from veterans; instead, the government absorbs the cost of the mortgage guaranty.

The highly liquid position of financial institutions was the second great impetus to the rapid expansion of single-family housing construction following World War II. In 1945, more than half of the assets of financial institutions were tied up in the no-risk but low-yielding government securities that institutions were obligated to purchase during World War II. At the end of the war, these bonds could be sold and the cash converted into mortgages, which provided a higher yield.

The greatest boom in housing construction in the history of this country, and possibly the world, occurred from 1945 to 1955. The two government housing programs (FHA and VA), the built-up demand for housing, and the liquid position of lenders were instrumental in this dramatic growth in housing. Since the end of World War II, mortgages have been the largest user of long-term credit in the entire American economy.

Housing Act of 1949

The Housing Act of 1949 is one of the most important pieces of social legislation in the past 50 years because of the national commitment made to provide "a decent home and suitable living environment for every American family." Much of the legislative action in the housing and mortgage lending field since then has been an attempt to fulfill that commendable but probably unrealistic goal.

The 1950s and early 1960s were a period of national optimism, economic growth, and, as far as mortgage lending is concerned, a relatively quiet period in the legislative arena. This period of tranquility soon dissipated in the face of an onslaught of such national crises as political assassinations, civil rights demonstrations, urban blight, and the war in Vietnam.

Department of Housing and Urban Development

The lack of adequate housing, a situation often associated with poverty, was partially addressed in 1965 by the consolidation of the many federal housing agencies into a new cabinet-level department, the Department of Housing and Urban Development (HUD). HUD was to be the focal point of much of the new legislation in the years to come as it assumed a dominant position in regulating real estate and mortgage lending.

The avalanche of legislation and regulation that was to so change mortgage lending began a few years after HUD was created, when the Housing and Urban Development Act (1968) was enacted. This was the first major legislation in the mortgage lending field in over a decade. The act committed the government to a goal of 26 million new housing starts in the next decade. At the time, many argued that this goal was not practical on either fiscal or political grounds. However, the act introduced a new concept in government programs for residential real estate by adopting the principle of subsidizing interest rates.

These government subsidy programs, combined with national economic growth, stimulated housing production in 1972 to more than three million units—the highest ever. With political pressure to increase housing production, the inevitable problems developed almost immediately. Report of possible scandals in subsidized housing began to appear in 1971, involving FHA officials and some mortgage lenders. These scandals were followed by congressional investigations, which spotlighted the unforeseen high costs of these programs.

In January of 1973, President Richard Nixon ordered a freeze on all subsidy programs. This was partially lifted later but only after a thorough review of government programs by a special task force created by HUD. This task force reviewed the history of government involvement in real estate and analyzed the impact of the various subsidy programs on housing. The task force concluded that the goal of providing home ownership for everyone was neither practical nor desirable when weighed against the cost.

The government's concept changed from subsidizing home ownership to subsidizing rent. The Housing and Community Development Act (1974) formalized this change with the Section 8 program. This program allows low- and moderate-income families to choose the rental unit in the community in which they want to live, with the government subsidizing the amount of fair market rent that is in excess of 25 percent of the family's monthly income. This program provides assistance both to families that could not afford the minimal housing expenses stipulated in prior programs and to families whose incomes were just over the maximum income limit to qualify for assistance in home purchasing.

Consumer Protection

The way residential mortgage lending is conducted today is controlled to a great extent by a series of federal laws and regulations. The Consumer Protection Act of 1968 was the first in a series of legislative acts that redefined the concept of consumer protection regarding mortgage lending, thus changing forever the way in which residential mortgage lending is conducted. Through the next three decades, the federal government has been striving to remove all inequities from residential mortgage lending. These actions have met with mostly good results, but occasionally inequities still appear. The various pieces of federal legislation are discussed in detail where appropriate throughout this book.

 **ROLE OF GOVERNMENT**

The government's role in the management of the nation's economy in general, and mortgage lending in particular, is one that has been analyzed and debated many times—and undoubtedly will continue to be in the future. There seems to be little argument that government, regardless of whether it is federal, state, or local, has an obligation to its citizens to provide adequate shelter for all—even if they cannot afford it themselves. There are many arguments, though, regarding how to provide this basic necessity. Over the past decade, the federal government tried helping people in need of shelter in a variety of ways, first by providing rent assistance, then mortgage assistance so people could purchase rather than rent, and, finally, by returning to subsidizing rent payments.

Recently, some commentators have suggested that excessive governmental interference has resulted in fewer families being able to afford the average-priced home. That may be true, but most governmental laws and regulations have had a commendable impact on real estate and mortgage lending. The Interstate Land Sales Full Disclosure Act (1968), which helped to prevent fraudulent land sales, is an obvious example. Many of these new laws and regulations were necessitated by excesses and failures on the part of the lending community. The contribution of some of these laws cannot be overstated. In fact, one governmental creation, the Federal Housing Administration, has provided the framework for a modern, vibrant mortgage lending system that has made this the best-housed nation in the world.

Following is a listing of the more important federal legislative acts impacting residential mortgage lending.

1913—Federal Reserve Act. Established the Federal Reserve System and authorized federally chartered commercial banks to make real estate loans.

1916—Federal Farm Loan Act. Provided for the formation of Federal Land Bank Associations as units of the Federal Land Bank System, which was given authority to generate funds for loans to farmers by the sale of bonds.

1932—Reconstruction Finance Act. Created the Reconstruction Finance Corporation, which was designed, among other things, to provide liquidity to commercial banks.

1932—Federal Home Loan Bank Act. Established the Federal Home Loan Bank Board and 12 regional banks to provide central credit facilities for home finance institutions that were members of the FHLB.

1932—Home Owners Loan Act. This act produced two results: (1) created the Home Owners Loan Corporation with authority to purchase defaulted home mortgages and to refinance as many as prudently feasible; (2) provided the basic lending authority for federally chartered savings and loan associations.

1934—National Housing Act. Authorized the creation of the Federal Housing Administration and Federal Savings and Loan Insurance Corporation.

1938—National Mortgage Association of Washington. This governmental agency, soon renamed the Federal National Mortgage Association, was authorized to provide secondary mortgage market support for FHA mortgages.

1944—Servicemen's Readjustment Act. Established within the VeteransAdministration as a mortgage guarantee program for qualified veterans.

1949—Housing Act. Stated that the national housing goal was to provide "a decent home and suitable living environment for every American family." Consolidated past lending programs of the Farmers Home Administration.

1961—Consolidated Farmers Home Administration Act. Extended authority for the agency to make mortgage loans to nonfarmers in rural areas.

1965—Housing and Urban Development Act. Consolidated many federal housing agencies into a new Department of Housing and Urban Development with expanded authority.

1966—Interest Rate Adjustment Act. Authorized the setting of maximum savings rates and the creation of a differential between the savings rates of commercial banks and thrift institutions.

1968—Fair Housing Act. Prohibited discrimination in real estate sales and mortgage lending based on race, color, national origin, and religion.

1968—Interstate Land Sales Full Disclosure Act. Required complete and full disclosure of all facts regarding interstate sale of real estate.

1968—Consumer Credit Protection Act. Contained Title I, better known as Truth-in-Lending, which authorized the Federal Reserve Board to formulate regulations (Reg Z) requiring advanced disclosure of the amount and type of finance charge and a calculation of the annual percentage rate. Title VI, better known as the Fair Credit Reporting Act, established disclosure requirements regarding the nature of credit information used in determining whether to grant a loan.

1968—Housing and Urban Development Act. This act put the existing Federal National Mortgage Association in private hands and authorized it to continue secondary mortgage market support. The act created a new governmental agency, the Government National Mortgage Association, and authorized it to continue the FNMA special assistance function and guarantee mortgage-backed securities.

1969—National Environmental Policy Act. Required the preparation of an Environmental Impact Statement for the Council on Environmental Quality in order to determine the environmental impact of real estate development.

1970—Emergency Home Finance Act. Created a new secondary mortgage market participant, the Federal Home Loan Mortgage Corporation, which had as its stated objective providing secondary mortgage support for conventional mortgages originated by thrift institutions. The act also gave FNMA authority to purchase conventional mortgages in addition to FHA/VA.

1974—Flood Disaster Protection Act. Effective in 1975, mortgage loans could not be made in a flood hazard area unless flood insurance had been purchased.

1974—Real Estate Settlement Procedures Act (RESPA) (as amended in 1976 and 1992). This act as amended required mortgage lenders to provide mortgage borrowers with an advance disclosure of loan settlement costs and charges. Further, this act prohibited kickbacks to any person for referring business. The 1976 amendment required lenders to provide applicants with a Good Faith Estimate of Settlement Costs and a HUD booklet. A Uniform Settlement Statement (HUD-1) must be furnished to the borrower before or at the settlement. The 1992 amendment extended RESPA to subordinate financing, effective 1993.

1974—Equal Credit Opportunity Act (ECOA) (as amended in 1976). This act as amended prohibited discrimination in lending on the basis of sex, marital status, age, race, color, national origin, religion, good faith reliance on consumer protection laws, or the fact that a borrower receives public assistance. In addition, if an application is rejected, the borrower must be notified within 30 days of the reason for rejection.

1975—Home Mortgage Disclosure Act (HMDA) as amended in 1992. This act required disclosure by most mortgage lenders of geographic distribution of loans in metropolitan statistical areas. The purpose was to establish lending patterns of lenders.

1976—RESPA amendment (see 1974).

1976—ECOA amendment (see 1974).

1978—Fair Lending Practices Regulations. These FHLB regulations required members to develop written underwriting standards, keep a loan registry, not deny loans because of age of dwelling or condition of neighborhood, and direct advertising to all segments of the community.

1978—Community Reinvestment Act. This act required FSLIC-insured institutions to adopt a community reinvestment statement, which delineates the community in which they will invest; maintain a public comment file; and post a CRA notice.

1979—Housing and Community Development Amendments. This legislation exempted FHA-insured mortgages from state and local usury ceilings. (Other concurrent legislation exempted VA and conventional mortgages.)

1980—Depository Institutions Deregulation and Monetary Control Act. Congress extended the savings interest rate control and thrift institution's ¼ of 1 percent differential for six years. The act also extended the federal override of state usury ceilings on certain mortgages. Other changes included simplified truth-in-lending standards and eased lending restrictions, including geographical limitations, loan-to-value ratios, and treatment of one-family loans exceeding specified dollar amounts.

1980—Omnibus Reconciliation Act. Limited the issuance of tax-exempt housing mortgage revenue bonds.

1982—Garn–St. Germain Depository Institutions Act. Preempted state due-on-sale loan restrictions; mandated phase-out of interest rate differential by January 1, 1984; provided FSLIC and FDIC assistance for institutions with deficient net worth; and allowed savings and loans to make consumer, commercial, and agricultural loans.

1984—Deficit Reduction Act. Extended the tax exemption for qualified mortgage subsidy bonds; created new reporting procedures for mortgage interest.

1986—Tax Reform Act. Reduced top corporate tax rate from 46 percent to 34 percent; reduced taxable income bad debt deduction from 40 percent to 8 percent; provided for 3-year carrybacks and 15-year carryforwards for savings institution net operating losses.

1987—Competitive Equality Banking Act. Set the FSLIC $10.8 billion recapitalization in motion, kept intact Savings Bank Life Insurance, and gave thrifts flexibility to form different types of holding companies.

1987—Housing and Community Development Act. Notice of availability of counseling must be given within 45 days of delinquency on single-family primary residence.

1989—Financial Institutions Reform, Recovery and Enforcement Act (FIRREA). Restructured the regulatory framework by eliminating FHLBB, FSLIC, and FADA; created the Office of Thrift Supervision (OTS) under the Treasury Department; enhanced FDIC to supervise safety and soundness of financial institutions, the Savings Institutions Insurance Fund, and the Bank Insurance Fund; created the Resolution Trust Corporation (RTC) to dispose of failed savings and loans; established new capital standards for thrifts.

1992—RESPA amendment (see 1974). Coverage of RESPA is extended to subordinate financing.

1992—HMDA amendment (see 1976). Mortgage companies and other non-
depository institutions required to comply with HMDA.

RECENT RESIDENTIAL MORTGAGE LENDING

The most productive boom in real estate construction and financing in the
United States has occurred during the past 30 years. More housing units and
other types of buildings have been constructed during this period than in all
the years since this country was founded. Much of the credit for this boom can
be attached to the availability of capital at a reasonable rate and the corresponding creation of the secondary mortgage market. For example, FNMA
was given expanded purchasing authority in 1970 and was joined by the Federal Home Loan Mortgage Corporation (FHLMC) in that year to provide secondary market facilities for conventional mortgages originated by savings and
loan institutions. While the housing boom changed the landscape of the American countryside, new office buildings, apartment complexes, and shopping
centers provided the amenities and services needed by the families in these
new homes.

   In the 1970s, providing or stimulating housing for low- and moderate-
income families was not the exclusive province of government at the federal
level. Before 1960, the state of New York had the only state housing agency,
but by 1975 nearly all states had some type of housing agency. Although some
states have used tax-exempt bonds to raise revenue to lend to home buyers at
below-market interest rates, many have fulfilled their social responsibility by
providing financing for multi-family units.

1980S: THE DECADE OF HISTORIC CHANGE

The decade of the 1980s will be remembered as the decade when the economy
went through startling changes and as a result, changed residential mortgage
lending and mortgage lenders. This period witnessed positive developments
such as the rapid growth of mortgage-backed securities, the evolution of alternative mortgage instruments, and, in general, more sources of needed capital.
All of these positive developments, combined with much lower interest rates,
resulted in one- to four-family originations of nearly $500 billion in both 1986
and 1987.

   However, the decade also witnessed double-digit inflation, a major recession, a record high for the Dow-Jones average, and then a crash exceeding
that of 1929. The decade ended with the near total collapse of the savings and
loan industry and the related taxpayer bailout of the Federal Savings and Loan
Insurance Corporation (FSLIC). All of these events produced drastic changes
for the nation's economy in general and for mortgage lending in particular.

Federal Reserve and the Money Supply

The 1980s began with the nation's economy clearly out of control. The Federal Reserve, responsible for managing and regulating interest rates and monetary supply, was forced in the fall of 1979 to bring about some order to the economy. Its fundamental decision was to stop attempting to regulate short-term interest rates and, instead, to exercise control over growth in the money supply. The theory was that control of the money supply would help reduce inflation and that this, in turn, would decrease upward pressure on interest rates as investors decreased their need for inflation protection.

The immediate result of this action was sharply higher interest rates. The most visible rate, the so-called prime rate, peaked at 21½ percent in 1981. Interest rates did come down fairly rapidly after that peak, partially as a result of the Federal Reserve action but primarily because of the serious recession that followed that action. The recession that followed, the worst since the Great Depression, resulted in unemployment reaching over 10 percent. This recession and the action of the Federal Reserve deflated the inflation balloon to the point where inflation in the mid-1980s fell to about 1 percent per year before turning up modestly at the end of the decade. As a reaction to control overinflation, the prime interest rate dropped sharply to 7½ percent by the spring of 1987 before turning up slightly.

With inflation under control and interest rates declining, the stock market rocketed to levels only dreamed of by the most optimistic of market watchers—the Dow-Jones average hit a record of 2722. Some market watchers were

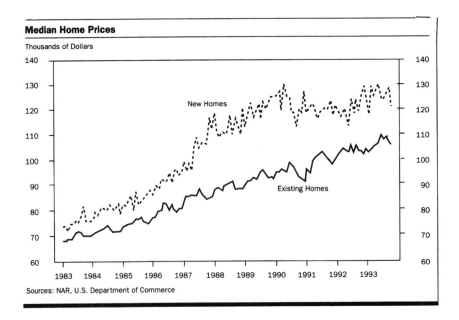

Median Home Prices

Thousands of Dollars

New Homes

Existing Homes

Sources: NAR, U.S. Department of Commerce

calling for 3000 by the end of the year, but what happened instead was a crash that exceeded (in points, but not percent) the 1929 crash. Wall Street was shocked by a 508-point drop in the Dow-Jones average on October 19, 1987. A week later the market dropped another 175 points. The sound heard around the world was the hard landing of other stock exchanges as they followed the lead of Wall Street.

The reasons for the crash of 1987 are many and varied, but the two principal ones are that the market was simply overvalued and that investors in the United States and abroad had lost faith in the ability of the United States government to control its huge deficit. The federal deficits for the second half of the 1980s averaged approximately $150 billion a year. These huge deficits have turned the United States into the world's largest debtor nation owing hundreds of billions of dollars to foreigners. The impact of the crash of 1987 and the 1990–91 recession chilled the home purchasing plans of many Americans and originations trailed off for the rest of the decade from the record years of 1986–87.

Financial Institutions Reform, Recovery and Enforcement Act (FIRREA)

By 1988, the problems of the savings and loan industry, which had been festering since the late 1970s, reached a climax. Many savings and loan associations in the 1980s were characterized by speculative lending, negative earnings, low capital, and poor management. These problems eventually culminated in the failure of many of these savings and loan associations and the insolvency of the Federal Savings and Loan Insurance Corporation (FSLIC)—the deposit insurance fund for savings and loan associations.

The failure of FSLIC precipitated a massive federal bailout of the insurance fund and the closing of hundreds of failed savings and loans. The 1989 law, which mandated these changes, was called the Financial Institutions Reform, Recovery, and Enforcement Act (FIRREA). The cost of this federal bailout is projected to be as high as $400–$500 billion over the life of the bonds sold to finance the bailout.

1990S: BOOM YEARS

The 1990s began with a recession that purged much of the spending excesses of the 1980s from the United States economy. Unemployment reached a little over 7 percent throughout the United States, but in some areas, especially New England and California, unemployment exceeded 10 percent. As the Cold War ended with the fall of Communism throughout Europe, the American defense budget was cut and cut again, resulting in tens of thousands of Americans losing their jobs in defense-related industries. With the economy in trouble

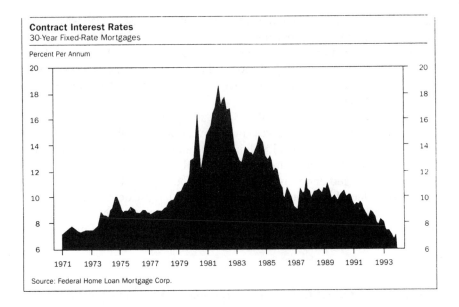

Contract Interest Rates
30-Year Fixed-Rate Mortgages

Percent Per Annum

Source: Federal Home Loan Mortgage Corp.

and unemployment up, consumers stopped spending. This change in consumer attitudes toward spending, when combined with a drop in inflation, convinced the Federal Reserve to lower interest rates in the hope this would stimulate business to expand and hire more workers.

At first, this drop in interest rates had another benefit, as Americans jumped to refinance their home mortgages at interest rates unheard of in decades. This wave of refinancings of homes during the years 1991–93 allowed millions of Americans to refinance their home mortgages at interest rates that were the lowest in 20 years. During one period late in 1993, 30-year fixed-rate mortgages were actually below 7 percent. It is estimated that American homeowners, as a result of these refinancings, will annually save tens of billions of dollars in mortgage payments. Much of the money saved from the lower mortgage payments will be used to purchase consumer goods, thus helping to stimulate the economy in general. In 1993, one- to four-family first mortgage originations reached the staggering level of $1.1 trillion! Of that amount, approximately 55 percent was from refinancing of existing mortgages. This was the first time ever that refinancings exceeded purchase money mortgages for a whole year.

Although mortgage originators profited greatly with the millions of mortgages refinanced, many mortgage servicers were hurt badly by the refinancings. These servicers had expected the refinanced loans to remain on the books for a long enough period of time to make a profit on servicing those loans. This expectation was not borne out as some consumers refinanced their mortgages two and three times within a three-year period. On the other hand, mortgage servicers will benefit from the refinanced loans since the new loans at lower rates (about a third of outstanding mortgages now carry rates that are historically low) will have a much longer life than normal. These servicers will enjoy a longer stream of servicing income; thus the value of the servicing of those refinanced mortgages has increased. An interesting sidebar to the story of the surge in refinancing is that the overall quality of loans serviced improved as delinquencies hit a 20-year low in 1993.

New Administration and Deficit Reduction

After the success of Desert Storm, it appeared President Bush would have little trouble with reelection, but the economy continued to deteriorate and other politicians entered the race for president. In a three-way race, Governor William Clinton, a Democrat from Arkansas, was elected president.

During President Clinton's first year in office an agreement was reached between the president and Congress on a deficit reduction package that, if not later modified by Congress, could help reduce the federal budget deficit gradually over a number of years. The financial markets reacted positively to Congress finally reaching some closure on deficit reduction and as a result, interest rates continued to decline throughout 1993.

Interest rates bottomed in late 1993 at 20-year lows and began a modest turn upward in 1994 led by Federal Reserve action designed to keep a lid on inflation. The result was fewer mortgages being refinanced, although purchase money mortgages did increase. As refinancing returns to the more normal 25–30 percent of originations, it is difficult to project originations reaching the level of 1993 for years to come even with the modest upturn in purchase money mortgages.

ROLE OF RESIDENTIAL MORTGAGE LENDING IN THE ECONOMY

2

The importance of housing, and therefore residential mortgage lending, to the nation's economic health is unquestionable. Economic commentators have contended from the time of the Great Depression that housing construction and related components (e.g., real estate sales, financing, furnishing, taxes, etc.) are among the most important integrals of the engine that (during most periods) powers the economy of the United States. The sharp drop in housing construction in 1989 and 1990 certainly contributed to the recession experienced in that time frame. Likewise, the substantial increase in housing construction in 1993–94 contributed significantly to the economic revival of the mid-1990s.

Examples of the economic importance of housing, and therefore residential mortgage financing, comes from the National Association of Home Builders (NAHB), which estimates that housing construction, sales, and financing account for one out of every 12 jobs in the United States. The NAHB calculates that the economic impact of the construction of 1,000 single-family houses creates nearly 1,800 worker-years of employment and over $60 million in wages.

Multiplier Effect of Housing

Over the past 50 years, housing has often provided the stimulus that produces economic growth in the American economy by the multiplier effect that results from construction and financing. It is generally accepted that housing generates about $4 in Gross Domestic Product (GDP) for every $1 of activity. NAHB expands on the economic impact of housing this way: "The servicing of housing in place—broadly defined to include brokerage services, rental housing management, mortgage lending and servicing, and repair and maintenance services—contributes another 7 percent to GDP."

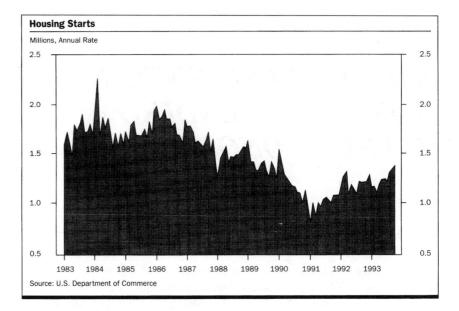

This economic stimulus is generated by:

- consumption of raw materials for construction of the home,
- wages earned by home builders, which are spent on food, clothing, cars, furniture, schooling, and taxes in addition to many other products and services,
- fees earned by real estate professionals when the homes are sold,
- interest earned by financial intermediaries on mortgage loans financing the construction and purchase of homes.

As is generally accepted, the ripple effect of a healthy home building industry stimulates the entire economy. Obviously, there can not be a healthy home building industry without mortgage lending.

Other Economic Benefits

Another economic benefit derived from residential mortgage lending is that it provides a means whereby an attractive return on savings can be generated for those individuals who are in the saving cycle of their lives. Residential mortgage lending could not provide these many economic benefits without the many and varied types of mortgage lenders. These lenders are discussed in detail in Chapter 3, The Mortgage Lenders.

Residential mortgage lending, in addition to being an important part of our nation's economy, also allows for the fulfillment of certain sociological

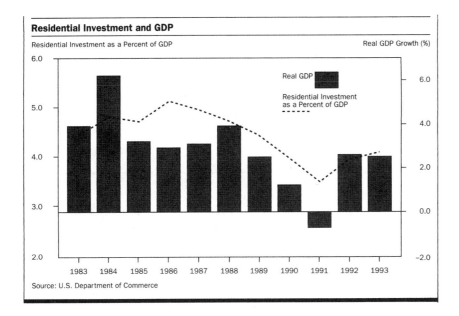

Residential Investment and GDP

Residential Investment as a Percent of GDP

Real GDP Growth (%)

Source: U.S. Department of Commerce

demands, principal among them obtaining the "American Dream"—owning a home. People who have their own home have a more substantial stake in their community and our nation's society, with many resulting benefits.

AVAILABILITY OF CREDIT

The health of the home building industry is often controlled by the availability of credit for home financing and by its cost. The demand for credit for housing grows every year. It is estimated that housing will require nearly a trillion dollars a year from the capital markets in the 1990s in order to meet the projected housing demands of consumers. This chapter examines how this money for housing is created and then made available to home buyers.

Importance of Savings to Housing

The common requisite for all residential mortgage lenders, whether depository institutions or not, is the accumulation of sufficient savings to produce the capital needed for mortgage loans. Unless financial intermediaries have access to sufficient savings, capital shortages result and credit restraints occur that affect all mortgage lenders, often with disastrous results. This has been the situation periodically in American economy history and, as a result, during those periods, housing starts and resales have dropped dramatically.

Secondary mortgage markets can assist housing somewhat during these periods of credit restraint by tapping the capital markets, but they cannot solve the basic problem of a lack of savings inflow to mortgage lenders.

Shortage of capital is not always the reason for falloffs in housing starts. The dramatic falloff in housing starts in 1989–91 was not the result of a shortage of capital for housing but rather a sharp drop in consumer confidence because of the Gulf War and a spreading recession.

CAPITAL FORMATION

The funds required for capital formation are derived primarily from the savings of individuals and businesses. This process of capital formation produces most of the capital used by the various segments of our economy. Business savings are defined as retained earnings and capital consumption allowances. They exceed personal savings by a substantial amount. However, the savings generated by individuals—either as deposits at financial institutions or as reserves in whole life insurance policies—account for approximately 90 percent of the funds used for residential mortgage lending.

Savings Rates

The importance of personal savings to residential mortgage lending cannot be overemphasized. Since the end of World War II, the personal savings rate has ranged from a low of about 3 percent of disposable income to a high of about 9 percent. These savings have permitted (except for brief periods of disintermediation) borrowers to obtain needed funds at reasonable rates. Through this process, the percentage of Americans who own the home in which they live reached an all-time high of 65 percent in the early 1980s (since then it has slipped to about 63 percent).

Savings inflows are not constant, and the savings function must compete with food, shelter, clothing, transportation, recreation, and other real or perceived demands for an individual's after-tax income. Those individuals who do save are usually motivated by such desires as accumulating funds for retirement, future security, major purchases such as a home, or a college education.

The reasons for declines in the savings rate (until just recently) include the low interest paid on passbook savings and the fact that the interest received was subject to federal, state, and (in some situations) city income taxes. Another reason for previous declines in savings rates has been inflation psychology. During the high inflation period of the early 1980s, many sophisticated individuals realized it was more prudent to borrow than save. They rationalized it made sense to borrow money now for immediate consumption and then pay back the money later with deflated dollars. That psychology, as it spread to many Americans in the early 1980s, led to a period of disintermediation—withdrawal of more money from financial intermediaries than was being deposited. During this period, capital was very short and as a result, interest rates were very high for residential mortgage loans.

Many potential savers believe that today's society offers fewer reasons for people to save than in the past. Many individuals believe, for example, that they can rely on company pensions or Social Security, or both, for retirement, thus they don't need to save. Others believe they need not accumulate additional savings because inflation has dramatically increased the equity in their home.

Recently, for a number of reasons, the savings rate has moved up moderately to about 4 percent of disposable personal income. The reasons for the increase in savings include:

- an aging population that normally saves more and borrows less,
- an erosion of confidence in the economy,
- lack of alternatives (e.g., stock market is too high)

Changes in the economy directly influence savings in many ways. For example, if the business cycle is down and unemployment increases, individuals may increase savings because of uncertainty over their employment. The result could be a savings inflow, which theoretically should cause interest rates to decline as more dollars chase less demand. On the other hand, with a downturn in the business cycle and an increase in unemployment, those who are unemployed may have to withdraw savings for living expenses. If the economy is expanding, savings may also accumulate since the demand for funds could reach a point where high interest rates attract more savings.

For a period of time, depository institutions could not attract savings during periods of high interest because limits were placed on the amount of interest that could be paid to savers. This is not the case now since limits on interest rates on savings have been deregulated and now move with the market. This change in itself will have a major impact on future availability of funds for residential mortgage lending.

MORTGAGE MARKETS

In our economy, the total financial market consists of the capital markets and the money markets. These two markets compete with each other for funds. The basic difference between the two markets is the maturity of the financial instruments. Money market instruments (U.S. Treasury bills, corporate commercial paper, etc.) mature in less than one year. Capital markets, on the other hand, are markets for long-term obligations. The mortgage market is only part of the complete capital market. Within the capital market, a specific demand for funds (e.g., mortgages) must compete with other instruments, such as corporate bonds. The competition is determined by the price a user of funds is willing to pay. The price of money is stated as the interest rate.

USERS OF CREDIT

In today's economic environment, the demand for credit is derived from three groups:

- business demand,
- consumer demand,
- government demand.

Businesses demand credit for financing inventory, accounts receivable, plant expansion and modernization, and occasionally for research and development. The magnitude of business loan demand is normally tied to the economic cycle. Business normally looks to commercial banks to provide needed capital, usually at the prime rate (or lower in some cases). If a business's credit rating is high enough, that business may look to sell commercial paper.

Consumer demand is also impacted by the economic cycle and employment. When interest rates are high, many consumers cannot qualify for a loan, thus demand falls off. Further, when unemployment increases, consumers become concerned for their employment, thus they tend to decrease borrowing. Consumer credit is used to purchase automobiles, furniture, clothing, and other durable and nondurable goods. In addition, consumer credit includes funds to purchase residential real estate (or to refinance existing home mortgages).

Finally, all levels of government have experienced insatiable appetites for borrowed funds from the late 1970s to the present time. These borrowed funds have been used primarily to finance the federal government's deficits, in addition to other local needs such as mortgage revenue bonds. The amount of borrowing by the federal government is controlled by the government's fiscal policy, which establishes spending and taxing levels. Regrettably, for all users of credit, the fiscal policy of the federal government has been to continue to spend more money than it collects.

INTEREST RATES

If the demand for available funds is high, the price for these funds (the interest rate) will probably be high as well. Therefore, the price of money is subject to supply and demand like any other commodity. For example, if the federal government is borrowing extensively to fund its deficits, the greater the demand for funds, and thus the higher mortgage interest rates will be.

Competition for Funds

As a general rule, any user of credit can obtain needed funds if he or she is willing to pay the price (interest rate) for those funds. But, when all users of credit are competing for funds at the same time, some users are in an unfavorable position. For example, if business demand for credit is high and business is willing to pay a price equal to that offered by mortgages, funds will generally flow to bonds to the detriment of mortgage lending.

The explanation for this preference for corporate debt lies in the unique characteristics of mortgage debt. Mortgage debt requires a higher yield because of the longer maturity, lack of uniformity in real estate laws, lower liquidity, and problems and delays of foreclosure. Although inflation and supply and demand for funds are most important factors in the rise and fall of interest rates, the degree of risk inherent in a mortgage loan or a bond offering also is influential. Of course, if the other major consumers of capital—the various levels of government—are also active in the capital markets, they will take all they need.

Public Debt vs. Private Debt

When any government—federal, state, or local—spends more money than it collects, it must borrow in the same markets in which other users of credit borrow. This includes issuers of corporate bonds and home buyers. In this manner government competes with other users of credit for the limited capital available. The federal government in particular has been in a severe deficit position over the past couple of decades, a condition that many economists believe was the basic cause of the persistent inflation of the early 1980s. This inflation and the continuing credit demands of the federal government resulted in high interest rates, which played havoc in both the money markets and the capital markets. As a result, all users of credit suffered during this period.

The reason why the federal government's borrowing has such a negative impact on other borrowers is that the federal government will always get as much money as it needs because of its unquestioned credit. Therefore, unless available credit is expanding at a rate that allows for the accommodation of all users of credit, excessive federal borrowing will have a crowding-out effect on less creditworthy borrowers.

As bad as the deficits of the 1970s and 1980s were, they pale in comparison to the projected deficits of the 1990s. The deficits for the early 1990s apparently will be in the range of $150–$200 billion per year. As large as these deficits are, they could have been much larger if Congress and President

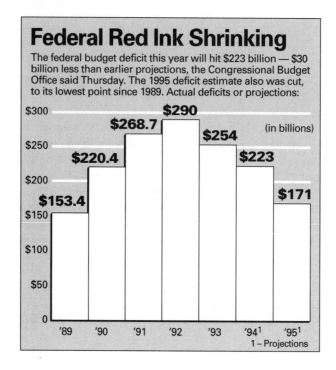

Federal Red Ink Shrinking

The federal budget deficit this year will hit $223 billion — $30 billion less than earlier projections, the Congressional Budget Office said Thursday. The 1995 deficit estimate also was cut, to its lowest point since 1989. Actual deficits or projections:

(in billions)

'89 — $153.4
'90 — $220.4
'91 — $268.7
'92 — $290
'93 — $254
'94[1] — $223
'95[1] — $171

1 – Projections

Clinton had not agreed to a deficit reduction package. Excessive federal deficits require massive borrowing, and the result is usually higher rates, which have a negative impact on all borrowers, especially home buyers.

Monetary Policy and Interest Rates

Another important element in determining interest rates is monetary policy. Monetary policy (as controlled by the Federal Reserve) occurs when the supply of money is controlled rather than interest rates. Thus, if the Federal Reserve wants to stimulate the economy, it would increase the supply of money. The fiscal policy of the federal government often forces the Federal Reserve to act in an attempt to moderate the impact of federal borrowing on the nation's economy.

FEDERAL RESERVE

In addition to its banking functions, the Federal Reserve has credit control responsibility over the nation's economy through financial institutions. The Federal Reserve has several methods of implementing this control:

- Reserve requirements. By increasing the amount of money a member institution must have in its reserve account, less money is available to be loaned. Conversely, if the Federal Reserve policy is to increase the amount of money in order to make credit easier to obtain, it can lower the reserve requirement.
- Open-market operations. This commonly used method allows the Federal Reserve to decrease the supply of money by selling treasury securities on the open market. The securities are paid for by checks drawn on commercial banks. This decreases their reserves, therefore reducing the amount of funds that can be loaned. If the Federal Reserve intends to increase the supply of money, it will buy the securities by issuing a check drawn upon itself.
- Discount rate. The Federal Reserve operates a service of discounting (paying less than par) commercial paper from member institutions. By discounting, the Federal Reserve provides funds that can be loaned. If the discount rate (considered to be the interest rate that a member institution pays the Federal Reserve) is increased, it becomes more difficult for an institution to borrow to obtain necessary reserves. Consequently, the interest rate a member institution must then charge a borrower increases. If the discount rate is lowered, borrowing is easier for a financial institution and the interest rate charged to a borrower could be lowered.

COUNTERCYCLICAL NATURE OF REAL ESTATE

During periods of high demand for credit (normally the apex of an economic cycle), the capital markets are usually unable to satisfy the combined demands for credit of individuals, government, and business. Mortgage lending usually suffers during such periods because the price of money, as indicated by the interest rate, is too high for most home buyers to qualify for a mortgage. In some situations in the past, mortgage interest rates may even be forced up against a state's usury ceiling, if one exists. Because real estate in general and mortgage lending in particular are the losers in a credit crunch, they have often been classified as countercyclical. The development of the secondary mortgage market has helped this situation a bit by being able to provide funds from the capital markets for housing during periods of high credit demand.

The countercyclicality of real estate means that real estate activity, and consequently mortgage lending, usually expands when the general business cycle is down and credit demand is low. The normal situation when the economic cycle is down is lower interest rates in general, which allow more borrowers to qualify for a mortgage loan. Conversely, as the economy begins to improve and demand for credit from other users increases, real estate activity begins to slow down as interest rates increase. This somewhat simplified explanation demonstrates the direct relationship between the availabiity of credit and real estate activity.

FINANCIAL INTERMEDIARIES

The more modern and clearly more descriptive term *financial intermediaries* describes that classification of economic units that previously were called financial institutions. Their principal economic function is to serve as the intermediary between the saver and the borrower. Both saver and borrower benefit from this arrangement. The saver, as will be explained, is able to earn a higher return on savings, while the borrower can obtain needed funds at a more reasonable rate. The term *financial intermediaries* includes these major economic units, among others:

- commercial banks,
- savings and loan institutions,
- mortgage companies,
- life insurance companies,
- mutual savings banks,
- finance companies,
- investment companies,
- credit unions,
- pension funds,
- money market funds,
- stockbrokers.

Financial intermediaries are essential to the entire economy but are especially crucial to mortgage lending, since they lend much of the funds required by home buyers, and those funds are accumulated almost exclusively from individual savers. The characteristics of these lenders will be examined later, but let us first examine how savers benefit from using these intermediaries.

How Savers Benefit

Many of the benefits to savers when dealing with financial intermediaries are obvious, such as higher yield, safety, and diversification. Others, such as economics of scale, variety of maturities, and specialization, are not. Higher yields result from the increased level of knowledge and experience intermediaries have over the average saver. The experts know where, how, and when to make safe, profitable investments. Safety is derived both from federal deposit insurance and from the informed investment decisions of the experts.

Diversification is also an element of safety that for a smaller saver can only be reached, without sacrificing yield, by the use of an intermediary.

How Mortgage Borrowers Benefit

The cost to a consumer in need of a mortgage loan is made lower by dealing with an intermediary. Instead of having to solicit many savers for funds, this mortgage borrower need only deal with one financial intermediary that has been able to pool the funds of many savers. The benefit to savers in this arrangement is a higher yield since a part of the saved cost of borrowing can be passed on to them, while a borrower will also benefit from this economy of scale. Each saver has different objectives in mind for savings deposited. Since financial intermediaries can also lend to borrowers with differing needs and for differing maturities, the match is beneficial to both parties. Finally, since many financial intermediaries specialize in a selected type of lending, they can provide that type of lending more cheaply than competitors, with a resulting benefit to both saver and borrower. An example of this type of specialization is thrift institutions and single-family mortgage lending.

Gross Profit Spread

Financial intermediaries are able to fulfill their important economic function by operating on a spread between their cost of funds (generally the interest on savings of individuals) and their portfolio yield (the interest earned on loans outstanding). As a general rule, savings institutions require a gross profit spread of 2 or 3 percent (200 or 300 basis points). As an example, if the average interest rate paid by a savings bank on all savings deposits is 5 percent, the average portfolio yield would need to be between 7 and 8 percent for that institution to be profitable.

Interest Rate Risk

The primary economic danger to financial intermediaries that are portfolio lenders, like some credit unions and savings institutions, is that interest rates will begin a rapid increase. The financial institution would have to match the rising rates on savings deposits in order to retain its deposits. It could then lend these funds out at what should be an increased mortgage rate. The problem is that even with the increased interest rate on current mortgage production, the entire mortgage portfolio may not have a sufficient yield to generate a profitable spread. Thus, even though an institution is currently lending at 200 to 300 basis points above its cost of funds, the portfolio yield may not be sufficient for a profitable spread; in fact, it may even be negative, as it was for savings institutions during the high interest rate period of 1981–83.

MORTGAGE LENDERS AND THE PRIMARY MORTGAGE MARKET _____

The primary economic function of a residential mortgage lender is to lend money for the purchase or refinancing of residences of all types in the primary mortgage market. This would include single-family detached housing, condominiums, cooperative housing, and two- to four-family housing. These loans are secured by either a first or second mortgage. The primary mortgage market is that market where funds are loaned (credit extended) directly to a borrower. This market is contrasted with the secondary mortgage market, where mortgages originated in the primary market are bought and sold. The secondary mortgage market is discussed in detail later in Chapter 10, The Secondary Mortgage Market.

Those financial intermediaries that are usually involved in the residential primary mortgage market include:

- mortgage bankers,
- mortgage brokers,
- commercial banks,
- savings and loan institutions,
- savings banks,
- credit unions,
- housing finance agencies.

These mortgage lenders, along with a few nontraditional mortgage lenders (such as Sears and GMAC), originate nearly all residential mortgage loans each year. Some of these mortgage lenders also hold mortgages in their own portfolios. Others, such as mortgage bankers, sell all of their originations to other lenders or into the secondary mortgage market. Some of these same lenders are also very active in commercial mortgage lending.

These lenders obtain the money for residential mortgage loans from the following sources:

- funds deposited by savers,
- funds borrowed from other financial intermediaries,
- sale of commercial paper (short-term promissory note),
- proceeds from the sale of mortgages or mortgage-backed securities.

Normally, all of the residential mortgage lenders are active on a day-to-day basis in the primary market, but during some stages of the economic cycle, one or more may temporarily drop out. When this occurs it is usually because of the high cost of funds to lend. By bringing together borrowers and savers from different economic sectors and geographic locations, mortgage lenders as financial intermediaries contribute to a more efficient allocation of the economy's resources. All of the mortgage lenders are discussed individually in detail in Chapter 3, The Mortgage Lenders.

_____ *MORTGAGE INVESTORS*

In addition to those mortgage lenders that hold mortgage debt in their own portfolios, a number of other financial intermediaries are important holders of mortgage debt. These intermediaries only hold residential mortgage debt (either individual loans or mortgage-backed securities); they do not originate any loans. Classified as mortgage investors, they include the following:

- Federal National Mortgage Association (Fannie Mae),
- Federal Home Loan Mortgage Corporation (Freddie Mac),
- retirement and pension funds,
- other federal agencies,
- state housing agencies,
- life insurance companies,
- individuals.

These investors acquire the mortgage debt they hold either directly from the mortgage lenders that originated them or through the operation of the secondary mortgage market. Some participants in the primary mortgage market will, on occasion, also buy loans from other originators. They are purchasing these mortgage loans from other originators because they believe they can acquire mortgage loans and/or servicing rights cheaper this way. For a discussion of the secondary mortgage market, see Chapter 10.

_____ *TRENDS IN MORTGAGE LENDING*

Residential mortgage lending continues to evolve rapidly. More changes are occurring now than at any other time since the 1930s. These changes affect:

- who the lenders are in the primary market,
- how residential loans are originated,
- how technology is used to enhance profits,
- how funds for mortgages are generated,
- how interest rates are calculated,
- how mortgages are sold and securitized,
- how mortgages are serviced and by whom,
- how borrowers are qualified,
- who the mortgage investors are in the secondary markets.

Some of these changes are discussed in this text. Others, such as who the lenders of tomorrow will be, are beyond the scope of a text of this type. The most meaningful changes in residential mortgage lending over the past 10 years include the following:

- demise of thrifts as the dominant originator of residential debt and the rise of the mortgage banker,
- widespread use of mortgage-backed securities to access the capital markets for additional funds for residential loans,
- adoption of alternative mortgage instruments by financial intermediaries to spread the risk of mortgage lending,
- explosion of refinancings in 1992–93 because of low interest rates and the resulting runoff of servicing.

These subjects are discussed in detail in later chapters.

Mortgage Revenue Bonds (MRB)

Prior to 1978, state housing finance agencies were the only government entities using tax-exempt MRBs to provide financing for mortgage borrowers. Their normal method of financing was to borrow money and then provide below-market-rate loans to low- and moderate-income groups.

The concept behind using tax-exempt MRBs for financing is quite simple. An issuer, whether state or city, is able to sell its tax-exempt bonds in the capital market with an interest rate substantially below taxable bonds because of the tax savings to investors. This money is then channeled through various mortgage lenders to mortgage borrowers. As a result of this low-cost borrowing, mortgagors often can obtain a loan two or three percentage points below the conventional market rate.

The various state programs in past years caused little reaction as they attempted to help the low- and moderate-income groups, but when new programs developed that were designed to assist middle-income groups, the concern of many segments of society became vocal. The Mortgage Subsidy Bond Act (1981) resulted from this rising concern. This act severely restricts the use of tax-exempt MRBs issued by state and local housing authorities. It limits eligibility of buyers and imposes purchase price ceilings and limitations on states' annual volumes.

Mortgage Credit Certificate (MCC)

The law extending authority for mortgage revenue bonds also provided state and local governments with an alternative to MRBs with which to assist first-time home buyers. This alternative provides for the issuance of MCCs to qualified home buyers, which allows them a nonrefundable tax credit of from 10 to 50 percent (as determined by the state or local government) of the interest paid on home mortgage indebtedness. MCCs are limited to first-time home buyers having a joint income below the local area median income and to the purchase of a home whose acquisition cost does not exceed 90 percent of the local average purchase price. The MCC concept is an attempt to ensure that the entire amount of the subsidy, in the form of tax credits, flows directly to first-time home buyers and not partially to others. Congress perceived that MRBs had a part of the subsidy flowing to tax-exempt investors and intermediaries, in addition to the home buyer. The MCC will provide the same subsidy or more as with the MRB to first-time home buyers and at a reduced revenue loss to the federal tax coffers. This subsidy is meant to complement the mortgage interest deduction, which provides greater benefits to higher income home buyers and little or no benefit to low-and middle-income taxpayers.

Under the law, state and local governments have the choice of issuing MRBs or MCCs or a combination of both. The aggregate annual amount of MCCs issued by a state may not exceed 20 percent of the authorized MRB volume for the state. The state's MRB volume is determined by an average of originations over the past three years or $200 million, whichever is greater.

Builder Bonds

Builder bonds are used frequently today as a means whereby builders can access the capital markets directly in order to obtain the funds needed by the purchasers of their homes. To builders, the obvious benefit of this financing technique is that they can sell more houses than they would otherwise. This is true even during those periods of the economic cycle when some of the traditional lenders are out of the market because of a lack of savings inflow. A builder (or group of builders) will use a mortgage banker or a similar organization to take local applications, underwrite the loan, and provide loan servicing.

As important as this direct access to the capital market is, another aspect is more important to some builders. The use of builder bonds to finance the purchase of houses allows a builder to report house sales on an installment basis for tax purposes and thus be able to defer most of the income tax until later years. The reason is that since the mortgage payments are spread out over 20 years or more, the house is paid for over that same period. Taxes are paid according to the amount of profit earned each year.

Builder bonds are mortgage-backed securities that are backed either by the individual mortgages on houses sold or by GNMA certificates that are purchased for the purpose of serving as collateral for a builder bond. For an extensive discussion of mortgage-backed securities, see Chapter 11, Mortgage-Backed Securities.

THE MORTGAGE LENDERS

3

The objective of this chapter is to examine those financial intermediaries—the mortgage lenders—that originate residential mortgage loans in the primary mortgage market. Care should be taken to understand that *originators* of mortgage debt are not necessarily *holders* of mortgage debt. Some mortgage lenders, such as credit unions, hold in their portfolios most of the mortgage debt they originate. On the other hand, mortgage bankers sell all of the loans they originate.

The term *financial intermediary* is applied to all mortgage lenders even though not all mortgage lenders are depository institutions. For example, mortgage bankers, who annually originate about half of all residential mortgage loans, are not depository institutions (i.e., they do not take deposits from savers). Mortgage bankers obtain funds for lending either by borrowing from other financial institutions or through the sale of commercial paper.

Before the Great Depression, wealthy individuals made up the largest classification of holders of residential debt. In today's highly sophisticated and segmented residential mortgage lending environment, financial intermediaries

HOLDERS OF ONE- TO FOUR-FAMILY MORTGAGE DEBT
(millions of dollars)

	Savings & Loans	Savings Banks	Commercial Banks	Federal Agencies	Mortgage Pools	All Others	Total
1980	$411.0	67.5	160.4	183.2	n.a.	144.0	965.1
1985	459.0	76.3	185.1	111.6	376.7	74.9	1,283.6
1990	458.3	36.6	388.0	132.5	1,005.3	322.6	2,343.3
1993*	331.7	91.2	479.5	222.7	1,337.5	376.2	2,838.8

*3rd quarter
Source: Department of Housing and Urban Development.

originate the mortgage loans that are either retained in portfolio or sold to other financial institutions—the holders of mortgage debt. Although individuals today still hold billions of dollars of residential debt, their percentage of the total residential mortgage debt is very small. This chapter focuses on a discussion of the major residential lenders in order of their origination volume, starting with mortgage bankers.

MORTGAGE BANKERS (MBs)

A discussion of residential mortgage lenders should start with mortgage bankers since they originate approximately half of all residential mortgage loans each year. In addition, mortgage bankers are servicing approximately 40 percent of the nearly $3 trillion in outstanding residential mortgage debt. Both of these figures represent major growth in the 1990s.

A mortgage company is usually identified as a mortgage banker (MB). The term *mortgage banker* is somewhat misleading since it implies that this lender is a depository for savings like other lenders. Mortgage bankers are not depositories for savings but are classified as intermediaries since they serve as a financial bridge between borrowers and lenders. As mentioned, MBs obtain the money they lend to home buyers by either borrowing the money from another intermediary (usually a commercial bank) or by the sale of commercial paper.

Mortgage Bankers, Not to Be Confused with Mortgage Brokers

Mortgage brokers are not the same type of mortgage lender as a mortgage banker. In a typical mortgage transaction involving a mortgage broker, the broker takes the application for a mortgage loan from a consumer and then sells that loan to another mortgage lender (which could be a mortgage banker) before the loan is closed. After the unclosed loan is sold, the mortgage broker has no continuing responsibility in regard to the loan. Mortgage bankers, on the other hand, sell all of the mortgages they originate (or purchase) and close but continue to service the loan after the sale.

The number of independent mortgage bankers is actually quite small (only a few hundred), but many more financial institutions that perform the mortgage banking function belong to the trade association, the Mortgage Bankers Association of America (MBA). Today, most of the largest 100 mortgage banking companies are owned by either commercial banks or thrift institutions. The majority of MBs are geographically located in traditional capital-deficit areas such as the South and West. These MBs continue to render a valuable service to both borrowers and mortgage investors by moving funds for mortgages from capital-surplus areas to areas where insufficient capital exists to meet the needs of home buyers.

Not A Portfolio Lender

Unlike other mortgage lenders, a mortgage banker does not intentionally hold mortgages for its own benefit. Since an MB does not have a traditional portfolio like other intermediaries, all residential mortgage loans are originated with the intent of selling the loans to mortgage investors either directly or through the secondary mortgage market. On occasion, an MB may originate a "mistake," which cannot be sold as a conforming loan to an established investor. When this happens, the MB will usually sell the loan to another investor at a discount rather than hold on to it.

Development of Mortgage Bankers

Mortgage companies, later called mortgage bankers, developed to fulfill a need for farm financing in the second half of the ninteenth century. Following the Civil War, the opening of new farmland in the Ohio Valley and further west required an infusion of credit from the capital-surplus areas of New England. Originally, a few real estate agents, attorneys, and some commercial bankers made the needed mortgage loan and then sold the loan to wealthy individuals or institutions in the East. This practice grew until farm mortgage lending specialists developed and formed the first mortgage companies. At the turn of the century approximately 200 mortgage companies existed. They originated farm mortgages with the following components: 50 percent loan-to-value interest only loans, with five-year maturities.

Following World War I, the migration from farms to the developing urban areas accelerated. A few of the more aggressive mortgage companies at this time began to make single-family mortgage loans. This new type of loan was similar to the farm mortgages made by mortgage companies for the previous 50 years in regard to loan-to-value ratios and term. These nonamortized mortgages, which normally required refinancing at the expiration of the term, were the principal reason why such a large number of families lost their homes in the Depression of the 1930s. The reason for the lost homes was the liquidity crisis, which prevented financial institutions from refinancing mortgage loans as they rolled over.

Government Programs

In the early 1930s, officials of the federal government realized that some basic economic changes were needed to prevent more serious political changes from occurring. The first step taken toward stabilizing the economy was to put a floor under depreciating real estate values. Not only was demand for real estate at a low point at this time, but real estate values were being forced down by the ever-increasing number of foreclosures. The Federal

Home Loan Bank System was begun in 1932 to help the savings and loan business, but the Home Owners Loan Corporation (HOLC) in 1933 allowed all lenders, including mortgage bankers, to exchange defaulted mortgages for government bonds. This program helped save many family homes as HOLC restructured mortgages and put them on an amortized basis. It also helped stabilize real estate values since foreclosed properties were no longer forcing down the market.

The Federal Housing Administration (FHA), created in 1934, provided the main stimulus to the formation of the modern mortgage banker. FHA established minimum standards for both the borrower and the real estate before it would insure a mortgage loan. FHA minimum standards prompted life insurance companies to seek permission from state insurance commissioners to make out-of-state loans with higher loan-to-value ratios and longer terms. State regulatory authorities eventually agreed to the request and mortgage bankers soon began originating FHA-insured mortgages for sale to life insurance companies.

FHA adopted the HOLC practice of amortizing mortgage loans to assist borrowers in budgeting mortgage payments. Amortized loans created a need for these loans to be serviced following their sale to investors. Servicing requires that the servicer collect the monthly principal and interest and forward the payment to an investor. This requirement for servicing was the linchpin that allowed the mortgage banker to be the dominant originator of FHA-insured mortgage loans. This dominant position for mortgage bankers in regard to FHA-insured mortgage loans remains constant even to the present time.

After the Second World War, Congress created another type of mortgage loan with governmental involvement—the Veterans Administration (VA) guaranteed loan. The mortgage bankers quickly became the dominant originator of this type of loan also. Both the FHA-insured mortgages and the VA-guaranteed mortgages originated by mortgage bankers were sold to and serviced for the Federal National Mortgage Association, which only bought FHA and VA mortgages until the early 1970s.

Modern Mortgage Banker

The evolution of the MB has produced a modern financial intermediary that is very capable of adapting to changes in economic and marketplace conditions. Today, many MBs have dual capabilities—single family housing and income property production—while some companies have decided to specialize in only one area. The modern mortgage banker specializing in originating residential mortgage loans performs some or all of the following functions:

- originates, processes, underwrites, and closes all types of residential mortgage loans,
- arranges construction financing,

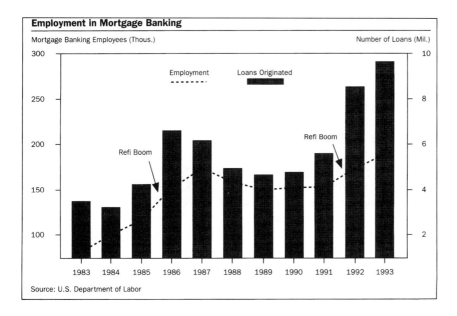

Employment in Mortgage Banking

Mortgage Banking Employees (Thous.) — Number of Loans (Mil.)

Employment ---- Loans Originated

Refi Boom

Refi Boom

Source: U.S. Department of Labor

- warehouses closed residential mortgage loans,
- sells residential loans, either as whole loans or participations,
- sells to private investors or secondary mortgage market,
- pools residential mortgages into mortgage-backed securities,
- services the loans after sale.

Organization and Regulation

Unlike other mortgage lenders, mortgage bankers are not chartered by either a state or the federal government, but instead they follow either the partnership or incorporation laws of the state in which the company is located. Today, many states have passed laws specifically aimed at mortgage bankers and mortgage brokers that require them to be licensed by the state in which they want to originate mortgages. If an MB is domiciled in one state and wants to do business in another state, it usually has to register as a mortgage banker in that other state also. MBs are also unique in that they are not subject to direct regulation or supervision of any federal agency.

If a mortgage banker is an FHA-approved lender, VA-approved lender, or an approved seller/servicer for FNMA or FHLMC, it is subject to periodic audits by those entities. HUD has attempted to exercise some control over MBs by issuing regulations governing several areas of concern, among them the way a mortgagee handles delinquency problems with a mortgagor. During the early 1980s, when merger activity between commercial banks and MBs was common, the Federal Reserve exercised some control by requiring approval prior to an ownership change.

Financing the Mortgage Banker

Mortgage bankers finance their lending activity differently than most other residential mortgage lenders. The reason is they have no funds deposited by savers to lend to mortgagors. An MB finances its residential mortgage lending activity by either the sale of commercial paper or by drawing on a line of credit with another lender—usually a commercial bank. Historically, the latter was the primary way of obtaining funds. Commercial paper is a short-term debt instrument with a maximum term of 180 to 270 days that carries a fixed rate of interest for a fixed term. MBs use this alternative during those periods in the economic cycle when the rate for commercial paper is lower than the prime rate.

Sale of Commercial Paper

In addition to a lower cost of borrowing, the use of commercial paper removes the need for compensating balances—funds left on deposit with a commercial bank to provide an increased incentive to lend funds. If a commercial bank lends its support to the commercial paper of an MB by backing it with an irrevocable letter of credit, the bank will require a fee and some compensating balances. On the other hand, if commercial paper is sold under the name of a holding company of a mortgage banker, no compensating balances are required. For this alternative to be used, the parent company must have an acceptable credit rating. The problem with selling commercial paper is that the market is quite volatile. During periods of tight money, only high-cost funds can be obtained and then only by those companies with the highest credit ratings.

Line of Credit and Warehousing

The second alternative used by mortgage bankers for obtaining funds to be loaned to residential mortgagors is by drawing on a line of credit with a commercial bank. This process is usually a part of a unique function performed by mortgage bankers—*warehousing*. Warehousing refers to the function of an MB holding mortgages in the "warehouse" on a short-term basis pending sale to an investor. These first mortgages held in the warehouse also serve as security for the revolving line of credit at a commercial bank. This process finances the MB's loans to borrowers and the MB's inventory of closed residential loans. The loan from the commercial bank will require that it be fully collateralized by closed mortgage loans retained by the MB until enough loans are grouped for sale to investors. The commercial bank's line of credit is repaid by the MB from the proceeds of periodic sales of mortgages to investors. Warehousing aptly describes the flow of closed mortgages into an MB, which are then used to secure the bank loan. The closed mortgages remain for 30 to 90 days in the warehouse until a group or pool of mortgages, typically in million-dollar units, is sold to an investor.

Commercial banks are attracted to this type of loan because it is short term and involves little risk. The risk is minimal because the mortgages serving as collateral are usually presold to an investor who is obligated to purchase by a commitment it has issued. Commercial banks usually require that this line of credit be supported by compensating balances, typically of 20 percent of the maximum line of credit. These required compensating balances may consist of tax and insurance escrows collected by the MB and deposited with the lending bank until needed.

Mortgage Banking Today

Whether performed by an independent mortgage banker or another type of mortgage lender, the "mortgage banking strategy" has become the predominant and preferred strategy for originating residential mortgage loans, minimizing risk, and growing a servicing portfolio. As mentioned, MBs originated over 50 percent of residential mortgage loans in the first half of the 1990s, and other lenders, such as commercial banks and thrifts, also followed the same strategy of originating loans, selling them, and growing a servicing portfolio.

The modern MB earns most of its revenue from four main sources:

- origination fees charged applicants,
- servicing fees paid by investors,
- marketing difference between interest rate on underlying mortgage and yield required by commitment,
- warehousing difference between interest rate on funds borrowed and loaned.

How these revenues are earned by MBs, and how profitable these various activities are, will be discussed in other chapters dealing specifically with those topics. See chapters on Origination, Marketing Residential Mortgage Loans, The Secondary Mortgage Market, and Mortgage Loan Administration.

COMMERCIAL BANKS (CBs)

Commercial banks (CBs) have both the largest collective membership, at about 11,000 (with 45,000 branches), and the greatest total assets ($3,500 billion in 1992) of all financial institutions. The assets of all CBs are more than twice those of all savings and loans, savings banks, and credit unions combined. CBs hold more one- to four-family mortgage loans—nearly $500 billion—than any other classification of financial institution (only mortgage pools have a larger dollar amount of one- to four-family mortgage loans). In 1993, CBs were the second largest originators of one- to four-family mortgages (about 25 percent) behind only mortgage bankers. They are also first in origination of income property loans and construction mortgages.

A commercial bank is a private financial institution organized to accumulate funds primarily through time and demand deposits and to make these funds available to finance the nation's commerce and industry. Over the past 20 years, commercial banks have expanded their real estate finance operations from what was mostly short-term mortgage loans to include many long-term mortgage loans.

Historical Development

Except for a one-year period following the enactment of the National Bank Act of 1863, federally chartered commercial banks were not allowed to make real estate loans until 1913. During the period from 1863 to 1913, state-chartered banks thrived since they were able to make real estate loans. Then in 1913, the Federal Reserve Act provided the authorization for federally chartered commercial banks to make mortgage loans. The typical mortgage loan provided by CBs during this early period was similar to those made by other lenders: a 50 percent loan-to-value ratio for a five-year term, with the principal payable at the end of the term and with interest payable semiannually.

Commercial banks in the 1930s were in a position similar to that of other financial institutions—lack of liquidity—and consequently many failed. (In fact, the number of commercial banks decreased during this period from more than 30,000 to about 16,000.) During the early months of President Franklin D. Roosevelt's first term, many new federal laws affecting the economy were enacted. The Federal Deposit Insurance Corporation (FDIC), authorized by the Banking Act of 1933, helped restore confidence in commercial banks and encouraged badly needed funds to flow back into bank vaults to provide liquidity for new loans. Currently, the Bank Insurance Fund (BIF), a part of FDIC, insures deposits in all commercial banks up to $100,000.

Organization and Regulation

Commercial banks are chartered either by the federal government (through the Comptroller of the Currency) or by a state banking agency. State chartered banks outnumber federally chartered banks by about two to one, although more assets are in the federally chartered CBs. State-chartered CBs may be members of the Federal Reserve System, but only 1,000 (10 percent) are members. All federally chartered CBs must be members, however. This central banking system, comprising 12 Federal Reserve districts, provides many services to its members such as issuing currency, holding bank reserves, discounting loans, and serving as a check clearinghouse. (For a discussion of how the Federal Reserve operates to control economic developments, see pages 30–31.)

CBs historically have been interested in maintaining a balance in the maturity of their source of funds and their loan portfolios. CB funds are primarily short term and derived from passbook savings and deposits in checking accounts. Because of the maturity of their funds, long-term lending of any type is generally not attractive. Most CBs are interested in commercial and industrial loans (over $650 billion at year-end 1993) that are normally short term and provide a better match between the maturity of assets (loans) and liabilities (deposits). When commercial loan demand is high, practically all CB funds flow to meet that demand and mortgage loans are neglected. During those periods in the business cycle when commercial loan demand is low, CBs have placed excess funds in real estate.

Mortgage Lending Activity

Larger commercial banks, as a general rule, are different from other major mortgage lenders in that they are not organized for, or philosophically inclined toward, residential mortgage lending. On the other hand, CBs located in smaller, more rural areas have a greater inclination toward residential mortgage lending. As a whole, CBs have increased their real estate lending activity (both residential and income property) by about 50 percent from 1984 to 1992. Part of the reason for this shift in emphasis is the capital requirements (50 percent risk weight) for single-family mortgage loans, which are half that required for commercial and industrial loans (100 percent risk weight). Put another way, a CB needs twice the capital to make commercial and industrial loans as needed for single-family mortgage lending.

Real estate financing activity has been very profitable to banks during certain phases of the business cycle. But, it has also been very damaging to banks at times because some of the mortgage loans that were made probably should not have been. In the second half of the 1980s, CBs made a major move into real estate. For example, in 1988–90, Citicorp was the largest originator of mortgage debt in this country. However, for some of the banks, this recent experience with real estate lending was not profitable. Many bank failures of the late 1980s and early 1990s, according to FDIC, were the result of poor real estate lending by the CBs.

Currently, CBs make all types of mortgage loans, but construction loans on residential and income properties comprise a large percentage of mortgage financing activity. On the bank's books, these loans are normally classified as ordinary commercial loans, not real estate loans. The interest rate is generally two to five points above the prime rate, depending on the borrower. These loans are attractive to CBs because of the yield and because the loan is short term (6 to 36 months), making it similar to the term of the bank's source of funds.

The board of governors of the Federal Reserve System issues regulations affecting real estate lending activity by member banks. State-chartered banks are governed by the regulations of the responsible state agency. These regulations usually are similar to those of the Federal Reserve. Current Federal Reserve regulations allow loans up to 90 percent of value to be amortized up to 30 years with no limit on the loan amount, although they are subject to the maximum loan limit in the secondary market. A bank can lend up to 70 percent of its deposits or 100 percent of capital and surplus, whichever is greater. CBs may have up to 10 percent of real estate loan units in a "basket," or nonconforming classification. Leasehold loans are allowed if the lease extends at least 10 years past the date of full amortization.

COMMERCIAL BANKS
RESIDENTIAL MORTGAGE LOANS HELD
(dollars in millions)

	FHA/VA *One- to Four-Family*	*Conventional* *One- to Four-Family*	*Multi-Family*	*Total*
1990	$8,581	$388,032	$20,244	$416,857
1993	$7,535	$479,505	$26,024	$513,064

Source: Department of Housing and Urban Development.

The mortgage lending activity of commercial banks is more diverse than that of other lenders. Banks not only engage in both government and conventional residential mortgage lending but also are the largest income-property lender. They are the largest mortgage lender for construction loans and help finance other lenders, especially MBs, by issuing lines of credit that allow for the warehousing of loans until needed for delivery to an investor.

CBs, like other mortgage lenders, originate residential mortgage loans for their own portfolios and for sale to others. Also, like other lenders, CBs purchase mortgages originated by others. In 1992, CBs sold $104 billion of mortgages and purchased $49 billion.

SAVINGS AND LOAN INSTITUTIONS (S&Ls)

The historical role of savings and loan institutions (S&Ls) in the nation's economy is the pooling of savings of individuals for investment, primarily in residential mortgages. This financial intermediary is still fulfilling that role today even though S&Ls have had great difficulty since the hyperinflation period of the early 1980s. Even with all of the problems facing S&Ls, in the mid-1990s, they were still originating 20 percent of the first mortgage loans made each year. At year-end 1993, S&Ls held nearly $333 billion in one- to four-family mortgage debt. As large as the amount is, it is a substantial decline from the $458 billion held at year-end 1990.

Although the name may be different in some states (e.g., homestead associations, building and loans, cooperatives, etc.), their role remains the same. S&Ls operate in all 50 states and numbered approximately 1,900 (with about 20,000 branches) at the end of 1993. The number of S&Ls has decreased rapidly over the past 12 years from about 4,100 as the savings and loan crisis and the resulting federal bailout closed many failed S&Ls.

S&Ls are no longer the largest private holder of residential mortgage debt (commercial banks overtook them in 1992), and they are no longer the largest originator of residential mortgage debt each year (mortgage bankers and commercial bankers are both larger). At year-end 1993, S&Ls originated 20 percent of one- to four-family residential mortgage debt. Before the decrease in the number of S&Ls, their origination was at about 50 percent of total one- to four-family mortgage debt each year.

Historical Development

From the founding of the first association in 1831 (Oxford Provident Building Association in Frankfort, Pennsylvania), S&Ls have spread across the United States, providing funds for the housing growth of the nation. For example, S&Ls provided much of the institutional financing of urban homes for middle-income Americans before the 1930s. Although the largest number of S&Ls was reached in 1927, when more than 12,000 were in existence, the contribution S&Ls have made toward providing financing for housing has been critical ever since.

The 1930s were years of dramatic change for S&Ls. More than half of those in existence failed during this decade and more than 25 percent of S&L mortgage assets were in default. In addition to the general economic depression, the major problem for all lenders during the 1930s was a lack of liquidity. This liquidity crisis was caused by the panic of the American public following the stock market crash and the failure of some banks, precipitating a rush to withdraw savings from all financial institutions. To help alleviate this liquidity problem, the Federal Home Loan Bank System (FHLB) was created by Congress in July 1932. The FHLB provided liquidity during periods of credit restraint for member S&Ls and served the industry in the way that the Federal Reserve System served the needs of commercial banks. The law provided for the creation of 12 regional banks, one to serve each geographic area. Many of the functions of the FHLBs were stripped away with the enactment of the Financial Institutions Reform, Recovery and Enforcement Act (FIRREA) in 1989.

Another important step toward the development of the modern S&L occurred with the creation of the Federal Savings and Loan Insurance Corporation (FSLIC) as authorized by Title IV of the National Housing Act of 1934. This step was vital for the restoration of faith in the safety of deposits in S&Ls and paved the way for new deposits, which were needed before any new mortgage loans could be made. Today, as a result of changes mandated by FIRREA, deposits in savings institutions are insured up to $100,000 by a successor to FSLIC called the Savings Association Insurance Fund (SAIF), which is a part of the Federal Deposit Insurance Fund (FDIC).

An Institution in Trouble

The 20 years before the enactment of FIRREA (1989) were periods of highs and lows for S&Ls. The 1970s witnessed steady growth in total assets and profitability, but during the 1980s, the S&L industry struggled for survival and many didn't make it. The reasons for the collapse of many S&Ls and of their insurance fund (FSLIC), with the resulting federal bailout, have been debated in many forums. The experts agreed that the primary reasons for the eventual collapse of S&Ls was the low-yielding, fixed-rate mortgages of the early 1980s, which, when combined with high inflation, created a negative spread between the cost of funds and the portfolio yield.

The S&L industry attempted to solve this problem by seeking and winning federal government/regulatory approval for deregulation of depository institutions, in addition to creative accounting changes that differed from GAAP (generally accepted accounting procedures). Further, S&Ls lobbied for and received regulatory permission to expand their activity into high-yield/high-risk lending. All of these changes were to occur without an increase in supervision. For a few years, these changes allowed S&Ls to improve their bottom line. But, these changes proved to be the undoing of many struggling S&Ls. The Tax Reform Act of 1986 probably was the beginning of the end. This act eliminated many of the tax benefits from real estate, which had made real estate an attractive investment for many. As a result of these tax law changes, builders and developers could not sell their property and many S&Ls that had financed these properties had to take them back. Earnings were once again under pressure and regulators were starting to look very carefully at earnings and loan portfolios. What they saw was a disaster developing—the S&L industry lost $20 billion in 1989 alone.

The National Association of Realtors recently summed up the problem this way: "Deregulation and new investment powers made financial and managerial demands that most thrift executives had not contemplated. Speculative investments, a regulatory system which failed to exercise controls, basic mismanagement and an unprecedented level of fraud and abuse perpetrated by many thrift executives resulted in the inevitable legislative backlash." That legislative backlash was FIRREA, which is estimated to cost the American taxpayer up to $400 billion over the life of the bonds sold to finance the S&L bailout.

Organization and Regulation

Savings and loan institutions may be chartered either by a state or by the federal government and can be either mutual or stock institutions. Recently, a fairly equal number were chartered by the states and by the federal government and an equal number were stock and mutual institutions.

The enactment of FIRREA in 1989 completely changed the way S&Ls were regulated. FIRREA restructured the regulatory framework by abolishing the Federal Home Loan Bank Board (but not the Federal Home Loan Banks) and FSLIC. FSLIC was replaced with Savings Associations Insurance Fund (SAIF), a part of FDIC. The FHLBB was replaced by the Office of Thrift Supervision (OTS), under the Treasury Department. FDIC was given extensive new powers to ensure the safety and soundness of financial institutions (but not credit unions) and was given the supervision of separate S&L (SAIF) and bank deposit insurance funds (BIF). Finally, this major piece of legislation created the Resolution Trust Corporation (RTC) to dispose of failed S&Ls and their assets.

S&Ls Today

Over the years, S&Ls have loaned hundreds of billions of dollars to millions of borrowers at the prevailing market rate for the purchase of homes. During the past decade, as the problem at S&Ls multiplied, the share of originations has decreased. But, notwithstanding all of these problems, S&Ls are still a major source of mortgage money. The surviving institutions (probably about 1,500) will once again place greater emphasis upon residential mortgage lending and less on commercial lending. The principal reason for this reliance on one- to four-family mortgage lending is that it requires less capital than other types of lending.

Today many S&Ls are active in the secondary mortgage market, both as buyers and as sellers. Beginning in 1987, S&Ls have been net sellers of mortgages in the secondary mortgage market. This development is significant in that it demonstrates a change in lending philosophy from one dominated by local concerns to one affected and shaped by the nation's economy. Some S&Ls have even formed mortgage banking subsidiaries to originate all types of loans for sale into the secondary mortgage market.

Because of their historical local focus and previously existing legal limitations on their lending area, many S&Ls did not become involved in either FHA-insured or VA-guaranteed mortgages. Instead, S&L deposits were invested in local conventional mortgages originated either for their own portfolios or for sale. Today, changes in the marketplace have forced S&Ls to originate all types of residential loans, including second mortgages.

SAVINGS BANKS (SBs)

Savings banks (SBs) have often been categorized as commercial banks and sometimes as S&Ls. Although an SB has some of the characteristics of both, it is actually a unique thrift institution. At year-end 1992, SBs held $91 billion in one- to four-family mortgage debt and another $11 billion in multi-family mortgage debt. In 1993, SBs originated about 4 percent of total one- to four-family first mortgages. Since SBs are thrift institutions, this percentage is quite cyclical, depending on savings inflow.

Historical Development

Like the first savings and loan, the first savings bank was founded in Pennsylvania. The Philadelphia Savings Fund Society (now called Meritor Savings Bank), the nation's largest savings bank, began in 1816 and was followed in 1817 by the Provident Institute for Savings in Boston.

Unlike the early building societies, these institutions were organized to provide ongoing facilities to encourage savings by the small wage earner, who had been virtually ignored by the other financial institutions. They were well received and began to spread throughout the New England states. By 1875 the number of SBs had reached a peak of 674. The SB concept never spread far from its origins, though, probably due to the development of S&Ls, which encouraged savings and housing, and the development of the savings account at commercial banks. Today, most of the approximately 300 savings banks are located in three states: Connecticut, Massachusetts, and New York.

Organization and Regulation

Until the early 1980s, all savings banks were mutual organizations and as such had no stockholders. Beginning in the early 1980s, many savings banks realized that they needed additional capital in order to compete in the new, deregulated environment. By 1994, nearly half of the savings banks were stock institutions and the trend appears to be in the direction of more mutuals converting to stock.

If an SB remains a mutual organization, all depositors share ownership, and it is managed by a self-perpetuating board of trustees, usually made up of prominent local business leaders. If the SB is a stock organization, then it is managed by a board of directors, representing the stockholders of the bank.

In 1979 changes in federal law allowed savings banks to be federally chartered. Before this time all SBs were state chartered. The majority of SBs are still state chartered but that may change as federal law evolves regarding capital requirements and portfolio structure. Since the vast majority of SBs are chartered by various states, the regulations that govern their operations vary from state to state. State regulations establish guidelines for deposits, reserves, and the extent of mortgage lending allowed, as well as maximum loan amounts, loan terms, and loan-to-value ratios. These limits are usually similar to those of S&Ls and are governed to a great extent by what the markets require, especially the secondary mortgage market. SB deposits are all insured by FDIC up to the $100,000 maximum.

Mortgage Lending Activity

Savings banks differ somewhat from S&Ls in that they were never encouraged by regulators to invest a set amount of money in mortgages. At the end of 1993, SBs had 50 percent of their assets in mortgage loans. Savings banks have had the authority to make other types of loans longer than S&Ls, and today most make consumer loans and commercial loans. Other assets include corporate stocks and bonds, U.S. Treasury and federal agency obligations, and state and local debt obligations.

In the current mortgage market, SBs originate both conventional and FHA/VA mortgages for their own portfolios. Since the majority of SBs are located in capital-surplus areas and therefore have more funds than are demanded locally, they often purchase low-risk FHA/VA and conventional mortgages from other mortgage lenders, particularly mortgage bankers, in capital-deficit areas of the country. Recently, much of this purchase has been in the form of mortgage-backed securities.

CREDIT UNIONS (CUs)

A credit union (CU) is a specialized thrift institution that serves nearly one out of every four Americans. Credit unions are one of the fastest-growing financial intermediaries in the American economy. At the end of 1994, the approximately 13,000 credit unions had more than $280 billion in assets and were becoming very sophisticated. Nearly 64 million Americans belong to a credit union, which normally represents a specific industry group or community—a common bond. The largest CU is the Navy Federal Credit Union, with 830,000 members and assets of nearly $7 billion.

Historical Development

Credit unions began in Germany during the middle of the nineteenth century. The principal objective of the founding fathers of the credit union movement was to combat usurious rates and to provide consumers with an opportunity to borrow at reasonable rates. The first credit union in the U.S. was organized in New Hampshire in 1908. CUs were chartered by state law only until the Federal Credit Union Act was passed in 1934. Slowly the various states enacted enabling legislation until in 1969, the number of CUs in the U.S. peaked at 23,876. Since then the number of CUs has declined as many smaller CUs merged into larger ones.

Many state chartered CUs have had the authority to make real estate loans for many years, but federally chartered CUs only acquired that right in 1978.

Credit unions operate somewhat differently than other thrift institutions. After providing for operating expenses and reserves, credit unions return their earnings to their members. CUs pay, on average, about 80 basis points more in dividends than competitors' savings products. This is one of the primary reasons for their popularity.

Organization and Regulation

All CUs are mutual organizations and, as such, are directed by a board of directors elected by the membership. The members of the board are all volunteers except in the situation where one member from management serves on the board. The management (excluding the board) of a CU consists of professionals who, as a general rule, are paid.

Approximately 60 percent of CUs are chartered by the federal government and as a result are regulated by the National Credit Union Administration (NCUA). State-chartered CUs usually have greater leeway in what they may do and how. Nearly all CUs are insured by the National Credit Union Share Insurance Fund (NCUIF) with the amount of insurance being the same as with FDIC. A small percent of CUs (less than 3 percent) are insured privately.

One recent problem CUs have experienced is the decline in the percentage of the assets invested in consumer loans, automobile loans in particular. This decrease in consumer loans is the result of increased competition from automobile manufacturers and other financial intermediaries. In the face of this increased competition and the resulting sea of liquidity, CUs turned to mortgage lending in earnest in the 1980s. Of course, the tax law changes introduced in 1986 encouraged other CUs to enter into mortgage lending.

Mortgage Lending Activity

Residential mortgage originations, both first and second loans, totaled $25 billion in 1993. First mortgage loans originated were approximately $15 billion, which represented less than 2 percent of total first mortgage originations. By the end of 1993, mortgage loans totaled 36 percent of credit union loans outstanding, up from 6.4 percent in 1984. According to the data compiled by NCUA, 50 percent of all credit unions were offering first-mortgage loans at the end of 1993, and nearly all of those with assets over $50 million were offering these loans.

1993 YEAR-END TOTALS
FOR FEDERAL INSURED CREDIT UNIONS
(in billions of dollars)

Assets	$277.2
Loans	152.3
Shares	247.0
Capital	27.0

Ratios

Loans/Shares	62 Percent
Capital/Assets	9.7 Percent

Source: National Credit Union Administration.

As with most new entrants to residential mortgage lending, most of the mortgages being originated by CUs are for their own portfolios. At the end of 1993, CUs held about $55 billion in mortgage loans in their portfolios. Estimates are that CUs sold about half the first mortgages they originated into the secondary mortgage market in 1993. Many credit unions didn't sell any loans, probably the result of their liquidity problems. A major change for credit unions in the 1990s is that most of their mortgages are now standardized mortgage products and can easily be sold to regular secondary market outlets or specialized ones like CUNA Mortgage, which purchases loans from credit unions only.

As credit unions continue to grow in total assets and in sophistication, it can be expected that they will increase their mortgage lending activities. These activities will naturally expand to increase sale of mortgages into the secondary mortgage market.

ORIGINATION ——————— *4*

The residential mortgage lending process begins with attracting potential borrowers to a mortgage lender, resulting, it is hoped, in a completed application for a mortgage loan. Mortgage lenders refer to this activity as loan origination. Residential mortgage loans are originated in the *primary mortgage market* (i.e., that market wherein credit is extended to a borrower[s]). Put another way, a primary mortgage market activity occurs when a mortgage lender agrees to extend credit to a borrower(s). This market is contrasted with the secondary mortgage market, where mortgage loans already originated are bought and sold. (See Chapter 10, The Secondary Mortgage Market.)

Obviously, all mortgage lenders perform the origination function. They may use different methods or employ alternative strategies to originate loans according to their own unique sources of funds, portfolio possibilities, fee income needs, staff resources, or other considerations, but to one degree or another, they all perform the origination function. *Mortgage investors*, on the other hand, only hold mortgages that they have purchased from one of the many types of mortgage lenders or from other investors.

The First Step

The first step in originating a residential mortgage loan is getting an applicant in the door. With increased competition for mortgage loans, this first step can be a real hurdle for some lenders. Identifying who the customer is and establishing how to attract that customer will be discussed in this chapter. The way a customer is treated once in the lender's door can determine whether that customer will continue the origination process with the lender. This initial treatment of a customer should be important to all mortgage lenders, since it may be what decides whether this applicant comes back for another mortgage loan later or recommends the lender to another consumer.

Mortgage lenders must be sensitive to the stress that most applicants are under when they enter a mortgage lender's office. The stress comes from the applicants having found their "dream home" and now having to apply for and wait for approval for the financing. Lenders need to understand this stress and that the process of applying for a residential loan is often an intimidating experience for many applicants. Lenders are often looked upon as adversaries by consumers, and if the origination function is not smooth or explained clearly and fully, it can further alienate an applicant. Lenders should understand that most applicants have either never applied for a mortgage loan before or have done so only rarely. Applicants must be treated with care and understanding, and the reasons for the various verifications, appraisal, survey, insurance, and other documentations fully explained. In addition, the applicant should be given an indication of the likely turnaround time for approval of the application.

Some lenders have the attitude that they are doing a mortgage applicant a favor by considering them for a mortgage loan. Those lenders that have been able to increase their market share over the past few years have been those that have recognized that a mortgage applicant is a customer and is entitled to courteous and fair treatment. With the entry of so many new residential mortgage originators into the market, the ability to treat customers courteously and fairly will be an important factor in determining a lender's market share.

Convenience for the Applicant

A fairly recent innovation has been the willingness of some mortgage lenders, especially mortgage bankers or brokers, to meet with applicants at any time and place that is most convenient for the applicant. This often takes the form of an originator meeting at the applicant's home at night or at the applicant's office. This accommodating approach is appreciated by the applicants and gets the attention of real estate salespeople as well. A related issue is whether a mortgage lender's origination personnel consider themselves "order takers" or "salespeople." Today's competitive residential lending market places a premium on salespeople, whereas order takers are a relic of the past.

Information Booklet

In a real estate transaction, time is usually of the essence; any delay can destroy the transaction. This is equally true for the financing of the transaction. Many lenders handle this timing issue by providing potential applicants with a marketing brochure that explains what information (e.g., W-2s, tax returns, divorce decree, credit card numbers, employment history, etc.) should be brought with them into the lender's office to apply for a loan. Having all the required information ready ensures that both the lender and the applicant are using their time in the best manner. This booklet can also be used to explain about housing and debt-to-income ratios, loan-to-value ratios, and other pertinent information a potential applicant should be aware of before completing an application. If the applicant has all or most of this information at application time, the process can move rapidly toward a decision.

Tracing the Progress of the Application

Once an application has been completed, it is quite normal for an applicant to wonder about the progress of the application or to have other questions while the application is being processed. Some mortgage lenders advise the applicant to talk to the loan originator when questions develop. Other lenders designate a loan processor with whom an applicant should discuss the mortgage loan. Neither approach is any better than the other; rather it depends on how the origination function is organized and whose time can best be spent answering the applicant's questions.

WHAT ATTRACTS CONSUMERS?

A few years ago, the Mortgage Bankers Association of American (MBA) conducted a survey of its membership to determine their opinion of what attracted consumers for a residential mortgage loan. The survey confirmed some old beliefs and introduced some new ones. One of the old beliefs confirmed was the importance of the realtor in determining where an applicant would seek a purchase money mortgage (not important for refinancings).

The three "attributes" considered the most important by mortgage lenders in attracting consumers were:

1. referral by real estate sales agents,
2. low interest rates on loans,
3. good company reputation.

The next five attributes were of about equal importance:

4. friendliness of loan officers,
5. previous experience with company/institution,
6. recognition of company/institution name,
7. availability of various loan products,
8. convenience of home or office application.

Finally, this survey established the importance of attracting the potential applicant while he or she is still "shopping around." Once an applicant has submitted an application elsewhere it is extremely difficult to get him or her to drop that application and apply with another lender.

How Loyal are Mortgage Borrowers?

During 1993, in the midst of that historic wave of refinancings, the MBA did another survey of its members and found that homeowners had little loyalty when it came to refinancing their mortgages. According to this survey, three out of five borrowers were taking their business elsewhere when they refinanced. As a result of this survey and others like it, some mortgage lenders developed a strategy of sending a letter to all of their existing mortgagors asking them to "call us first" if they are considering refinancings. Other mortgage lenders simply made sure that they were offering attractive interest rates and doing effective marketing to let all potential borrowers know their rates, including existing borrowers. To put the concepts for successfully attracting and retaining mortgage consumers into a nutshell, consumers are looking for a lender:

- with the right mortgage product at an attractive rate,
- that handles the application in a timely manner,
- that gives quality service.

METHODS OF ORIGINATION

In today's rapidly evolving primary mortgage market, three strategies or methods of loan origination are used:

- retail loan origination,
- wholesale loan origination,
- combination of retail and wholesale.

Recent data indicates that most mortgage lenders continue to follow the traditional retail strategy, while a growing minority uses the wholesale strategy, with a few, larger lenders using a combination of the two.

These three strategies will be discussed in some detail, with particular emphasis placed on the advantages and disadvantages of each.

Retail Loan Origination

Most borrowers are familiar with retail loan origination. It is still the strategy or method used by most mortgage lenders today, especially smaller financial institutions. Larger lenders tend to have a more diverse approach. The retail method of loan origination occurs when a mortgage lender itself performs directly all of the steps or functions during the origination process. These origination steps are discussed in detail later in this chapter.

Importance of the real estate agent   The principal customer or client of most mortgage lenders is the local realtor (i.e., for purchase money mortgages). Ultimately, of course, the customer is the mortgage borrower, but initially the realtor is the one who directs most borrowers to a mortgage lender. For any retail lender, good relations with realtors are essential. The National Association of Realtors and others have estimated that 80 to 90 percent of home buyers followed the recommendation of the real estate agent who sold them their home as to which lender to apply to for a home mortgage loan.

It is customary in today's competitive real estate sales market for real estate agents to routinely advise consumers about current home financing options and to recommend lenders who can fulfill the consumer's financing needs. Real estate agents will usually only recommend those mortgage lenders who act promptly and treat the applicants sent to them in a courteous and timely manner. Once a mortgage lender has developed a negative image within the real estate sales community, it is difficult to change that image and convince realtors to send new applicants. Those mortgage lenders that provide quality service to the real estate agents, and ultimately the consumer, are the lenders that will increase market share.

Except in small markets or in refinancing situations, borrowers seldom seek out or identify a lender on their own. For this reason, it is essential to a lender's market share that it maintain a good working relationship with local real estate salespeople.

During periods of increased refinancing activity, real estate salespeople are less important, but relationships must be maintained for the next cycle when purchase money mortgages are important again. During refinancing

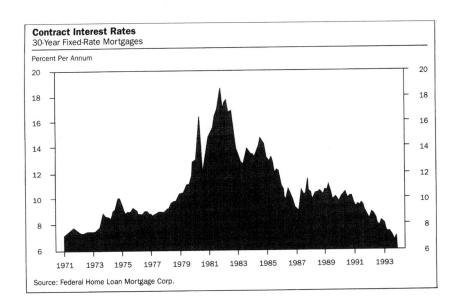

Contract Interest Rates
30-Year Fixed-Rate Mortgages

Percent Per Annum

Source: Federal Home Loan Mortgage Corp.

ONE- TO FOUR-FAMILY MORTGAGE ORIGINATIONS
1980–1994

	Total Dollar Volume ($ in billions)	% of Total, Refinancings	Loan Size	ARM Share % of Conv.
1980	134	n.a.	50,717	n.a.
1981	98	n.a.	52,819	n.a.
1982	97	n.a.	54,197	n.a.
1983	202	n.a.	58,669	n.a.
1984	204	n.a.	63,418	62
1985	290	18	68,549	51
1986	499	32	75,965	30
1987	507	29	83,903	43
1988	446	18	92,517	58
1989	453	19	99,535	38
1990	458	13	98,056	28
1991	562	30	102,031	23
1992	894	48	105,962	20
1993	1,060	55	111,031	20
1994	750 (est.)	30 (est.)	117,368 (est.)	25 (est.)

Source: U.S. Department of Housing and Urban Development, Survey of Lending Activity.

frenzies (e.g., 1992–93), interest rates and reputation of mortgage lenders attract the most business.

Commission loan agents   In today's highly competitive primary mortgage marketplace, most retail lenders employ commissioned loan officers or loan representatives to solicit business from realtors or, in some cases, builders. Mortgage bankers and brokers have traditionally used commissions as the way to both compensate and motivate their originators. Other lenders, primarily smaller thrifts and credit unions, pay their originators a salary only. Some lenders will use a combination of salary and commissions.

The commission normally given to a retail mortgage loan originator is ½ of 1 percent of the loan amount (or, as normally stated, 50 basis points). This commission is payable, of course, only if the loan can be made according to the policies and procedures of the lender and finally closes. Some lenders will give a smaller commission per loan until a certain quota has been reached and then increase the commission to a higher amount, say 60 basis points.

With the introduction of many new, nontraditional mortgage lenders (e.g., Sears and GMAC) into an already crowded marketplace, developing ways to meet the competition has become the backbone of all mortgage lenders' game plans. This concern for market share has forced many lenders to change their lending philosophy from being simply an order taker to being an

ONE- TO FOUR-FAMILY MORTGAGE ORIGINATIONS
MARKET SHARE BY LENDER GROUP

	Mortgage Co's (%)	Commercial Banks (%)	Thrifts (%)	Others (%)
1980	22	22	50	6
1981	24	22	47	7
1982	29	26	40	5
1983	30	22	46	2
1984	23	21	53	3
1985	38	20	40	2
1986	35	22	41	2
1987	33	25	41	1
1988	33	23	42	2
1989	37	27	35	1
1990	35	33	30	2
1991	47	27	25	1
1992	49	26	24	1
1993	53	25	21	1

Source: Department of Housing and Urban Development.

aggressive seller of their mortgage products. Lenders with commissioned loan agents logically seem to be the lenders that will succeed in holding on to their market share, and probably grow, at the expense of lenders with only salaried loan officers. Increased compensation is still the best reward for increased productivity.

Functions Performed by Retail Lenders   The retail mortgage lender directly performs the following origination functions:

- completes application with borrower,
- orders all employment, income, and deposit verifications,
- orders appraisal,
- orders credit report,
- prepares loan for underwriting,
- underwrites the loan application,
- approves or rejects the loan application,
- closes and funds approved loan,
- portfolios or warehouses/sells loan.

Historically, the vast majority of residential mortgage loans has been originated in this manner. Today, many smaller mortgage lenders, especially financial institutions, still use this method predominantly. An obvious benefit

TOP FIVE RESIDENTIAL MORTGAGE ORIGINATORS IN 1993
(dollars in billions)

Rank	'93 Volume	'92 Volume	Percent Increase
1. Countrywide Funding	$49.5	$30.5	62.3
2. Prudential Home Mortgage	43.2	28.5	51.5
3. Norwest Mortgage	33.7	20.9	61.2
4. Fleet Mortgage Group	24.0	19.6	22.4
5. North American Mortgage	17.6	11.7	50.4

The totals include both retail and wholesale originations.
Source: Inside Mortgage Finance, the Mortgage Market Statistical Annual for 1994.

to retail lenders in originating mortgage loans themselves is that they can establish a long-term relationship with mortgage borrowers, which can prove profitable in future transactions. These future transactions can be either mortgage loans or other consumer loans.

Origination income   Most retail mortgage lenders charge an application fee or origination points, or both, to offset some or all of the expenses incurred in performing the various origination functions. If the borrower charges an application fee, that fee is usually large enough to pay for the credit report, appraisal, and any other direct out-of-pocket expense a lender has in processing the loan application. The use of application fees has given way to charging origination points at most lenders, but some charge both. The marketplace will determine which fees are charged and how much.

Origination points are often used by lenders for revenue to:

- offset personnel and office expenses,
- increase yield on mortgages to secondary market requirements,
- produce current income.

Estimates for the cost of processing a residential mortgage loan (not including the 50 basis points paid to a loan originator) range from 60 to 120 basis points. Keeping these costs as low as possible is the goal of all mortgage lenders. As a general rule, increasing loan volume helps to drive down the cost of processing.

Some mortgage lenders have concluded that they can put loans on the books cheaper by buying residential mortgage loans from brokers rather than incurring the expense of processing the loans themselves.

FASB #91   In its Statement of Financial Accounting Standards (#91), the Financial Accounting Standards Board (FASB) has ruled that any origination points that are not offset by actual expenses incurred in originating the loan must be amortized over the loan contract period or, if it can be clearly established, the expected life of the loan. This ruling has changed the way many lenders look at origination points. Those lenders that sell loans immediately into the secondary mortgage market (e.g., mortgage bankers and others) are affected the least since they can take any fee income into current income immediately after the sale of any loan. But portfolio lenders (e.g., thrifts and credit unions) will have to amortize much of that fee income over the expected life of the loan. Thrifts in particular may be hurt by this ruling since many have become comfortable using these fees to boost current income.

Points and interest rate trade-offs   The long-term result of this FASB ruling may be a return to the low- or no-point lending of the 1970s. No-point lending does not necessarily interfere with a lender's overall yield since it can increase the interest rate to offset the loss of fee income. As a general rule, a 1 percent origination fee equals an increase in yield of ⅛ of 1 percent; thus, a quote of 10 percent and 2 points is approximately the same to a borrower as a 10¼ percent quote with no points.

Retail branch office   A retail mortgage lender is primarily interested in giving the best possible service to its customers—local realtors and mortgage applicants. A convenient location for loan origination offices is probably the most basic "service" to applicants, but it can be one of the most important rendered. Location is also important to a retail lender in regard to walk-in business. Although the percentage of this type of business to total originations is generally small, walk-in business for a new mortgage and refinancing can be just the additional business that makes a branch profitable. Therefore, each branch origination office should be easily reached by automobile or public transportation and be in a highly visible location, preferably on a ground floor.

Depending on whether loan processing is centralized or not, a branch office houses the loan origination personnel and appropriate staff support. If loan processing is not centralized, loan processors will be located at each branch office. Mortgage loan volume per retail office varies widely depending on many factors, but a valid goal is to produce 30 to 40 loans per production employee (including loan processors) per year. An office with a staff of nine— a branch manager who handles closings, a secretary, three loan originators, three loan processors, and one underwriter—should produce 300 to 350 loans a year. At an average annual loan balance of $110,000, loan production for the office should exceed $33 million.

Wholesale Loan Origination

Over the past 15 years, the natural cycle of mortgage lending has been magnified by a number of unpredictable factors. These factors have contributed to changes in the way many mortgage lenders approach residential mortgage origination.

These factors include, among others:

- greater volatility in mortgage interest rates (e.g., fixed rates that ranged from 9 percent in 1979 to 18 percent in 1982 and down to below 7 percent in 1993),
- massive swings in one- to four-family mortgage originations from year to year (e.g., range from $187 billion in 1979 to $97 billion in 1982 and then up to over a trillion dollars in 1993),
- increased geographical cycle of originations as one area and then another became hot and then cooled off,
- new, dynamic origination competition from traditional and nontraditional lenders,
- cheaper and more sophisticated technological support for mortgage lending,
- greater valuation of servicing rights.

All of these factors, along with other factors unique to individual lenders, have contributed to the growth of *wholesale mortgage lending* by some mortgage lenders. This method of producing loans is sometimes referred to as "third party-origination," or TPO. In recent years, as much as 40 to 50 percent of residential mortgage loans has been originated using this strategy. These third-party originators have increased in numbers as the demand for their products has increased. It is estimated that their numbers increased from around 7,000 in 1987 to over 14,000 in the boom year of 1993. The third-party originators are mortgage brokers and loan correspondents who sell mortgages they originate to acquiring mortgage lenders called wholesale lenders.

Mortgage brokers and loan correspondents   This method or strategy of loan origination occurs when a mortgage lender acquires a loan, processed to one degree or another, from another lender that has originated the loan. The primary reason for purchasing a mortgage loan originated by another lender is the purchasing mortgage lender's belief that it can originate mortgages (and/or servicing) cheaper that way. The "other lender" from whom loans are purchased is normally either a mortgage broker or a loan correspondent. The difference between these two lenders is that a mortgage broker usually has not begun either the processing or underwriting of the loan, while a loan correspondent typically has closed and funded the loan.

Functions performed   The extent of loan processing by a broker varies depending on the needs of the originating lender and the acquiring lender. In many situations, the broker completes the application with the borrower and orders the various verifications. This material is then shipped to the acquiring lender (referred to as a wholesaler) which will then make the underwriting decision.

Table funding   Loan correspondents, on the other hand, normally complete the loan processing and make an underwriting decision. The loan correspondent may or may not fund the loan. If the loan is funded by the acquiring lender, the transaction is called *table funding*. Table funding occurs when a broker closes a mortgage loan with funds belonging to an acquiring lender and immediately assigns the loans to that lender. This activity gives the originator the opportunity to say it is a direct lender since it can close loans with its own funds. These originators believe that by funding the loan at closing, they acquire a marketing advantage over other brokers.

Upon purchase, the acquiring lender may reunderwrite the individual mortgage, or some or all of the mortgages, if in a package. The extent of underwriting by the acquiring lender will depend to a great extent on the amount of business it has previously done with the loan correspondent.

If the loan is not closed before the correspondent sells the loan to the investor, the correspondent is most concerned with the turnaround time for an underwriting decision from the acquiring investor. The loan correspondent is normally looking for a 48-hour decision time. This is important to the originating lender since it may have to renegotiate with the applicant if the loan is declined as originally submitted. The ability of the wholesaler to fund quickly after the underwriting decision is also of great importance to the originating lender.

What motivates the originating lender?   The originating lender is not interested in holding the loans or in selling them into the secondary mortgage market. This lender has determined that it can operate more profitably by originating loans for other lenders without the inherent interest rate risk associated with holding mortgages for a short or long period of time. This lender will almost always be originating against commitments that have been obtained from those lenders that rely on them for production.

Fees and premiums   The originating lender retains any application fee and will probably collect as large an origination fee as the market will bear. It is the originating lender's responsibility to pay the originating agent the 50 basis point commission and also to have the staff necessary to process the loan. In addition to the fee income generated from the origination process, often an originating lender also receives a fee called a "servicing release premium" from the acquiring lender. This fee is a recognition that value (the value inherent in servicing a mortgage) is being transferred to the acquiring lender.

After the loans have been acquired and underwritten, the acquiring lender will close the loan in its own name and either put the loan in its portfolio or sell it in the secondary mortgage market.

Affinity groups   Another variation on the wholesale theme is the concept of one mortgage lender serving the mortgage lending needs of an "affinity group." This arrangement involves a mortgage lender that links up with a large corporation or membership group (such as a credit union) as the preferred provider of mortgage loans. The benefits of this type of arrangement are mutual: The mortgage lender is endorsed by the sponsor, and the borrowers usually are treated better and may get a more attractive deal. Mortgage lenders are also interested in arrangements of this type because the new business is usually in addition to their own business; thus the economies of scale become even more attractive. As a general rule, the arrangement between the mortgage lender and the affinity group contains provisions that prevent the lender from selling the servicing rights to another lender.

Advantages and disadvantages of wholesale lending   As with most types of business strategies or methods of doing business, there are advantages and disadvantages for each. This is particularly true for the wholesale method of loan origination. The greatest advantage of wholesale loan origination to the acquiring mortgage lender is that it provides them with an inexpensive method of quickly originating a high volume of mortgage loans. This method is assumed by these lenders to be less expensive than retail lending for a number of reasons including the ability to acquire loans without the need for a large loan processing staff. Some experts indicate that from 60 to 70 percent of the cost of originating a mortgage loan involves personnel expenses. If some or all of the originating functions are performed by the originating lender, the acquiring mortgage lender assumes they will enhance their own profitability.

An important item to be considered in determining which approach is most appropriate for a particular lender is the expected number of loans produced per production employee. The rule of thumb for retail mortgage lending is yearly production of approximately 30 to 35 loans per production employee. A recent study suggests that the direct cost of producing a mortgage loan using the retail strategy is approximately $1,700 per loan. For nonretail production, the direct cost per loan averaged approximately $500 per loan. The nonretail production figure is approximately 100 to 110 loans per production employee. This major difference in productivity is explained by a retail lender needing to have more employees to perform all of the origination functions while a mortgage broker or loan correspondent only performs certain functions.

Another important advantage a wholesale lender has is the ability to move quickly into and out of markets that are changing. Since a wholesale lender does not have to be concerned with brick and mortar expenses or with acquiring personnel for a new office, it can quickly move into a geographical area that is attractive even if it is on the other side of the country. In addition, if a market deteriorates quickly, a wholesale lender can simply decide not to purchase any loans in that area; it does not have to be concerned with either selling its physical assets or relocating its personnel.

Unlike the retail lender, the wholesale lender does not have to be concerned with the attractiveness or the location of its offices. Not only will this lender need far fewer offices (each office can serve a very large geographical region), none are needed for direct face-to-face contact with applicants. As a result, offices can be less visible and thus less costly.

Wholesale lenders are usually quite interested in rapid growth in their servicing portfolio. These institutions desire large portfolios in order to obtain the economies of scale that can produce profits approaching 40 percent of servicing revenue. To these lenders the quickest way to increase their servicing portfolios is to acquire large blocks of loans through the wholesale approach, sell the loans immediately into the secondary mortgage market, and strip off the servicing rights.

Quality control   The strongest negative factor to wholesale lending is the issue of quality control. If a mortgage lender does not process or underwrite a mortgage loan, that lender's ability to control the quality of the loans is greatly reduced. Many wholesale lenders have addressed this issue by dealing only with well-established, reputable brokers or correspondents. Because the acquiring mortgage lender has these quality control problems, these lenders generally have higher underwriting and quality control expenses than retail lenders. They face the need of increased spot checking of appraisals and verifications in order to manage quality. Since these loans are probably sold in the secondary mortgage market, the wholesale lender could see its servicing profits greatly diminished, with increased servicing expenses if quality controls are not in place and strictly adhered to.

Unlike a retail lender, an acquiring lender does not receive any application or processing fee and normally receives none or just a small part of the origination points. This reduced fee is not a critical item to the wholesale lender since it does not have the expenses of a retail lender. The best example of an expense that an acquiring lender does not have to pay is the 50 basis points commission to an origination agent.

MORTGAGE INSTRUMENTS ————————— 5

The recent explosive growth of the many types of alternative mortgage instruments is the result of fundamental changes in the way homes are financed. During the period between the Great Depression and the early 1980s, practically all residential real estate loan transactions were financed with the use of the standard fixed-rate mortgage. Today, residential real estate is financed by either the standard fixed-rate mortgage or by one of the various alternative mortgage instruments. Depending on interest rates, alternative mortgage instruments have been used for as many as 60 percent of all residential mortgage loans or as low as 20 percent. Because residential mortgage interest rates have been relatively low during the first half of the 1990s, fixed-rate mortgages have once again been the product most mortgage consumers select. This can be expected to change if mortgage interest rates once again turn up meaningfully. If rates do move up significantly, consumers will again be interested in the various alternative mortgage instruments. Before reviewing these new instruments, a discussion of the standard fixed-rate mortgage is required.

————————————— *STANDARD FIXED-RATE MORTGAGE*

The standard fixed-rate mortgage was the product of an earlier financial upheaval, the Great Depression of the 1930s, which changed the way homes were financed at that time. Before this innovation, most homes were financed by a term mortgage with the entire principal due at the end (or term) of the loan. It was normal practice for these loans to be rolled over into another loan at the end of the term. However, as a result of this practice, many homeowners lost their homes during the economic emergency of the early 1930s because traditional lenders were unable to refinance these mortgages as they came due. This inability to refinance was the result of a severe national liquidity crisis.

The liquidity crisis was brought about by massive bank and thrift failures caused by a combination of bad loans and savers' panic withdrawals of their deposits. The resulting losses to depositors during this predepositor insurance period destroyed savers' confidence in financial institutions until deposit insurance arrived a few years later. As a means of addressing the national wave of foreclosures, the Home Owners Loan Corporation (HOLC), a federal agency, began exchanging government bonds for defaulted mortgages. If HOLC believed a loan it received was basically a sound one and only in default because of the liquidity crisis, that loan would be reconstituted as a 20-year loan with a self-amortizing monthly payment of principal and interest. This became the standard fixed-rate mortgage, which was used almost exclusively until recently and which allowed this nation to have such a high home ownership rate.

Direct Reduction Instrument

The standard fixed-rate mortgage is a monthly amortized, direct reduction instrument. This means that equal monthly payments for the term of the loan are used to directly reduce the amount owed by first paying interest on the loan due since the last payment and then using the remainder to reduce principal. This periodic reduction of principal combined with the fact that a borrower knows exactly how much is due each month are the two most important features of the standard fixed-rate mortgage.

The direct reduction of principal is also important for another reason. It allows for a considerable savings in the total amount of interest a borrower would have to pay if interest were calculated on the entire amount of principal, as occurs with a term loan. As noted earlier, term loans allow for no principal repayment during the term—only periodic interest payments, with the entire principal due at the end of the term. The savings to a borrower (before taxes) using an amortized loan as opposed to a term loan are seen in the following example.

Example: $1,000 loan at 10 percent interest to be repaid in five years with annual year-end payments compared to the same loan repaid on an amortized basis.

	Term Loan				Amortized Loan		
Year	Interest	Principal	Total	Year	Interest	Principal	Total
1	$100.00	–0–	$100.00	1	$100.00	163.80	$263.80
2	100.00	–0–	100.00	2	83.62	180.18	263.80
3	100.00	–0–	100.00	3	63.60	198.20	263.80
4	100.00	–0–	100.00	4	45.79	218.01	263.80
5	100.00	1,000.00	1,100.00	5	23.99	239.81	263.80
	$500.00	$1,000.00	$1,500.00		$319.00	$1,000.00	$1,319.00

Thus, with the standard fixed-rate mortgage, the monthly mortgage payment would remain the same from the first payment until the next to last (the last could be slightly different), even though much of the first payment went to interest and practically all of the last went to principal. If the example was for a longer term, say 30 years, practically all of the first payment would go to interest.

This type of mortgage served both borrower and lender well from the 1930s until the middle 1970s. For those who obtained one of these mortgages in the early 1970s or before, the fixed nature of their monthly mortgage payment was obviously a beneficial feature during the high inflation period of the late 1970s and early 1980s. What was good for those fortunate borrowers was nearly ruinous for mortgage lenders after 1978. The billions of dollars in these fixed-rate mortgages was also a deterrent to new borrowers, who had to pay higher rates for mortgages than would have been expected in order to help offset low-yielding mortgages.

MORTGAGE LENDERS' DILEMMA

For those portfolio lenders active in residential lending, primarily savings and loans, savings banks, and some commercial banks, the path that eventually led to financial ruin for some was initially quite smooth and profitable. These institutions had served savers and borrowers well over the past 50 years as they borrowed money at 5 or 5½ percent and loaned it out to homebuyers at 7 or 7½ percent. The 150 to 250 basis point spread between a lender's cost of funds and the yield on its portfolio allowed for all operating expenses and an attractive profit. Through the process of financial intermediation, these institutions built up loan portfolios of 20- to 30-year mortgages worth hundreds of billions of dollars. It was this huge portfolio of low-yielding mortgages that became the nearly fatal characteristic of thrift institutions in the early 1980s.

Two events occurred during the late 1970s and early 1980s that changed how mortgage lenders would operate: rapid increases in inflation and increased competition for depositors' savings. The result was a doubling of the cost of funds to lenders in just a period of months. Since thrifts were primarily mortgage lenders and did not have the benefit of a variable-rate asset structure, as did many commercial banks with commercial loans, they suffered greatly.

Many portfolio lenders found themselves paying more for deposits than they were earning on the mortgage portfolios. Many lenders that normally worked with a positive spread of 200 to 250 basis points were now faced with a negative spread of over 100 basis points. As a direct result of these unforeseeable events, many lending institutions were forced to close their doors or to merge with other institutions. All mortgage lenders were forced to reexamine how they would lend on mortgages in the future.

As a consequence of this near disaster for those mortgage lenders that portfolioed mortgage loans, many surviving mortgage lenders retreated from the standard fixed-rate mortgage to one of a number of alternative mortgage instruments. These alternative mortgage instruments were attractive because they allowed for some periodic adjustment to interest rates in a changing financial environment. Even those mortgage lenders that sold some or all of their production into the secondary mortgage market needed new mortgage instruments so that their investors would be protected from interest rate risk. The feature that lenders were looking for in these alternative mortgage instruments was a way of sharing with borrowers some of the risk of lending in an uncertain economic environment.

1990s: Return of the Fixed-Rate Mortgage

Although many lenders vowed they would never again originate and portfolio fixed-rate mortgages after the disaster of the early 1980s, these same lenders were forced to change their minds when long-term, fixed rates tumbled in the late 1980s and early 1990s. As rates on long-term, fixed-rate mortgages dropped to 20-year lows, consumers refinanced their existing mortgages and over 80 percent of them selected fixed-rate mortgages of varying maturities.

SHARING THE RISK

In order for residential mortgage lenders to remain active in the mortgage market on a daily basis, they must have ways of meeting interest rate shifts in a profitable manner. Some mortgage lenders have solved the problem of interest rate risk by selling some or all of the fixed-rate mortgages they originate. Other portfolio lenders have decided they can obtain a greater spread between their cost of funds and portfolio yield by retaining the fixed-rate mortgages with their higher initial yield in their mortgage portfolio.

During periods of interest rate volatility, mortgage borrowers will be offered more variable-rate mortgages at attractive rates by mortgage lenders as those lenders move to protect themselves from interest rate risk. All mortgage lenders should develop strategies allowing future lending activity to produce a sufficient spread between cost of funds and portfolio yield to cover the following:

- cost of funds/interest expenses,
- cost of loan processing,
- operating expenses,
- reasonable profit.

In the past, many mortgage lenders borrowed short and loaned long by using market-sensitive savings to finance 20- to 30-year mortgages. Hopefully, with the bitter lesson of the 1980s behind them, lenders have become more sophisticated and have learned how better to match the maturity of their liabilities with their assets. The improvement in lenders' asset/liability management is evidenced by the increased use of certificates of deposit of longer maturity and by the use of alternative mortgage instruments. Many different types of alternative mortgage instruments have evolved since the first type was used in California in the early 1970s. The more common are discussed in the following sections.

ALTERNATIVE MORTGAGE INSTRUMENTS

Adjustable Rate Mortgage (ARM)

The most popular form of alternative mortgage instrument is the adjustable rate mortgage (ARM). Over the past 10 years, the percentage of residential mortgage loans that were ARMs has been as high as 60 percent when interest rates were high and as low as 20 percent when interest rates were low. An ARM is basically an alternative mortgage instrument with the interest rate adjusting periodically to some predetermined index, with the payment increasing or decreasing accordingly.

Alternative mortgage instruments, common around the world, were first used in this country in the early 1970s by state-chartered savings and loan institutions in California. These thrifts initially had only qualified success with these instruments. Many borrowers rejected these early ARMs because they were afraid that their interest rates would increase rapidly and thus they continued to select fixed-rate mortgages. Only after mortgage lenders began putting caps on how far interest rates could adjust each year and over the life of the loan were borrowers willing to try these new instruments.

Structure of an ARM: Adjustment period   The period of time in which the interest rate and payment can change is called the "adjustment period." ARMs can have adjustment periods of varied length, but the most common are the one-year, three-year, and five-year adjustment periods. Therefore, an ARM with a one-year adjustment period is called a one-year ARM. The one-year ARM is, by far, the most popular of the various ARMs offered today. One of the reasons for the popularity of this ARM is that it usually has the lowest interest rate of all the various ARMs. As a general rule, the shorter the interval between adjustments, the lower the initial interest rate.

Index   The concept behind an ARM is that it will produce an interest rate that moves as interest rates in general move, thus providing the portfolio lender

Date __April 3__, 19__95__

Loan No. __N0123445__

ADJUSTABLE RATE MORTGAGE LOAN ADJUSTMENT NOTICE

This notice is to inform you of:

__XX__   An adjustment to your interest rate **with** a corresponding adjustment to your payment

_____   An adjustment(s) to your interest rate **without** a corresponding adjustment(s) to your payment

The interest rate on your loan with __Tolland Bank__
secured by a __mortgage__ _____ on property located at __123 Tolland Ave.,__
__Tolland, CT__ _____ is scheduled to be adjusted on __May 1, 1995__, 19____.
The index on which your interest rate is based is __one year Treasury adjusted to a constant maturity__

You should be aware of the following interest rate adjustment information concerning your Adjustable Rate Mortgage Loan. (The checked statements below reflect interest rate and payment adjustments as they apply to this notice. Those left blank do not apply.)

☒☒ Your new interest rate will be __7.00__ %, which is based on an index value of __4.25__ %.
☒☐ Your previous rate was __6.75__ %, which was based on an index value of __4.00__ %.
☐ The new interest rate does not reflect a change of _____ percentage points in the index value which
     was not added because of _____.
☒☒ Your new payment will be $ __1,245.89__
☐ Your new loan balance is $ __88,989.90__
☐ Your ☐ new ☐ existing payment will not be sufficient to cover the interest due and the difference will be
     added to the loan amount. The payment amount needed to pay your loan in full by the end of the term at
     the new interest rate is $_____.
☐ The following interest rate adjustment(s) have been implemented this year without changing your payment:
     _____
     _____
     _____

     These interest rates were based on the following index values: _____
     _____

If you have any questions about this notice, please contact:

__Ted Williams__
NAME
__Loan Officer__
__Boston Mortgage Company__
TITLE

__800-406-1941__
PHONE NUMBER

43077 7/88
AML Adjustment Notice
T-I-L Disclosure (10/88)   **BORROWER**

with some protection against interest rate risk. In order to accomplish this, the interest rate for the ARM is tied to an "index." The index must be beyond the control of the lender; thus it cannot be the lenders' cost of funds. As a general rule, the index is tied either to a general cost of funds (e.g., the 11th District of the FHLB), or to a Treasury security with a like period of maturity (e.g., a one-year ARM indexed to the one-year Treasury bill). The most common index is the one-year Treasury bill (adjusted to a constant maturity).

The following are some representative ARM indices:

- Six-month Treasury Bill. Based on the weekly auction rates on six-month (26-week) Treasury bills. Generally considered the most responsive of all indices to changes in market interest rates and thus the most volatile.
- One-Year Constant Maturity Treasury. This index is calculated by taking the average of all Treasury securities having one year remaining until maturity. This index is very responsive to market interest rate changes and therefore is volatile. Most popular of all indices.
- Three- and Five-Year Treasury. Similar to the one-year Treasury in that each is adjusted to a constant maturity. These have become less popular over recent years because the discount from a fixed-rate mortgage is much less with these indices.
- Federal Home Loan District Bank Cost of Funds (COF). Based on the total of all interest/dividends paid or accrued by thrift institutions in a particular district. The most common COF index is the 11th District (West Coast) of the FHLB. This index has lost some appeal since it is now understood to be a trailing index in that it lags behind recent interest rate movements.
- National Contract Rate on Purchase of Previously Occupied Homes. Based on a weighted average of initial contract mortgage rates charged by major lenders on newly originated, conventional, fixed- and adjustable-rate mortgages on previously occupied homes. Probably the least volatile of indices. Not used very often.

Other indices are used occasionally, such as LIBOR (London Inter-Bank Offering Rate) used for ARMs sold in Europe, and a fairly new CD interest rate index that is the average of commercial bank certificates of deposit. All of the indices can be tracked by use of the Federal Reserve Board's statistical release H.15.

Margin   In order to establish what the interest rate on an ARM will be, lenders add to the index rate another figure called the "margin." The margin originally was to correspond to that lenders' operating expenses, but it is now market driven. Recently margins have ranged between 200 and 300 basis points—the average is about 275 basis points. This is an important number for a consumer to establish before entering into any ARM transaction. Once the margin is established, it is set for the life of the loan.

$$\text{Index Rate} + \text{Margin} = \text{ARM Interest Rate}$$

Interest rate caps   In addition to the requirement (Truth-in-Lending amendment) that all ARMs entered into after December 8, 1987, must have an interest rate ceiling, most ARMs today have other *caps*. Interest rate caps place a limit on the amount the interest rate can increase. The introduction of caps was what made ARMs acceptable to most consumers. Two types of interest rate caps are used today to make ARMs attractive to consumers:

- *periodic cap*, which limits the interest rate increase (or decrease) from one adjustment period to the next—1- or 2-percent caps are the most common,
- *life-time cap*, which limits the interest rate increase (or decrease) over the life of the loan—5- or 6-percent caps are the most common life-time caps.

A few ARMs have payment caps that limit the monthly payment increase at each adjustment period, usually to a certain percentage of the previous payment. A payment cap that has been recently used is a 7½-percent payment cap, which means that payment cannot increase more than that amount each adjustment period. Payment caps are not very popular because they usually produce "negative amortization" (deferred interest). This occurs when the monthly mortgage payment isn't sufficient to pay all the interest due on the mortgage; thus the mortgage balance is increasing, not decreasing as would be expected. These loans may not be salable on the secondary mortgage market because of investors' concern that these mortgages have increased risk of delinquency.

Discounts   In order to make ARMs more attractive to more consumers, most lenders lower the initial interest rate (and thus the payment rate) from that called for by adding together the index and the margin. This initial rate is called a "discounted" rate and may be 200 basis points or more below the full indexed rate. If the rate is 300 basis points or more, the rate is called a "teaser" rate. Mortgage borrowers should be wary of teaser rates since they often require large loan fees or have larger than normal margins. Mortgage lenders must be careful that they make the correct annual percentage rate (APR) disclosure when offering a discounted ARM. The correct annual percentage rate disclosure for a discounted ARM is a *composite* APR. A composite APR reflects the initial payment rate and the rate that would have resulted from the use of the full index (as it existed at closing) for the remaining term.

Composite APR Example: XYZ Savings Bank offers its one-year ARM at an initial payment rate of 6.00 percent even though the full indexed accrual rate called for a rate of 8.00 percent. In order to correctly disclose the APR, the bank will use a composite APR that reflects the 6.00 percent rate for a year and the 8.00 percent rate for the remaining term.

Spread Offering a discounted ARM is important to a lender if that lender wants to originate ARMs. There must be enough of a difference between what the fixed rate mortgage is offered at and the rate for the ARM. If no difference exists, few borrowers would select an ARM because those borrower would be taking on the risk of interest rates increasing. Therefore, lenders must compensate borrowers by making the initial payment rate of an ARM attractive as compared with the fixed-rate mortgage. This spread is usually from 200 to 300 basis points below that at which the fixed-rate mortgage is offered. As interest rates for all types of residential mortgages increase, the amount of spread between the fixed-rate and ARMs necessary to attract borrowers to the ARM will decrease since consumers expect rates to drop in the future.

Sometimes a seller or builder will pay a lender money so a borrower can get a lower initial rate. A transaction of this type is called a "buy down" and is discussed in detail later. The reason these buydowns occur is that the borrower will be able to qualify for the mortgage at the payment rate rather than the fully indexed accrual rate (FIAR) rate.

The risk to a borrower with an ARM with a discounted rate is that payment rate may still go up at the adjustment period even if the index does not. See the following example.

Example: A borrower wants to buy a house by putting 10 percent down and borrowing $100,000. The mortgage lender is offering two mortgage choices:

1. a one-year ARM indexed to the one-year Treasury (adjusted to a constant maturity) with a 250 basis point margin and 2 and 6 percent caps, or
2. a 30-year fixed-rate mortgage at 10 percent.

With the one-year index at 7 percent, the ARM interest rate is established as follows:

Index	7.00 percent
Margin	2.50 percent
Fully Indexed Accrual Rate (FIAR)	9.50 percent

But the 30-year fixed-rate is at 10 percent and the lender realizes few borrower will select the ARM at the fully indexed rate since it carries interest rate risk. The lender, therefore, offers the ARM at 200 basis points lower than the 30-year fixed-rate. The result is a payment rate discounted for the first year to 8 percent (not the 9.50 percent FIAR).

One year later however, even if the one-year Treasury index stays the same, the payment rate will increase. The payment rate the second year will be 9.50 percent. This new payment rate is established by adding the index (7 percent) to the margin (250 basis points) producing the new payment rate (9.50). The increase of 1.5 percent over the initial payment rate is less than the 2-percent annual cap and as a result is the new payment rate.

In order to protect consumers, Congress passed an amendment to Regulation Z (Truth-in-Lending) that requires that lenders provide the following information if a consumer applies for an ARM loan on the borrower's principal dwelling:

- the interest rate ceiling,
- a booklet explaining ARMs (Consumer Handbook on Adjustable Rate Mortgages),
- 15-year historical example of how rates would have changed,
- worst-case example assuming a $10,000 loan.

Biweekly Mortgages

Developed during the middle of the 1980s, the biweekly mortgage is a popular instrument that some homeowners use for shortening the life of their mortgage debt and saving on the total interest paid over the life of the mortgage. A biweekly mortgage is a fixed-rate, level-payment, fully amortizing mortgage that requires the borrower to make payments every two weeks rather than monthly—for a total of 26 payments a year. Each biweekly payment is exactly half the amount that would be payable under a comparable monthly payment mortgage. Thus, the 26 bi-weekly payments are equivalent to 13 monthly payments a year. The benefits to consumers of such a payment schedule are many. These benefits include:

- a payment schedule that fits the budget of those who are paid on a weekly or biweekly basis,
- a more frequent payment schedule substantially reduces the total interest paid over the life of the loan,
- the life of the loan is meaningfully shortened.

Example: Assume a $100,000 mortgage at 8 percent for 30 years.

Loan Product	Periodic Payment	Term
• 30-year, monthly payment	$733.77	360 months
• Biweekly payment	$366.89	272 months

Interest saved with the biweekly mortgage = $46,300.86

BI-WEEKLY PAYMENT NOTE RIDER

This BI-WEEKLY PAYMENT NOTE RIDER is made this_____day of_____, 19_____, and is incorporated into and shall be deemed to amend and supplement the Note made by the undersigned (the "Borrower") to_____ (the "Lender") and dated the same date as this BI-WEEKLY PAYMENT NOTE RIDER.

ADDITIONAL COVENANTS. In addition to the covenants and agreements made in the Note, Borrower and Lender further covenant and agree as follows:

3. PAYMENTS

A) Time and Place of Payments

I will pay principal and interest by making payments every two (2) weeks ("Bi-Weekly").

I will make my bi-weekly payments beginning_____, 19_____. I will make these payments every two (2) weeks until I have paid all of the principal and interest and any other charges described below that I may owe under this Note. My bi-weekly payments will be applied to interest before principal. If on_____, _____, I still owe amounts under this Note, I will pay those amounts in full on that date, which is called the "maturity date".

I will make my bi-weekly payments at _____ or a different place if required by the Note Holder.

B) Amount of Bi-Weekly Payments

My bi-weekly payment will be in the amount of U.S. $_____.

4. BORROWER'S RIGHT TO REPAY

I have the right to make payments of principal at any time before they are due. A payment of principal only is known as a "prepayment". When I make a prepayment, I will tell the Note Holder in writing that I am doing so.

I may make a full prepayment or partial prepayments without paying any prepayment charge. The Note Holder will use all of my prepayments to reduce the amount of principal that I owe under this Note. If I make a partial prepayment, there will be no changes in the due date or in the amount of my bi-weekly payment unless the Note Holder agrees in writing to those changes.

6. BORROWER'S FAILURE TO PAY AS REQUIRED

A) Late Charge for Overdue Payments

If the Note Holder has not received the full amount of any bi-weekly payment by the end of_____calendar days after the date it is due, I will pay a late charge to the Note Holder. The amount of the charge will be_____% of my overdue bi-weekly payment of principal and interest. I will pay this late charge promptly but only once on each late payment.

B) Default

If I do not pay the full amount of my bi-weekly payment on the date it is due, I will be in default.

BY SIGNING BELOW, Borrower accepts and agrees to the terms and covenants contained in this Bi-Weekly Payment Note Rider.

The mortgage life is shortened and the interest paid substantially decreased because with biweekly payments a borrower is paying off more of the mortgage principal in a year than would occur with monthly payments. The payment is calculated on a 30-year amortization schedule at the market rate for a biweekly mortgage, which usually is at a 25 to 50 basis point reduction from regular 30-year mortgages. The increased number of payments allow for more principal to be paid before the next scheduled payment, thus reducing the interest and the effective mortgage life. Because the principal is paid off faster, the loan matures in a shorter length of time.

The negative aspects of the biweekly mortgage are minor as far as the borrower is concerned. These negative aspects mainly center around coordinating the mortgage payment with the borrower's payday. Lenders have helped to make this easier for borrowers by setting up checking accounts that are debited every 14 days for the mortgage payment. Many borrowers have their paychecks deposited directly into these checking accounts, thus making the payment process even easier.

The major negative aspect as far as lenders are concerned is the increased cost associated with processing and calculating the increased number of payments. Some lenders have calculated that it costs $10 to process each payment; however, this may not remain an issue as lenders become more sophisticated with computer processing. Interest on biweekly mortgages is calculated using simple interest (365 rather than 360 days). A lender must have the capacity to reamortize the loan after each payment.

The underwriting requirements for a biweekly mortgage are the same as for any other mortgage except, to qualify borrowers, the biweekly principal and interest payment are adjusted to the equivalent monthly payment. Uniform biweekly notes and payment riders are available and should be used if a lender wants to be able to sell these mortgages. Fannie Mae buys 15- and 30-year biweekly mortgages through its Standard Commitment Window and will consider 10- and 20-year biweekly mortgages on a negotiated basis.

Buy Downs

Buy downs became popular during the extremely high interest rate period of the early 1980s. This concept is designed to address the issue of affordability of housing and not the issue of protecting lenders' relative yields. Although market interest rates cannot be changed (the market dictates what they will be), the effective rate to a home buyer can be changed by buying down the market rate to a rate which will allow a potential home buyer to qualify for a loan. This buydown happens when a builder, home seller, parent of a buyer, or home buyer prepays a portion of the interest a lender will earn over the life of the loan. This one-time nonrefundable payment is either paid directly to the lender in one lump sum or put into an interest-earning account that a lender debits monthly to subsidize the reduced monthly payment.

Through this method, mortgage payments can be bought down for a temporary period—usually 1 to 10 years—or permanently. The buy down can be structured in many ways: for example, a reduced monthly payment could remain constant over the life of the loan, increase yearly, or increase only once.

If a buy down is a permanent one, a home buyer is qualified for the loan on the ability to make the established monthly payment. If the buy down is only temporary, as most are, the buyer is qualified on ability to make the initial lower payment rather than ability to meet the increased payment. This benefit allows many more families to qualify for a mortgage loan.

Convertible Mortgages

The main attraction of this mortgage is that it appears to combine the best features of the fixed-rate and the adjustable-rate mortgage. This mortgage, sometimes called a convertible ARM, allows a borrower to start out with the lower payment rate that makes ARMs attractive. Later, if it is to the borrower's advantage, the existing ARM can be converted to a fixed-rate mortgage.

The attractive features of any ARM include, as we have already discussed, an interest rate that is normally 200 to 300 basis points below the fixed-rate interest rate and yearly and lifetime caps on interest rate increases. As with most standard ARMs, borrowers using this mortgage are qualified at the lower ARM payment rate (usually with a certain minimum rate, e.g., 7 percent), which, of course, allows for more borrowers to qualify for a mortgage loan.

The one feature of a fixed-rate mortgage that makes this type of loan so attractive to consumers and that is missing with a standard ARM is that the interest rate is capped at the rate set at closing. This attractive feature is normally found only in fixed-rate mortgages. Of course, if interest rates should drop, an ARM mortgagor is going to benefit from the drop in rates while the fixed-rate holder would have to refinance to enjoy the interest rate drop.

Converting to a fixed rate   A convertible mortgage affords the borrower the opportunity, for a period of time, to convert the ARM to a fixed-rate mortgage in the future. The time frame within which to convert depends on the mortgage instrument, but most instruments allow the borrower to convert anytime after the thirteenth month and until the sixtieth month. The opportunity need only be used if the borrower decides it would be beneficial to convert. At first glance the ability to convert may not appear to be of great value to a borrower since a borrower could always refinance the existing ARM and obtain a new fixed-rate mortgage. The problem with that strategy is the cost of refinancing. It is generally acknowledged that the cost of refinancing is from 2 to 4 percent of the outstanding balance. That can amount to many thousands of dollars.

AGREEMENT TO CONVERT

This Agreement is made this ____ day of _____, 19____, by and between_____
_____ (the "Lender")
and _____ (the
"Borrower") and modifies and amends certain terms of Borrower's indebtedness evidenced by a Convertible ARM Note
(the "Note") to Lender dated _____, 19____, which is secured by a Mortgage, Deed of Trust or Security
Deed (the "Security Instrument") of the same date and covering the property described in the Security Instrument and
located at:

_____

[Property Address]

In consideration of Borrower's exercise of Borrower's option to convert Borrower's adjustable interest rate loan to a
fixed interest rate loan pursuant to the provisions of the Note and the Convertible ARM Rider to the Security Instrument,
the Note is hereby modified and amended as follows:

I. Section 2 is changed to read:

2. INTEREST

Interest will be charged on unpaid principal until the full amount of principal has been paid.

I will pay interest at a yearly rate of _____% both before and after any default described in Section 8(B)
of this Note.

II. Section 3(B) is changed to read:

(B) Amount of My Monthly Payments

Each of my monthly payments beginning with the payment due _____, 19____, will be in the
amount of U.S. $_____.

III. Sections 3(C), 4 and 5 are deleted in their entirety.

IV. Section 6 is changed to read:

6. BORROWER'S RIGHT TO PREPAY

I have the right to make payments of principal at any time before they are due. A payment of principal only is
known as a "prepayment." When I make a prepayment, I will tell the Note Holder in writing that I am doing so.

I may make a full prepayment or partial prepayments without paying any prepayment charge. The Note
Holder will use all of my prepayments to reduce the amount of principal that I owe under this Note. If I make a
partial prepayment, there will be no changes in the due dates of my monthly payments unless the Note Holder
agrees in writing to those changes.

In addition to the modifications to the Note stated above, Borrower understands that, upon the Borrower's signing this
Agreement, the Lender will have the option to require immediate payment in full of all the sums secured by the Security
Instrument if all or any part of the Property or any interest in it is sold or transferred without Lender's prior written consent,
as provided in Uniform Covenant 17 of the Security Instrument.

Except as stated in this Agreement, Borrower's promise to pay and the covenants and agreements under the Note and
under the Security Instrument continue without change.

In Witnesss Whereof, Borrower and Lender have executed this Agreement.

_____   _____ (Seal)
Name of Lender   —Borrower

By: _____   _____ (Seal)
                                                                                                —Borrower

Its: _____   _____ (Seal)
                                                                                                —Borrower

MULTISTATE AGREEMENT TO CONVERT—Single Family—FHLMC Uniform Instrument   **Form 3180 8/88**

With the convertible ARM, the borrower can convert and may only have to pay a fixed amount—say $250 to $500. If the loan has been sold into the secondary mortgage market, an additional fee may be charged.

When would a borrower choose this ARM over a normal ARM or a fixed-rate mortgage? That answer depends mostly on whether the borrower can qualify for a fixed-rate mortgage. In addition, a borrower must decide whether the spread between the mortgage alternatives makes one more attractive than another.

A convertible ARM usually has an interest rate 25 to 50 basis points more than a normal ARM. The convertible ARM makes sense to a borrower if the borrower expects interest rates to drop over the next couple of years. If that occurs, the borrower will have benefited from the lower ARM interest rate initially, and after converting, the benefit of locking in the fixed rate for the life of the mortgage.

Graduated Payment Mortgage (GPM)

The GPM is an instrument that was specifically designed to provide borrowers with an opportunity to match their expected increase in income with a mortgage payment that is initially low but increases yearly. This instrument is not designed to address the issue of sheltering lenders from interest rate shifts. It does, however, help alleviate the problem of how to qualify more potential homeowners for mortgages. Many otherwise qualified potential homeowners are unable to qualify for a standard fixed-rate mortgage because their current income is not sufficient; however, if their conservatively estimated future income could be factored in they could qualify.

With a GPM, the interest rate and the term of the loan are set, as with a standard fixed-rate mortgage. The difference is that the initial monthly payment begins at a lower level than it would with a standard mortgage. The result is monthly payments that are not sufficient to fully amortize the loan. Since the payments do not fully amortize the loan, the borrower, in effect, is borrowing the difference between the payment being made and the interest actually due. The amount of accrued but unpaid interest is added to the outstanding principal amount. Through this negative amortization, the outstanding principal balance actually increases for a period of time, rather than decreasing as with a standard mortgage.

The following year the monthly payment increases at a predetermined rate, say 7½ percent, with additional increases occurring each year for a set number of years. Depending on the plan selected, as the yearly increases occur, at some point the monthly payments will equal or exceed the payment under a standard mortgage. At that point negative amortization stops but the payment increases will have to continue until they reach a level that will fully amortize the outstanding balance over the remaining years of the loan.

Example: Comparison of fixed-rate mortgage payment to GPM payment. Assume for comparison a $75,000 house, 20 percent down payment, $60,000 loan at 12 percent for 30 years. Add 2½ percent of market value for taxes and insurance = $156 per month.

Standard Fixed-Rate Monthly Payment	*Year*	*Five-year GPM 7½ Increase Monthly Payment*
$617.17	1	$474.83
617.17	2	510.45
617.17	3	548.73
617.17	4	589.88
617.17	5	634.12
617.17	6–30	681.68
$162,172.71	Total interest paid	$177,577.04

When the $156 per month for taxes and insurance is added, the necessary family income to qualify for this standard fixed-rate mortgage is $2,750 per month.

With the same $156 for taxes and insurance added, the necessary family income to qualify for this five-year GPM is $2,250 per month.

From the example, two important points emerge. First, the amount of family income to qualify for a GPM is substantially less and therefore more families can qualify. Of course, if family income does not increase at the hoped-for rate, the burden of a 7½-percent mortgage payment increase may result in a default. The second point is that the total amount of interest paid is increased with a GPM. This is the result of the negative amortization during the early years of the mortgage when principal is increasing rather than decreasing as with a fully amortized mortgage.

In addition to conventional GPMs, the Department of Housing and Urban Development has an insured GPM (Sec. 245) that is basically the same as described here.

Price Level Adjusted Mortgage (PLAM)

A PLAM is one of the more recent alternative mortgage instruments and one that holds much promise, especially if a period of hyperinflation should reappear. The underlying concept of a PLAM is that the "real" mortgage payment remains constant over the life of the mortgage. This means that the rate at which interest is charged to a borrower is guaranteed to provide a lender with a "real" return above inflation.

Under a standard mortgage, the mortgage payment is at a level sufficient to return to the lender the following: principal plus interest plus an inflation premium to make up for the decrease in the value of the money repaid. This "inflation premium" adds several hundred basis points to a typical standard mortgage payment—possibly more during higher inflation periods.

The PLAM is designed to address this problem of real return and offers a solution that benefits both borrower and lender. A PLAM takes the expensive guesswork out of lending in an inflationary economy. The real return is guaranteed by increasing the monthly mortgage payment at the same rate as the increase in inflation (or stated differently, by the decrease in the value of money) as measured by an appropriate index such as the Consumer Price Index. The outstanding principal balance is also adjusted to constant dollars. The adjustments to both the monthly payments and the outstanding principal are on a yearly basis.

The basis assumption with a PLAM, as with many other alternative mortgage instruments, is that household income will increase at or near the inflation rate. Therefore, as the mortgage payment increases, the same percentage of monthly income will be used to meet that payment.

Two-Step or Reset Mortgage

The two-step or reset mortgage is a relatively new alternative mortgage instrument developed after the convertible mortgage and shares some of the same features. This alternative provides a borrower with the certainty of a fixed-rate mortgage for a period of time (usually 5 or 7 years) and then the rate adjusts to a *new* fixed-rate (indexed to the 10-year Treasury, weekly average) with the payment remaining at that rate for the remaining 25 or 23 years. The advantage to the consumer of this mortgage is that it starts out low (lower than a 30-year fixed-rate mortgage) and remains at that low rate for 5 or 7 years with any increase in rates capped at 6 percent (Fannie Mae's program). A consumer may only be planning to stay in the home for that 5 or 7 years; thus they benefit from the lower rate.

Reverse Annuity Mortgage (RAM)

The RAM is designed to enable older retired homeowners who are probably on fixed incomes to use the equity in their homes (probably totally paid for) as a source of supplemental income while still retaining that ownership. One of the many RAMs available today is Fannie Mae's Home Equity Conversion Mortgage, which is an FHA-insured reverse mortgage. This program is open to homeowners who are at least 62 years of age who own their homes free and clear, or nearly so, and who wish to use the equity in their homes to cover part of their expenses after retirement. The loan is an ARM with the rates adjusted either annually or monthly with caps on increases.

Other RAMs work as follows: a lender has the house appraised and then lends a certain percentage of the current value. The loan itself is to be paid to the homeowner in the form of a monthly annuity. This annuity is either from the mortgage lender directly or else the proceeds of the loan are used to purchase an annuity from a life insurance company. The annuity provides monthly payments for the life of the loan or the life of the annuitant(s) depending on how the RAM is structured. Throughout the time of the loan, the homeowner owns and lives in the house.

A lender's security for a RAM is the same as with a standard mortgage: the home itself. If the homeowner (or owners) dies before the term, the estate is liable for the debt. Of course, if the house is sold before death, the debt must be paid off.

If, when the loan comes to term, the homeowner (or owners) is still alive, a new RAM can be created, assuming that the property has appreciated. The proceeds from the new RAM first repay the old one and the difference purchases a new annuity for the homeowner.

Although this mortgage concept has not been used much to date, it may become a necessary part of future mortgage lending as the American public grows older, especially if double-digit inflation returns.

Ten-, 15- or 20-Year Mortgages

Until recently, most American homeowners had become conditioned to making monthly mortgage payments on a 30-year mortgage. However, over the last couple of years this situation has changed to the point that the 30-year mortgage makes up less than half the mortgages being originated. Many homeowners refinanced their existing 30-year mortgages (as a result of the unprecedented drop in long-term mortgage rates) with 10-, 15-, or 20-year mortgages. These homeowners had been paying out a certain dollar amount each month, and when they refinanced they were willing to continue paying at that dollar amount. But, at the same dollar amount, loans would pay off sooner at the lower interest rates. The beneficial result to borrowers of the shorter-term mortgage is a substantial saving on total interest paid over the term of the mortgage loan.

PROCESSING THE RESIDENTIAL MORTGAGE LOAN

6

The residential mortgage loan processing function includes all actions and procedures that occur from the time a potential borrower submits an application through the time the loan is presented to an underwriter for a decision as to whether to grant the loan. The speedy, professional completion of this function is crucial to any mortgage lender and may be the determining factor in whether the residential mortgage lending operation is successful and profitable.

As a general rule, loan processing takes the longest time of all the steps in producing a closed residential mortgage loan. Until recently, this step could take up to 45 days, but the trend is toward faster loan processing. Today, some mortgage lenders advertise they will get an answer to the applicant within 10 days or less.

The first step in the process toward a closed mortgage loan is the initial interview. The importance of this initial contact with potential borrowers cannot be overemphasized and, if this contact is handled correctly, it can save both borrower and mortgage lender considerable time and money. The reason this step is so important is that this contact can establish early on whether a potential borrower is qualified for a mortgage loan. The person conducting this interview, most often called the loan officer, should be careful to not give the impression they are making a credit decision, only that they are explaining the general nature of the financial obligations inherent in a mortgage loan.

Be Careful Not to Discourage an Application

Although a lender cannot refuse an application if a potential borrower wants to submit one, most individuals will not apply for a mortgage loan if they realize they will not qualify after having the financial obligations of a mortgage loan explained to them. Therefore, this initial interview should establish whether the basic qualifications are present for an application to be taken. A lender must be careful, though, that they not discourage potential borrowers from applying for a mortgage loan if they so desire. Further, as mentioned, mortgage lenders must be careful that this initial interview not imply a credit decision and not be explicitly represented as one. If a lender, at this stage of the process, tells potential applicants that based upon their income they do not qualify, that is a credit decision requiring a notice of adverse action. (Adverse action will be discussed later.)

APPLICATION

The application is the most important document in the residential mortgage lending process. Every step that follows is done to verify the information provided in the application. At this point, it is important to emphasize that all lenders should use the FNMA/FHLMC Uniform Residential Loan Application, even if at the time of origination it is believed the loan will stay in a lender's portfolio.

Use of the Uniform Application

If market conditions reach a point where a lender must sell existing loans out of its portfolio into the secondary mortgage market and it has not used the uniform documentation, that lender may have a much more difficult time selling those mortgages. Additionally, the use of a lender's own forms may place a lender in violation of the various consumer protection laws if they are not drafted correctly. The FNMA/FHLMC Uniform Application has been accepted as meeting all consumer protection requirements.

Most applicants, even if they have applied for mortgage loans before, have no idea of the amount of information they will be asked to provide a mortgage lender before that lender can make a decision on a loan request. In order to speed up processing, a lender should distribute to real estate brokers and/or applicants a brochure that lists the information an applicant should bring to the lender at time of application.

Information to Bring When Applying for a Mortgage Loan

This brochure should request information on the following topics:

- names in which title to the property will be held and how title will be held (e.g., joint tenants),

- address of property to be purchased—copy of Contract of Sale should be included to provide legal description,
- birthdate and Social Security number of applicant(s) for use by credit bureau,
- principal residence address for previous two years; if not at present address for two years, previous address,
- financial information an applicant should bring to interview/application includes:
  —borrower (and co-borrower, if applicable) proof of income (in the form of paycheck stubs and W-2s),
  —any supplemental income,
  —if self-employed, signed income tax returns for previous two years and a Profit & Loss Statement prepared by an accountant,
  —creditor and account number information: credit cards, revolving charge, past mortgages, etc.,
  —name(s) and address(es) of current employer(s), and if employed less than two years, previous employers,
- list of liquid assets and where held with account numbers and addresses (usually in the form of monthly statements for savings, checking, or mutual fund accounts).

Mailing Out Application Forms

Although it is strongly recommended that all mortgage loan applications be completed in a face-to-face interview, circumstances sometimes require that an application be completed through the mail. These circumstances almost always involve an applicant from out of town who can't return for a face-to-face interview. When this situation presents itself, a lending institution needs to be as specific as possible in a transmittal letter concerning directions on:

- how to complete the application,
- requesting additional information,
- signing the various verifications.

The letter to the applicant should provide specific instructions to sign the forms that will thereby authorize banks, employers, and others to provide the desired information to a lender. When the signed verifications are received from the applicant, the lender will in turn mail them out to the various institutions and employers identified in the application.

After all required information has been received from an applicant, a mortgage lender will generate a typed final application form for the borrower to sign at closing. Both applications (the initial application and typed final application signed at closing) should be kept in the loan file. Of course, as with a face-to-face application, all of the federally mandated consumer protection forms and documents must be provided to an applicant who is using the mail.

CONSUMER PROTECTION

Because of actual and perceived inequities in the way mortgage applicants are handled, the federal government has, over the years, enacted a series of rules and regulations governing how the application, processing, and underwriting of mortgage loans (among other loans) must be handled. Regrettably, recent data from Home Mortgage Disclosure Act (HMDA) reports filed by mortgage lenders with the federal government suggests that inequities may still exist with mortgage lenders.

The Boston Fed Study

After the HMDA data was reported in the late 1980s, the Federal Reserve Bank of Boston ran a very comprehensive statistical analysis of lending patterns by race and concluded that "old style" discrimination did not exist. The study concluded that qualified applicants of any race were approved for loans, while clearly unqualified applicants were denied loans regardless of race. However, when the approval rate for less-qualified applicants was considered, white applicants were more likely to be approved for a mortgage loan than African Americans.

Because the results of recent HMDA data show a discrepancy between declination rates for whites and minorities, every mortgage lender must strive to ensure that all mortgage applicants are treated equally. If our pluralistic society is going to work, all participants regardless of their origin, race, religion, or other differences must be treated equally when they seek mortgage financings.

The relevant consumer safeguards are summarized in the following section. All mortgage lending personnel are urged to become familiar with all of these regulations.

EQUAL CREDIT OPPORTUNITY ACT (ECOA)

The provisions of ECOA, sometimes referred to as Regulation B, became effective on October 28, 1974, and were initially limited to prohibiting discrimination on the basis of sex or marital status. The prohibited bases of discrimination were broadened in 1976 when the ECOA amendments became law.

The basic rule of ECOA is "that creditor shall not discriminate against an applicant on a prohibited basis regarding any aspect of a credit transaction." The prohibited bases are:

- race,
- color,

- religion,
- national origin,
- sex,
- marital status,
- age,
- the fact that all or part of an applicant's income is derived from any public assistance program,
- the fact that an applicant has in good faith exercised any rights under the Consumer Credit Protection Act or any similar state law.

These prohibited bases are sometimes referred to as the "nifty nine" and apply to all mortgage lenders. A few states and some regulators (such as NCUA, the credit union regulator) have added prohibitions, usually dealing with the physically and mentally challenged and with sexual orientation.

EQUAL OPPORTUNITY LENDER

To Our Applicant:

You are hereby provided the following "Equal Credit Opportunity Act" notice as required under Section 202.9 (a) (2).

The Federal Equal Credit Opportunity Act prohibits creditors from discriminating against credit applicants on the basis of race, color, religion, national origin, sex, marital status, age (provided that the applicant has the capacity to enter into a binding contract); because all or part of the applicant's income derives from any public assistance program; or because the applicant has in good faith exercised any right under the Consumer Credit Protection Act. The Federal agency that administers compliance with this law concerning this creditor is:

Delivery of the above Notice is hereby acknowledged.

Applicant's Signature,
or Mailed By: _____ Date _____

45020 (rev. 1/91)
ECOA-1 Equal Credit Opportunity Act Notice

©1991 SAF Systems & Forms, Inc.
Chicago, IL • 1-800-323-3000

As a general rule, most mortgage lenders have had little difficulty in adhering to ECOA. On the other hand, each year some mortgage lender is sued for a real or perceived violation of ECOA. As a result, all mortgage lending personnel must be familiar with the provisions of this act.

Encouraging Applications

All mortgage lenders must be careful to encourage potential borrowers to make application for a mortgage loan. This should be interpreted to mean that all inquiries concerning whether a potential borrower would qualify for a mortgage loan should be answered by stating that credit decisions can only be made based on a written loan application. This should be followed up with an invitation to make application.

It is important that lenders realize that an application does not necessarily (legally) have to be in writing. The requirement that an adverse action letter be sent to all who have "applied" for mortgage credit applies equally to oral requests for credit. Lenders can prevent themselves from unintentionally violating the adverse action letter requirement by stating to all who request credit decisions orally that they can only be made based on a written application. Caution is required so that a lender's actual practices do not contradict written policies concerning oral applications.

Monitoring Information

Loan originators or loan processors who take loan applications should be prepared to answer questions from applicants as to why the FNMA/FHLMC application requests information relating to race, national origin, and sex. Some applicants, especially minorities, may express their uneasiness with these questions. The lender must explain that the information is only for government monitoring purposes and is not part of the criteria used when determining whether to grant a loan. The applicant must also be told that this information need not be supplied, but if it is not, then the loan officer must supply this information based on visual observation.

The chart displayed on page 105 shows that the 1990s began with a heavy emphasis on equality in lending. Several regulatory agencies have conducted investigations into discriminatory lending practices at targeted lending institutions. At this time progress has been made identifying the effects of these practices. However, altering the causes is still an ongoing project.

Marital Status

The marital status of an applicant or applicants may be requested for a mortgage loan. This information is important to a lender because of the different requirements in some states for establishing a secured interest in real estate depending on whether a person is married or not. However, in establishing marital status, the only eligible terms that can be used by a lender are whether the applicant is married, unmarried, or separated.

A lender may never ask questions about an applicant's spouse unless:

- the spouse will be contractually liable,
- the applicant is relying on the spouse's income to qualify,
- the applicant resides in a community property state or the security is in such a state,
- the applicant is relying on alimony, child support, or separate maintenance payments from a spouse or former spouse.

Notification of Adverse Action

As previously noted, applicants must be notified within 30 days after receipt of a completed application whether the loan has been:

- approved substantially as requested,
- determined to be incomplete,
- denied (creditor is taking "adverse action")

The approval should be in the form of a commitment letter or notes in the loan file indicating how the applicant was notified of the lender's approval. Lenders are urged to consider the many benefits of using a commitment letter to inform applicants that they have been accepted for a mortgage loan.

If the application is incomplete after 30 days, the lender must send a notice of incomplete application and specify what information is missing.

When a lender denies an application—that is, takes adverse action—the following four written notices must be made to the applicant:

- a statement of the action taken,
- a statement of the specific reasons for the action taken,
- the Equal Credit Opportunity Act notice,
- the name and address of the lender's federal compliance agency.

Generally all four of these notices are combined into one form.

An application is considered complete when all required information has been received by the lender. If the application is rejected, the lender must state a specific reason for the rejection. In addition, the lender must deliver these notices to the applicant within 90 days after the lender has made a counteroffer and the applicant has not expressly accepted it.

TRUTH-IN-LENDING

The Consumer Credit Protection Act of 1968 contained Title I, better known as Truth-in-Lending (or Regulation Z). This legislation requires that all lenders, including mortgage lenders, disclose to borrowers exactly how much the credit applied for is going to cost them. Under these regulations a lender is required to make certain disclosures concerning the extension of credit to a borrower:

- disclose the Annual Percentage Rate (APR),
- provide information about the total finance charges,
- inform the borrower of the right of rescission in certain transactions.

Annual Percentage Rate (APR)

The most meaningful disclosure required by Truth-in-Lending is of the Annual Percentage Rate (APR). The APR is the annual interest rate the mortgage borrower will actually pay after all other upfront fees and charges associated with the loan are taken into consideration. The APR must be computed and disclosed with an accuracy to the nearest $\frac{1}{8}$ of 1 percent for a regular loan. For example, an exact APR of 7.16 could be stated as exactly that or could properly be rounded to the nearest $\frac{1}{8}$ percent, resulting in an APR of 7.125 percent. A mortgage lender may not avoid calculating and disclosing the actual APR by simply stating that the rate does not exceed 8 percent or by quoting a rate that would be meaningfully higher than the actual APR. A lender can compute the APR on the basis of either a 360- or 365-day year. The APR and the finance charge discussed following must be disclosed to the applicant in a preliminary manner within three business days of the application.

Finance Charges

In addition to the APR disclosure, a mortgage lender is required to provide within three business days after a written application a good faith estimate of the amount financed. The amount financed includes the principal loan amount, any other amount that is financed by the lender, and the finance charge. The finance charge is "the dollar amount the credit will cost you." The good faith estimate of settlement costs required for those loans subject to RESPA may be substituted for this disclosure if it provides all of the required information. Most mortgage lenders use one form for these two disclosures.

Charges that must be disclosed to a borrower include all fees that are required as a condition of the loan, such as the following:

- prepaid interest (from the day of closing until the end of that month),
- loan discount fee,

LOAN NUMBER:

APPLICANT(S):

A PHH GROUP COMPANY

QUESTIONS AND ANSWERS ABOUT "TRUTH-IN-LENDING" STATEMENT

Federal law provides that you receive a "Truth-in-Lending Disclosure Statement." Study it carefully as well as the other information about your loan we gave you. Your loan is an important transaction. Following are some of the most frequently asked questions about the Truth-in-Lending Statement and their answers. Additional information can be obtained from your real estate agent or mortgage loan officer.

Q.   What is a Truth-in-Lending Disclosure Statement and Why Do I Receive It?

A.   Your Disclosure Statement provides information which Federal law requires us to give you. The purpose of the statement is to give you information about your loan and help you shop for credit.

Q.   What is the ANNUAL PERCENTAGE RATE?

A.   The Annual Percentage Rate, or A.P.R., is the cost of your credit expressed in terms of an annual rate. Because you may be paying "points" and other closing costs, the A.P.R. disclosed is often higher than the interest rate on your loan. The A.P.R. can be compared to other loans for which you may have applied and give you a fair method of comparing price.

Q.   What is the AMOUNT FINANCED?

A.   The amount financed is the mortgage amount applied for *minus* prepaid finance charges and any required deposit balance. Prepaid finance charges include items such as loan origination fee, commitment or placement fee (points), adjusted interest, and initial mortgage insurance premium. The Amount Financed represents a *net* figure used to allow you to accurately assess the amount of credit actually provided.

Q.   Does this mean I will get a lower mortgage than I applied for?

A.   No. If your loan is approved for the amount you applied for, that's how much will be credited toward your home purchase or refinance at settlement.

Q.   Why is the ANNUAL PERCENTAGE RATE different from the interest rate for which I applied? Why is the AMOUNT FINANCED different?

A.   The Amount Financed is lower than the amount you applied for because it represents a *net* figure. If someone applied for a mortgage of $50,000 and their prepaid finance charges total $2,000, the amount financed would be shown as $48,000, or $50,000 minus $2,000.

The A.P.R. is computed from this *lower* figure, based on what your proposed payments would be. In a $50,000 loan with $2,000 in prepaid finance charges, and an interest rate of 14%, the payments would be $592.44 (principal and interest) on a loan with a thirty year term. Since the A.P.R. is based on the *net* amount financed, rather than on the actual mortgage amount, and since the payment amount remains the same, the A.P.R. is higher than the interest rate. It would be 14.62%. If this applicant's loan were approved he would still receive a $50,000 loan for thirty years with monthly payments @ 14% of $592.44.

Q.   How will my payments be affected by the Disclosure Statement?

A.   The Disclosure Statement only discloses your estimated payments. The interest rate determines what your monthly principal and interest payment will be.

Q.   What is the FINANCE CHARGE?

A.   The Finance Charge is the cost of credit. It is the total amount of interest calculated at the interest rate over the life of the loan, plus prepaid finance charges and the total amount of mortgage insurance charged over the life of the loan. This figure is *estimated* on the disclosure statement given with your application.

Q.   What is the TOTAL OF PAYMENTS?

A.   This figure indicates the total amount you will have paid, including principal, interest, prepaid finance charges, and mortgage insurance if you make the minimum required payments for the entire term of the loan. This figure is *estimated* on the Disclosure Statement and is estimated in any adjustable rate transaction.

Q.   My statement says that if I pay the loan off early, I will not be entitled to a refund of part of the finance charge. What does this mean?

A.   This means that you will be charged interest for the period of time in which you used the money loaned to you. Your *prepaid* finance charges are not refundable. Neither is any interest which has already been paid. If you pay the loan off early, you should not have to pay the full amount of the "finance charges" shown on the disclosure. This charge represents an estimate of the full amount the loan would cost you if the minimum required payments were made each month through the life of the loan.

Q.   Why must I sign the Disclosure Statement?

A.   Lenders are required by law to provide the information on this statement to you in a timely manner. Your signature merely indicates that you have received this information, and does not obligate either you or the Lender in any way.

- origination fee,
- mortgage insurance premiums,
- principal repayment (amortization schedule).

Typical closing costs (fees paid to a third party) that need *not* be included in the finance charge include:

- appraisal fee,
- credit report fee,
- title examination fee, title insurance,
- lawyer fees,
- property survey.

Composite APR

When the loan under discussion is a fixed-rate loan, the APR and finance charge disclosures are relatively simple. If the loan is a closed-end adjustable-rate mortgage on the borrower's principal dwelling, the disclosures are a bit more complicated. The disclosures become more complicated because the total finance charge cannot be calculated since future changes in the interest rate are unknown.

The commentary section of Regulation Z, Truth-in-Lending, explains a method of computing the Annual Percentage Rate as it relates to discounted adjustable-rate transactions. This discussion describes the calculations a mortgage lender will have to perform to correctly disclose the APR when the initial interest rate is below the index plus the margin. These calculations blend the initial interest rate with the adjusted rate, when following a set of prescribed criteria. This blended rate is called the "Composite APR."

Most lenders fulfill their Truth-in-Lending requirements for adjustable-rate mortgages by first disclosing that the interest rate, payment, or term can change. Next, the lender discloses the APR and total finance charges using the initial interest rate and then using a narrative to explain what future increases in the interest rate will mean to the borrower. This narrative should contain a description of the index and margin that will determine future increases and disclose any limits of yearly and lifetime rate increases.

Also, the lender must provide an explanation of how the consumer may calculate payments based on a $10,000 example. Finally, a lender must provide a 15 year historical example of a how the index plus margin would have produced changes in interest rate and payments.

Right of Rescission

Truth-in-Lending regulations also require that mortgage lenders disclose to borrowers who are refinancing an existing home mortgage or getting a second mortgage (either open- or closed-ended) that they have three business days in which to rescind the loan transaction if they so desire. Mortgage processors should understand that this right does not attach to a purchase money mortgage. This right of rescission is intended to provide borrowers with a limited cooling-off period during which they can cancel the whole transaction and get all funds expended back from the lender.

REAL ESTATE SETTLEMENT PROCEDURES ACT (RESPA)

RESPA became law in 1974 (later amended in 1976 and 1992) and applies to all federally related mortgage loans, which means practically all purchase money residential mortgages. The purpose of RESPA is to inform borrowers of the costs that are associated with the loan and loan closing. The knowledge gives them the opportunity to shop for the best deal. RESPA does not apply to the following transactions:

- a construction loan, except where the construction loan is used as, or converted to, a permanent loan to finance the purchase by a first user,
- a bonafide transfer of the loan obligation in the secondary market; HUD considers the *real* source of funding and the *real* interest of the settlement lender.

The 1992 revisions to RESPA eliminated several previously existing exemptions to the regulation and provided some further requirements for mortgage broker fees, use of computerized loan applications, and business arrangements. Loans involving subordinated financing are now included in the RESPA regulations.

RESPA requires a lender to deliver or place in the mail, no later than three business days after, not including the day the application is received, a copy of HUD's current *Special Information Booklet*. This publication describes and explains the typical settlement costs that are incurred when closing a residential mortgage loan. Most mortgage lenders give their applicants this booklet at the time the loan application is taken.

In addition, RESPA requires a mortgage lender to provide within three business days a "good faith estimate of the settlement costs" that a borrower will incur at closing. This estimate does not have to be exactly what the final closing statement will show at closing but must truly be a good faith estimate.

The items that normally are found in the closing statement include among others:

- appraisal fee,
- commitment fee,

- credit report,
- settlement or closing fee,
- title insurance,
- survey,
- recording fee,
- pest inspection,
- underwriting fee.

Mortgage Broker Fees

RESPA contains very broad prohibitions against kickbacks and un-earned fees. The 1992 revisions to RESPA contain some regulations concerning the payment of fees to brokers who provide computerized loan origination services, table funding services, and exclusive services to a lender. While RESPA is not perfectly clear in regulating these areas, the requirement to disclose broker fees is mandatory. Whether the broker is closing the mortgage in its name or in the name of another lender, the broker must disclose the fees paid by the consumer for these services.

Appraisal Request

RESPA gives mortgage applicants the right to request of the lender a copy of the appraisal used in their loan package. If the request is formally made by an applicant—generally in writing—the lender must provide the applicant with a copy of the appraisal. It should be noted that the appraisal still belongs to the lender. Simply because an applicant paid for the appraisal doesn't give him or her ownership of the appraisal. Further, an appraiser will not be allowed to discuss an appraisal with the applicant; the appraiser can only review the appraisal with the client—the lender.

HUD-1

Finally, RESPA provides a borrower with the right to inspect the Uniform Settlement Statement (HUD-1) on the business day before settlement. This two-page form is completed by the closing agent and lists all the charges paid by both the seller and buyer. Both parties must sign this form and the lender will keep the original in the loan file.

Notice of Transfer of Mortgage Servicing

This disclosure is in reality a two-part process. At loan application the applicant(s) must be given (and return signed) a Servicing Disclosure Statement. This form discloses the servicing activities of the lender and the odds of

NAVY FEDERAL CREDIT UNION

RESPA GOOD FAITH ESTIMATES OF SETTLEMENT COSTS AND FEDERAL TRUTH-IN-LENDING DISCLOSURE

| MEMBER'S NAME GEORGE P ANDERSON
MARTHA A. ANDERSON | NFCU ACCOUNT NO. SUFFIX
0123456/012345/001/10 | DATE
07/16/92 |
| PROPERTY ADDRESS
3459 EAGLE ROCK COURT, ANNANDALE, VIRGINIA 22030-4151 | TYPE OF LOAN
VA LOAN | |

You have applied to Navy Federal Credit Union for a proposed mortgage loan in the amount of 151,650.00 to be repaid at a simple interest rate of 9.500 % for a term of 360 months. The following RESPA Good Faith Estimates of Settlement Costs include all settlement service charges you must pay, but IT MAY NOT COVER ALL ITEMS YOU HAVE TO PAY IN CASH AT SETTLEMENT – FOR EXAMPLE, DEPOSIT IN ESCROW FOR REAL ESTATE TAXES AND INSURANCE. YOU MAY WANT TO ASK ABOUT THE COST OF ANY ITEMS YOU MUST PAY THAT ARE NOT SHOWN ON THIS FORM. YOU MAY BE REQUIRED TO PAY OTHER ADDITIONAL AMOUNTS AT SETTLEMENT. For further explanation of the charges, consult your booklet entitled "A Homebuyer's Guide to Settlement Costs."

LINE NO. ON HUD-1	SETTLEMENT SERVICE	CHARGES INCLUDED IN AMOUNT FINANCED OR PREPAID FINANCE CHARGES	CHARGES EXCLUDED FROM AMOUNT FINANCED
801	Loan Origination Fee .750	$ 1,137.38 e	$ e
802	Loan Discount 1.000	$ PAID BY SELLER e	$ e
803	Appraisal Fee	$ e	$ e
901	Interest Based on 39.47 per day for 16 days	$ INCLUDED WITH FIRST PAYMENT e	$ e
902	Mortgage Insurance Premium 1.125 VA-FUNDING FEE	$ 1,687.50 e	$ e
1002	Mortgage Insurance ___ months at ___ per mo.	$ N/A e	$ e
1101	Settlement Fee	$ e	$ N/A e
1107	Attorney's Fee (may include 1102 through 1106)	$ e	$ e
1108	Title Insurance	$ e	$ e
1201	Recording Fees	$ e	$ e
1202	City/County Tax Stamps	$ e	$ e
1203	State Tax	$ e	$ e
1301	Survey	$ e	$ e
	TOTALS	(A) 2,824.88 e	

EXPLANATION OF AMOUNT FINANCED

The Loan Amount of 151,650.00 e less the total (column A) of the Prepaid Finance Charges of 2,824.88 equals the Amount Financed of 148,825.12 e.

AMOUNT FINANCED is 148,825.12 e, the amount of credit provided to you or on your behalf.

FINANCE CHARGE is 310,854.85 e, the dollar amount the credit will cost you, if you pay as scheduled. This figure includes e 308,029.97 mortgage interest plus 2,824.88 prepaid finance charges and N/A e of mortgage insurance premiums not included in prepaid finance charges.

TOTAL OF PAYMENTS is 459,679.97 e, the amount you will have paid when you have made all payments as scheduled. This figure includes the FINANCE CHARGE plus the AMOUNT FINANCED.

ANNUAL PERCENTAGE RATE is 9.716 % and is the cost of your credit as a yearly rate. Includes interest adjusted from settlement

YOUR PAYMENT SCHEDULE WILL BE:

Number of Payments	Amount of Payments (principal and interest only)	When Payments Are Due
1 e	$ 1,906.68 * e	09/01/92 e
359	1,275.16	MONTHLY THEREAFTER

☐ Your loan will also include monthly payments of ☐ FHA Mortgage Insurance ☐ Private Mortgage Insurance as follows: NONE

LATE CHARGE: You will be charged 4% of the monthly payment for principal and interest only if a payment is not received within 15 days of the first of the month due date.

INSURANCE: Property hazard insurance is required as a condition of this loan. The required insurance may be purchased from any insurance company of your choice that is acceptable to NFCU. The minimum amount is your loan amount or the replacement cost of the dwelling, whichever is less.

PREPAYMENT: If you pay off early, you will not have to pay a penalty. (In addition, if you pay off early, you may be entitled to a refund.)

ASSUMPTION: If you are obtaining a VA guaranteed or FHA insured mortgage loan, someone buying your home in the future may be allowed, subject to conditions, to assume the remainder of your mortgage on the original terms. NFCU *conventional loans* however, *are not assumable.*

SECURITY: You are giving a security interest in the property being purchased.

See your mortgage documents for any additional information they may contain about nonpayment, default, any required repayment of the obligation in full before the scheduled date and prepayment funds.

e means an estimate

NFCU 204M (2-80)

06011992

_____ _____
DATE DATE

the applicant's loan being sold. When their loan is sold a second disclosure is sent to the borrowers detailing who is the new owner of their mortgage. This second disclosure must be sent no fewer than 15 days prior to the loan sale or transfer.

These notices must contain certain information. They must contain the effective date of the transfer of the servicing to the new servicer and the name, address, and toll-free or collect-call phone number of the new servicer. Also, these notices must contain the toll-free or collect-call number of the person or department for both the present servicer and the new servicer who will answer questions about this transfer. Finally, the regulation specifies that during the 60 days following this transfer a mortgage payment received prior to the due date by the old servicer cannot be considered late by the new servicer.

FLOOD DISASTER PROTECTION ACT

The Flood Disaster Protection Act requires lenders to inform borrowers whether their property is in a flood hazard area. If the property is in a flood hazard area, borrowers are to be advised that in order to obtain a mortgage they have to be covered by flood insurance. Mortgage lenders have two pre-scribed notification requirements pursuant to the Flood Disaster Protection Act depending on whether the property is located in a community participating in the National Flood Insurance Program. If so located in a special flood hazard area, the lender is required to notify the purchaser of this fact and also whether flood disaster insurance is available in that community. If this insurance is available, the lender must require the borrower to obtain the insurance. If flood insurance is not available, the lender can make the loan if it sees fit, but usually it will not.

Mortgage lenders need to remember that they are legally responsible for determining whether the property is in a flood disaster area, even if they rely on the appraiser to so inform them.

FAIR CREDIT REPORTING ACT

The Fair Credit Reporting Act regulates the users and the use of consumer credit information. The purpose of this law is to ensure that accurate credit information is used when credit decisions are made. Mortgage lenders are able to underwrite a mortgage application only when they have complete information. Much of the required information comes from a credit report. This legislation, which directly impacts credit reporting agencies and how credit information is obtained, also requires lenders to handle this credit information correctly. Basically, this requires mortgage lenders to only request credit in-

LOAN NUMBER:

APPLICANT(S):

PROPERTY ADDRESS:

Notice Required under the Fair Credit Reporting Act

In compliance with the Fair Credit Reporting Act, we are informing you that an investigative report will be made. We are also informing you that you have a right to make a written request, within a reasonable period of time after you receive this notice, for an additional disclosure of the nature and scope of the investigation requested. To save you the trouble of writing, we are furnishing this additional information as follows:

The nature and scope of the investigation requested may include information obtained through personal interviews concerning residence verification, number of dependents, employment, occupation, general health, habits, reputation and mode of living.

Notice under the Equal Credit Opportunity Act

The Federal Equal Credit Opportunity Act prohibits creditors from discriminating against credit applicants on the basis of race, color, religion, national origin, sex, marital status, age (provided that the applicant has the capacity to enter into a binding contract); because all or part of the applicant's income derives from any public assistance program; or because the applicant has in good faith exercised any right under the Consumer Credit Protection Act. The Federal agency that administers compliance with this law concerning a creditor is the Federal Trade Commission, Equal Credit Opportunity, Washington, D.C. 20580, (202) 724-1140.

You, as a borrower, have the following rights when answering questions:

You do **not** have to reveal any information regarding courtesy titles; i.e., you do not have to state whether you are Miss, Mr., Mrs., or Ms. Your first name and surname (whether birth-given, obtained through marriage, or a combined surname) is sufficient.

You do **not** have to reveal any information regarding the receipt of alimony, child support, or separate maintenance income if you do not chose to have it considered as a basis for repaying this loan.

When answering questions pertaining to marriage, you need **only** reveal whether you are married, separated, or unmarried. (Unmarried includes single, divorced, or widowed.)

Certain information regarding your race/national origin and sex will be asked. This information is requested by the Federal Government in order to monitor compliance with Federal anti-discrimination statutes which prohibit creditors from discriminating against applicants for these reasons. You do **not** have to give this information; it is voluntary. If you chose **not** to furnish this information, you **must** initial the application in the space provided. Your decision will in no way affect the approval or rejection of your application.

Notice Required by the Right to Financial Privacy Act

If you are applying for an FHA or VA loan, this is notice to you as required by the Right to Financial Privacy Act of 1978 that the Department of HUD or a VA Loan Guaranty Service or Division (whichever is appropriate) has a right of access to financial records held by financial institutions in connection with the consideration or administration of assistance to you.

Financial records involving your transaction will be available to the Department of HUD or to a VA Loan Guaranty Service or Division (whichever is appropriate) without further notice or authorization, but will not be disclosed or released to another government agency or department without your consent except as required or permitted by law.

ACKNOWLEDGEMENT

I do hereby certify that I have read and do understand the Notices set forth above, and that I have been notified of my rights by the Lender.

formation on those individuals who have given their permission for their credit to be reviewed. The standardized mortgage application contains that authorization.

If a mortgage lender turns down an applicant because of poor credit as established by the credit report, the lender must notify the applicant of this fact and provide the name, address, and phone number of the reporting credit bureau. This notice should also inform the applicant of the right to discuss or question any information on the credit report with the credit bureau.

Under no circumstances should the lender discuss the contents of the credit report with the applicant until the applicant has been given a copy of the credit report. Many credit bureaus will automatically send a copy of a Residential Mortgage Credit Report to an applicant if the report contains negative credit information.

Any discussions about the accuracy of the credit report should be between the applicant and the credit bureau, not with the mortgage lender.

Lenders should give applicants the time and chance to cure any problems with their credit reports since credit bureaus do make mistakes and at times will report on the wrong person.

HOME MORTGAGE DISCLOSURE ACT (HMDA)

The Home Mortgage Disclosure Act (HMDA), known as Regulation C, requires mortgage lenders to keep a record and report annually on the disposition of all of their mortgage applications. Mortgage lenders must report the type of real estate loans they made and where they made them so that the federal government can determine if that lender is refusing to make loans in certain urban areas (whether they are "redlining"). This information is contained in the Loan/Application Register, and it is usually the loan processor's responsibility to maintain this register. The type of information that is registered includes the following:

1. application or loan information
   - type of loan applied for,
   - purpose of loan,
   - occupancy status,
   - action taken,
2. applicant information
   - race or national origin,
   - sex,
3. type of purchaser (of mortgage loan, if sold),
4. reasons for denial (if appropriate).

This record keeping is also important because the federal government can examine these records for consumer protection violations. As shown in the following chart, this information is often aggregated by the government to gauge lending discrimination.

HMDA AGGREGATE STATISTICS—ALL MORTGAGE LENDERS

	1991 Applications Denied	1992 Applications Denied
Black	35.5%	30.3%
Native American/Alaskan	24.6%	20.5%
Hispanic	28.5%	27.0%
Joint (white/minority)	19.0%	15.7%
White	16.7%	12.7%
Asian/Pacific Islander	18.0%	16.3%
Other	23.2%	23.5%
All applications	19.6%	15.7%

Source: NCUA.

QUALIFYING AN APPLICANT

Income of Applicant(s)

An applicant's income (in some situations combined with that of a co-applicant) provides the means for the repayment of the mortgage debt and other household and long-term debts in addition to everyday expenses. Not only is the amount of that income important, but the prospect for continuation of that income must be determined.

In determining whether the income is sufficient to fulfill all existing debt and the mortgage applied for, five possible sources of income should be analyzed:

- wage or salary income,
- self-employment income,
- rental/interest/investment/commission income,
- child support/alimony/separate maintenance income,
- retirement/pension/disability/welfare income.

As will be discussed later, the manner in which a lender can inquire about these sources of income is limited by certain laws, particularly the Equal Credit Opportunity Act.

The income that is most commonly relied upon is wage or salary income. This income should be verified for the previous two years. The Request for Verification of Employment (VOE) form requests the following information from an employer:

PHH US Mortgage   55 Haddonfield Road   Telephone
Corporation   Cherry Hill, NJ 08002   1 800 446 0963

AUTHORIZATION TO OBTAIN INFORMATION

I authorize PHH US Mortgage Corporation to request verification of my bank accounts, other assets, employment earnings records and also to order a consumer credit report. I further authorize my banks and employer(s) to accept a copy of this document as their authorization to release such information.

Customer Signature: _____

Address: _____

_____

Customer Signature: _____

Address: _____

_____

This information is confidential and will only be used to process your mortgage loan application.

- date of employment,
- amount of current income,
- type of income,
- present position,
- probability of continued employment.

The amount of income usually is not an item of controversy, but the type of income may generate controversy. If all income is derived from commis-

FannieMae

Request for Verification of Employment

Privacy Act Notice: This information is to be used by the agency collecting it or its assignees whether you qualify as a prospective mortgagor under its program. It will not be disclosed outside the agency except as required and permitted by law. You do not have to provide this information, but if you do not your application for approval as a prospective mortgagor or borrower may be delayed or rejected. The information requested in this form is authorized by Title 38, USC, Chapter 37 (if VA); by 12 USC, Section 1701 et.seq. (if HUD/FHA); by 42 USC, Section 1452b (if HUD/CPD); and Title 42 USC, 1471 et.seq., or 7 USC, 1921 et.seq. (if USDA/FmHA).

Instructions: Lender - Complete items 1 through 7. Have applicant complete item 8. Forward directly to employer named in item 1.
Employer - Please complete either Part II or Part III as applicable. Complete Part IV and return directly to lender named in item 2.
The form is to be transmitted directly to the lender and is not to be transmitted through the applicant or any other party.

Part I -- Request

1. To (Name and address of employer)	2. From (Name and address of lender)
PROMACS **5806 SUFFOLK RD** **MADISON WI 53711**	**AnchorBank, s.s.b.** **25 W. Main Street** **Madison, WI 53703**

I certify that this verification has been sent directly to the employer and has not passed through the hands of the applicant or any other interested party.

3. Signature of Lender	4. Title **Pamela A. Allen** **LN PROCESSING SPECIALIST** **(608) 252-8993**	5. Date **01/28/94**	6. Lender's Number (Optional)

I have applied for a mortgage loan and stated that I am now or was formerly employed by you. My signature below authorizes verification of this information.

7. Name and Address of Applicant (include employee or badge number) **MICHAEL J. ROBERTSON** **5806 SUFFOLK RD.** **MADISON, WIS. 53711**	8. Signature of Applicant **SEE ATTACHED**

Part II -- Verification of Present Employment

9. Applicant's Date of Employment	10. Present Position	11. Probability of Continued Employment
5-17-91	**President / COO**	**Excellent**

12A. Current **Gross Base Pay** (Enter Amount and Check Period)		13. For Military Personnel Only		14. If Overtime or Bonus is Applicable, Is Its Continuance Likely?
[X] Annual [ ] Hourly		Pay Grade		Overtime [ ] Yes [X] No
[ ] Monthly [ ] Other (Specify)		Type	Monthly Amount	Bonus [ ] Yes [X] No
$ **54,500** [ ] Weekly		Base Pay	$	15. If paid hourly -- average hours per week

12B. **Gross Earnings**			

Type	Year To Date	Past Year 19 ___	Past Year 19 ___			
	Thru ___ 19 ___			Rations	$	
Base Pay	$ **31,500**	$ **58,000**	$ **28,650**	Flight or Hazard	$	16. Date of applicant's next pay increase **Unknown**
Overtime	$	$	$	Clothing	$	17. Projected amount of next pay increase
Commissions	$	$	$	Quarters	$	**Unknown**
				Pro Pay	$	18. Date of applicant's last pay increase
Bonus	$	$	$	Overseas or Combat	$	
Total	$ **31,500**	$ **58,000**	$ **28,650**	Variable Housing Allowance	$	19. Amount of last pay increase

20. Remarks (If employee was off work for any length of time, please indicate time period and reason)

Part III - Verification of Previous Employment

21. Date Hired	23. Salary/Wage at Termination Per (Year) (Month) (Week)
22. Date Terminated	Base _____ Overtime _____ Commissions _____ Bonus _____
24. Reason for Leaving	25. Position Held

Part IV - Authorized Signature
Federal statutes provide severe penalties for any fraud, intentional misrepresentation, or criminal connivance or conspiracy purposed to influence the issuance of any guaranty or insurance by the VA Secretary, the U.S.D.A., FmHA/FHA Commissioner, or the HUD/CPD Assistant Secretary.

26. Signature of Employer	27. Title (Please print or type) **Owner**	28. Date
29. Print or type name signed in item 26 **C. R. Hemingway**	30. Phone No. **277-8870**	**7-25-93**

0015149   24   PAA   Anchor Form LF104   Fannie Mae   Form 1005 Mar 90   LF104

sions, an obvious problem exists regarding the possibility of lower sales income in subsequent years, which would not support the continuation of the commission income at the present level. As a rule, averaging the past two or three years establishes the average level as "normal." This income can then be given full consideration. If income derived from overtime or part-time work is necessary to qualify the loan, a lender should establish whether the additional income is expected to continue and whether the amount of that income is reasonable for the additional employment.

The same VOE form should be used to verify previous employment if the current employment is less than two years.

Self-Employment

Even though the self-employed are in the highest risk category for default, these applicants must be treated basically the same as others. The difficulty in verifying the income of the self-employed is obvious. A loan processor must be extremely careful that enough information is made available so that the underwriter will be able to analyze the risk.

A lender should require signed copies of the prior two year's 1040s with all schedules, plus a current accountant-prepared profit and loss statement and a balance sheet evidencing a stable or increasing income stream. Self-employment income is considered stable income if the borrower has been self-employed for two or more years, during which time the income was stable or increasing. Also, a borrower who owns 25 percent or more of a company is considered to be self-employed and falls under these requirements.

When computing the income available for the proposed mortgage and other debts in addition to living expenses, net income from tax returns is used. Depending on the business a borrower is in, depreciation and other paper losses may be added back to net income to arrive at a figure for available income.

Interest and Dividends

Interest and/or dividend income may be used as income if it is properly documented and has been received for the past two years. An average of the past two years' interest income will be used to qualify the borrower. Copies of brokers' statements or of the interest/dividend checks, photocopies of tax returns, or other account statements may be used to document this income. A lender should take care to determine if any of these funds will be used for making the down payment or for paying moving expenses. Assets used for down payments aren't available to generate interest or dividend income.

Rental Income

Rental income is often relied upon by borrowers in qualifying for a mortgage loan. This income is easy to verify by obtaining copies of the lease agreement or tax returns. In order to allow for maintenance, taxes, and a vacancy factor, many lender's underwriting guidelines will allow only 75 percent of rental income to count towards qualifying for the mortgage loan.

Child Support, Alimony, or Separate Maintenance

In today's society, more and more borrowers are claiming child support, alimony, or separate maintenance as additional income. This income can be used as long as proof exists that payment has been made in a regular manner and is based on a written agreement or court order. A mortgage lender must be mindful of the ECOA requirements when asking about this type of income. Basically, ECOA requires a lender to inform the applicant that it can use this type of income but the applicant doesn't have to divulge it if he or she doesn't want to.

Pension, Retirement, and Social Security

An applicant can rely on pensions, retirement, or Social Security to qualify for a mortgage loan. As with any type of income, it must be verifiable. This type of income is usually easy to verify by letter from the company or organization providing the income or by a copy of the checks received.

Welfare Payments

The ECOA states emphatically that all income must be treated equally when an applicant is trying to qualify for a mortgage loan. That includes welfare payments or aid to dependent children income. The lender should, of course, verify the amount and how long it will last when determining if sufficient income exists to approve the application.

Other Assets

In addition to verifying the income of an applicant, the assets of that applicant or co-applicant are important to an underwriter in determining whether a loan should be made. These assets, which must be verified, will be used for the down payment, for any pre-paid items such as credit report, appraisal, closing costs, and moving expense, and for those many other expenses associated with moving into a new house. A Request for Verification of Deposit (VOD) form should be used to verify savings and checking accounts.

 **FannieMae**

REQUEST FOR VERIFICATION OF DEPOSIT

Privacy Act Notice: This information is to be used by the agency collecting it or its assignees in determining whether you qualify as a prospective mortgagor under its program. It will not be disclosed outside the agency except as required and permitted by law. You do not have to provide this information, but if you do not your application for approval as a prospective mortgagor or borrower may be delayed or rejected. The information requested in this form is authorized by Title 38, USC, Chapter 37 (If VA); by 12 USC, Section 1701 et.seq. (If HUD/FHA); by 42 USC, Section 1452b (If HUD/CPD); and Title 42 USC, 1471 et.seq. or 7 USC, 1921 et.seq. (If USDA/FmHA).

Instructions: Lender - Complete Items 1 through 8. Have applicant(s) complete Item 9. Forward directly to depository named in Item 1.
Depository - Please complete Items 10 through 18 and return DIRECTLY to lender named in Item 2.
The form is to be transmitted directly to the lender and is not to be transmitted through the applicant(s) or any other party.

Part I - Request

1. To (Name and address of depository)	2. From (Name and address of lender)
CUNA CREDIT UNION **401 S YELLOWSTONE DR** **MADIOSN WI 53719**	**AnchorBank, s.s.b.** **25 W. Main Street** **Madison, WI 53703**

I certify that this verification has been sent directly to the bank or depository and has not passed through the hands of the applicant or any other party.

3. Signature of lender	4. Title	5. Date	6. Lender's No. (optional)
Pam Allen	Pamela A. Allen **LN PROCESSING SPECIALIST** (608) 252-8993	01/28/94	

7. Information To Be Verified

Type of Account	Account in Name of	Account Number	Balance
SAV	MICHAEL J OR AUDREY F ROBERTSON	59104000	12,273.70
CHKG	MICHAEL J OR AUDREY F ROBERTSON	59104000	2,924.87
SAVG	MICHAEL J OR AUDREY F ROBERTSON	80472004	2,553.49
CHKG	MICHAEL J OR AUDREY F ROBERTSON	80472004	1,014.73

TO DEPOSITORY: I/We have applied for a mortgage loan and stated in my financial statement that the balance on deposit with you is as shown above. You are authorized to verify this information and to supply the lender identified above with the information requested in Items 10 through 13. Your response is solely a matter of courtesy for which no responsibility is attached to your institution or any of your officers.

8. Name and Address of Applicant(s)	9. Signature of Applicant(s)
MICHAEL J OR AUDREY F ROBERTSON **5806 SUFFOLK RD.** **MADISON, WIS. 53711**	**SEE ATTACHED**

To Be Completed by Depository
Part II - Verification of Depository

10. Deposit Accounts of Applicant(s)

Type of Account	Account Number	Current Balance	Average Balance For Previous Two Months	Date Opened
Sav	59104000	12,273	10,565	6-15-85
Chk	59104000	2,924	2,345	6-15-85
Sav	80472004	2,553	2,085	8-10-87

11. Loans Outstanding To Applicant(s)

Loan Number	Date of Loan	Original Amount	Current Balance	(Monthly/Quarterly)	Secured By	Late Payments
All Paid						

12. Please include any additional information which may be of assistance in determination of credit worthiness. (Please include information on loans paid-in-full in Item 11 above.)

13. If the name(s) on the account(s) differ from those listed in Item 7, please supply the name(s) on the account(s) as reflected by your records.

Part III - Authorized Signature
Federal statutes provide severe penalties for any fraud, intentional misrepresentation, or criminal connivance or conspiracy purposed to influence the issuance of any guaranty or insurance by the VA Secretary, the U.S.D.A., FmHA/FHA Commissioner, or the HUD/CPD Assistant Secretary.

14. Signature of Depository Representative	15. Title (Please print or type)	16. Date
Mary Jackson		
17. Please print or type name signed in item 14	18. Phone No.	
Mary Jackson	277-5590	7-19-93

0015149   24   PAA   Form LF1A1   Fannie Mae Form 1006 Mar.90   LF107

110

If any of the funds used by an applicant come from relatives or others, a gift letter must appear in the file. This letter, signed by the donor, states that the funds are truly a gift and need not be repaid. The loan processor should verify that these funds exist and be able to trace and document where these funds came from.

RESIDENTIAL MORTGAGE CREDIT REPORT

Of great concern to any mortgage lender is how an applicant(s) has handled credit responsibilities in the past. This is established by a credit report. The credit report must be issued by an independent credit reporting agency and must be less than 90 days old.

The type of credit report used for a loan that will be salable on the secondary mortgage market is a *Residential Mortgage Credit Report.* This report should be ordered for and become a part of each residential mortgage loan application. This specialized report provides a mortgage lender with more information than can be found on a simpler standard factual credit report. The additional information provided by this report includes the following:

- credit information from two national credit repositories,
- a check of public records for divorce, liens, judgments, etc.,
- verification (if possible) of current employment and address of employer,
- list of credit inquiries within previous 90 days.

This report must also contain a certification that it meets the standards of the FNMA, FHLMC, VA, and HUD. The credit information provides a report on how debts have been handled by the applicant in the past. This report lists all of the applicant's debts for the past seven years by creditor's name, date account was opened, high credit, current status, required payment, unpaid balance, and payment history.

The payment history appears in a "number of times past due" format. When a mortgage lender orders a credit report, it should be ordered using the full name of the applicant(s) and their Social Security number(s). If the applicants are co-borrowers and not married to each other, then separate credit reports must be provided.

If an applicant has demonstrated, by the credit report, a difficulty in handling financial obligations, the amount of current income and its relationship to outstanding obligations is most crucial. This is especially true if the debt was a type of installment debt similar to a mortgage loan. In some situations, a mortgage lender may not be able to justify a loan to an applicant regardless of current income because of past credit problems. In all situations, an applicant should be advised that if the loan is turned down because of adverse credit information, he or she can contact the credit bureau that furnished the derogatory information for additional information.

Derogatory Items

If any of the derogatory items listed following appear on the credit report, the loan processor should require a letter explaining the specific reason for the credit problem as if the situation still exists. This information is critical to the underwriter's final loan determination. These items include:

- derogatory ratings,
- bankruptcy,
- suits,
- judgments,
- late payments,
- concealed liabilities,
- numerous recent inquiries.

A mortgage lender must be aware of the Fair Credit Reporting Act and the limitations that are placed on credit information gathering. That law, as mentioned earlier, is designed to ensure the fair and accurate reporting of information regarding consumer credit. A mortgage lender seeking credit information from a consumer reporting agency must certify the purpose for which the information is sought and use it for no other purpose. This act prohibits investigative reports based on interviews with neighbors and others relating to character, general reputation, mode of living, and other subjective areas.

At the time a lender orders a credit report, it should indicate to the credit agency or bureau the type of loan (i.e., conventional, FHA, or VA) and should be sure that the credit reporting agency is approved by FHA or VA. The report from a reporting agency should be used as a verification of information supplied on the application. The credit bureau relies on its own files, various national repositories of credit information, and the public record.

When a credit report is received, the lender should check it against the application and look for discrepancies. Some are almost certain to occur since many applicants cannot remember all details exactly, but if major deletions or erroneous information of a serious nature are present, the applicant should be asked to explain. An applicant may not be aware of some of the information contained in a credit report. If the applicant believes a mistake has been made, the applicant should be advised to discuss the information with the credit bureau. On occasion, wrong information is transmitted and can often be corrected by a discussion between the applicant and the credit bureau.

TITLE INSURANCE

The purpose of title insurance is to protect the mortgage lender against any defects in the title of the mortgagor. Title insurance (or a title opinion by an attorney) is required for all residential mortgage loans that will be sold into the secondary mortgage market.

As a general rule, after the loan has been approved, a loan processor will order a preliminary title report. This report lists the current owners and any liens or encumbrances against the property. The final title insurance policy is not received until after the loan has closed so that it will show the mortgage lender's position. This report will be discussed further in Chapter 13, Closing the Residential Loan.

FINAL CHECK

Before sending a residential mortgage loan file on to an underwriter, a loan processor should review the file to ascertain that all required documents are present and properly prepared. This will include the following:

1. application: both final typed and preliminary application,
2. completed verification for:
   - employment(s) (and former employment if needed),
   - deposit(s),
   - past mortgages or landlords,
3. Residential Mortgage Credit Report,
4. Uniform Residential Appraisal Report,
5. evidence that all federally mandated consumer protection requirements have been followed for:
   - ECOA,
   - RESPA,
   - Truth-in-Lending,
   - flood insurance,
   - others (if applicable),
6. money collected for:
   - credit report,
   - appraisal,
   - other third-party expenditures.

When a loan processor has reviewed the file and is satisfied that all relevant information is available for an underwriting decision to be made, the file should be forwarded to an underwriter as expeditiously as possible.

It is not recommended that the person who processed a loan be the same person who underwrites the loan. The chances for fraud in this situation are too great. If a lending institution is so small that it cannot afford a qualified underwriter, it should use the various underwriting services offered by an independent underwriting service or by one of the private mortgage insurance companies.

UNDERWRITING THE RESIDENTIAL MORTGAGE LOAN

7

The term *underwriting* is used in many segments of the American economy to describe the process of analyzing information relating to risk and making a decision whether or not to accept that risk. In real estate, underwriting is an integral part of the mortgage lending process, regardless of the type of loan or the type of property securing the mortgage. Although similarities exist in the underwriting of the different types of residential mortgage loans (conventional, FHA, VA), the differences are more procedural and not of great significance.

This chapter reviews the steps and examines the basic issues involved in underwriting a residential mortgage loan, with the desired result being that the loan conforms to the standards of the secondary mortgage market.

UNDERSTANDING RISK

All mortgage loans involve the risk of possible financial loss to a mortgage lender or investor. The underwriting involved to determine this risk requires the gathering and analysis of much information about both the applicant and the real estate that will secure the mortgage loan. Underwriting a residential mortgage loan can, and often does, involve more than just what is done by the originating mortgage lender. On any single residential loan, three separate underwriting reviews could occur at various stages of the mortgage lending cycle by the following parties:

1. A *mortgage lender* analyzes the risk and determines whether to lend funds at a certain interest rate to a borrower for a period of time secured by a certain piece of real estate.
2. A *mortgage insurer* or *guarantor* determines if mortgage insurance is to be written or a guarantee made based on the loan as submitted.

3. A *permanent investor* determines if the mortgage or mortgages as submitted will be purchased.

Each of these underwriters analyzes the loan package, estimates the risk to the institution being represented, and determines if the benefits are sufficient to balance the risk. Mortgage lending is a risk business and a lender must be willing to take a business risk to earn a fee or make a profit and therefore satisfy the real estate financing needs of borrowers. All mortgage lenders have a responsibility to attempt to satisfy any request for a mortgage loan as long as the risk is fully analyzed and deemed acceptable. The duty to make a loan, if at all possible, must be balanced by a mortgage lender's duty to protect loaned funds, which are the savings of depositors or the investments of shareholders.

UNDERWRITING BY A MORTGAGE LENDER

Of the three stages mentioned, mortgage lenders have the most difficult underwriting task because they face the delinquency problems that can result from improperly underwritten mortgages. A mortgage banker has a unique problem. Unlike other mortgage lenders, a mortgage banker underwrites a loan knowing that the loan must be sold to a permanent investor either directly or through the secondary mortgage market. If a loan is not attractive as made, because of poor processing or poor underwriting, that loan may not be marketable at a reasonable price. This can involve considerable loss to a mortgage banker.

Since most mortgage lenders have the option of placing mortgages they originate into their own portfolios, their loss potential for a poorly underwritten mortgage is less than that of a mortgage banker. All lenders, of course, share the danger that a poorly underwritten mortgage may become delinquent.

If a default occurs, the cost of either curing the default or foreclosing could eliminate present or future profits made from either marketing or servicing. For example, loss could result from a poorly underwritten mortgage if the defaulted loan is in a pool of mortgages securing a GNMA mortgage-backed security. In this situation, the originating mortgage lender (if also the servicer) must pay the monthly accrued principal and interest to the security holder from its own funds. As is evident, the underwriting phase in the mortgage lending cycle can have a lasting effect, obligating the originating mortgage lender to exercise professional expertise in underwriting.

UNDERWRITING GUIDELINES

Unfortunately, no single uniform set of underwriting guidelines exists for all residential mortgage loans. To a great extent, the underwriting guidelines of both Fannie Mae and Freddie Mac are the core standards that most lenders attempt to follow. Even those lenders who don't intend to sell loans to these two secondary mortgage market players should attempt to follow these well-conceived underwriting guidelines. In the past, most lenders have had to adopt and follow different underwriting rules, regulations, and formulas depending on whether a residential mortgage loan would be sold to an investor or kept in portfolio and whether the loan is conventional, FHA-insured, or VA-guaranteed. Many of these differences are not of major significance in underwriting but instead affect loan processing.

It is important to realize that only guidelines exist—not specific, precise formulas that can be applied to every applicant. Underwriting is an art, not a science, and the successful underwriter is one who can analyze all relevant material and approve a mortgage applicant while protecting the assets of others.

Underwriting, Discrimination, and the Federal Government

The 1970s witnessed the federal government becoming very involved in the fairness of certain underwriting guidelines. The government wanted to end all discriminatory lending practices and to ensure that each individual would be treated equally when applying for a mortgage loan. In essence, the burden shifted from the applicant demonstrating that he or she was qualified for a mortgage loan to the lender establishing that the applicant was not so qualified. This shift in the underwriting concept makes a mortgage lender liable for civil and/or criminal penalties if the letter and spirit of the various antidiscrimination laws are not followed exactly.

Regrettably, in the 1990s this issue is still challenging mortgage lenders. Data derived in the early 1990s from records mortgage lenders are required to maintain and submit to their federal regulator (required by the Home Mortgage Disclosure Act) reveal that minorities are still rejected for mortgage loans at a much higher rate than whites. As a result of this data, the federal government has placed renewed emphasis on determining why the same pattern of declinations continued even after the enactment of many consumer and discrimination safeguards. The 1992 Housing and Community Development Act required government-sponsored enterprises (GSE) to promote nondiscriminatory lending practices in their underwriting. It also required GSEs to discourage discrimination by loan originators. As a result, HUD may call upon the agencies to help monitor originators for signs of discrimination.

A part of the federal government's strategy to encourage lending to minorities was the enactment of the Community Reinvestment Act (CRA), which required lenders to serve their local communities. In a few situations, mortgage lenders who had not served the local community's borrowing needs, and therefore had poor Community Reinvestment Act (CRA) results, had their requests for charter revisions denied by their federal regulator. In other situations, lenders with poor CRA results were denied the opportunity to purchase other lending institutions.

All mortgage lenders have an obligation to make sure that their mortgage lending underwriting standards don't produce unintended discrimination resulting in fewer minorities receiving residential mortgage loans.

Loan-to-Value Ratios

The loan-to-value ratio (LTV) is probably the most important of all the ratios when underwriting a residential mortgage loan. The lower the LTV ratio the safer the loan is for a lender. The reason is that the lower the LTV ratio, the higher the equity investment the borrower will have in the property and thus the more that borrower has to lose. The LTV is calculated as follows:

$$\frac{\text{Mortgage Amount}}{\text{Lesser of Sales Price or Appraised Value}} = \text{LTV}$$

One of the reasons loans with LTV ratios of 95 percent have fallen on disfavor with some lenders is because a borrower has no equity in the property if the loan goes bad shortly after being made. The reason for this is, according to the Mortgage Guaranty Insurance Corporation, that "once default occurs, there is a better than 50 percent chance of foreclosure, largely because of the borrower's inability to sell the property at a price high enough to cover the remaining loan balance plus selling costs and delinquent interest."

This situation is made worse if the property is located in a real estate market where property values are declining, such as Texas in the early 1980s and New England during the early 1990s.

Various studies support this position and have established that a 90 percent LTV ratio loan is twice as likely as an 80 percent LTV ratio loan to default, and a 95 percent LTV ratio loan has nearly three times the default risk as an 80 percent LTV ratio loan. A 97 percent LTV ratio loan (a section 203 FHA loan), according to these same studies, was nearly six times more risky than an 80 percent LTV ratio loan.

It should be obvious that any loan with a LTV ratio of over 80 percent should be supported by some type of mortgage insurance. Mortgage insurance is discussed in detail in Chapter 8.

Down Payment (Equity)

Where can the money for a down payment come from—anywhere? The money for the down payment (or the equity) can come from any "liquid investment" source. That source could be money in a financial institution, in stocks and bonds, or from the sale of real estate. The existence and history of these funds should be established by a Verification of Deposit (VOD). The major issues with the VOD for the underwriter are:

- when was the account opened?
- how long have the funds been there?
- in what name(s) is it held?

Deposits in joint accounts and recently opened new accounts often hide loans from family members.

As a general rule, the secondary mortgage market is interested in establishing that an applicant has been able to save most of the down payment for the mortgage loan. If the LTV ratio is below 80 percent, the down payment could be gifted, but if the LTV ratio is over 80 percent, at least 5 percent of the purchase price must have been saved by the borrower. Exceptions to this general rule do exist, such as under certain "affordable housing" programs that allow for a 3/2 split, whereby the borrower only has to produce 3 percent of the purchase price from savings while the remaining 2 percent can come from another source, such as an employer. In all situations, the borrower is expected to be able to establish how the required money was saved.

As mentioned, some or all of the down payment could be from a gift, but it is essential that it be a true gift and that there is no expectation that the money be repaid. A legally binding gift letter must be signed by the grantor, and the source of the funds given must be established. In addition, the transfer of the gift money must be documented.

Income Ratios

An underwriter is concerned about both the ability to repay the mortgage debt and the willingness to do so. First, the issue of ability to repay is considered.

The most important test of whether an applicant can afford a particular mortgage loan is by computing the various income ratios. These ratios, established by either the secondary mortgage market or the insuring/guaranteeing entities, have evolved through the years after reviewing millions of mortgage loans as realistic guidelines for making mortgage loans with a low risk of default. The so-called mortgage debt ratio (or *front-end* ratio, as it is sometimes called) is arrived at by computing the percentage of monthly income necessary to meet the monthly housing expense.

The monthly housing expense is determined in various ways, depending on whether a loan is conventional, FHA, or VA. The percentage of income that can be used for these expenses also varies depending on the type of loan. When computing the monthly housing expense on a conventional loan, the following monthly charges or monthly share of annual expenses are added (if applicable):

- principal,
- interest,

- hazard insurance,
- real estate tax,
- mortgage insurance premium,
- homeowners' association fee,
- ground rents,
- any payment on an existing or proposed second mortgage.

The ratio of housing debt to gross monthly income is the same for all loans regardless of the LTV ratio or whether the loan is an ARM or FRM. As a result, the total of the applicable items included in the monthly housing expense should not exceed 28 percent of gross monthly income. Gross monthly income means income before deductions of any type.

In some situations, if no long-term debts exist, a lender may be able to justify higher ratios for housing expenses, but care must be taken that the loan can still meet investors' requirements.

Example: Ed and Jane Smith want to borrow $92,000 in order to purchase a single-family detached house appraised at $115,000. He earns $35,000 a year as a bricklayer and she earns $25,000 as an assistant professor of English. The only long-term debt is a car payment of $400 a month with 25 months remaining.

Calculations

Gross monthly income (borrower)			$2,917
Gross monthly income (co-borrower)			$2,083
Substantiated other gross income			–0–
Total Monthly Income			$5,000
Monthly housing expense:			
Principal & interest (7.5% for 30 years)			$643.28
Private mortgage insurance			–0–
Insurance escrow			$ 35.00
Tax escrow			$155.00
Other			–0–
Total housing expense:			$833.28
Total of all long-term debts			$400.00
Total of all monthly payments			$1,233.28
Mortgage Debt Ratio:	$833.28 / $5,000	=	16.67%
Total Debt Ratio:	$1,233.28 / $5,000	=	24.67%

Long-term debts Individuals often have other monthly contractual debt obligations in addition to mortgage payments. The ratio of these combined debts to gross monthly income must be calculated separately. This ratio is called the total debt ratio or *back-end* debt ratio. For example the total payments for the following:

- monthly housing expenses,
- revolving charges,
- other payments on installment debts that have more than 10 remaining payments,
- any alimony or child support payments,

should not total more than 36 percent of gross monthly income.

Higher ratios may be justified by mitigating factors, such as:

- demonstrated ability of an applicant to allocate a higher percent of gross income to housing expenses,
- larger down payment than normal,
- demonstrated ability of an applicant to accumulate savings and maintain a good credit rating,
- a large net worth,
- potential for increased earnings because of education or profession.

FHA-insured loan   If the loan requested is FHA-insured, the income ratios are slightly higher than with a conventional loan. Before 1990, FHA used net income when calculating ratios but has since decided to adopt the more universal gross income calculations. The new FHA ratios are:

- 29 percent for the mortgage payment ratio,
- 41 percent for the total debt ratio.

VA-guaranteed loan   The VA uses a modified residual method in qualifying a veteran for a mortgage loan, and this result is then double-checked against a total debt-to-income ratio of 41 percent. The residual income standards are based on a Department of Labor Consumer Expenditure Survey with regional differences.

Loans with ratio between 41.1 and 45 percent would be acceptable provided the residual was at least 20 percent over the appropriate standard. The VA also accepts some deviations if written justifications exist and are acceptable.

Employment

An evaluation must be made of the employment of the applicant and co-applicant and the probability that it will continue. For most applicants, the income that will repay the mortgage loan is derived from being employed. An underwriter will consult the Verification of Employment (VOE) form in the file, which should provide all the information needed about an employed individual.

The important points for the underwriter to review carefully on the VOE include the following:

- salary/wage correspond with the application,
- probability of continued employment is acceptable,
- overtime/bonus income is likely to continue,
- dates of employment correspond with the application,
- name and signature of employer is on the form.

If the applicant has been employed at the current employer for less than two years, a VOE from the former employer is necessary. For a self-employed person, the accounting forms discussed earlier should be used.

An applicant who has demonstrated job stability and is in a line of work with a promising future should be considered favorably by an underwriter. The education of an applicant or co-applicant and whether he or she is in a profession with strong growth potential may actually be enough to influence a close underwriting call. This would make a "tough loan" a "makeable" one.

In today's society, changing jobs, especially if the new job is for more pay and is in the same field of endeavor, is a positive characteristic. On the other hand, extensive job changes without advancement or pay increases may be indicative of future financial instability. Gaps in employment may indicate possible future employment problems and should be adequately explained.

Willingness to Repay

A key factor in underwriting an application for a mortgage loan is how an applicant has handled credit in the past. Ability to repay has already been discussed; here we are analyzing a borrower's willingness to repay. The primary way of establishing willingness to repay is by careful review of the credit report. The credit report that should be used for first mortgages is the Residential Mortgage Credit Report. This credit report was discussed in detail in the chapter on loan processing.

If an underwriter can determine that an applicant has had a credit history of meeting payments according to contract terms, then that application should be considered in a positive manner. If, on the other hand, the credit history shows credit problems such as slow payment, then an underwriter needs to analyze the credit history very carefully. If an applicant has declared bankruptcy, it is incumbent on an underwriter to have complete information in order to make an informed loan decision.

Self-Employed Income Analysis

Borrower Name

Property Address

General Instructions: This form is to be used as a guide in Underwriting the Self-employed borrower. The underwriter has a choice in analyzing the Individual Tax return by either the Schedule Analysis Method or the Adjusted Gross Income (AGI) Method.

The Schedule Analysis Method derives total income by analyzing Schedule C, D, E, and F for stable continuing self-employed income.

Schedule Analysis Method

		19__	19__	19__
A.	Individual Tax Return (Form 1040)			
1.	Schedule C:			
	a. Net Profit or Loss			
	b. Depletion	(+)		
	c. Depreciation	(+)		
	d. Less: 20% Exclusion for Meals and Entertainment	(−)		
2.	Schedule D Recurring Capital Gains	(+)		
3.	Schedule E Part II: Partnership/S Corporation Income (Loss)**			
4.	Schedule F a. Net Profit or Loss			
	b. Depreciation	(+)		
5.	Schedule 2106 Total Expenses	(−)		
6.	W-2 income from Corporation	(+)		
7.	Total			

**Partnership Income (Loss) = [From IRS Schedule K-1 (Form 1065)]
Ordinary Income (Loss) (+) Guaranteed Payments
S Corporation Income (Loss) = [From IRS Schedule K-1 (Form 1120-s)]
Ordinary Income (Loss) + Other Income (Loss)

		19__	19__	19__
B.	Corporate Tax Return Form (1120) - Corporate Income to qualify the borrower will be considered only if the borrower can provide evidence of access to the funds			
1.	Taxable Income (Tax and Payments Section)	(+)		
2.	Total Tax (Tax and Payments Section)	(−)		
3.	Depreciation (Deductions Section)	(+)		
4.	Depletion (Deductions Section)	(+)		
5.	Mortgages, notes, bonds payable in less than one year (Balance Sheets Section)	(−)		
6.	Subtotal			
7.	Times individual percentage of ownership	X____%	X____%	X____%
8.	Subtotal			
9.	Dividend Income reflected on borrower's individual income tax returns	(−)		
10.	Total Income available to borrower			

		19__	19__	19__
C.	S Corporation Tax Returns (Form 1120s) or Partnership Tax Returns (Form 1065) - Partnership or S Corporation income to qualify the borrower will be considered only if the borrower can provide evidence of access to the funds.			
1.	Depreciation (Deductions Section)	(+)		
2.	Depletion (Deductions Section)	(+)		
3.	Mortgages, notes, bonds payable in less than one year (Balance Sheets Section)	(−)		
4.	Subtotal			
5.	Times individual percentage of ownership	X____%	X____%	X____%
6.	Total income available to borrower			
	Total Income Available (add A, B, C)	I	II	III

D. Year-to-Date Profit and Loss
Year-to-date income to qualify the borrower will be considered only if that income is in line with the previous year's earnings or if audited financial statements are provided.

1.	Salary/Draws to Individual			$_____
2.	Total Allowable add back	$_____ X _____%	of individual ownership =	$_____
3.	Total net profit	$_____ X _____%	of individual ownership =	$_____
4.	Total			$_____

Combined Total I, II, III, YTD = $_____ divided by _____ months = $_____ Monthly Average

This form is only a reference to help organize information from the tax returns. You must refer to the selling guide for our complete underwriting requirements on the self-employed.

Fannie Mae
Form 1084A Nov. 89

EQUIFAX *The Information Source*   REAL ESTATE SERVICES

ACCOUNT NO. BBQ 352123230498
ACCOUNT NAME Dominion Bankshares
REPORT ORDERED BY Janis Williams
DATE ORDERED 12/14/92
DATE MAILED 12/18/92
INDIVIDUAL OR JOINT REPORT Joint
TYPE REPORT (CASE OR FILE NO.) Residential
SOURCE CBI/CSC, TRW
REPORT PREPARED BY Lorie Jamison
PRICE (plus applicable sales tax) $43.86

RESIDENTIAL MORTGAGE CREDIT REPORT PREPARED FOR

Dominion Bankshares Mortgage Corporation
12300 Twinbrook Pkwy.
Rockville, MD

GENERAL INFORMATION

1.	APPLICANT'S NAME AND AGE / SPOUSE'S NAME AND AGE	MILLER, Theodore A. - 29 yrs./Vicki L. - 29 yrs.
2.	CURRENT ADDRESS	2024 Georgian Park Pl., Wheaton, MD
3.	LENGTH OF TIME AT PRESENT ADDRESS / OWN?	1½ years/rent
4.	PREVIOUS ADDRESS	2101 S. Sipley St., Alexandria, VA
5.	APPLICANT'S SS # / SPOUSE'S SS #	081-60-4823 / 075-54-6256
6.	MARITAL STATUS / DEPENDENTS	Married / None

APPLICANT'S EMPLOYMENT

7.	NAME OF EMPLOYER / ADDRESS	U.S. Naval Research Lab. Wash. D.C. 20735
8.	POSITION HELD / LENGTH OF EMPLOYMENT	Res. Physicist - 3 years
9.	SOURCE AND DATE OF VERIFICATION / INCOME	Personnel - 12-15-92 / $4,000 p/m
10.	PREVIOUS EMPLOYMENT	n/a

SPOUSE'S EMPLOYMENT

11.	NAME OF EMPLOYER / ADDRESS	N.I.H. 9000 Rockville Pike, Bethesda, MD 20892
12.	POSITION HELD / LENGTH OF EMPLOYMENT	Chemist - 4 years
13.	SOURCE AND DATE OF VERIFICATION / INCOME	Cheri Roundtree / 12/15/92 - $24.71 hr.
14.	PREVIOUS EMPLOYMENT	n/a

CREDIT HISTORY

CREDIT GRANTOR	DATE OPENED	LAST DATE REPORTED	HIGHEST CREDIT	BALANCE OWING	PAST DUE AMOUNT	CURRENT RATING	TERMS	30 DAYS	60 DAYS	90 DAYS	DATE LAST PAST DUE
NRL Fed. Credit Union 242568-B	04-91	10-92	6531	4092	0	I-1	164	0	0	0	–
State University of NY	NOT VERIFIED, REQUIRES WRITTEN AUTHORIZATION										
Bankeast 5413826554321	01-90	11-92	1500	192	0	R-1	10	0	0	0	–
Georgian & Woods (Landlord)	07-91	12-92	735	0	0	O-1	735	0	0	0	–
Crestar Bank 9238199532	10-89	09-92	832	0	0	R-1	0	0	0	0	–

Accounts under co-borrower:

CREDIT GRANTOR	DATE OPENED	LAST DATE REPORTED	HIGHEST CREDIT	BALANCE OWING	PAST DUE AMOUNT	CURRENT RATING	TERMS	30 DAYS	60 DAYS	90 DAYS	DATE LAST PAST DUE
Citibank VISA 412201159872	01-88	11-92	5600	87	0	R-1	20	0	0	0	–
Discover Card 60110846603	10-88	11-92	2300	78	0	R-1	20	0	0	0	–
Baybank 28492734998563892	09-88	06-91	500	0	0	R-1	0	0	0	0	–
Filenes 3722943234799	05-89	10-92	54	0	0	R-1	0	0	0	0	–

Inquiries made in the last 90 days: None

Previous residence:
  2101 S. Sipley Street, Alexandria, VA - 2 years

Public Records: NONE FOUND

Prepared by: Equifax - Real Estate Services
             854 East Wiggins AVe. Schaumburg, IL 60234 (800-555-1234)

** END OF REPORT **

* Please Wait, initializing *
* Testing phone line *

Form 22228—11/90 Equifax Services Inc USA

Bankruptcy

The fact that a bankruptcy exists in an applicant's credit history does not in itself lead to a negative response to an application. The reasons for the bankruptcy and the type of filing are the most important factors for an underwriter to consider. For example, if the bankruptcy was caused by unemployment, extensive medical bills, or other circumstances beyond the control of the applicant and these facts can be verified, the bankruptcy should not be the reason for a credit denial. As a general rule, if a bankruptcy exists in the credit history, additional credit may be extended if two years of excellent credit history have been maintained since the discharge.

A common form of bankruptcy is a wage earner's petition. A wage earner's petition under Chapter 13 of the Bankruptcy Law provides for partial or full repayment of debts over a period of time, usually two to five years. When all payments have been satisfactorily made, underwriters should consider that accomplishment as reestablishing credit. Occasionally a mortgage application is made before full discharge. In such a situation, the approval of the bankruptcy judge may be required. Certain other bankruptcies, such as those over seven years old, should not be given excessive consideration.

Past Foreclosures or Deed in Lieu

If the applicant has a past foreclosure or has entered into an agreement for a deed in lieu of foreclosure, that applicant has indicated a problem handling credit. The secondary mortgage market requires that these applicants have three years of excellent credit history since the foreclosure or deed in lieu before they can be considered for a mortgage loan. This type of credit problem is serious because it involved a mortgage loan—the same type of loan the borrower has applied for.

Property Guidelines

The next stage in underwriting a residential mortgage loan involves an analysis of the real estate that will secure the mortgage debt. Although it is expected that the income of a borrower is available to fulfill the mortgage obligation, a mortgage lender must protect both its own position and that of any investor by having adequate security for the debt. The adequacy of the security is established by an appraisal.

An appraisal is an opinion or estimate of market value made by an appraiser who is either an independent fee appraiser or employed by a mortgage lender. An appraisal not only helps establish the adequacy of the security but also establishes the value of security upon which the loan-to-value ratio is applied (see Chapter 12, Residential Real Estate Appraisal).

Redlining   An underwriter must analyze the appraisal as carefully as any other information. But the underwriter must not designate any area or neighborhood as unacceptable or allow any appraiser to do so; in other words, a lender will not "redline." (Redlining is defined as the withdrawal of mortgage funds from an area due to perceived risks in that area, based on racial, social, religious, or ethnic factors.) Instead, a lender should make a sound, supportable judgment based upon the written appraisal for a given piece of real estate and whether that value provides sufficient security.

The following are some of the items found on the appraisal that should be carefully reviewed by the underwriter:

1. Location. Location is always the most critical of all evaluating factors.
   a. Property must be residential in nature and not any type of agricultural property.
   b. Adequate sewage and water facilities and other utilities are present.
   c. Property is readily accessible by an all-weather road
   d. No danger is posed to health and safety from immediate surroundings (including environmental hazards).
2. Physical security. The age, equipment, architectural design, quality of construction, floor plan, and site features are considered in establishing the adequacy and future value of the physical security.
   a. Evidence of compliance with local codes should be in file for underwriter's review.
   b. Topography, shape, size, and drainage of a lot are equally important.
   c. View amenities, easements, and other encroachments may have either a positive or negative influence on market value.
3. Local government.
   a. The amount of property tax can have a great effect on future marketability.
   b. Building codes, deed restrictions, and zoning ordinances help to maintain housing standards and promote a high degree of homogeneity.
4. Comparable sales. Critical section for residential real estate loans.
   a. Ascertain that the comparables are truly similar to the subject in regard to location, type of real estate and time of sale.
   b. Determine if the adjustments exceed 10 percent for any line item.
   c. Determine if the total of all adjustments, disregarding plus and minus signs, exceeds 25 percent.

In order to permit the sale of the loan into the secondary mortgage market and to satisfy certain regulatory requirements, the Uniform Residential Appraisal Report (URAR), such as FHLMC Form 70, should be used.

UNDERWRITING SYSTEMS

Two systems exist for evaluating the creditworthiness of an applicant. Practically all mortgage lenders use the judgmental system, which relies on trained underwriters to evaluate each application on a case-by-case basis. This means that the same standards are applied to each application in the same manner. Although exceptions are allowed, the reason for the exception must be clearly demonstrable. For example, if a larger-than-normal down payment is made, then an increased total debt ratio of 40 percent of gross monthly income may be acceptable. The second system attempts to determine the creditworthiness of an applicant by assigning points to certain attributes and facts. These systems are not illegal or discriminatory, although ECOA regulations state that these systems must be "demonstrably and statistically sound and empirically derived." Because of the complexities and potential for unintended discrimination, few if any mortgage lenders are currently using this second system. However, several larger mortgage lenders are exploring so-called "smart systems" as a method to speed service and cut underwriting costs.

UNDERWRITING GUIDELINES AND LOAN APPLICATION REGISTER

The underwriting standards used by a lender should be clearly written, nondiscriminatory, and available for review by the general public. These standards should be periodically reviewed to ensure continuing compliance with evolving legislation and good business practices. All mortgage lenders (excluding credit unions) also need to be concerned about the Community Reinvestment Act (CRA), which establishes guidelines for taking care of the credit needs of the community.

The Home Mortgage Disclosure Act (HMDA) requires all mortgage lenders to maintain a Loan Application Register, within which they retain important information on each application for a mortgage loan. The information to be retained must include:

- name(s) of applicant,
- amount of loan requested,
- zip code and census tract of property,
- sex, race, marital status, age of applicant,
- interest rate,
- terms and fees,
- loan-to-value ratio,
- year dwelling was built,
- disposition of the application.

This information allows both regulators and the public to determine whether lending standards are being applied in a discriminatory manner.

THE UNDERWRITING DECISION

When all information relating to an applicant's financial capabilities, credit characteristics, and physical security are present, a decision must be made to accept, reject, or modify the mortgage loan application. This decision must be sent to an applicant within 30 days of the date of application.

If the application is accepted, a mortgage lender should send a commitment letter to the approved applicant and explain the procedures that will be followed in connection with loan closing.

NOTICE OF INCOMPLETE APPLICATION AND REQUEST FOR ADDITIONAL INFORMATION

Applicant Name: _Marshall W. Dennis_   Date: 9/13/95
Applicant Address: _3001 Greenhall Lane_   Transaction Reference: 1275
City, State, Zip: _Northbrook, ILL. 30122_

Dear Applicant:

Thank you for your application for credit. The following information is needed to make a decision on your application.

We need to receive your Federal Tax returns for the past two years.

We need to receive this information by _____10/1/95_____
                                                                                (Date)
If we do not receive it by that date, we will regrettably be unable to give further consideration to your credit request.

Sincerely,

Jack Nolle

STATEMENT OF CREDIT DENIAL, TERMINATION, OR CHANGE

Date:

Applicant's Name: __Francis Stavola__   Date __2/1/95__

Applicant's Address: __529 Ridge Rd., Wethersfield, CT   60606__

Description of Account, Transaction, or
Requested Credit: __Residential Mortgage Loan__

Description of Action Taken: __Application rejected__

PART I. PRINCIPAL REASON(S) FOR CREDIT DENIAL, TERMINATION, OR OTHER ACTION TAKEN CONCERNING CREDIT.

THIS SECTION MUST BE COMPLETED IN ALL INSTANCES

☐ Credit application incomplete
☐ Insufficient number of credit references provided
☐ Unacceptable type of credit references provided
☐ Unable to verify credit references
☐ Temporary or irregular employment
☐ Unable to verify employment
☐ Length of employment
☐ Income insufficient for amount of credit requested
☐ Other, specify: _____
☐ Other, specify: _____

XX Excessive obligations in relation to income
☐ Unable to verify income
☐ Length of residence
☐ Temporary residence
☐ Unable to verify residence
☐ No credit file
☐ Limited credit experience
☐ Poor credit performance with us
☐ Delinquent past or present credit obligations with others

☐ Garnishment, attachment, foreclosure, repossession, collection action, or judgment.
☐ Bankruptcy
☐ Value, or type of collateral not sufficient
☐ Inadequate down payment
☐ No deposit relationship with us
☐ We do not grant credit to any applicant on the terms and conditions you have requested.

PART II.   DISCLOSURE OF USE OF INFORMATION OBTAINED FROM AN OUTSIDE SOURCE. This section should be completed if the credit decision was based in whole or in part on information that has been obtained from an outside source.

XX Our credit decision was based in whole or in part on information obtained from the consumer reporting agency listed below. You have a right under the Fair Credit Reporting Act to know the information contained in your credit file at the consumer reporting agency. The consumer reporting agency played no part in our decision and is unable to supply specific reasons why we have denied credit to you.

__Connecticut Credit Bureau__
Name of Consumer Reporting Agency

__123 Main St.__
Street Address

__New Haven, Conn.   60709__
City, State, Zip

__203-456-7890__
Telephone Number

☐ Our credit decision was based in whole or in part on information obtained from an outside source other than a consumer reporting agency. Under the Fair Credit Reporting Act, you have the right to make a written request, no later than 60 days after you receive this notice, for disclosure of the nature of this information.

If you have any questions regarding this notice, you should contact:

__Northwoods Mortgage Company__
Institution Name

__2468 North St.__
Street Address

__Wethersfield, CT   60609__
City, State, Zip

__800-456-0987__ Telephone Number

Notice:

The Federal Equal Credit Opportunity Act prohibits creditors from discriminating against credit applicants on the basis of race, color, religion, national origin, sex, marital status, age (provided the applicant has the capacity to enter into a binding contract); because all or part of the applicant's income derives from any public assistance program; or because the applicant has in good faith exercised any right under the Consumer Credit Protection Act. The federal agency that administers compliance with this law concerning this creditor is:

Occassionally, an underwriter is unable to make a decision on an application because one or more important pieces of information is missing. In that situation a request for additional information is sent to the applicant.

If the application is modified by any action, such as offering less credit or credit at different terms, and that counteroffer is accepted, the loan proceeds as with a normal loan acceptance.

On the other hand, if an application is rejected, an applicant must be notified of the rejection, provided with the ECOA notice of nondiscrimination, and informed that the reason for rejection will be given if requested. This is usually accomplished by a Statement of Credit Denial.

Although all underwriters should attempt to approve a loan application if at all prudently possible, the approval of a loan that will become delinquent is a disservice to the borrower, the mortgage lender, and those the lender represents.

MORTGAGE INSURANCE ══ *8*

Insurance of any type is designed to spread the economic risk or loss from a particular hazard over a large group—that is, the insured group. Mortgage insurance is a financial guarantee provided to a mortgage lender in return for a premium paid, usually by a mortgage borrower (however, there are some exceptions), which insures a lender against all or most of the losses that would be suffered if a borrower defaults on the mortgage obligation. This function is performed by all types of mortgage insurance or guarantee, whether it be government sponsored or private.

The various classifications of mortgage insurance or guarantees are:

- Federal Housing Administration (FHA) insurance,
- Veterans Administration (VA) guarantee,
- Private mortgage insurance (MI).

The social benefit derived from mortgage insurance is that it allows for more people to purchase homes. The reason is that lenders are willing to accept smaller down payments than the normal 20 percent if one of the types of mortgage insurance is present. Since lower down payments are required, more people are capable of saving the reduced amount and thus purchasing a home of their own. In addition, the use of mortgage insurance disperses the risk and makes mortgage investments more attractive to mortgage investors. Before examining current government and private mortgage programs, a brief review of the historical development of mortgage insurance will help to develop an understanding of present practices.

The Beginning

Early title insurance companies began mortgage insurance in the 1890s by insuring the repayment of mortgages in addition to the validity of title. The first statutory law providing for this type of insurance was enacted in New York state in 1904.

The social and demographic changes in the United States that emerged after 1900 (particularly following World War I) led mortgage lending into a more important position in the American economy. As mortgage lending became more prevalent and important, mortgage insurance became more accepted and desired. Because of this increased interest, title insurance companies became involved in providing this financial service as a no-cost add-on to title insurance.

The residential mortgage lending and title insurance business was practiced differently then from the way it is practiced today. It was customary during this period for a mortgage company to exchange a new mortgage for a defaulted one or to buy back a troubled loan sold to an investor. As the real estate boom of the 1920s continued, this custom gave way to the actual guaranteeing of principal and interest by a new entity—the mortgage guaranty company.

During their peak years (1925–32), as many as 50 of these companies were in operation, located primarily in the state of New York. These companies prospered by originating and selling mortgages with a guarantee to institutional investors or to individual investors as mortgage participation bonds. The units sold to individual investors were usually in $500 or $1,000 denominations. Yield and apparent safety made the units very attractive. A trustee would hold the mortgages and be responsible for foreclosure if any default in payment occurred. The prevailing viewpoint during this period was that real estate values would continue to appreciate, and if any lax underwriting or appraising occurred, the resulting questionable mortgage would be saved by inflation. This optimism affected the investing public. Large portions of accumulated savings were invested in mortgage bonds issued by apparently successful mortgage guaranty companies.

Due to the general optimism about the economy and the laissez-faire attitude of the government, these mortgage guaranty companies were virtually unregulated. Lack of regulation often led to poor underwriting, self-dealing, fraud, and ultimately a lack of adequate reserves to meet any meaningful emergency.

Even before the stock market crash of 1929, the real estate industry was in serious trouble. Real estate values started to drop and foreclosures resulted, which further depressed values. It was inevitable that these companies would not survive the bank holiday declared by President Roosevelt in March 1933. Many billions of dollars were lost by institutional investors with similarly tragic results to private investors because of the failure of these companies. The collapse left such an ugly mark on the real estate finance industry that private mortgage insurance did not reappear for almost 25 years.

GOVERNMENT (FHA) INSURANCE

The years immediately following the stock market crash witnessed much debate on the proper role of the government in the nation's economy. Many in Congress urged action; others were against it. Most, however, agreed that government action would benefit real estate by helping to put a floor under real estate prices. Those in favor of stimulation reasoned that expanding waves from a healthy real estate industry would have a multiplier effect on the remainder of a depressed economy. The National Housing Act (1934) contained provisions to help stimulate the construction industry. The act created the Federal Housing Administration (FHA) to encourage lenders to make real estate mortgages again by providing government-backed mortgage insurance as protection. Title I of this law provided insurance, initially free, to lenders who would loan money for home improvements and repairs.

Title II provided for the establishment of a Mutual Mortgage Insurance Fund to be funded by premiums paid by mortgagors out of which any claims by the protected lenders could be satisfied. Initially, the mortgagor paid an annual insurance premium of 1/2 of 1 percent based on the original amount. This insurance premium has changed through the years, but the current practice of paying a 2.25 percent fee the first year and an annual 1/2 of 1 percent of the original loan amount for up to 30 years has been in effect since 1994.

The basic program under this act was Section 203(b), designed to provide government insurance to lenders who made loans on one- to four-family houses. (Through the years, most have been single family.) This program is still successfully helping to meet the national housing needs after helping to provide housing for more than 21 million families.

FHA-INSURED HOME MORTGAGES
(in millions of dollars)

Year	Amount
1960	$ 4,601
1965	7,465
1970	8,114
1975	6,165
1980	16,458
1985	23,964
1987	81,881
1990	51,864
1992	48,315
1993	79,100

Source: Federal Housing Administration.

Now a part of the Department of Housing and Urban Development (HUD), FHA has other insurance programs, each designed to meet a specific need. But the Mutual Mortgage Insurance Fund remains the largest and most important.

Early Opposition

Initially, the legislation to establish FHA was faced with opposition from some thrift institutions that believed that the federal government should not get involved in housing. Even after enactment, FHA did not meet with great acceptance among financial centers, since many felt that mortgage insurance as a concept was discredited or that government should not get involved in what was basically a private enterprise.

History, however, has proven this to be a shortsighted belief, especially in view of the many changes for which FHA has paved the way in real estate finance. As an example, FHA insurance has allowed for the development of a national mortgage market by providing for the transferability, and thus the liquidity, of mortgage instruments. The FHA-insured mortgage was attractive to many investors because it established property and borrower standards with a corresponding reduction in risk.

The FHA mortgage insurance program allowed life insurance companies to justify a successful request, to state insurance commissioners, for the purchase of loans with higher loan-to-value ratios and with lower down payments. The program also gave them the opportunity to lend across the nation. With this new authorization, life insurance companies could lend in those areas of the country that desperately needed capital. Subsequently they could receive a higher yield than what was previously available in the capital-surplus area of New England, where most of the major life insurance companies were located. Mortgage companies were the principal intermediaries for moving this capital from capital-surplus areas to capital-deficit areas by originating mortgages with FHA insurance and then selling them to life insurance companies.

Mortgage Lending Benefits Derived from FHA

One of the primary reasons for the increase in home ownership (from about 40 percent of all homes occupied in 1930 to about 63 percent in 1994) is the leadership provided by FHA, which:

- established property and borrower lending standards,
- reintroduced mortgage insurance,
- led to self-amortizing mortgage loans,
- accepted higher loan-to-value ratios,
- agreed to longer mortgage terms.

These factors contributed not only to the higher percentage of home-ownership but also to a financial environment conducive to a rebirth of private mortgage insurance.

FHA-insured mortgage loans can be originated by any of the various mortgage intermediaries, although as a practical matter, about 75 percent of all FHA mortgages are originated by mortgage bankers. Initially, this high percentage of origination was due to the local lending philosophy of the other mortgage lenders and the correspondent system that developed between mortgage bankers and life insurance companies. Most FHA-insured mortgages are still originated by mortgage bankers.

FHA Insurance Today

FHA and its various insurance programs have been in existence for over 50 years and have assisted approximately 21 million families that might not otherwise have been able to purchase a home. In 1993, FHA insurance backed more than $79.1 billion worth of mortgages for over 1 million buyers (40 percent of this total was refinancings). This volume represented about 7 percent of total originations for 1993.

During the past 60-plus years, FHA has often been a leader in innovation and has helped shape the way residential mortgage lending is done today. These years have not all been smooth, as witnessed by the dramatic falloff in loans insured during the 1970s and early 1980s. Some of the reasons for this decline in insured loans were:

- internal reorganization and change of FHA's status within HUD,
- fraud, abuse, and influence peddling by some lenders and loan originators,
- excessive government red tape and paperwork delay.

These issues were addressed, and the amount of FHA insurance began to increase, reaching record levels in the second half of the 1980s. But then another problem developed. By the end of the 1980s, Congress realized that radical changes had to occur to remedy persistent high default and foreclosure rates. These changes included:

- higher insurance premiums,
- underwriting changes (use of gross income),
- elimination of investor loans.

FHA in the 1990s

After nearly 1 million Americans used various FHA programs in 1993, the federal government increased the appropriation level for 1994 and 1995 hoping that FHA market share would increase to 1.2 million. Today, as in prior years, the most important FHA program is Section 203(b). The maximum loan amount permitted and other requirements periodically change, but the most recent limits for high-cost areas is $151,725.

The low down payment requirement for an FHA mortgage is what makes this program so popular. To establish the downpayment, all of the acquisition costs most be considered. Acquisition cost includes the contract price of the property or appraised value (whichever is lower), plus allowable closing costs for the purchase. FHA allows a borrower to finance the origination fee, survey, appraisal, title insurance and up to $200 of the home inspection cost. However, the loan maximum is 97.75 percent of the home price if the home price is greater than $50,000 (98.75 percent if the home price is less than $50,000).

The maximum term is 30 years, and the loan is assumable (with some limitations) with no prepayment penalty to a qualified borrower.

Example: If Mr. and Mrs. O. K. Bymee want to purchase a home that has a total acquisition cost (including some closing costs) of $140,000, their down payment would be:

3 percent of $25,000	= $ 750
5 percent of next $100,000	= $5,000
10 percent of last $15,000	= $1,500
Total down payment	= $7,250
Loan-to-value ratio	= 94.8 percent

Not only are the down payment requirements for an FHA mortgage attractive to potential mortgage applicants, the underwriting standards are more generous than a conventional mortgage. The percent of gross income that can be used for housing expenses is 29 percent, and the ratio of long-term debt to gross income is up to 41 percent. In addition, FHA permits the use of bonafide gifts for the entire down payment.

U.S. DEPARTMENT OF HOUSING AND URBAN DEVELOPMENT
HOUSING — FEDERAL HOUSING COMMISSIONER

Mortgage Insurance Certificate

FHA Case No.
352:222222-2

Section
703(b)

Mortgagor's Name *(Last Name First)*
Jones, Jon & Linda

Mortgage Amount
$84,078

Property Address
205 Smith Street

City, State and ZIP Code
Perth Amboy, NJ   08861

This Certificate, when endorsed in the block below, is evidence of insurance of the mortgage loan described herein under the indicated Section of the National Housing Act *(12 USC 1701 et seq.)* and Regulations of the Department of Housing and Urban Development Published at 24 CFR 200.1 et seq.

Margaretten & Company, Inc.
271 Maple Street
P.O. Box 3021
Perth Amboy, NJ   08862

Endorsed for insurance by an Authorized Agent of the Federal Housing Commissioner.

MORTGAGEE'S NAME AND ADDRESS

(Signature)   *(Date)* 1/16/89

(REMOVE CERTIFICATE BEFORE SIGNING)   (HB 4045.1) HUD-59100.1 (12-83)

Previous Edition May Be Used Until Exhausted

FHA Insurance Premium

In 1991, the amount of the mortgage insurance premium was changed to allow for sufficient revenues to the Mutual Insurance Fund, which was suffering increasing losses. This fund had been badly depleted in the 1980s as FHA loan defaults per year were as high as 11 percent. Through the years, this fund has been put back on strong footing and as a result, the premium has dropped back down. For an FHA loan with less than 10 percent down, the upfront premium dropped from 3 percent to 2.25 percent in April 1994.

VETERANS ADMINISTRATION: VA-GUARANTEED LOAN

As a gesture to returning World War II veterans, Congress enacted the Servicemen's Readjustment Act (1944), which authorized the Veterans Administration (VA) to guarantee loans (among other benefits) made to eligible veterans. This guaranteed loan program, now administered by the Department of Veterans Affairs, no longer represents a large segment of originations each year, but it still serves the needs of many active and retired military personnel.

The original guarantee was for the first 50 percent of the loan amount or $2,000, whichever was less. This has been increased through the years to the current guarantee limit of $46,000. (The VA guarantee now ranges from 50 percent for mortgages with original loan amounts of $45,000 or less to 25 percent for mortgages with original loan amounts up to $184,000, with the guarantee limited to the maximum of $46,000.)

HISTORY OF INCREASES IN VA, MAXIMUM GUARANTEES

Change Date	Increased to
September 16, 1940	$ 4,000.00
April 20, 1950	7,500.00
May 7, 1968	12,500.00
January 1, 1975	17,500.00
January 1, 1978	25,000.00
October 7, 1980	27,500.00
February 1, 1988	36,000.00
January 1, 1990	46,000.00*

* Only available on purchases when the loan amount is in excess of $144,000. Otherwise, the maximum guarantee is $36,000.

HUD / VA Addendum to Uniform Residential Loan Application

| | OMB Approval Nos. | VA: | 2900-0144 |
| | | HUD: | 2502-0059 (exp. 3/31/94) |

Part I - Identifying Information (mark the type of application)

1. ☐ VA Application for Home Loan Guaranty   ☐ HUD/FHA Application for Insurance under the National Housing Act

| 2. Agency Case Number (include any suffix): | 3. Lender's Case Number: | 4. Section of the Act : (for HUD cases) |

5. Borrower's Name & Present Address (include zip code):

| 7. Loan Amount (include the UFMIP if for HUD or Funding Fee if for VA): $ | 8. Interest Rate: % | 9. Proposed Maturity: yrs.   mos. |

6. Property Address (including name of subdivision, lot & block no. & zip code):

| 10. Discount Amount: (only if borrower is permitted to pay) | 11. Amount of Up Front Premium: $ | 12a. Amount of Annual Premium: $ /month | 12b. Term of Annual Premium: months |

| 13. Lender's I.D. Code: | 14. Sponsor / Agent I.D. Code: |

15. Lender's Name & Address (include zip code)

16. Name & Address of Sponsor / Agent:

(Type or Print all entries clearly)

17. Lender's Telephone Number:
(   )

VA: The veteran and the lender hereby apply to the Secretary of Veterans Affairs for Guaranty of the loan described here under Section 3710, Chapter 37, Title 38, United States Code, to the full extent permitted by the veteran's entitlement and severally agree that the Regulations promulgated pursuant to Chapter 37, and in effect on the date of the loan shall govern the rights, duties, and liabilities of the parties.

18. First Time Homebuyer?	19. VA Only: Title will be Vested in	20. Purpose of Loan (blocks 9 - 12 are for VA loans only)

a. ☐ Yes   b. ☐ No

☐ Veteran
☐ Veteran & Spouse
☐ Other (specify):

1) ☐ Purchase Existing Home Previously Occupied
2) ☐ Finance Improvements to Existing Property
3) ☐ Refinance (Refi.)
4) ☐ Purchase New Condo. Unit
5) ☐ Purchase Existing Condo. Unit
6) ☐ Purchase Existing Home Not Previously Occupied
7) ☐ Construct Home (proceeds to be paid out during construction)
8) ☐ Finance Co-op Purchase
9) ☐ Purchase Permanently Sited Manufactured Home
10) ☐ Purchase Permanently Sited Manufactured Home & Lot
11) ☐ Refi. Permanently Sited Manufactured Home to Buy Lot
12) ☐ Refi. Permanently Sited Manufactured Home/Lot Loan

Part II - Lender's Certification

21. The undersigned lender makes the following certifications to induce the Department of Veterans Affairs to issue a certificate of commitment to guarantee the subject loan or a Loan Guaranty Certificate under Title 38, U.S. Code, or to induce the Department of Housing and Urban Development - Federal Housing Commissioner to issue a firm commitment for mortgage insurance or a Mortgage Insurance Certificate under the National Housing Act.

A. The loan terms furnished in the Uniform Residential Loan Application and this Addendum are true, accurate and complete.

B. The information contained in the Uniform Residential Loan Application and this Addendum was obtained directly from the borrower by a full-time employee of the undersigned lender or its duly authorized agent and is true to the best of the lender's knowledge and belief.

C. The credit report submitted on the subject borrower (and co-borrower, if any) was ordered by the undersigned lender or its duly authorized agent directly from the credit bureau which prepared the report and was received directly from said credit bureau.

D. The verification of employment and verification of deposits were requested and received by the lender or its duly authorized agent without passing through the hands of any third persons and are true to the best of the lender's knowledge and belief.

E. The Uniform Residential Loan Application and this Addendum were signed by the borrower after all sections were completed.

F. This proposed loan to the named borrower meets the income and credit requirements of the governing law in the judgment of the undersigned.

G. To the best of my knowledge and belief, I and my firm and its principals: (1) are not presently debarred, suspended, proposed for debarment, declared ineligible, or voluntarily excluded from covered transactions by any Federal department or agency; (2) have not, within a three-year period preceding this proposal, been convicted of or had a civil judgment rendered against them for (a) commission of fraud or a criminal offense in connection with obtaining, attempting to obtain, or performing a public (Federal, State or local) transaction or contract under a public transaction; (b) violation of Federal or State antitrust statutes or commission of embezzlement, theft, forgery, bribery, falsification or destruction of records, making false statements, or receiving stolen property; (3) are not presently indicted for or otherwise criminally or civilly charged by a governmental entity (Federal, State or local) with commission of any of the offenses enumerated in paragraph G(2) of this certification; and (4) have not, within a three-year period preceding this application/proposal, had one or more public transactions (Federal, State or local) terminated for cause or default.

Items "H" through "J" are to be completed as applicable for VA loans only.

H. The names and functions of any duly authorized agents who developed on behalf of the lender any of the information or supporting credit data submitted are as follows:

Name & Address:

Function: (e.g., obtained information on the Uniform Residential Loan Application, ordered credit report, verifications of employment, deposits, etc.)

If no agent is shown above, the undersigned lender affirmatively certifies that all information and supporting credit data were obtained directly by the lender.

I. The undersigned lender understands and agrees that it is responsible for the omissions, errors, or acts of agents identified in item H as to the functions with which they are identified.

J. The proposed loan conforms otherwise with the applicable provisions of Title 38, U.S. Code, and of the regulations concerning guaranty or insurance of loans to veterans.

| Signature & Title of Officer of Lender: | Date: |
| X | |

Many differences exist between VA-guaranteed lending and conventional lending, but most of the differences are of minimal importance, such as the way VA establishes value of real estate. The VA requires an appraisal to establish the "reasonable value" of the real estate and, based upon that appraisal (or the sales price, if lower), issues a Certificate of Reasonable Value (CRV). The maximum guarantee is based upon the loan amount, not the appraised value. Another difference is the underwriting debt-to-income ratio, which is slightly higher for a VA-guaranteed loan (41 percent) than for a conventional loan. This underwriting difference and others were discussed in greater detail in Chapter 7, Underwriting the Residential Mortgage Loan.

VA Down Payment

Originally, this program was designed to allow a veteran to buy a home with no money down. It still operates on that concept although a veteran now must pay a "funding fee," and a down payment might be required if the loan amount exceeds a certain limit.

VA FUNDING FEE
FIRST TIME USER

Purchase

The funding fee is based on the amount of downpayment:

Down Payment	Funding Fee (Percent of Loan Amount)
• no down payment to 4.99%	= 2 percent fee
• 5 percent to less than 10 percent down	= 1.50 percent fee
• 10 percent and over	= 1.25 percent fee
• all refinances	= 0.500 percent fee

Refinance

• Standard/cash out	= 2.00 percent fee
• Interest rate reduction	= .50 percent fee

Special reservist add .75 percent to each category except interest rate reduction.

Currently, a veteran (or any other eligible person) can buy a home costing up to $184,000 with no down payment with a mortgage guaranteed by the VA, assuming income is sufficient to support the mortgage payment. The current maximum guarantee ($46,000) is the reason lenders will accept no down payment. Although a lender makes a $184,000 mortgage, only $138,000 ($184,000 − $46,000 = $138,000), or 75 percent of its value, is made with

Form Approved
OMB No. 2900-0045

| [X] VA REQUEST FOR DETERMINATION OF REASONABLE VALUE (Real Estate) | HUD Section of Act | 1. CASE NUMBER |
| [ ] HUD APPLICATION FOR PROPERTY APPRAISAL AND COMMITMENT | | ▶ LH123456DC |

2. PROPERTY ADDRESS (include ZIP code and county)	3. LEGAL DESCRIPTION	4. TITLE LIMITATIONS AND RESTRICTIVE COVENANTS
3459 EAGLE ROCK COURT ▶ANNANDALE , VA 22030-4151 COUNTY OF FAIRFAX	LOT 10, SEC 3, GREENBRIAR COUNTY OF FAIRFAX	USUAL UTILITY EASEMENTS BUILDING RESTRICTION LINE

▶ 1 [ ] CONDOMINIUM 2 [X] PLANNED UNIT DEVELOPMENT

5. NAME AND ADDRESS OF FIRM OR PERSON MAKING REQUEST/APPLICATION (include ZIP code)	6. LOT DIMENSIONS:
▶NAVY FEDERAL CREDIT UNION • P.O. BOX 3328 SECURITY PLACE MERRIFIELD , VA 221193328	▶100 X 200

1 [ ] IRREGULAR   SQ/FT 2 [ ] ACRES:

7. UTILITIES (✓)▶	ELEC.	GAS	WATER	SAN. SEWER
1. PUBLIC	X	X	X	X
2. COMMUNITY				
3. INDIVIDUAL				

ATTN: CHONG SUMNER
(703) 255-7340

B E Q U I P.	1 [X] RANGE/ OVEN	4 [X] CLOTHES WASHER	7 [X] VENT FAN
	2 [X] REFRIG.	5 [X] DRYER	8 [X] W/W CARPET
	3 [X] DISH- WASHER	6 [X] GARBAGE DISP.	9 [ ]

9. BUILDING STATUS ▶	10. BUILDING TYPE ▶	11. FACTORY FABRICATED?	12A. NO. OF BUILDINGS	12B. NO. OF LIVING UNITS	13A. STREET ACCESS	13B. STREET MAINT.
1 [ ] PROPOSED 3 [ ] UNDER CONSTRUCTION 4 [X] EXISTING 2 [ ] SUBSTANTIAL REHABILITATION 5 [ ] ALTERATIONS, IMPROVE-MENTS, OR REPAIRS	1 [X] DETACHED 3 [ ] ROW 2 [ ] SEMI-DETACHED 4 [ ] APT. UNIT	1 [ ] YES 2 [X] NO	1	1	1 [X] PRIVATE 2 [X] PUBLIC	1 [ ] PRIVATE 2 [ ] PUBLIC

14A. CONSTRUCTION WARRANTY INCLUDED?	14B. NAME OF WARRANTY PROGRAM	14C. EXPIRATION DATE (Month, day, year)	15. CONSTR. COMPLETED (Mo., yr.)
1 [ ] YES 2 [X] NO (If "Yes," complete items 14B and C also.)			01/85

16. NAME OF OWNER	17. PROPERTY:	18. RENT (if applic.)
LEWIS HODGES	[X] OCCUPIED BY OWNER [ ] NEVER OCCUPIED [ ] VACANT [ ] OCCUPIED BY TENANT (Complete item 18 also)	$ _____ /MONTH

19. NAME OF OCCUPANT	20. NAME OF BROKER	DATE AND TIME AVAILABLE FOR INSPECTION
OWNER 703/545-2674	REMAX 703/756-3525	[ ] AM [ ] PM
CALL ^FIRST/OWNER 703/458-7375 703/856-6723	25. ORIGINATOR'S IDENT. NO. 15700600007	26. SPONSOR'S IDENT. NO.	27. INSTITUTION'S CASE NO. 06011992

28. PURCHASER'S NAME AND ADDRESS (Complete mailing address, include ZIP code)	EQUAL OPPORTUNITY IN HOUSING
GEORGE P ANDERSON MARTHA A ANDERSON 820 FOLLIN LANE VIENNA, VA 22180	NOTE - Federal laws and regulations prohibit discrimination because of race, color, religion, sex, or national origin in the sale or rental of residential property. Numerous State statutes and local ordinances also prohibit such discrimination. In addition, section 805 of the Civil Rights Act of 1968 prohibits discriminatory practices in connection with the financing of housing. If HUD/VA finds there is noncompliance with any antidiscrimination laws or regulations, it may discontinue business with the violator.

29. NEW OR PROPOSED CONSTRUCTION – *Complete items 29A through 29G for new or proposed construction cases only.*

A. COMPLIANCE INSPECTIONS WILL BE OR WERE MADE BY:	B. PLANS (check one)	C. PLANS SUBMITTED PREVIOUSLY UNDER CASE NO.
[ ] FHA [ ] VA [ ] NONE MADE	[ ] FIRST SUBMISSION [ ] REPEAT CASE (if checked, complete item 29C.)	
D. NAME AND ADDRESS OF BUILDER	E. TELEPHONE NO. F. NAME AND ADDRESS OF WARRANTOR	G. TELEPHONE NO.

30. COMMENTS ON SPECIAL ASSESSMENTS OR HOMEOWNERS ASSOCIATION CHARGES NONE	31. ANNUAL REAL ESTATE TAXES $ 1,800.00	33. LEASEHOLD CASES (Complete if applicable)
	32. MINERAL RIGHTS RESERVED? [ ] YES (Explain) [X] NO	LEASE IS [ ] 99 YEARS [ ] RENEWABLE [ ] HUD/VA APPROVED	EXPIRES (Date) ANNUAL GROUND RENT $

34. SALE PRICE OF PROPERTY	34A. IS BUYER PURCHASING LOT SEPARATELY?	35. REFINANCING–AMOUNT OF PROPOSED LOAN	36. PROPOSED SALE CONTRACT ATTACHED	37. CONTRACT NUMBER PREVIOUSLY APPROVED BY VA THAT WILL BE USED
$ 180,000.00	[ ] YES [X] NO (If "Yes," see instruction page under "Sale Price.") $		[X] YES [ ] NO	

CERTIFICATIONS FOR SUBMISSIONS TO HUD

In submitting this application for a conditional commitment for mortgage insurance, it is agreed and understood by the parties involved in the transaction that if at the time of application for a Firm Commitment the identity of the seller has changed, the application for a Firm Commitment will be rejected and the application for a Conditional Commitment will be reprocessed upon request by the mortgagee.
It is further agreed and understood that in submitting the request for a Firm Commitment for mortgage insurance, the seller, the purchaser and the broker involved in the transaction shall each certify that the terms of the contract for purchase are true to his or her best knowledge and belief, and that any other agreement entered into by any of these parties in connection with this transaction is attached to the sales agreement.

BUILDER/SELLER'S AGREEMENT. All Houses: The undersigned agrees to deliver to the purchaser a statement of appraised value on Form HUD-92800.5B. Proposed Construction: The undersigned agrees, upon sale or conveyance of title within one year from date of initial occupancy, to deliver to the purchaser Form HUD-92544, warranting that the house is constructed in substantial conformity with the plans and specifications on which HUD based its value and to furnish HUD a conformed copy with the purchaser's receipt thereon that the original warranty was delivered to him/her. All Houses: In consideration of the issuance of the commitment requested by this application, I (we) hereby agree that any deposit or down payment made in connection with the purchase of the property described above, whether received by the undersigned or an agent of the undersigned, shall upon receipt be deposited in escrow or in trust or in a special account which is not subject to the claims of my creditors and where it will be maintained until it has been disbursed for the benefit of the purchaser or otherwise disposed of in accordance with the terms of the contract of sale.

| Signature of: [ ] Mortgagee [ ] Builder [ ] Seller [X] Other X | Date | 19 |

MORTGAGEE'S CERTIFICATE: The undersigned mortgagee certifies that to the best of his/her knowledge, all statements made in this application and the supporting documents are true, correct and complete.

| Signature and Title of Mortgage Officer: X | Date | 19 |

CERTIFICATIONS FOR SUBMISSIONS TO VA

1. On receipt of "Certificate of Reasonable Value" or advice from the Veterans Administration that a "Certificate of Reasonable Value" will not be issued, we agree to forward to the appraiser the approved fee which we are holding for this purpose.
2. CERTIFICATION REQUIRED ON CONSTRUCTION UNDER FHA SUPERVISION (Strike out inappropriate phrases in parentheses)

I hereby certify that plans and specifications and related exhibits, including acceptable FHA Change Orders, if any, supplied to VA in this case, are identical to those (submitted to)(to be submitted to)(approved by) FHA, and that FHA inspections (have been) (will be) made pursuant to FHA approval for mortgage insurance on the basis of proposed construction under Sec _____

38. SIGNATURE OF PERSON AUTHORIZING THIS REQUEST C. SUMNER	39. TITLE SUPERVISOR MTG SECTION	40. TELEPHONE NUMBER (703) 255-7340	41. DATE 06/02/92
42. DATE OF ASSIGNMENT 06/05/92	43. NAME OF APPRAISER ROBERT R. PALMER	(703) 657-8775	

WARNING Section 1010 of title 18, U.S.C. provides: "Whoever for the purpose of...influencing such Administration...makes, passes, utters or publishes any statement knowing the same to be false...shall be fined not more than $5,000 or imprisoned not more than two years or both."

VA FORM 26-1805, AUG 1986   SUPERSEDES VA FORM 26-1805/HUD FORM 92800-1, JUN 1984, WHICH WILL NOT BE USED.

2618058

NFCU 526M (8-89)

any risk. If foreclosure is necessary, the real estate should bring at least the $138,000 the lender had at risk. This amount, combined with the $46,000 guarantee, should make the lender whole.

If a veteran wanted to buy a home appraised at more than $184,000, a lender would probably require a down payment equal to 25 percent of the amount in excess of $184,000 to keep the loan within the 75 percent loan-to-value ratio.

The continuing popularity of VA-guaranteed mortgages is shown by the more than $41 billion of activity in 1993. That figure represented a nearly 65 percent increase over 1992 activity.

Eligibility

VA-guaranteed loans are only available to qualified current or former armed service personnel, unremarried surviving spouse of a veteran whose death was caused by a service-related injury or ailment, or spouse of member of the armed services who has been either missing in action or a prisoner of war for more than 90 days.

VA-GUARANTEED
HOME MORTGAGE LOANS MADE
(dollars in millions)

Year	Number	Amount
1960	145,000	$ 1,985
1965	164,000	2,652
1970	186,187	3,682
1975	288,163	8,072
1980	289,164	14,653
1985	170,015	11,262
1987	474,391	34,783
1990	196,166	15,768
1992	265,895	22,956
1993	458,000 (est.)	41,600

Source: Department of Veterans Affairs Trends Report.

A veteran is eligible for a VA-guaranteed mortgage if the service record indicates active service:

- World War II: 90 days between 9-16-40 and 7-25-47
- Pre-Korean: 181 days between 7-26-46 and 6-26-50
- Korean Conflict: 90 days between 6-27-50 and 1-31-55

Veterans Administration — **Certificate of Eligibility**

9829879

FOR LOAN GUARANTY BENEFITS

NAME OF VETERAN *(First, Middle, Last)*		SERVICE SERIAL NUMBER/SOCIAL SECURITY NUMBER
DAVID PRESTON WALTERS	CANCELLED	123 45 6789

ENTITLEMENT CODE	BRANCH OF SERVICE	DATE OF BIRTH
4	ARMY	1/2/45

IS ELIGIBLE FOR THE BENEFITS OF CHAPTER 37, TITLE 38, U.S. CODE, AND HAS THE AMOUNT OF ENTITLEMENT SHOWN AS AVAILABLE ON THE REVERSE, SUBJECT TO THE STATEMENT BELOW, IF CHECKED.

☐   Valid unless discharged or released subsequent to date of this certificate. A certification of continuous active duty as of date of note required.

ADMINISTRATOR OF VETERANS AFFAIRS

Mary Barbarin

(Signature of Authorized Agent)

30 JUL 1987

(Date Issued)

Veterans Administration
Regional Office
(Issuing Office)
701 Loyola Avenue
New Orleans, LA 70113

- Post-Korean: 181 days between 2-1-55 and 8-4-64
- Vietnam Era: 90 days between 8-5-64 and 5-7-75
- Post-Vietnam: 181 days between 5-8-75 and 9-7-80
- Pre-Desert Storm: 24 months between 9-8-80 and 8-22-90
- Desert Storm: 90 days between 8-22-90 and present
- Post-Desert Storm: 24 months' continuous service

Veterans who believe they are eligible for a VA-guaranteed loan must apply to the VA for a *Certificate of Eligibility,* which establishes eligibility and the amount of the guarantee available. The 1974 law that increased the guarantee also provided for restoration of veterans' entitlement.

Restoration of Veterans' Entitlement

Before the law was changed, once a veteran's entitlement was used it could not be restored. A 1974 law provided for partial and, in some situations, full restoration of benefits. This change was partially motivated by Congress' desire to stimulate housing during that economic downturn.

A veteran's entitlement can be restored if:

- real estate was sold for reasons of health or condemnation,
- real estate was destroyed by fire or a natural hazard,
- loan was paid in full.

Eligibility is also restored by the veteran obtaining a release of liability. A veteran's entitlement is restored to the extent it was not used.

Example: A veteran purchased a home in January 1970 for $25,000. The maximum entitlement at that time was $12,500. This veteran wants to purchase another home today for $120,000 using the remaining entitlement.

$$\begin{array}{r} \$25,000 \\ \underline{\times .60} \\ \$15,000 \end{array}$$

  $25,000 loan amount on first home
  × .60
  $15,000 amount of entitlement used

The amount of guarantee used exceeds the amount available, but the amount is 50 percent of the purchase price, which exceeds the 25 percent required by a lender.

Maximum loan available now is established by subtracting the entitlement used from the current entitlement:

  $36,000 current entitlement
  −12,500 entitlement used
   23,500 remaining entitlement
     × 4
  $94,000 maximum loan with no down payment

In this case, the veteran will have to put $6,000 down ($100,000 price − $94,000 maximum loan = $6,000 ÷ 25 percent down payment = $1,500).

Assumptions

Unlike most conventional loans, a VA-guaranteed loan can be assumed without an increase in the mortgage interest rate. This feature makes homes with VA-guaranteed loans more attractive to purchasers, especially during periods of rising interest rates. The purchaser does not have to be a veteran, although the purchaser must be judged to be a creditworthy borrower. As mentioned, the interest rate is not increased but the VA charges the assumptor a modest funding fee equal to .05 percent of the outstanding loan balance.

VA No-Bids

The VA's normal way of handling foreclosures changed in the late 1980s to the detriment of mortgage lenders. Before this change, the VA would acquire the title to foreclosed property after the foreclosure sale for an amount up to the guarantee. VA would then market the foreclosed property hoping to recoup as much of the guaranteed amount as possible. VA learned that in many cases it actually lost more money by taking title to the property and attempting to sell it. As a result, VA now requires an appraisal before the foreclosure sale. If that appraisal indicates a value that will produce a loss to the VA greater than its guarantee, the VA will issue "nonspecific" bidding instructions. The effect of this "no-bid" is the servicer acquires the property at foreclosure and must market the property themselves. The VA provides no more than the maximum amount of its guarantee.

PRIVATE MORTGAGE INSURANCE

After a lapse of a quarter of a century, private mortgage insurance companies (PMIs, or simply MIs) returned as the FHA mortgage insurance programs proved successful. The first of the reborn MIs was the Mortgage Guaranty Insurance Corporation (MGIC), organized in 1957 under a Wisconsin state law passed in 1956. For many years MGIC was the largest MI, but today GE Capital Mortgage Insurance Companies have the largest market share and insurance in force.

The return of private mortgage insurance was important for potential home buyers who had difficulty saving the 20 percent down payment normally required by a mortgage lender. Lenders would approve a mortgage with a smaller down payment if the mortgage was covered by private mortgage insurance.

The reasons for the rebirth of the MIs and their impressive growth since then include:

- extensive use of the secondary market by mortgage bankers,
- secondary mortgage market requirement that all loans over 80 percent LTV ratio must be supported by mortgage insurance,
- slow loan processing with government programs,
- low loan limits for FHA mortgages,
- interest in low down payment conventional loans.

Of great importance to the rapid growth of MIs was the Emergency Home Finance Act (1970), which authorized FNMA and FHLMC to purchase conventional mortgages. If these loans had a loan-to-value ratio in excess of 80 percent, mortgage insurance was required to cover the lender's exposure down to 75 percent of value (lower of sales price or appraisal). These high-ratio conventional mortgages became increasingly popular in the 1970s, and once these mortgages could be traded in the secondary market, most mortgage lenders, in particular savings associations, began to offer them.

The coverage used to lower exposure for a lender down to 75 percent, as allowed by FNMA and FHLMC, is as follows:

80.01–85 LTV = 12 percent coverage
85.01–90 LTV = 17 percent coverage
90.01–95 LTV = 25 percent coverage

In certain situations, lenders may require more extensive coverage to below the normal 75 percent for certain loan products and in certain geographical areas.

The formula for determining this coverage is explained in the following example.

Example for: Determining Coverage:

The following formula determines the amount of mortgage insurance required:

$$\frac{\text{Loan amount} - 75\% \text{ of value}}{\text{Loan amount}} = \text{Required percentage coverage}$$

– or –

If a property is appraised at $100,000 and the borrower wants to put 10 percent down:

$$\frac{\$90,000 - \$75,000}{\$90,000} = \$15,000$$

$$= 16.66 \text{ or } 17 \text{ percent}$$

Strengths of MIs Today

Strong regulatory control, coupled with sound actuarial reserves, missing in the old mortgage insurance business, are now present with the new MIs. All MIs are carefully regulated by the laws of the state in which they are organized as well as the states where they do business. The regulating entity is normally the state insurance commission or department. Rating agencies, such as Moody's, Fitch, and Standard and Poor's, also rate the MIs.

The specific regulations vary among the states but generally provide that an MI company can insure first liens on one-to four-family residences that do not exceed 95 percent of fair-market value.

Authority has been expanded to include the various alternative mortgage instruments. Before an MI can begin insuring loans, it must meet minimum limits for paid-in capital and surplus. Then its insurance exposure is limited to 25 times the value of its capital, surplus, and contingency reserves. In other words, they set aside $1 of capital for every $25 of risk they insure. Insured risk is defined as the percentage share of each loan that is actually covered by the individual insurance policy.

MIs must maintain three types of reserves:

1. Unearned Premium Reserve. Premiums received but unearned for the term of a policy are placed in this reserve.
2. Loss Reserve. This reserve is established for losses or potential losses on a case-by-case basis as the company learns of defaults and foreclosures.
3. Contingency Reserve. This is a special reserve required by law to protect mortgage lenders against the type of catastrophic loss that can occur in severe economic periods. Half of each premium dollar received goes into this reserve and cannot be used by an MI company for 10 years, unless losses in a calendar year exceed 35 percent of earned premiums and the insurance commissioner of the state where the insurer is domiciled concurs in the withdrawal.

Contracting with a Mortgage Insurance Company

Before a mortgage lender can do business with an MI, the lender must be approved in regard to its capacity to process, underwrite, and especially service (if required) the high-ratio loans to be insured. An approved lender is issued a master policy and can get an individual insurance commitment within a day or two of submitting the application package for the individual loan. Generally, the MIs screen mortgage lenders applying for master policies and look for experience in originating and servicing first mortgage loans. This application process includes interviews with mortgage processing, underwriting, and servicing staff, as well as company management. Obviously, the MIs want to assure themselves that the loans they will insure have been originated in a thorough and professional manner. But also they wish to establish that the servicing lender has the experience to manage the ongoing insurance policy requirements.

TOTAL INDUSTRY ASSETS AND RESERVES
(dollars in thousands)

Total Industry	1989	1990	1991	1992
Admitted assets	$3,444,974	$3,476,654	$4,065,119	$5,113,366
Unearned reserve prem.	446,941	516,527	626,988	766,351
Loss reserve	801,949	833,970	678,415	798,912
Contingency reserve	528,545	671,406	948,582	1,317,844

Source: Mortgage Insurance Companies of America.

MORTGAGE INSURANCE APPLICATION

GE Capital
Mortgage Insurance

This Application must be filled out entirely before a commitment/certificate can be issued.

LENDER NAME AND ADDRESS

Dominion Bankshares Mortgage Corp.
12300 Twinbrook Pky.
Rockville, MD. 20852-0000
            ORG B22432

Master Policy No. _____
                    Full 10 Digit Number

Borrower Name: <u>Theodore A. & Vicki L. Miller</u>
Base Loan Amount: $ <u>171,000</u>   Base LTV <u>90</u> %

Front-End Zero (Financed Premium)
Premium Financed $_____   Loan Term ____ Yrs.
Total Loan Amount $ <u>171,000</u>   Total LTV <u>90</u> %
(Total LTV, including Financed Premium, must not exceed 95%.)

LOAN INFORMATION

Type of Certificate: <u>X</u> Primary ____ Pool ____ Both   If a Brokered Loan, Broker Name: _____

Property Use: <u>X</u> Primary Res. ____ Second Home ____ Investment   If Conduit Program, Conduit Name: _____

MORTGAGE INSURANCE INFORMATION

Annual Premium Plans:
<u>X</u> Standard
____ Front-End Zero (First-Year)
____ Front-End Lite

Single Premium Plan:
____ Single premium coverage
for ____ years
____ Front-End Zero (One-Time
coverage down to 80% LTV)

Standard Coverage:
____12% <u>X</u>17% ____20% ____22% ____25% ____30% ____Other ____%
____ Advantage to 75% Exposure   Premium financed ____ Yes ____ No   Renewals: ____ Amortized <u>X</u> Level

MORTGAGE INSTRUMENT DESCRIPTION (Detailed instructions appear on the BACK of this form.)

<u>X</u> Fixed Payment (For fixed payment loans only the top two lines of this section need to be completed.)
____ Balloon or call option: number of years _____
Non-Fixed Payment
____ Negative Amortization: ____ None ____ Potential
____ Fixed Rate, Non-Fixed Payment [GEM, Temporary Buydown, etc.]
____ Adjustable Rate Mortgage (ARM)

ARM Index:
____ 6 Mo. T. Bill—Auction Average (1D)   ____ FHLBB Monthly Median COF (3A)   Other _____
____ 1 Yr. T. Security—Constant Maturity (2A)   ____ FHLBB 11th District COF (3C)   _____

MAXIMUM GROSS MARGIN _____ % (MANDATORY FOR ALL ARMs)

Payment/Interest Rate Data:	Payment	Interest	Buydown Data:
Initial Rate:	____%	____%	Amount of subsidy $_____
Qualifying Rate:	____%		Source: ____ Builder/Seller (S) ____ Borrower (B)
Months until first Adjustment:	____	____	____ Employer (E) ____ Other (O) _____
Frequency of Adjustment:	____ mos.	____ mos.	Application of funds:
Per Adjustment Cap:	____%*	____%	____ 3-2-1% (3) ____ 1-0% (1)
Lifetime Cap:		____%	____ 2-1-0% (2) ____ Other (O)
Prescheduled Payment Increase:	____%		*Including optional payment cap

DOCUMENTATION REQUIRED

<u>X</u> Signed Loan Application   <u>X</u> Appraisal, Photos, Legal Description
<u>X</u> Credit Report   <u>X</u> Good Faith Estimate
<u>X</u> V.O.E.   <u>X</u> Sales Contract/Offer to Purchase
<u>X</u> V.O.D.

If Applicable:
____ Federal Tax Returns
____ Payment History on Present Mortgage
____ Lease Agreement
____ Gift Letter
____ Verification of "other" income (i.e. child support, alimony)

Lender represents and, except where prohibited by law, warrants that the statements and information contained in this Application and in all supporting documentation are accurate and complete and that the lender is not aware of any allowances or inducements that have been or are being given to the borrower(s) in connection with this transaction except those described in this Application and the supporting documentation, and acknowledges that GE will rely on such information and statements in issuing any commitment/certificate. This Application and all supporting documentation are hereby made a part of, and are incorporated by reference into, the Master Policy under which the commitment/certificate is issued.

LENDER RESPONSE:
Please complete for immediate commitment reply.

<u>Julie Davidson</u>   <u>555-8923</u>
Person to notify of disposition   Area code/telephone number

____GE's PowerLine

_____   <u>1/9/93</u>
Authorized signature   Date

Form 202 (REV. 5/88)

GE Capital
Mortgage Insurance

GENERAL ELECTRIC MORTGAGE INSURANCE CORPORATION   (The "Company)
PO Box 1415 Merrifield, Va. 22116
2000 Corporate Ridge
McLean, Va. 22102

COMMITMENT/CERTIFICATE OF INSURANCE

In consideration of the premium hereinafter set forth and in reliance upon the statements made in the application, the Company hereby issues this Commitment for Insurance to you, and tenders to you a Certificate of Insurance for the mortgage loan herein described subject to the terms and conditions of your Master Policy identified below, and subject to any Special Conditions that may be set forth below.

INITIAL PREMIUM	COMMITMENT EXPIRATION DATE	COMMITMENT EFFECTIVE DATE	MASTER POLICY NO.	COMMITMENT NO.
684.00	07/10/93	01/11/93	B2244322	81-0079234-5

INSURED'S NAME AND ADDRESS:	BORROWER NAME AND PROPERTY ADDRESS:
Dominion Bankshares Mortgage Corporation 12300 Twinbrook Pky. Rockville, MD 20852	MILLER, Theodore A. MILLER, Vicki L. 4463 Loveday Street Silver Spring, MD 20902

INSURED AMOUNT	SALES PRICE	APPRAISED VALUE	TERM OF LOAN	COVERAGE
171,000	190,000	190,000	360 months	Top 17%

INITIAL PREMIUM RATE	RENEWAL RATE	RENEWAL TYPE	PREMIUM PLAN	TERM OF COVERAGE
.40000	.340000	Level	500	1 year

PREMIUM SCHEDULE •   .40 of 1% of original loan amount for 1 year with annual renewal at
.34 of 1% of original loan amount for the next 9 renewal years.
Thereafter at .25 of 1% of original loan amount.

SPECIAL CONDITIONS •

Calculation assumes a term from closing of 360 months using initial principal and interest payment.

MORTGAGE INSURANCE INFORMATION •

TOTAL PREMIUM	BASIS PTS	MONTHLY PAYMENT/RATE			
$14,467.80	27	FIRST: $48.45	/ .34000 %	LAST: $35.63	/ .25000 %

PLEASE NOTE: Premium is due within 10 days of Loan Closing Date/Certificate Effective Date indicated below.

INSTRUCTION TO LENDERS: Please complete the following information relative to the closing of the loan and mail this Commitment together with your premium remittance to the Company. Insurance coverage as set forth above shall become effective as of the loan closing date or such later date as mutually agreed to by you and the Company. Any revision or modification of the terms and conditions set forth in this Commitment, or failure to satisfy any Special Conditions specified above, without prior written consent of the Company, will invalidate this Commitment and the related insurance coverage.

SECRETARY _~Richard A. Miller~_   AUTHORIZED REPRESENTATIVE _____

INSURED'S CERTIFICATION: By tender of premium and submission of this completed Commitment/Certificate, the Insured represents and certifies that the above loan transaction has been consummated in accordance with the loan documents provided to the Company by the Insured, any Special Conditions set forth in this Commitment have been satisfied, and the applicable premium has been paid.

LENDER'S LOAN NUMBER	LOAN CLOSING DATE CERTIFICATE EFFECTIVE DATE	REMITTED PREMIUM	DATE OF SIGNATURE

CC (4/89)   **COMPLETE AND RETURN TO THE COMPANY**   BY: _____
                                                                   AUTHORIZED REPRESENTATIVE OF LENDER

Evolving MI Business

After a third of a century of progress and service, MIs have recently evolved into one of the more innovative members of the real estate finance business. In addition to the function of insuring mortgage loans of all types, MIs are:

- serving as intermediaries between sellers of mortgage loans and investors,
- extensively involved in private mortgage-backed securities,
- operating conduits that pool and sell privately insured mortgage-backed securities,
- assisting in the portfolio restructuring of lenders,
- offering cutting-edge technology products and services,
- developing innovative, affordable housing programs.

Many of these added functions are logical extensions of the mortgage insurance business and have assisted in the tremendous growth of MIs over the past 20 years. For example, the bringing together of originators and investors is facilitated by the large number of MI company salespeople calling on lenders and the existence of many satellite underwriting offices across the country. This secondary market assistance is provided free or at a reduced fee, but the hope of the MI company is that this service and others will be repaid with additional insurance business.

1980s: Difficult Years

The 1980s were difficult years for the MI industry as the number of defaults and foreclosures increased dramatically. The decade ended with the MI industry paying claims to mortgage lenders in the billions of dollars. This large amount is strong evidence of the value of mortgage insurance during periods of economic downturn and deflation in housing values. If these losses had not been absorbed by MIs, then lenders would have had to suffer the losses, with the resulting economic chaos. As it was, the losses were too much for some MIs and they either stopped writing new business or merged with larger, better capitalized MIs.

TOTAL INDUSTRY PRE-TAX PROFIT & LOSS
(dollars in thousands)

Total Industry	1989	1990	1991	1992
Underwriting income/loss	($247,519)	$58,647	$149,968	$252,272
Investment income	$261,168	$243,544	$284,975	$361,150
Other income	($12,999)	($11,509)	($6,991)	($386)
Operating income/loss	$650	$290,682	$427,952	$613,036

Source: Mortgage Insurance Companies of America.

Claims

Both mortgage lenders and mortgage insurers are very interested in the quality of mortgage loans made. Investors are also interested, but presumably the loans they purchase either will be low loan-to-value ratio loans or will be insured. It is the function of an MI to analyze the risk and charge a premium based on that risk. The MI can then spread that risk over a large number of geographically dispersed loans. Until the early 1980s, this process worked well, and all parties to the transaction, MIs, mortgage lenders, and homeowners, benefited as a result.

In the 1980s the situation changed, and the MI industry suffered spectacular losses, with $5 billion paid out in claims to policyholders. The changes that occurred were the dramatic increases in inflation and interest rates, which resulted in a general slowing of property appreciation. These problems were followed by the collapse of the energy-oriented economies in the Southwest. These problems resulted in many homeowners not being able to sell their property and pay off their mortgages to avoid foreclosure. This slowing of property appreciation, combined with the expansion of 95 percent loan-to-value lending, coupled with exotic ARM loan programs, significantly raised the claims incidence for MIs. Many of the MIs discovered, to their financial disappointment, that the level of claims on loans written in the early 1980s were five or six times that of loans written in the 1970s.

As a result of these staggering losses to the MI companies, some confrontations developed between MI companies and mortgage lenders. Some of these confrontations that developed were over questionable origination and servicing practices of mortgage lenders, which resulted in losses to the MI companies. The Mortgage Insurance Companies of America (MICA) estimates that during this period 5 out of every 1,000 policyholders experienced a denial of claim because of some irregularities.

Because mortgage lending is a risky business, defaults by mortgage borrowers will occur even in the best of times.

When a default is not cured (usually through the sale of the home and the subsequent payoff of the mortgage), a claim on an MI could result. Claims are settled in three ways:

1. the MI company reimburses the lender the percentage of loss specified in the policy, or
2. at its option, the MI pays the lender the entire loan amount and takes title to the property, later selling the property to mitigate the loss to the MI,
3. preapproved sales.

Mortgage Insurance Claims Settlement Example: Assume a home appraised at $100,000 is purchased with a 10 percent down payment at a fixed rate of 8 percent interest over 30 years. Default has occurred and a claim against the MI company is filed. The MI had 17 percent coverage.

Principal balance	$88,500
Accumulated interest from default at 8 percent	3,500
	$91,800
Attorney fees—3 percent	2,754
Property taxes	700
Hazard insurance	250
Preservation of property	250
Statutory disbursements	100
	$95,854
Escrow funds	(350)
Other funds	( )
CLAIM TOTAL	$95,504
PERCENTAGE W/COVERAGE	× .17
PAYOFF	$16,295

As an alternative approach, the MI could pay the claim off ($95,504), take title to the property, and sell it. Assuming the property sold for $85,000:

Sales price	$85,000
Less 6 percent sale commission	5,100
Less expenses	1,000
Less carrying cost of money	2,000
	$76,900
Payoff to lender	95,504
Proceeds of sale	76,900
NET LOSS	18,604

PRIVATE MORTGAGE INSURANCE COMPANIES

The major private mortgage insurance firms in North America are members of the industry's own trade association, the Mortgage Insurance Companies of

America (MICA). The association consists of the following domestic, Canadian, and Australian private mortgage insurance companies:

- American Guaranty Corporation—Chicago, IL
- Commonwealth Mortgage Assurance Company—Philadelphia, PA
- GE Capital Mortgage Insurance Companies—Raleigh, NC
- Mortgage Guaranty Insurance Corporation—Milwaukee, WI
- PMI Mortgage Insurance Company—San Francisco, CA
- Republic Mortgage Insurance Company—Winston-Salem, NC
- Triad Guaranty Insurance Corporation—Winston-Salem, NC
- United Guaranty Corporation—Greensboro, NC
- The Mortgage Insurance Company of Canada—Toronto, Ontario

MARKETING RESIDENTIAL MORTGAGE LOANS ——————— *9*

The marketing function of residential mortgage loans includes selling loans, obtaining investor commitments, managing interest rate risk, and preparing and shipping loan packages. In this day, when most mortgage lenders sell some or all of their loan production, the ability to market successfully is crucial to profitability and market share.

This chapter examines the process and the various alternatives for marketing residential mortgage loans that have already been closed. It does not discuss the marketing issue of how best to originate mortgage loans, which was discussed in Chapter 4, Origination.

This chapter is interrelated with Chapter 10, The Secondary Mortgage Market, and Chapter 11, Mortgage-Backed Securities; thus, frequent reference is made to them.

DEVELOPMENT OF MARKETING

The marketing of residential mortgage loans has become increasingly important for all types of mortgage lenders. The growth of the secondary mortgage market, with transactions each year approaching $600 billion, bears witness to that importance. Before 1961, the only originating lender concerned about marketing loans was the mortgage banker. Practically all other mortgage originators were portfolio lenders.

In 1961, savings and loan institutions were authorized to buy and sell whole loans originated outside their normal lending area, and with that change the marketing of residential loans took on greater importance. The Depository Institutions Deregulation and Monetary Control Act (1980) completed the evolution as it revised federal lending regulations to the extent that any federally chartered financial institution could buy and sell whole loans or participations under the exact terms as if originating such a loan.

MARKETING ALTERNATIVES

In today's sophisticated mortgage market, all mortgage lenders have various alternatives for placement of their loan production. These alternatives include:

1. retaining loan production in their own portfolios
2. selling whole loans or participations to government-related secondary mortgage market entities—FNMA/FHLMC,
3. selling whole loans or participations to private secondary market entities,
4. directly issuing mortgage-backed securities (MBS),
5. selling loans to conduits for packaging into MBS.

These alternatives are available to all mortgage lenders, but some will opt not to use one or more for various reasons. A mortgage banker, for example, will never retain production in its portfolio. Some thrifts, on the other hand, may opt for this alternative most of the time. Credit unions are also examples of lenders that keep much of their production in their own portfolios. Except in those situations in which a lender will not consider one or more alternatives (e.g., a mortgage banker and portfolio lending), a mortgage lender should consider all alternatives before selecting the most advantageous.

Retaining Production in Portfolio

For many years, retaining production in portfolio was the only option available to thrifts and commercial banks, and it served them well. In the early 1960s a few thrifts began selling some of their loan production, but until the late 1970s most thrifts were primarily portfolio lenders. In fact, one type of thrift, the mutual savings bank, which is located primarily in the capital-surplus Northeast, could not generate sufficient loan production and as a result had to balance savings deposits with mortgages purchased from mortgage bankers. Savings banks as a result had their mortgage portfolios made up of their own production supplemented by that of mortgage bankers.

In this highly volatile interest rate environment, which has existed since 1978, portfolio lending has obvious pitfalls. The number of thrifts that have closed or merged since 1980 illustrates vividly the result of those dangers. They failed because their portfolio yield could not keep pace with their cost of funds, among other reasons. The spread between cost of funds and portfolio yield needs to be between 200 and 300 basis points for profitable lending. For the period 1981–83 the spread for most thrifts was negative, resulting in financial failure for the weakest and shrinking net worth for the remainder. If these thrifts had sold the mortgages originated before this period, they would not have faced this interest rate risk.

Even though the trend is clearly toward selling some or all of current production, it is expected that some mortgage lenders in the 1990s will continue to portfolio loans. Some of them, such as credit unions, have valid reasons for keeping some mortgages in their portfolios. Credit unions are having a problem putting all of the share deposits to work, so they keep many of their mortgages in portfolio to put that excess liquidity to work. Other lenders have similar problems or see similar investment opportunities in their own mortgages. (Of course, these mortgages should still be salable so that if a need ever develops, these lenders will be able to sell.)

In the more sophisticated mortgage market of the 1990s, those institutions that opt to be portfolio lenders have some ways to protect themselves. As mentioned earlier, the principal dangers to a portfolio lender are increasing interest rates (which increase the cost of funds) and a portfolio of fixed-rate mortgages (which does not respond to changed market conditions). These dangers can be minimized by better asset/liability management. That means lengthening the maturity of liabilities (deposits) and shortening the maturity of assets (mortgages) and/or indexing the interest rates on those assets. This is achieved by longer terms for certificates of deposit and the use of adjustable rate mortgages or similar instruments. These suggested changes will help all lenders but especially those mortgage lenders that opt for portfolio lending.

Selling Production to FNMA/FHLMC

All mortgage originators are now authorized to sell to both of these government-related agencies. Both buy whole loans or participations and fixed-rate or adjustable-rate mortgages. An extensive review of the programs, fees, and commitment requirements for both FNMA and FHLMC is made in Chapter 10, The Secondary Mortgage Market.

The attractiveness to a mortgage lender of selling loans to either of these entities is based on the following factors:

- no portfolio risk from changing interest rates,
- increased ability to meet local housing demand,
- instant liquidity,
- increased servicing volume and income,
- potential for marketing profit,
- participation leverage.

As previously discussed, mortgage bankers must sell their loan production to some investor. Although they can choose from many investors, they usually sell that production that does not go into GNMA mortgage-backed securities to these two government-related agencies. Other lenders, on the other hand, can sell to either of these agencies or to other investors, or they can retain loan production in their portfolios. The deciding factors include price, servicing fees, underwriting requirements, and commitments outstanding.

Direct Sales to Private Secondary Mortgage Market Entities

The direct sale by mortgage bankers to private investors of loans originated in one part of the country and sold in another was the only alternative to portfolio lending until the start of FNMA in 1938. Mortgage companies in the late 1890s were originating farm mortgages in the Ohio Valley and selling those loans to wealthy individuals or life insurance companies located in the Northeastern states. This activity started the loan correspondent system and produced the first use of commitments in mortgage lending. The various types and the use of commitments is discussed in a later section.

Oftentimes, when the term *secondary mortgage market* is used, mortgage lenders automatically think of FNMA or FHLMC, but there also exists a thriving private secondary mortgage market. Although FNMA and FHLMC account for about 65 percent of secondary mortgage market activity, the remaining 35 percent involves the following players:

- commercial banks,
- savings banks,
- savings and loan institutions,
- life insurance companies,
- pension funds,
- private conduits.

Mortgage bankers, at times, also purchase mortgages originated by other lenders but never for their own portfolios. This purchase activity is always to fill an outstanding commitment or to issue GNMA mortgage-backed securities. All mortgage lenders, including mortgage bankers, periodically purchase mortgages from other lenders servicing released (i.e., whereby the selling lender transfers the servicing of the loans to the purchasing lender). These mortgages in turn are sold to the government-related agencies with the servicing rights retained. In this way, mortgage lenders are able to grow their servicing portfolio without the expense of origination. Some mortgage lenders are purchasing mortgage loans from other lenders because of a permanent or temporary imbalance of deposits and loan production.

Details of Sale

The direct sale to private secondary mortgage market players can be either on a continuous basis supported by outstanding commitments or on a case-by-case negotiated basis.

DETAILS OF A SALE

Whether a direct sale is the result of a continuing relationship or of a negotiated transaction, the details of the sale include the following items:

1. Type of mortgage loans to be delivered
   a. FHA, VA, or conventional
   b. whole loan or participation
2. Total dollar amount of this sale
3. Yield (net) to the investor
4. Servicing requirements and fees
   a. servicing fee
   b. whether released or retained
5. Commitment fees (if any) charged to seller
   a. how much
   b. refundable or not
6. Delivery requirements to purchaser
   a. immediate delivery
   b. future delivery and when
7. Underwriting standards to be used
   a. FNMA/FHLMC standards
   b. other standards (whose)
8. Type of loan documentation to be used
9. Recourse to seller
   a. whether for mortgage default
   b. whether for breach of warranties
10. Method of monthly remittance to investor
11. Loan characteristics of mortgages to be delivered
    a. type of properties
       —single-family detached
       —one- to four-family
       —condominiums
       —cooperatives
       —second homes
    b. location (geographically)
    c. maximum loan amounts per mortgage loan
    d. coupon rates of loans
    e. loan-to-value maximums
    f. mortgage insurance required
12. Other requirements to be negotiated.

As a general rule, these private, secondary market purchasers use the same underwriting and documentation requirements as FNMA and FHLMC. At times, though, they may vary these requirements slightly, such as increasing ratios by a percent or two, to make themselves more competitive with FNMA and FHLMC.

The principal advantage to a mortgage lender of these direct transactions with private investors is that those mortgage loans that cannot be sold to FNMA or FHLMC because the loan is nonconforming (above the statutory loan limit) or has other unique features can still be sold. In addition, the marketing profit to an originating lender may be greater in a direct sale on a negotiated basis than in the more competitive environment of dealing with FNMA or FHLMC.

Directly Issuing Mortgage-Backed Securities

Until 1977, the MBS field was the exclusive turf of government and government-related agencies. This changed in 1977, when the Bank of America issued the first private MBS. Since then many other private concerns, including many different types of mortgage lenders, have issued MBS. This entire subject is covered extensively in Chapter 11, Mortgage-Backed Securities.

Even though mortgage bankers do not have the problem of securing existing portfolios, they have been very active in direct-issue MBS. Practically all of the GNMA mortgage-backed securities that have been issued to date are backed by FHA/VA loans originated or purchased from other lenders by mortgage bankers. By 1991, all types of mortgage lenders, with the possible exception of credit unions, have directly issued MBS. Those that have not are usually those that are not sophisticated enough to do it themselves, and as a result they have used conduits instead.

Selling Loan Production to Conduits for Packaging into MBS

The number of conduits in the marketplace that will buy loans from mortgage lenders and then package those mortgages with other mortgages from other lenders is growing every year. One example, CUNA Mortgage Corporation, buys mortgages only from credit unions and in turn sells those mortgages to FNMA or FHLMC, which then issues MBS. Wall Street companies and mortgage insurance companies have also been active in purchasing mortgages from many lenders and then directly issuing MBS themselves.

PIPELINE MANAGEMENT

If a mortgage originator is planning to sell some or all of the mortgage loans it originates, that lender must be concerned about the interest rate risk inherent in originating mortgage loans. This interest rate risk occurs between the time a lender commits to an interest rate to the borrower and the time that lender receives a commitment to sell that loan with a certain yield into the secondary market. The time spread of the interest rate risk (i.e., price risk) could be zero (if the lender immediately gets a commitment to sell the mortgage loan) or could be months (if the lender holds the loan(s) in the "warehouse" for a period before obtaining a commitment to sell them). Managing this interest rate risk is often referred to as "pipeline management." The term *pipeline* is used to portray and explain the "flow" of a mortgage from application to sale. The management part is derived from controlling or limiting the risk while the loans are in the pipeline.

Locking Rates at Application

In a perfect world, a lender would only commit on interest rates to borrowers at, or very near, closing of the mortgage loan to avoid a potential mismatch between when rates are committed first to the borrower and then to investors. But, if one lender is willing to commit to applicants at application, other lenders are normally forced by market pressures to do the same thing even though they would prefer not to. A problem many lenders have to face is what to do if rates drop after the lender has committed to a rate to the applicant. Do they require the applicant to close at the rate agreed to? What if the applicant refuses and goes to another lender with lower rates? If the transaction is a purchase money mortgage, an applicant may not have the time to shop for another mortgage and wait for the verification time, but if the mortgage is to refinance an existing mortgage, the applicant is not under any time constraints and may look for another lender with lower rates.

Many lenders have decided that the better business practice is to close the loan at the lower rate. If they don't and the applicant goes to another lender, the first lender may find it can only replace the lost loan with a new loan at the lower rate anyway. Some lenders attempt to manage the situation in which rates drop before closing by charging a fee for locking rates at application. This strategy can work if other lenders charge a fee to lock rates, but if only one lender charges a fee, applicants may take their business to those lenders who don't charge a fee for the lock.

Interest Rate Volatility

Even in periods of relative interest rate stability as existed in the U.S. during the early 1990s, mortgage interest rates rose and fell over short periods of time and those changes were significant enough to painfully hurt a lender that was uncovered by commitments for future delivery. For example, between January 15 and February 15, 1992, mortgage rates increased 110 basis points. To illustrate this risk, assume a lender committed to an applicant at a certain interest rate on January 15 and closed that loan four weeks later without having protected itself from interest rate movements. If that lender had to sell the mortgage loan, the price the lender would receive from an investor would have to be discounted to make up for the difference in yield.

This risk can be better understood by examining the following chart.

Assume $1 million package of 30-year, fixed-rate mortgages originated at 7.00 percent. Yields required in the secondary market have increased to:

Yields Required	Discount Factor	$ Value of Package
7.00 percent	100.00	$1,000,000
7.50 percent	96.31	963,100
8.00 percent	92.80	928,000

The pipeline should be viewed as consisting of two segments:

- *production segment*—period of time between taking the loan application and the closing of the loan,
- *inventory segment*—period of time between closing and sale of the loan.

The distinction is important since a lender has a different risk in a loan that has not and may not close and one that has closed.

At first glance it would appear that the best strategy is to simply provide an interest rate commitment to the borrower and obtain a commitment to deliver a net yield to an investor at the same time. The problem with this strategy is the loan may not close, either because the applicant doesn't qualify or interest rates drop and the applicant doesn't want to close at the rate quoted at application. This risk of a loan not closing is called *fallout risk*, which means a lender has a commitment to deliver loans at a certain net yield but doesn't have the loans yet.

Some lenders manage their pipeline risk by establishing what percentage of their applications will always close, no matter what happens to interest rates, and obtaining commitments to sell those loans at the same time they commit to the applicants. If the lender's history is that 50 percent of applicants will always close, while 10 percent never close, that lender has an easier problem in having to manage only 40 percent of the pipeline and not 100 percent. As the loans flow through the pipeline and get closer to closing without falling out, the lender can increase the amount of coverage on those loans by obtaining investor commitments so that by the time the loans close, the lender has nearly 100 percent coverage.

Another pipeline risk a lender has is *product risk*. Product risk is created by a lender obtaining commitments to deliver one type of loan (e.g., 15-year, fixed-rate mortgage) but not being able to close that type of loan. This risk is created because investors don't always value different loan products the same way as interest rates change directions. (For example, if rates are declining, an

ARM loan is less attractive to investors than is a fixed-rate mortgage. If rates are rising, just the opposite is true.)

Pipeline Reports

Before a lender can manage the pipeline risk successfully, management must have the necessary tools, and the most important tool is information. The loan processing system should contain a module that allows for the preparation of reports management can use to track the following information:

- dollar amount of loans in the pipeline,
- types of loans,
- interest rates committed to applicants,
- when loans are expected to close,
- any outstanding commitments to investors.

Once management has the appropriate pipeline reports it will be able to manage the risks inherent in the mortgages in the pipeline. There are two basic methods for managing the price and product risk inherent in mortgages in the pipeline. The most obvious is to obtain from investors commitments to buy the loans at a certain yield sometime in the future—a *forward sale*. Most lenders use this method to protect themselves. A few of the large originators use *substitute sales* to protect themselves. Substitute sales are accomplished with debt market instruments, such as futures contracts, which are sold at an agreed-upon price for delivery on a specified future date. Before the contract expires, the lender purchases an equivalent security to offset the existing position. The normal result is a loss in one market is offset by a gain in the other market, thus protecting the original transaction. These transactions can be expensive and don't always work. For that reason, few lenders use substitute sales. The vast majority are served well by obtaining commitments for forward sales.

MORTGAGE LOAN COMMITMENTS

Commitments are critical to successful mortgage lending in the 1990s for those lenders that sell mortgages. A commitment is an undertaking by either a mortgage lender to make a loan or an investor to buy a loan. A commitment is legally binding as a contract if it agrees completely with the loan application or the offer to sell. If a commitment varies the terms of an application or offer, then it becomes a counteroffer and must be accepted by the borrower or seller before a binding contract can result.

Commitments from investors to buy mortgage production are essential for successful marketing. During the early 1970s, a few mortgage lenders would originate mortgages for later sale without a commitment from a permanent investor to purchase those loans. Because interest rates moved so slowly during that period, the interest rate exposure of an originator was limited. But, practices changed later in that decade as interest rates became more volatile. After a few mortgage bankers were forced out of business because of severe losses occasioned by not having their production covered, the business changed. The normal course of activity changed to mortgage bankers protecting the majority of loan production from interest rate swings by obtaining commitments for future delivery.

For all practical purposes, that was the end of the practice of not covering loan originations by either a firm (mandatory) or standby commitment. Of course, those mortgage lenders that do not originate loans for sale (for their own portfolios instead) still continue to originate loans without the need of protection from commitments to sell.

A firm commitment assures the mortgage borrower or seller of loans that the loan or sale will occur if certain conditions as set forth in the commitment are met. A further discussion of mortgage loan commitments to borrowers appears in Chapter 3.

A standby commitment obligates the issuer to purchase mortgages at a certain yield for a certain period of time, but it does not obligate the originator to whom it is issued to deliver any loans. Both parties recognize the likelihood that the mortgage loans may not be delivered and that the standby is a type of insurance for the mortgage originator. This process is valuable to an issuer because it is a fee generator. The fees required for both types of commitments are, as a general rule, established by the marketplace. Standby fees are usually twice as much as those required for mandatory delivery. This is because an investor must be compensated for holding funds at the ready to purchase loans that may or may not be delivered.

PRICING IN THE SECONDARY MORTGAGE MARKET

The price an investor will pay for a mortgage loan (i.e., the yield on the mortgage) determines the value of that loan in the secondary market. Put another way, the secondary mortgage market players (meaning in this context, Fannie Mae and Freddie Mac), through posted yields, establish the price they will pay for a net yield (or pass-through rate) on a residential mortgage. Investors will buy mortgage loans at:

- par (100 percent of face value),
- discount (e.g., price of 98 for a 9 percent net yield equals 9.184 yield),
- premium (e.g., price of 102 for a 9 percent net yield equals 8.823 yield).

Pricing information is available from a number of sources, including Fannie Mae's MORNET and Freddie Mac's MIDANET.

Other sources of residential mortgage rates and yields include:

- Telerate,
- Knight-Ridder Money Center Index,
- Bloomberg Wire Service,
- Reuter Mortgage Service.

Remittance Options

In addition to the net yield on a mortgage, the price paid by an investor for a residential mortgage loan is also affected by the *remittance option* selected by the servicer. Once a loan has been sold to an investor, the principal and interest payments (minus any servicing fee) belong to the investor. How and when the principal and interest (P & I) collected by the servicer is remitted to the investor obviously impacts the price the investor pays for the loan. The options a servicer has for remittance include:

- sending P & I as collected,
- sending P & I when a certain dollar level is reached,
- sending P & I at some date in the future (e.g., fifteenth of month after collected).

The longer it takes for an investor to receive the principal and interest, the lower the price the investor is willing to pay for a loan. Some mortgage lenders are willing to take a slightly lower price for their mortgages when they sell (e.g., they have selected a longer period to remit the payments) because they believe they can make more money on the use of the P & I before it is remitted.

HOW IS YIELD CALCULATED?

What Is Current Yield?

Yield is defined as the return on an investment over a specified period of time, usually expressed as a percentage of the original investment amount. Mortgage loans are generally sold based on the yield (often net) of the mortgage or loan package to the investor. The establishment of some yields (e.g., yield to maturity) is neither an easy nor an exact task. Yield to maturity, for example, is impacted by defaults, foreclosures, and principal prepayments. When investors have a large enough package, they can establish *to a degree* the impact of these events. Mortgage-backed securities are marketed to investors based on certain assumptions regarding yield to maturity. These assumptions are discussed in greater detail in Chapter 11, Mortgage-Backed Securities.

Our concern in this chapter is determining current yield. Yield is determined by dividing the annualized income by the money invested, for example,

$$\frac{\$90{,}000 \text{ annualized income}}{\$1{,}000{,}000 \text{ invested}} = 9\text{-percent yield}$$

Put another way, what would an investor pay to receive $90,000 annually when the investor is looking for a 9-percent yield?

$$\frac{\$90{,}000}{9 \text{ percent}} = \$1{,}000{,}000$$

If the investor, with the same amount of annual income, wanted a 10-percent yield the calculation would be as follows:

$$\frac{\$90{,}000}{10 \text{ percent}} = \$900{,}000$$

Thus, if an investor paid $900,000 for a $90,000 annualized income, the yield to the investor would be 10 percent.

Net Yield

As a general rule, when yield to an investor is negotiated it refers to a *net yield* to that investor. Therefore, if a mortgage lender originates a package of mortgages at 9.00 percent and wants to retain 25 basis points for servicing, the net yield to an investor would be 8.75 percent. Put another way, if the net yield requirement for an investor with delivery in 60 days is currently 8.75 percent, the originating lender will want to originate mortgages with an average coupon rate of 9.00 percent. If the investor charges a commitment fee, the fee must also be subtracted in order to correctly establish the yield for the lender. Yield conversion tables are required to arrive at an exact yield, but as a general rule, a 1 percent commitment fee equals 14 basis points.

Weighted Average Yield

Seldom does the mortgage market rate remain constant long enough for a lender to originate a package of loans with the same coupon (interest) rate.

If a lender has mortgages with varying interest rates, the yield to an investor is calculated on a weighted average basis. For example, assume a lender has an outstanding commitment requiring delivery of $10 million in mortgages with a net yield to the investor of 9.00 percent. The following calculations will occur:

1. Lender determines which loans in the pipeline will be used to fulfill commitment. Assume:

$5 million at 9½ percent
3 million at 9¼ percent
2 million at 9 percent
$10 million

2. Yields are then converted into annualized income:

$5 million × 9½ percent = $475,000
3 million × 9¼ percent = 277,500
2 million × 9 percent   = 180,000
$932,500 annual income

3. Divide annualized income by loan package to establish weighted average yield:

$$\frac{\$932,500}{\$10,000,000} = .09325$$

In this example, minus the 25 basis point servicing fee, the weighted average yield of .09075 is more than the commitment of .09 net yield to the lender. When an originator is faced with this situation, it can do the following:

• keep the difference as excess servicing,
• sell the loans at a slight premium, or
• substitute a few more 9 percent mortgages to bring the yield down.

Price for a Package

Once a package of loans has been put together, the yield can be adjusted by the price paid by the investor for the package. Assume an originator has put together a $10 million package of fixed-rate mortgages for sale to an investor with a weighted average yield of 8.75 percent. Further, assume that the originating lender thought rates would remain steady so did not obtain a forward delivery commitment. As a result, now that the package is ready for delivery, the market requires a 8.75 net yield. The package of mortgages must be discounted to produce the required net yield to the investor. (With an 8.75 *weighted average yield* on the underlying mortgages, minus the 25 basis points servicing fee, the mortgages deliver a net yield to the investor of 8.50.) In this case, minus the servicing fee, the annualized income would be $850,000; thus the calculation would be as follows:

$$\frac{850,000}{.0875} = .9714$$

Thus, the package will be sold at a discounted price of .9714, or

$$\frac{850,000}{.9714} = 8.75 \text{ yield}$$

Occasionally, a mortgage originator wants to sell mortgages (probably from portfolio) with coupon rates higher than those required in the secondary market. In those situations, the loans could be sold at a premium. Assume the investor's required net yield is 8.50 and the lender wants to sell $10,000,000 of mortgages with a weighted average yield of 9.00 percent. After subtracting the 25 basis point servicing fee, the net yield would be 8.75 percent, or $875,000;

$$\frac{\$875,000}{.0850} = \$10,294.117, \text{ or a price of } 102.94$$

THE SECONDARY
MORTGAGE MARKET ⸺ *10*

This chapter examines the role secondary mortgage markets play in residential mortgage lending and reviews the major participants in that market. The major players include the two government-sponsored enterprises, Fannie Mae (Federal National Mortgage Association) and Freddie Mac (Federal Home Loan Mortgage Corporation), which together purchase approximately 50 to 60 percent of the one- to four-family mortgage loans originated each year. These government-sponsored enterprises (GSEs) are so identified because the federal government was involved in the creation of both of these now-private corporations. The importance of the GSE classification is that the debts of the GSEs are treated in the marketplace as "United States Agency" securities and thus are sold at lower rates, even though neither is now a part of the federal government. On the other hand, the Government National Mortgage Association (Ginnie Mae, discussed in Chapter 11, Mortgage-Backed Securities) is an actual federal agency (under the Department of Housing and Urban Development) and thus carries the "full faith and credit of the federal government." All three of these organizations are sometimes referred to as the "government-sponsored" secondary mortgage market to distinguish them from the private secondary mortgage market.

Marketing of residential mortgages and the activity of the secondary mortgage market have taken on new importance since the near disaster faced by thrifts in the early 1980s. The size of the secondary mortgage market is now nearly as large as the primary market was just a few years ago. In the first half of the 1990s, for example, for every four mortgage loans originated in the primary market, approximately three were sold into the various secondary mortgage market outlets. Total secondary mortgage market transactions for 1993 were just under $800 billion, a figure higher than originations in the primary market for any year before 1992.

Most Originations Should Be Capable of Being Sold

Today, the vast majority of mortgage loans produced by mortgage originators are *conforming* loans, which means they conform to the standards of the secondary mortgage market. (The term *conforming* mortgage is also used to describe the maximum original principal balance that a GSE secondary mortgage market player can purchase.) Today, the majority of mortgage originators realize that most mortgage loans should be capable of being traded in the secondary mortgage market even though the intent at origination is for those loans to be placed in a lender's portfolio.

Nonconforming Mortgages

Mortgage lenders, especially portfolio lenders, should understand that originating some nonstandard mortgages (or, as these mortgages are sometimes called, Grade B or C paper) can assist them in meeting the housing finance needs of their community. This can especially be true for low-income borrowers or first-time home buyers. But, these lenders should limit their portfolio exposure to these mortgages to a comfortable level or have an investor that is interested in purchasing these mortgages. As should be obvious, mortgage lenders that originate mortgages not suitable for sale in the secondary mortgage market at a reasonable price face the possibility of disaster when interest rates move up or when liquidity is needed, for whatever reason.

Some lenders believe that since all loans can ultimately be sold, they need not worry if their mortgage loans don't meet the requirements or standards of the secondary market. That belief is partially justifiable. All mortgage loans can be sold to someone, but the discounted price these loans command may be so low that a sale isn't really a viable option.

Generic Mortgage Banking

Sound modern asset management dictates that all mortgage lenders involved in residential lending should also be engaged in what is generically called *mortgage banking*. This prudent approach should be followed even if current economic conditions and investment philosophy dictate retaining some or all residential mortgage loan production in portfolio. The term *mortgage banking* refers to the process of originating mortgages that are capable of being sold (even if not actually sold) into the secondary mortgage market.

Growth of Residential Lending and the Secondary Mortgage Markets

One of the most important reasons for the sharp increase in real estate lending activity since the end of World War II has been the demand for and the supply of mortgage money at reasonable rates. The demand for housing credit resulted from the pent-up housing needs and the population growth in the Sunbelt states. This geographical area did not have sufficient capital to meet credit demands; therefore, easy availability of capital was essential for continued economic growth. During periods of tight money or credit restraints, such as existed in the 1970s and 1980s, the activity of the secondary market provides the funds needed for a large portion of the residential lending that occurs.

Today, the activity of the secondary market is greater than ever and provides the foundation for all residential mortgage lending in this country. As the need for more and cheaper credit for housing grows in the 1990s, it is estimated that 80 percent of this credit will be funded by the secondary market. In particular, the use of mortgage-backed securities will allow for a direct path of needed funds from the capital markets to the mortgage markets.

PRIMARY MARKETS AND SECONDARY MARKETS

The distinction between the primary and the secondary mortgage markets is not always clear, especially today with so much of originations being funded from sources other than deposits at financial intermediaries. However, most authorities agree that a *primary market* exists when a lender extends funds directly to a borrower. This process includes origination, processing, underwriting, closing, and possibly marketing of the loan. This same process occurs, of course, whether a lender is originating the mortgage for its own portfolio, for direct sale to an investor, or for sale into the secondary mortgage market.

The *secondary market*, on the other hand, is that market wherein existing mortgages are bought and sold. The most common transaction in this market occurs when a mortgage originator sells existing mortgages to one of the government-sponsored enterprises. This activity could occur as part of the normal course of business for a mortgage lender or be utilized only during periods of credit restraints. Thus, the primary market involves an extension of credit to borrower, and the secondary market a sale of that credit instrument.

ECONOMIC FUNCTIONS OF THE SECONDARY MORTGAGE MARKET

In order to provide the needed economic assistance to mortgage lending, the secondary mortgage market performs these five important economic functions:

1. *Provides liquidity.* Assuming the mortgages are of sufficient quality, any originator, portfolio lender, or investor can sell its mortgages in the mar-

SECONDARY MORTGAGE MARKET
AND
TRADING MORTGAGES FOR CASH

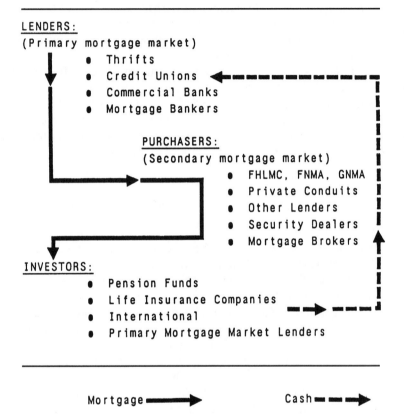

LENDERS:
(Primary mortgage market)
- Thrifts
- Credit Unions
- Commercial Banks
- Mortgage Bankers

PURCHASERS:
(Secondary mortgage market)
- FHLMC, FNMA, GNMA
- Private Conduits
- Other Lenders
- Security Dealers
- Mortgage Brokers

INVESTORS:
- Pension Funds
- Life Insurance Companies
- International
- Primary Mortgage Market Lenders

Mortgage ➡   Cash ➡

ket at any time. This ability allows a seller to meet any immediate needs for capital, (e.g., to meet deposit withdrawals, policy loans, or other demands). Many investors who have not traditionally invested in residential mortgage loans (such as pension funds, trust accounts, and others) are now beginning to invest because the required liquidity for mortgages is present. These investors, attracted by higher yields available with mortgages, realize that a ready market exists if they are forced to liquidate their holdings.

2. *Moderates the cyclical flow of mortgage capital.* During periods of general capital shortage, the funds available for residential mortgages are usually very scarce and real estate activity slows down. Institutions operating in the secondary market during these periods purchase existing mortgages from primary mortgage lenders, and in this way they provide

funds for additional mortgages to be originated. This availability of capital for mortgages helps to lessen the countercyclical nature of real estate. Today, the secondary mortgage market also serves as a link between the mortgage market and the capital market by the sale of mortgage-backed securities.

3. *Assists the flow of capital from surplus areas to deficit areas.* The operations of the secondary market allow an investor in a capital-surplus area, such as New England, to invest in mortgages originated in a capital-deficit area, such as the South or West, thus providing capital for needed mortgage activity. Capital-surplus areas are the older, slower-growing areas of the country, which have a surplus of capital exceeding the demand of home buyers. Capital-deficit areas are those where the demand for housing credit exceeds the supply of capital created by the savings of individuals.

4. *Lessens the geographical spread in interest rates and allows for portfolio diversification.* The mobility of capital allows for a moderation of the geographical differences in mortgage interest rates since capital will flow to areas of high interest, thus pressuring rates downward. In addition, regional risk (e.g., a large industry closing) is spread to more investors, thus lessening its effect.

5. *Increases profitability by increased mortgage lending activity.* As a lender sells mortgage loans, it can originate more mortgages with the proceeds of the sale and repeat the cycle again, eventually generating economies of scale in both the origination and service side of the business.

COMPETITION IN THE SECONDARY MORTGAGE MARKET

Before an examination of the two major players in the secondary mortgage market is attempted, the concept of competition between these two players and others should be examined. Just as competition in the primary mortgage market is intense, so is competition in the secondary markets. At the present time, the two giants, Fannie Mae and Freddie Mac, pretty much have the battlefield to themselves. But, it is important to mention, these two players command only 50 to 60 percent of the one- to four-family mortgage loans originated each year. That may equal about 65 to 70 percent of the loans sold. Therefore, there are other private corporations that are buying mortgage loans probably for their portfolios, or so the purchaser can issue mortgage-backed securities.

The significant advantages Fannie Mae and Freddie Mac enjoy because of the size of their activities and their GSE status have served thus far to prevent any significant penetration by other entities into the secondary market for conforming mortgages. Ginnie Mae provides a mechanism for lenders to sell FHA/VA mortgages into the secondary mortgage market, but FHA/VA mortgages have been a shrinking percentage of one- to four-family mortgage originations over recent years.

Fannie Mae and Freddie Mac Compete Directly

These two GSEs compete intensely and directly with each other year in and year out. These two former government agencies are now structured in a similar fashion and have, basically, the same business plan. Mortgage lenders should be approved to do business with both of these corporations since at any given time, the product mix, price, or services rendered may be better at one than the other. However, that could change the following week or month.

FEDERAL NATIONAL MORTGAGE ASSOCIATION (FNMA) ⸻

Any discussion of the secondary mortgage markets must start with the Federal National Mortgage Association, also known as "Fannie Mae." Fannie Mae was the most active participant in the secondary markets historically and currently is the largest holder of residential mortgage debt ($200 billion) in the world.

Fannie Mae is a congressionally chartered, shareholder-owned, privately managed corporation that is the fifth largest corporation in the U.S. Currently Fannie Mae purchases residential mortgages from nearly 3,000 originators across the U.S., including mortgage bankers, commercial banks, thrifts, housing finance agencies, and credit unions. It has been estimated that Fannie Mae, since its formation in 1938, has provided over $1 trillion to finance home mortgages for nearly 20 million families.

The importance of an effective secondary market has been recognized since 1924, when a bill was introduced in Congress to establish a system of national home loan banks that could purchase first mortgages. The legislation failed to become law. The first federal attempt to establish and assist a national mortgage market was the Reconstruction Finance Corporation (RFC), created in 1935 and followed in 1938 by a wholly owned subsidiary, the National Mortgage Association of Washington, soon renamed the Federal National Mortgage Association.

Separation of Ginnie Mae

In 1950, Fannie Mae was transferred to the Department of Housing and Urban Development (HUD) and was later partitioned into two separate corporations by an amendment to the Housing and Urban Development Act of 1968. This was done to permit the "new" Fannie Mae to more actively support

Fannie/Freddie Share of Single-family Conventional Mortgage Debt Outstanding

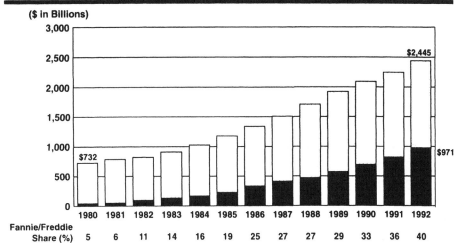

| Fannie/Freddie Share (%) | 5 | 6 | 11 | 14 | 16 | 19 | 25 | 27 | 27 | 29 | 33 | 36 | 40 |

the mortgage market outside the federal budget. The new entity, named the Government National Mortgage Association (GNMA, or "Ginnie Mae") remained in HUD and retained the special assistance and loan liquidation functions of the old Fannie Mae. Ginnie Mae is discussed in greater detail in a later section.

The new Fannie Mae corporation was to be basically private, though some regulatory control remained with HUD. In addition, Fannie Mae retained a $2.25 billion line of credit with the U.S. Treasury. It also retained the Federal National Mortgage Association's name as well as the assets and responsibilities for secondary market operations. Today, the corporation is run by an 18-member board of directors, consisting of 13 selected by stockholders and 5 appointed by the President of the United States.

From its beginning until 1970, Fannie Mae only purchased FHA/VA mortgages that were originated predominantly by mortgage bankers. In 1970, Congress (in the same bill that created the Federal Home Loan Mortgage Corporation) authorized Fannie Mae to purchase conventional mortgages. The first conventional mortgages were purchased in 1971, and today, Fannie Mae purchases more conventional mortgages than any other type of mortgage loan.

In 1992, new legislation was signed that strengthened the government-sponsored mission of FNMA and FHLMC and modernized the regulatory framework applicable to these two corporations. This legislation also ushered in a new era of modernized capital standards for the two GSEs. These new capital standards help to ensure that the two GSEs would be able to meet adverse interest rate scenarios and still continue serving the needs of home buyers across the U.S.

Today, Fannie Mae, along with Freddie Mac and private investors, provides the means by which funds can flow from the capital markets to the mortgage markets, usually in the form of mortgage-backed securities. These funds are then used by mortgage lenders to finance home purchases.

How Fannie Mae Finances Its Operations

Fannie Mae finances its secondary market operations by tapping the private capital markets using short-, medium-, and long-term obligations. Currently, the largest portion of the debt is short term. During recent years, callable debentures have become the most important funding vehicle for the corporation, thus providing some interest rate protection. Purchasers of Fannie Mae debentures include international concerns (largest purchasers), pension funds, local government, and individuals.

Fannie Mae's Earnings

Although Fannie Mae produces income from three sources, the first two are by far the most important:

- *net interest income*—the spread between its borrowing costs and the yield on its mortgage investment,
- *guaranty fees*—the fee charged for providing a guaranty that the principal and interest will be paid on a timely basis,
- *fee income*—from financial and information services such as the issuance of Real Estate Mortgage Investment Conduits (REMICs).

Fannie Mae earned nearly $2 billion in 1993. This continued the trend of record earnings of recent years, which is a substantial improvement over 1982, when FNMA lost a total (net) of $105 million.

SECONDARY MARKET OPERATIONS

Fannie Mae, like other institutions in the secondary mortgage market, has made extensive changes in its programs and in the way it operates in an attempt to adapt to changing economic conditions. These changes occur often, even monthly; therefore, any discussion of Fannie Mae's current programs runs the risk of being dated quickly. Recognizing that risk, a text without at least an overview of current practices and programs of Fannie Mae would appear to diminish the importance of this major player in the secondary mortgage market.

Fannie Mae purchases mortgages only from approved Seller/Servicers that have obtained delivery commitments. To become a Fannie Mae approved

Seller/Servicer, a lender must have a minimum net worth of $250,000. Fannie Mae requires an appropriate level of experience on a lender's part and periodically reviews the volume of loan originations and amount of serviced loans. Fannie Mae wants assurance that a lender's quality control system contains written procedures, identifies discrepancies, and takes corrective action.

Obtaining Commitments

In order to actually sell mortgage loans to Fannie Mae (Freddie Mac acts in a similar way), a mortgage originator must obtain a contract from the investors that spells out the details of the transaction—the product to be sold, the price, and the delivery terms. This contract is called a *commitment*. Commitments are obtained by agreeing to sell loans at a specific net yield with delivery within a commitment period. (Fannie Mae offers 10-, 30-, 60-, and 90-day commitments.) The net yield (which does not include the required servicing fee by a servicer) for specific loan products is quoted over the telephone or is available via various financial information systems (such as MOR-NET, Telerate, or Bloomberg). Commitments were discussed extensively in Chapter 9, Marketing Residential Mortgage Loans.

The servicing fee, which Fannie Mae requires a lender to collect, ranges from 25 to 50 basis points depending on the type of mortgage and the volume and experience of the mortgage lender.

FNMA ACTIVITY
(in millions of dollars)

Year	Purchases	Sales	Year-end Portfolio	MBS Issued
1960	$ 980	$ 42	$ 2,903	—
1965	757	46	2,520	—
1970	5,078	—	15,502	—
1975	4,263	2	31,824	—
1980	8,099	—	57,327	—
1985	21,510	1,301	98,282	23,649
1990	23,959	5,800	113,875	96,700
1993	92,300	6,900	189,800	221,400

Source: FNMA.

MORTGAGE LOANS FANNIE MAE WILL BUY

Fannie Mae offers standard purchase and negotiated purchase programs for many different types of mortgage loans, including both fixed-rate and adjustable-rate loans. The mortgages that Fannie Mae will buy for cash or swap for MBSs include current production and seasoned loans:

- 10-, 15-, 20-, 30-year conventional and FHA/VA fixed-rate mortgages,
- 1- and 3-year ARMs indexed to Treasury securities or 11th District COF,
- 15- and 30-year biweeklies,
- 5- and 7-year two steps,
- 7-year balloons with refinance option.

If a lender does not find the program it wants, it may also negotiate a special transaction with Fannie Mae.

FANNIE MAE YEAR-END 1993
RESIDENTIAL MORTGAGE PORTFOLIO

• Conventional, long-term, fixed-rate	43 percent
• Conventional, intermediate-term, fixed-rate	33 percent
• Adjustable-rate	10 percent
• FHA/VA	5 percent
• Multi-family	9 percent
	100 percent

Source: 1993 FNMA Annual Report.

Fannie Mae may only purchase single-family mortgage loans with a maximum original principal balance up to the conforming loan limit—which in 1994 was $203,150. This is the same limit for FHLMC (Alaska, Hawaii, and the Virgin Islands are 50 percent higher). Higher limits apply to loans secured by dwelling units for two, three, or four families.

Fannie Mae purchases whole loans or participation interests in 5 percent increments between 50 and 95 percent. Eligible properties include first mortgages on one- to four-family owner-occupied principal residences, second homes, and investment properties. First mortgages can be secured by units in condominiums, cooperatives, and planned unit developments (and manufactured housing in some cases).

Maximum Loan-to-Value Ratios for Standard Purchases

The following maximum loan-to-value ratios apply to Fannie Mae's standard purchases:

- 95 percent for fixed-rate mortgages if owner-occupied principal residence,
- 90 percent for adjustable-rate if owner-occupied principal residence,

- 90 percent for fixed- and adjustable-rate on owner-occupied refinances,
- 80 percent for investment properties and second homes.

Mortgage Insurance Requirements

Both secondary mortgage market investors require mortgage insurance on all conventional first mortgage loans if the loan-to-value ratio at the time of purchase is greater than 80 percent.

DELIVERY REQUIREMENTS

During much of Fannie Mae's history, most of its programs were optional delivery. These contracts resulted in Fannie Mae being on the receiving end of a "put" contract and were not always beneficial to Fannie Mae's financial position. Practically all of Fannie Mae's programs now require mandatory delivery of at least 95 percent of the commitment amount. On occasion, a mortgage lender may be unable to fulfill a commitment. In that situation the lender can "buy back" the commitment by paying a fee that compensates Fannie Mae for the lost yield. The "buy back" is called a *pair-off*. On the other hand, if an outstanding commitment has at least one additional dollar outstanding, another loan can be delivered under that commitment.

As mentioned earlier, most of the standard products no longer require the lender to pay a commitment fee. For a standby commitment, Fannie Mae will charge a modest fee.

FEDERAL HOME LOAN MORTGAGE CORPORATION (FHLMC)

The second major player in the so-called "organized" secondary mortgage market is the Federal Home Loan Mortgage Corporation (FHLMC), also known as Freddie Mac. The Emergency Home Finance Act of 1970, in addition to giving FNMA the power to purchase conventional mortgages, authorized the establishment of a new secondary market player. Because it was originally a government-sponsored enterprise, it carries the GSE designation. This player was originally intended to provide secondary market facilities for members of the Federal Home Loan Bank System, which meant savings and loan associations. The corporation's initial capital was from the sale of $100 million of nonvoting common shares to the 12 district Federal Home Loan Banks (FHLB). The charter of Freddie Mac has been modified to include all mortgage lenders; therefore, any originator of mortgage loans that meets the financial and experience qualifications of Freddie Mac may sell to this GSE.

Today, Freddie Mac is a publicly owned corporation similar to Fannie Mae with 60 million shares outstanding and listed on the New York Stock Exchange. Freddie Mac is managed by a board of directors consisting of 18 members, 13 of whom are elected by the shareholders and 5 appointed by the President of the United States.

A part of the enabling legislation authorized Freddie Mac to request that the FHLB guarantee Freddie Mac debts or help it raise funds. This authorization has not been used to date. Although Freddie Mac is not formally a part of the federal government, its ties to the FHLB have led investors to classify it as a quasi-governmental agency. As a result, its debt offerings, like Fannie Mae, sell at governmental or near-governmental rates.

Largest Purchaser of Conventional Loans

Since its beginning, Freddie Mac has been the largest purchaser of conventional loans with total purchases and mortgage-backed securities issued approaching $1 trillion by year-end 1993. In 1993, Freddie Mac purchased approximately $229 billion worth of mortgages from various lenders. These loans were purchased from the over 5,000 lenders approved to do business with Freddie Mac. Fulfilling its secondary mortgage market function in addition to its purchases, Freddie Mac issued nearly $209 billion in original issue mortgage securities in 1993.

In 1992, Freddie Mac made a major strategic decision to begin adding loans to its own portfolio. This action allows Freddie Mac to have the same strategic alternatives available to Fannie Mae during periods of volatile interest rates. At the end of 1993, Freddie Mac had a residential mortgage portfolio of approximately $55 billion.

Business Overview

Freddie Mac finances most of its mortgage purchases with the sale of guaranteed mortgage securities called Mortgage Participation Certificates (PC), for which Freddie Mac ultimately assumes the risk of borrower default. Mortgages financed in this way are referred to as the "sold portfolio."

Freddie Mac's Earnings

Freddie Mac's revenue base consists of three components:

1. Management and guarantee fees, which consist of the fee income or effective spread earned on the corporation's sold portfolio. The effective spread is the difference between the effective interest rate received on

sold mortgages and the effective rate paid to the holders of mortgage securities.

2. Net return on Freddie Mac's retained mortgage and investment portfolios.

3. Net float benefit or loss, which is the difference between interest earned and interest paid on cash flows generated by the sold portfolio held by Freddie Mac pending remittance to investors. Float arises due to inherent timing differences between the remittance of principal and interest payments to Freddie Mac by mortgage servicers and the pass-through of such payments to security holders.

Secondary Market Operations

Similar to Fannie Mae, before a lender sells loans to Freddie Mac it must become an approved seller/servicer. The major difference between the two is that Freddie Mac requires a high net worth before granting approval to deal with a lender. As of January 1, 1993, a lender must have a net worth of at least $1 million. Lenders telephone special numbers to receive current quotes on yield requirements. If a lender decides to obtain a commitment, it gives its identification number and tells the operator the type and amount of loans(s) the lender wants to sell and the delivery period desired. The operator confirms the commitment over the phone and mails two copies of the written contract to the lender. When received, the lender signs and returns the contract within 24 hours. The yield to Freddie Mac is a net yield: that is, it does not include the lender's servicing fee.

Freddie Mac also offers "master commitments," which allow a mortgage seller the opportunity to sell mortgages over a specified period of time that typically covers 6 to 12 months. Once a seller decides to deliver a specified amount of mortgages to Freddie Mac in accordance with the master commitment, a separate purchase contract is executed for the specific delivery and sale.

Mortgage Characteristics

FHLMC, under either the Cash Program or the Guarantor Program, offers to purchase from approved sellers the following residential mortgage loans:

- 15-, 20-, and 30-year fixed-rate mortgages,
- 5- and 7-year balloon/reset mortgages,
- 1-, 3-, and 5-year adjustable-rate mortgages.

CONFORMING LOAN LIMITS
FOR FANNIE MAE AND FREDDIE MAC

1975	$ 55,000*
1977	75,000*
1980	93,750*
1981	98,500
1982	107,000
1983	108,300
1984	114,000
1985	115,300
1986	133,250
1987	153,100
1988	168,700
1989	187,600
1990	187,450
1991	191,250
1992	202,300
1993	203,150
1994	203,150

* Determined by Congress.
Source: Fannie Mae and Freddie Mac.

Financing Mortgage Purchases

Freddie Mac finances its secondary mortgage market operations some-what differently than Fannie Mae. Rather than finance its purchases with debt securities in the capital market, as does Fannie Mae, Freddie Mac issues mortgage-backed securities. One of the early successes was the Guarantor Program, under which a mortgage lender sold mortgages to Freddie Mac and, in turn, Freddie Mac sold back to the lender an MBS secured by those same mortgages. For this action, Freddie Mac earned a guarantee fee.

In effect, Freddie Mac finances its mortgage purchases with capital generated from the sale of either whole mortgages (rarely) or participations (generally) in groups of mortgages. It effectively buys and sells mortgages on a constant basis. Some capital is generated by the sale of debt securities.

The practical result of this activity is the sale of so-called Participation Certificates (PC), which are sold to thrift institutions, pension funds, and others. PCs are mortgage-backed securities that have the timely payment of principal and interest guaranteed by Freddie Mac. These PCs give the investor an undivided interest in the pooled mortgages.

Freddie Mac's most important recent mortgage securitization program development has been the Gold Mortgage Participation Certificate (Gold). Under the program, introduced in 1990, investors receive borrowers' mortgage payments more quickly than under previous PC programs. See Chapter 11 for a complete discussion of mortgage-backed securities.

Delivery Requirements

Freddie Mac, similar to Fannie Mae, expects a mortgage lender to deliver the dollar amount of mortgages they contracted to deliver when they obtained a commitment. Though their requirements are slightly different, both secondary mortgage market investors allow a slight variance up or down from the commitment amount.

DOCUMENTS DELIVERED TO SECONDARY MARKET INVESTORS

After agreeing to purchase a mortgage, neither Freddie Mac nor Fannie Mae wants to keep all the documents a mortgage lender finds necessary to have when processing a mortgage loan. As a general rule, they only want the mortgage, note, assignment of the mortgage, and a loan schedule whereby the characteristics of the mortgage(s) sold are listed. The mortgage lender, on the other hand, must keep these documents either in their original form or recorded on microfilm. These documents must be available at all times if an investor wants to perform its own quality control audit or if the loan becomes delinquent.

RECOURSE

Mortgage lenders that sell mortgage loans to Fannie Mae or Freddie Mac (or, for that matter, to other investors) face the possibility of *recourse*. Recourse can be defined as the contingent liability a seller of a mortgage loan has to repurchase the loan if the sale of the loan breaches one of the warranties or representations the seller made when the loan was sold. For instance, a seller of a mortgage loan warrants to Fannie Mae that a loan sold was originated according to Fannie Mae's Seller/Servicer manual. If the loan was not originated according to the requirements, then the seller faces the risk of having to repurchase the loan. Sometimes an investor's quality control efforts identify a deficient loan and the seller is ordered to immediately repurchase the loan. If it is not identified in this manner and the loan never becomes delinquent, then no one is harmed and nothing happens. But, if the loan was not originated according to the requirements of the investor and the loan does become delinquent and a causal connection can be drawn between the delinquency and breach of warranty, then the seller will be required to repurchase the loan.

With or Without Recourse?

A seller has the option of selling a mortgage loan with or without recourse. If the seller finds an investor who will purchase mortgages with *no recourse*, the net yield to that investor will be higher than normal. Therefore, the seller's decision is whether or not to give up yield to acquire no contingent liability to repurchase mortgages. On the other hand, a seller could also contract that loans are sold with *full recourse*, which means if the loan ever becomes delinquent, the seller will repurchase the loan even if the seller did nothing wrong. This type of an arrangement is strongly recommended against (except for the most sophisticated lenders) because a seller could be forced to repurchase many mortgages that had defaulted (possibly because of economic events, such as a factory closing), which could put that seller out of business.

In conclusion, three levels of recourse exist:

1. *full recourse*—seller must repurchase the loan if loan becomes delinquent for whatever reason,
2. *normal recourse*—seller must repurchase after delinquency but only if seller did not process or underwrite the loan according to the investor's requirements,
3. *no recourse*—seller is not obligated to repurchase any loans, even if delinquent, but gives up yield to the investor (net yield is 10–15 basis points higher).

Most loans sold into the secondary mortgage market are with normal recourse. Although investors don't want to disclose how many loans are forced back on sellers, it has been suggested that the percentage of delinquent loans repurchased by seller is around 8–10 percent.

SECONDARY MARKET FRAUD ISSUES

Although both Fannie Mae and Freddie Mac (and other investors) attempt to address the risk of fraud when purchasing mortgages by their underwriting and servicing guidelines and requirements, certain types of fraud are difficult to address. Mortgage fraud takes many forms in both the origination and secondary market sales environment. From the secondary market sales side, some of the more common types include:

- double selling—selling loans to one investor that have already been sold to another investor,

- sale of nonexistent mortgages—illusory loans evidenced by falsified documents and not secured by any interest in real estate,
- deceptive underwriting practices—for example, overstating a borrower's income,
- conversion of funds—funds held for an investor's benefit in custodial accounts.

PRIVATE SECONDARY MORTGAGE MARKET

In addition to the government and government-related agencies, private companies have recently become quite active as well as important in the secondary mortgage market. Reasons for the emergence of the private secondary mortgage market include the following:

- deregulation and a shift in political sentiment to less government,
- government-related agencies borrowing in the capital markets at the same time as excessive federal deficits drive up interest rates and thus crowd some other borrowers out,
- perception of unfair competition, since government-related agencies borrow more cheaply than private companies,
- growth of primary and secondary mortgage markets provides profit opportunities for private entities.

Much of the activity by these private entities is with those mortgage loans classified as nonconforming. These loans are so classified because they exceed the set statutory limit above which FNMA and FHLMC cannot purchase mortgages. The private companies cannot compete with FNMA and FHLMC on loans below that limit because government-related agencies have a substantial advantage with their lower cost of funds.

UNIFORM DOCUMENTATION

In order for mortgages to be readily salable in the secondary market, a degree of uniformity must exist. Before FHLMC joined FNMA in the secondary market the required uniformity existed because all mortgages sold in the secondary market were either FHA-insured or VA-guaranteed. After 1970, conventional mortgages could also be bought and sold in the secondary market and a need developed for uniform documentation.

Both FNMA and FHLMC have worked diligently to produce the state-by-state uniform documents that all mortgage lenders should use for all originations. GNMA has also adopted these forms, which include among others:

- mortgage note,
- deed of trust,
- mortgage,
- loan application,
- appraisal form,
- verification documents.

These forms can also be used for VA-guaranteed mortgages if a VA-guaranteed loan rider is added to the mortgage or deed of trust to make the mortgage instrument conform to special VA requirements. These forms regretably cannot be used for FHA-insured loans; FHA-approved forms must be used. This may change in the future.

These uniform forms may contain some minor variations to comply with different state laws.

MORTGAGE-BACKED SECURITIES ════════════ *11*

After the benchmark year of 1993, when one- to four-family mortgage originations topped $1 trillion for the first time ever, residential origination volume dropped back moderately as interest rates rose. But, demographics for the second half of the 1990s point to a steady demand for housing and therefore residential mortgage credit. Mortgage economists project one- to four-family residential mortgage originations to average $700 to $900 billion annually for the second half of the 1990s. Even in an economic environment without excessive federal deficits and their resulting demands on credit, this projected growth cannot be met by traditional sources of capital. Mortgage-backed securities (MBSs) provide one of the few ways to meet this demand.

IMPORTANCE OF MBS TODAY

In the 1980s and 1990s, the use of MBSs became an important tool for mortgage lenders and secondary mortgage market players because of the increased amount of housing that could be financed via MBSs. Further, MBSs have been important to financial institutions because of capital requirements placed on them by their regulators. Because MBSs are considered safer than most other investments an institution can have in its portfolio, the capital requirements for MBSs are lower than for most other investments. In fact, because Ginnie Mae MBSs carry the "full faith and credit of the U.S. Government," the *capital requirements* for them are the same as for Treasury securities—zero. Fannie Maes and Freddie Macs carry a very low capital requirement—much less than for whole loans. As a result of these lower capital requirements, many financial institutions have securitized some or all of their residential mortgage portfolio.

The magnitude of MBS usage is unmistakable when the MBS volume of the secondary market players over the past couple of years is examined. Fannie Mae and Freddie Mac combined were issuing $400 to $450 billion of MBSs each year by the middle of the 1990s and more than $ 1.5 trillion in agency MBSs were held by investors. This chapter provides an introduction to mortgage-backed securities and a review of the recent developments in this important tool for providing financing for American homeowners.

CONCEPT OF MBSs

The basic concept behind MBSs is simple: to provide a way for more capital to flow into housing. Disintermediation among the *traditional mortgage lenders* in the late 1960s and early 1970s resulted in a shortage of capital for housing and focused attention on the need to develop additional sources of finance. The traditional mortgage lenders of this time were the mortgage companies, savings and loan associations, savings banks, and commercial banks. As economists and demographers in the late 1960s projected the arrival of the "baby boomers" into the housing market over following decades, they realized with alarm that the traditional mortgage lenders would not be able to provide the needed funds for home purchasers; thus, the need for additional sources of residential mortgage funds.

These additional sources were the so-called *nontraditional mortgage lenders* (i.e., those institutions that traditionally had not invested in mortgages) such as pension funds, retirement systems, and life insurance companies and trusts, among others. The challenge was to provide a way for these nontraditional mortgage lenders to get involved in residential mortgage financing. The answer was to be mortgage-backed securities.

How Successful Have MBSs Been?

In 1970, the traditional mortgage lenders (not including mortgage companies that sold all their originations) held 78 percent of the outstanding one- to four-family residential mortgage debt. In contrast, at the end of 1993 these same investors held only 32 percent of the outstanding debt. The other 68 percent was divided between federal agencies (Fannie Mae and Freddie Mac) with 8 percent, all other holders with 13 percent, and, finally, MBSs with 47 percent of total outstanding residential mortgage debt. MBSs now constitute the largest classification of holders of residential debt, with an estimated $1,500 billion outstanding at the end of 1994.

MBS: An Old Idea

This critical need for more capital was addressed by reviving an old idea—the use of a capital market instrument backed by a pool of mortgages. This concept had been used in the 1920s by some large mortgage insurance companies that sold participation bonds to the general public. Neither these mortgage insurance companies nor the bonds they guaranteed survived the Great Depression. Because of the severity of the losses caused by these bonds, MBSs were dormant for nearly 50 years.

Why Were Nontraditional Investors Afraid of Mortgages?

Nontraditional mortgage investors were not interested in residential mortgage debt before MBSs because of the cumbersome nature of mortgage investments and the high cost for each transaction. In addition, these investors were concerned about the following more basic drawbacks:

- diverse state real estate and mortgage laws (e.g., foreclosure, redemption),
- lack of liquidity (ability to sell quickly) of mortgages,
- lack of day-to-day evaluation of mortgages,
- monthly cash flow of principal and interest that required monthly reinvestment decisions.

Considering that the alternatives to mortgages were government and corporate bonds with little default risk, substantially lower administrative expenses, and fewer state-related differences to worry about, it is not surprising that these investors had little interest in mortgages before MBSs.

MBS: A Capital Market Security

What was needed was a way to make mortgage debt a more attractive investment for more investors. The tool used to make mortgage debt attractive was an instrument investors were already familiar with—a capital market security. That's the whole key to the success of MBSs: a capital market instrument that is understood by investors and readily traded in capital markets.

Types of MBSs

If all of the various types of MBSs are considered, all represent either an equity or a creditor position for an investor. That is to say, MBSs either provide an investor with an undivided ownership interest in a pool of mortgages or the pool of mortgages secures a debt.

Pass-through Certificates

In the first type, an equity position, the investor has a fractional undivided ownership in a pool of mortgages represented by an investment trust. (The trust does not actually manage the mortgages; therefore, no federal income taxes are due from the trust.) The pool of mortgages is created when a mortgage lender assembles a group of mortgages that are alike in type of mortgage instrument, term, and interest rate. The security issuer or pool sponsor is usually one of the traditional originators of residential mortgages. Mortgage bankers have issued more MBS than any other, but recently savings and loans, commercial banks, sponsors of conduits, and Wall Street have increased their activity.

When a mortgage lender structures a mortgage pool, the individual loans are actually sold; thus pass-through certificates involve a sale of assets and are not a debt instrument that would be carried on the books of the issuer. The MBS is then sold to investors who now are the owners of an undivided interest in the pool of mortgages. The monthly principal, interest, and any prepayments from the mortgagors are collected by a servicer (usually the issuer) and are then passed through to the investors.

The pass-through payments can be made in one of three ways depending on the type of security. The simplest type is the *straight pass-through,* which is used primarily in private placements. With this instrument, principal and interest are paid to an investor when collected, but if a default by a mortgagor occurs, the investor's cash flow is reduced by that amount.

Some of the early GNMA (Ginnie Mae) MBSs were of the second type, the *partially modified pass-through*. With this type, the monthly principal and interest due an investor is paid as collected, but if a default occurs, an issuer is only obligated to pass through a predetermined percentage of what is owed.

Neither of these first two were very attractive to investors since they required greater certainty of cash flow in order for mortgages to be considered as investments. The third form, the *modified pass-through*, became the instrument accepted in the marketplace and is the one used almost exclusively today.

The modified pass-through is the MBS that best meets the needs of investors since it offers near certainty of monthly cash flow. This certainty is an absolute guarantee in some situations; witness the *full faith and credit of the federal government* backing the monthly payment of principal and interest for the GNMA. With this instrument, the issuer of a certificate is required to pass through to investors principal and interest *even if not collected*. If the investor is unable to pass through this amount, then the GNMA (or Fannie Mae or Freddie Mac, if they provided the guarantee) will make the payment. This makes the instrument very attractive to investors since monthly cash flow is ensured. Many mortgage investors, including pension funds (the most sought after), invested heavily in GNMAs because of the full faith and credit of the federal government, making them the most popular pass-through for the non-traditional mortgage investors.

GOVERNMENT NATIONAL MORTGAGE ASSOCIATION (GNMA)

To understand MBSs more fully, one must start with the Government National Mortgage Association (GNMA), or as it's called, Ginnie Mae. As mentioned, GNMA was not the first to use mortgage-backed securities. The first MBS was issued in the 1920s. Because many financial institutions and individual investors lost considerable money with these instruments, the return of mortgage-backed security might not have been so successful if the federal government were not involved as a guarantor.

The way a GNMA mortgage-backed security works is as follows. First, an issuer, most often a mortgage banker, seeks a commitment from GNMA to guarantee a pool of acceptable FHA, Farmers Home Administration (FmHA), or VA mortgages. (Originally, only fixed-rate mortgages were used in MBSs, but now adjustable-rate mortgages can make up the pool.) After receiving the guarantee, a security is issued, backed by a pool of FHA, FmHA, or VA mortgages that have either been originated for this purpose, taken out of portfolio, or purchased on the secondary market. These mortgages are then placed in a custodian account as collateral for a GNMA-guaranteed security. This MBS is sold through a securities dealer to investors based on the guarantee that the issuer will pay all principal and interest due even if not collected. This guarantee of timely payment of principal and interest by the issuer is backed by GNMA, which in return is backed by the full faith and credit of the federal government.

Rate of MBS Is Lower Than Coupon Rate of Underlying Mortgages

The face rate of a GNMA mortgage-backed security is 50 basis points less than the coupon rate of the mortgages underlying the security. Originally, all GNMA MBSs issued required that all of the mortgages in the pool have the same interest rate. (The GNMA II MBSs allow a 1-percent spread.) If all of the mortgages in a pool carry a coupon rate of 9 percent, then the face rate of the GNMA MBS will be 50 basis points less, or $8\frac{1}{2}$ percent.

The split of the 50 basis points is 44 basis points going to the servicer and 6 basis points to GNMA. These fees are to compensate:

- the servicer, for its risk of making monthly payments to investors even if not collected from the borrower,
- GNMA, for its guarantee, backing up the servicer.

The first GNMA MBS was sold by the Associated Mortgage Company to the state of New Jersey pension fund in 1970. That is of interest not only from a historical viewpoint but also because the parties represented the two financial institutions most heavily involved in MBSs.

In 1990, Ginnie Mae began to guaranty securities backed by adjustable-rate mortgages. Although this type of MBS has not grown as rapidly as the fixed-rate MBS market, by 1994, it was growing at the rate of about $80 billion a year, and Ginnie Mae had a 26-percent market share. By the end of 1994, nearly $450 billion Ginnie Mae MBSs of all types were outstanding.

CONVENTIONAL MBSs

Since the late 1970s, housing finance has been evolving rapidly due to the changes brought about by deregulation of financial institutions, a bout of in-flation, and changes in capital requirements, among others. Portfolio lending is no longer the advisable strategy it once was for many lenders. Most resi-dential mortgage originators follow the mortgage banking strategy, which emphasizes originating mortgage loans for sale into the secondary mortgage market and the securitizing of mortgage portfolios. To accomplish this task, many lenders have turned to conventional MBSs. Conventional MBSs have allowed mortgage originators to tap the capital markets as a source of funds for housing. A conventional MBS is one that contains only conventional mort-gages (can be either fixed rate or adjustable rate, but not mixed together). The underlying conventional mortgages may or may not have private mortgage insurance.

A conventional MBS issuer may remit principal, interest, and any prin-cipal repayments to investors on a specific date of the month when collected or possibly the next month. Since mortgagors typically pay their mortgages on or about the first, this delay in payment results in a slight decrease in yield to an investor. This float can be very profitable to issuers based upon the amount of MBSs they have issued. Offsetting this slight decrease in yield to an investor because of the float is the monthly cash flow, which increases the bond equivalent yield since a bond typically has interest paid semi-annually.

Example: A pool of 15-percent mortgages (30-year fully amortized) with a 25-day delay in first payment will deliver a mortgage yield of 14.82 percent. This assumes that the pool is priced at par and prepayment is 12 years. If com-pared with a 15-percent corporate bond paying interest semi-annually, the yield would be 15.29 percent.

Mortgage Insurance

An investor in a conventional MBS has at least four layers of protection for its monthly cash flow.

1. The most important protection comes from the *pool insurance* covering the initial aggregate principal balance of all mortgages in the pool. For example, if an investor requires a prime pool rated "AAA," a rating agency will require a 7-percent coverage. This policy would protect investors against loss caused by a default on any mortgage loan or loans up to 7 percent of the initial balance. The total dollar amount of coverage remains the same throughout the pool's life minus any claims paid.
2. Investors are also protected by a *special hazard insurance policy,* which typically is 1 percent of initial aggregate principal balance. This protects against certain risks (e.g., earthquakes) not covered in individual hazard insurance policies.
3. Each individual loan, especially if it has a loan-to-value ratio in excess of 80 percent, will probably be covered by an *individual mortgage insurance policy,* which protects the lender against default. It is common for the originating lender to also become the security issuer; thus, this protection helps protect an MBS investor.
4. Finally, the *homeowner's equity* provides some degree of protection to investors.

When all of these factors are combined with the contractual obligation of the security issuer to pay the monthly principal, interest, and principal prepayments to an investor, conventional MBS investors have a very secure investment.

The most important of the three items reviewed by a rating agency is the amount of pool insurance and the financial strength of the mortgage insurance company providing it. Although various exotic techniques have been used to provide the desired pool protection in order to obtain a particular credit rating, normally this protection has come from pool insurance issued by a private mortgage insurance company. Because an investor may have to look to this insurance, the financial strength of the mortgage insurance company is examined by the rating agency.

Frequency of Expected Foreclosure

The amount of insurance depends on the level of creditworthiness desired by an issuer. Since an investment grade rating requires 100% repayment of principal with interest, the rating agency must determine the frequency of expected foreclosure and the severity of loss based on experience. The frequency of expected foreclosure is assumed from a "worst case" situation similar to that which existed in the Great Depression. The severity of loss is derived from actual loss experience assuming a 25-percent cash outlay for foreclosure-related expenses.

Example: For a AAA credit rating, a rating agency assumes a 15-percent frequency of foreclosure and a 47-percent severity of loss. Thus, 15 percent $\times$ 47 percent = 7-percent coverage required. That means that the amount of pool insurance required for an AAA rating is 7 percent of the initial aggregate mortgage principal of the pool.

For a AA credit rating, a 10-percent frequency and a 40-percent loss is assumed. Thus, 10-percent $\times$ 40-percent = 4-percent coverage required for a AA credit rating.

Note that a higher credit rating requires more insurance to cover the assumption of greater risk.

Credit Rating

The rating a private conventional MBS receives from a rating agency is very important since that rating helps establish the yield requirements of investors. Ratings depend on three major items:

- type of mortgages in the pool,
- experience of the servicer,
- pool mortgage insurance.

The so-called prime pool, which gets the highest rating, consists of mortgages that fit within the parameters established by a rating agency in the following table. Other types of properties can be in a pool, but the required amount of pool insurance will be higher since the perceived risk is higher.

CHARACTERISTICS OF PRIME MORTGAGE COLLATERAL POOL

Mortgage Security:	First lien on single-family (one-unit) detached properties.
Mortgage Payment:	Fixed-rate, level payment, fully amortizing loans.
Mortgagor Status:	Mortgagor's primary residences.
Location of Properties:	Well-dispersed throughout an area having a strong diversified economic base.
Mortgage Size:	Less than FNMA/FHLMC maximums.
Loan-to-Value:	80 percent or less.
Mortgage Documentation:	FNMA/FHLMC uniform documents.

Since a conventional MBS is a pass-through, an investor is ensured its monthly cash flow from the servicer. If the servicer does not collect it from the mortgagors, the servicer pays it out of its own pocket. Thus, the financial strength of the servicer is also of concern to the rating agency.

Mortgage Bonds

In contrast with the equity position an investor has with a pass-through, a mortgage bond puts an investor in a creditor position with a pool of mortgages serving as collateral. Since the issuer is in a debtor position, mortgage bonds are carried on the balance sheet as a liability. Two types of bonds have been used: the pay-through or cash flow bond and the straight or traditional bond. The Collateralized Mortgage Obligation is a type of bond but is unique enough that it is discussed separately.

Pay-Through Bond

The primary difference between the two mortgage bonds is how the mortgages are given value. With the pay-through bond, the mortgages serve as the source of cash flow to pay off the bond. The monthly principal and interest collected from the mortgagor—the cash flow—is used to make the bond interest payment. That payment can be monthly, quarterly, or semi-annually.

Pay-through bonds have the ability to stand on their own since the cash flow necessary to make the bond interest payment comes from the mortgages that are serving as the security. The cash flow generated by the underlying mortgages is put in the hands of a fiduciary—a trustee. This action removes the possibility that the funds could be seized by creditors of the issuer if the issuer gets into financial difficulty. Therefore, with the cash flow going to a trustee, the money is able to flow through to investors.

Straight Bond

Generally, whenever any debt instrument is issued investors require some security. The security for a pay-through bond is the cash flow from a pool of mortgages. Contrast that type with the so-called straight bond, which also puts the investor in a creditor position. The straight bond investor has in effect loaned money to the issuer. This debt obligation is very similar to a corporate bond, but the security is the market value of a pool of mortgages.

For example, if a $50-million bond is issued, the issuer will put as many mortgages into the pool as necessary to produce a market value of $50 million. This could require $100 million at 7 percent if the market rate is 14 percent.

Obviously, with this type of bond there is an underlying risk that the market might change quickly. In the early 1980s, mortgage yields in the marketplace could change 100 basis points in a month. In that situation, an investor that owned this type of bond would see the value of the security plummet. In order to protect investors, issuers were required to keep in the pool a sufficient number of mortgages with a market value equal to the issue outstanding. If the value of the mortgages in the pool drops because the market yield is increasing, the issuer is obligated to put more mortgages into the pool. In early issues the trustee would in effect "mark to market" the mortgages in the pool every six months. The current practice is to evaluate the mortgages in the pool quarterly with the issuer obligated to put more mortgages into the pool if the market value has decreased.

ISSUERS OF CONVENTIONAL MBSs

Federal Home Loan Mortgage Corporation (FHLMC)

Freddie Mac, as it is normally called, was the first issuer of conventional MBSs in 1971, when it sold Participation Certificates (PCs) backed by conventional loans purchased from savings and loan associations. Today, Freddie Mac continues to issue PCs, but they can be backed by conventional mortgages (fixed rate or adjustable rate) purchased under the cash program from any mortgage lender. The guarantee on the timely payment of principal and interest on PCs issued by Freddie Mac is in its own name and not that of the federal government, thus there has always been a slight decrease in the yield to investors when compared to Ginnie Mae securities.

At the end of 1994, approximately $500 billion of Freddie Mac PCs were outstanding. Of that total, approximately 12 percent were ARM securities.

Federal National Mortgage Association (FNMA)

Fannie Mae, as it is normally called, was a decade behind Freddie Mac when it issued its first MBS in October 1981 but now has surpassed its primary competitor. Fannie Mae backs MBSs consisting of either fixed-rate or adjustable-rate type mortgages, which can be either conventional or FHA/VA mortgages. By the end of 1994, Fannie Mae had over $550 billion in MBSs outstanding. Of that total, approximately 9 percent were ARM securities.

In 1987 Fannie Mae introduced a new concept with its "Fannie Majors" program under which mortgage originators could combine their mortgage loans into a multiple lender MBS. The lender received back a portion of the larger MBS equal to the principal amount of mortgages they had contributed to the pool. This process provided the benefits of geographical diversification to small lenders.

MORTGAGE-BACKED SECURITIES OUTSTANDING BY TYPE (DOLLARS IN BILLIONS)

Year	GNMA	FHLMC	FNMA	Private	Total
1980	$ 94	$ 17	$ 0	N.A.	$ 111
1985	212	100	55	N.A.	367
1990	401	316	300	$ 53	1,070
1992	420	408	445	132	1,405
1994 (est.)	440	480	550	205	1,675

Sources: GNMA, FNMA, FHLMC, Merrill Lynch.

Both Fannie Mae and Freddie Mac can only issue MBSs backed by mortgages (fixed rate or adjustable rate) with a principal balance below their conforming loan limit. Critics of Fannie Mae and Freddie Mac state that these government-related agencies have an unfair advantage over private competitors in the MBS area in particular and the secondary mortgage market in general. The advantages these government-sponsored enterprises have include access to capital markets at government or near-government rates and exemptions from many securities laws.

The federal government has supported the growth of a private secondary mortgage market and MBSs in the 1990s by introducing legislation to remove some of the advantages these government-related agencies had in the past.

Private Issuers of MBSs

Many private MBSs are sponsored by or affiliated with private mortgage insurance companies that use the conduit concept. Other private issuers are Wall Street companies and large financial institutions. A *conduit* works by channeling the originations of a number of traditional mortgage originators into a single security. This is attractive to investors because it provides them with greater economic and geographical diversity in the mortgage pools. Mortgage insurance companies are interested in sponsoring these conduits because both primary mortgage insurance and pool insurance are normally required. The mortgage insurance companies hope this insurance is purchased from them.

Privately issued MBSs have grown rapidly in the 1990s and currently have outstanding over $175 billion in securities representing about 11 percent of total MBSs outstanding.

Prepayment Considerations

Normally, when evaluating capital market securities the yield to maturity is the most important consideration. But with MBSs a prepayment factor seriously impacts all yield calculations. Prepayments occur because people move and sell their homes, refinance, or have other reasons for not letting a mortgage run the full 30 years. For many years, investors used the prepayment assumptions derived from FHA experience. The *FHA experience* is explained by the conclusions drawn from actual FHA studies on the average life of 30-year fixed-rate mortgages. For example, if all FHA mortgages originated in 1960 are examined, the propensity for prepayment can be established, since all have now been paid off. Some of these mortgages were paid off only months after being originated, others paid off after 1, 10, or 20 years, and some were not paid off until the full 30 years had expired. From these studies, it was concluded that 30-year FHA mortgages show a propensity to be repaid in 12 years. Therefore, a pool of mortgages backed by FHA and VA mortgages is going to show the same propensity for repayment as the mortgages in the pool. Based on such studies, it was assumed that a GNMA mortgage-backed security will prepay in 12 years and the yield is calculated on that assumption.

This assumption has been challenged and shown to be very inaccurate during certain interest rate cycles. Further, conventional mortgages have demonstrated a different propensity to prepay than FHA/VA mortgages. For example, when an MBS is said to have a 200-percent experience, it means the pool prepays twice as fast as a pool of FHA/VA mortgages. The assumption also varies based upon when the mortgage was originated. For example, the propensity to prepay a fixed-rate mortgage originated in 1982 at a rate of 17 percent was probably one or two years. On the other hand, fixed-rate mortgages originated in 1993, when rates were as low as 6.75, will have an average life closer to the old FHA assumption of 12 years.

PSA Model

In 1985, the Public Securities Association developed a new model for measuring prepayments—the PSA model. This model is used more often today because it better represents the differences between seasoned securities and new securities. For example, seasoned mortgages have been shown to have a more stable prepayment rate, while new mortgages display very low but increasing prepayment rates over the early months and years of their lives. Securities representing these mortgages should show the same propensity. The PSA model has provided interesting conclusions about the average life of 30-year mortgages. Recently, the model has shown that the average life of a 30-year fixed-rate mortgage originated after 1987 has been less than 5 years. That very short average life is the direct result of the major downward movement of interest rates over that period of time. As rates begin to head upward again, the average life is expected to also increase.

Mortgage-backed securities have accomplished what they were designed to do. They have allowed more dollars to flow into housing. But they are not a perfect invention. There are still some very basic conceptual problems with MBSs. Probably the most important is the irregular cash flow. This refers not to the monthly cash flow but to prepayments. The biggest problem with prepayments is that they usually come at the wrong time. Mortgagors tend to start prepaying when interest rates are falling just when an investor wants to be able to lock in a yield. On the other hand, when interest rates are going up and an investor would like to get some of the money back so it can be reinvested at a higher yield, prepayments fall off.

Call protection is another problem overhanging MBSs. The issue of call protection is also tied into monthly cash flow of principal and interest for some investors. Many investors would like to have an issuer reinvest the cash flow rather than having it flow through. In other words, if an investor puts money out at 10 percent and then interest rates drop, the investor will get the monthly payment of principal and interest, but it probably cannot reinvest it at 10 percent. In this situation, an investor would like some protection on its yield. The problem is that providing active management of an investment trust for mortgages in order to protect yield would incur some tax liabilities.

There are five items to keep in mind when discussing conceptual problems with MBSs. Already discussed are the reinvestment and prepayment risks. There are three others:

1. The market price could change, although that's a risk with any type of commodity subject to market price.
2. Credit risk can also impact liquidity and price of MBSs. Although this risk is not as strong now, in 1981–82 questions surfaced about some of the security issuers. The credit risk concerns the ability of a servicer to make required payments if mortgagors default.
3. A liquidity risk exists, which concerns the ability to resell a security. There is no liquidity risk with GNMA, FNMA, or FHLMC because of their real or perceived link with the federal government, but as more financial and nonfinancial institutions issue MBSs there may be some initial liquidity risk until the marketplace has fully accepted the integrity of the issuer.

_____ *COLLATERALIZED MORTGAGE OBLIGATION (CMO)*

As has been mentioned, the lack of any call protection was a major impediment preventing nontraditional mortgage investors and others from becoming extensive purchasers of MBSs. This problem has been addressed to a degree by Collateralized Mortgage Obligations (CMOs), which were introduced by FHLMC in 1983.

These debt instruments have been described as serial pay-through bonds that allow for any nonscheduled payments (prepayments) to be distributed first to one of the various classes of holders.

As an example, the first FHLMC CMO has three classes of holders with different maturities:

Class I   3.2 years maturity
Class II   8.6 years maturity
Class III   20.4 years maturity

Through semi-annual sinking fund payments, Class I bonds are fully retired before any principal reduction occurs in Class II or III. In other words, all principal payments go to one class until it is fully retired and then to the next. The maturity of each class is derived from the scheduled mortgage cash flow and the prepayment assumptions based on the characteristics of the mortgages in the pool. The PSA model is used to predict prepayments rather than the older, less accurate FHA experience. By investing in CMOs, investors have some degree of assurance that their investment will earn the stated yield and not be "called" before maturity. This has been a successful answer to the call issue, and many other issuers have joined FHLMC in issuing CMOs.

Problems with CMOs

The desired result with CMOs was to provide call protection to investors while avoiding "active management," which would trigger taxation. The Internal Revenue Service challenged the sought-after tax status in the so-called Sears Regulation, which resulted in a Sears CMO offering being denied trust tax status. In order for CMOs to get the desired tax status, the offering had to resemble a debt obligation, but this form created certain accounting problems for some issuers. The problem was that debt usually has to be carried on the balance sheet of the issuer, and this was difficult for issuers with capital problems.

REAL ESTATE MORTGAGE INVESTMENT TRUSTS (REMIC)

The 1986 Tax Reform Act provides that any issuer that meets the requirements of the law may be treated as a trust for taxation purposes. The primary purpose of the REMIC legislation was to provide more efficient and flexible financing arrangements than those that existed for CMOs under the prior tax law. The provisions of this law became effective January 1, 1987, and provided that CMOs may continue to be used until January 1, 1992, after which only REMIC would be used. The requirements that issuers had to meet related to the type of mortgages that qualified for REMICs and the trust status and how the cash not yet distributed to security holders could be invested.

Issuers of REMIC are allowed to treat these securities as the sale of assets and not as a debt obligation, which might create capital inadequacy issues. The law did provide, however, for REMIC transactions to be treated as debt for accounting purposes while reporting it as a sale of assets for tax purposes. These new provisions result in taxation only on the security holders.

Another important provision of the Tax Reform Act was that thrifts who purchased REMICs could include these securities in the classification of qualified real estate investments for thrifts. This allows for thrifts to qualify for the bad debt deduction tax benefit.

The Tax Reform Act also changed the existing law, which had stipulated that foreign purchasers of pass-through securities were subject to a 30-percent withholding tax. By the removal of this withholding tax, REMICs became much more attractive to foreign purchasers.

SELLING MBSs TO INVESTORS

To date, three ways of offering MBSs to investors have been used. A private placement is an offering of a security usually to only one investor, although more than one could be involved. Terms are negotiated up front directly between the issuer and the investor. The negotiations establish the type of security, type of coupon, yield, geographic diversity, and discount. Because terms are negotiated up front, the mortgages that will be in the pool may not yet have been originated; thus, delivery will be sometime in the future, possibly not for six to nine months. Since it's a private placement and not an offering to the public, there is no requirement for Securities and Exchange Commission (SEC) registration. This fact can save money and time, although many investors may still require SEC registration since they may want to market these securities in the future. Also, there is no requirement for a bond rating with a private placement, but if an investor wants to sell these bonds later a rating would be important. The underwriting fee is fairly modest: 25 to 100 basis points. Usually the first time a new type of MBS is issued, it is sold in a private placement. Later, once there is some experience with the new MBS and market acceptance, the new type of MBS can become a public issue.

A public-institutional offering is one made to a fairly large number of financial institutions. In this situation, the terms are negotiated between the issuer and the underwriter. After terms are established the underwriter sells these terms to interested institutions. Since the mortgages have probably already been originated, delivery can be almost immediate. This is a public issue; therefore, an SEC requirement exists along with a bond rating for marketability. The underwriting fee for this offering is still a fairly modest 50 to 100 basis points.

Finally, there is the public-retail offering. This has not been as popular recently but could be an area for future expansion. These MBSs are sold both to institutions and individual investors. Some of the bonds offered in the late 1970s were public-retail, but now about the only public-retail offerings are revenue bonds. Since this is a public offering, SEC registration is required, as well as a bond rating. Underwriters have been taking 250 to 500 basis points as a fee in public-retail offerings, and this has drastically cut the yield to the individual and thus acceptance.

RESIDENTIAL REAL ESTATE APPRAISAL ——— *12*

Throughout the economic activity of humankind, no meaningful business decision is made, nor does any significant investment of any type occur, without an appraisal first being made. The purpose of all appraisals is to establish an estimate of value. As is discussed later, there are many different types of appraisals designed for many different types of investment decisions.

The objective of this chapter is to provide an overview of the fundamentals of residential real estate appraisals, define the standard terminology used, and explain the common methodology of estimating value. Because of important recent developments in this field, new students of residential mortgage lending are encouraged to do additional reading or take further course work in appraising residential real estate. Care should be exercised in realizing that what is sought in a residential appraisal is a clearly described estimate of value by a well-trained professional.

VALUE

Value is generally defined as the relationship between an object desired and the person desiring it. It is the ability of one commodity to command another commodity, usually money, in exchange. Tying value to price, one can say that value, stated as a price, is that point where supply and demand coincide or intersect. In other words, the value of an object to an individual is generally equal to the price paid for the object by the same individual. It is also quite subjective. You or I might not pay the same price for this same object; thus its value to us is different.

PURPOSE OF THE APPRAISAL

In order to properly underwrite a residential mortgage loan application, an appraisal of the property being proposed as security is required. The primary

201

purpose of an appraisal to a mortgage lender is to estimate the value of the real estate. Not only is the appraisal a requirement of state and federal laws and regulations, but it is a requirement to sell the loan in the secondary mortgage market.

UNIFORM RESIDENTIAL APPRAISAL REPORT

Appraisers and the appraisal process were under intense scrutiny in the mid- to late 1980s because of the extremely high residential delinquency rates and resulting losses to the mortgage industry. Individual mortgage companies, investors, and mortgage insurance companies all experienced terrible losses because of higher than anticipated real estate losses. Many of these important players in the real estate lending business blamed the high losses on inflated and poorly prepared appraisals. The Federal National Mortgage Association and several private mortgage insurance companies were among the more vocal in their criticism of the current level of appraisal practices. As a result of this criticism and a desire to improve their profession, the various appraisal organizations worked with the five government agencies involved in residential real estate to develop a single form acceptable to all agencies.

By the fall of 1986 a new appraisal form, known as the Uniform Residential Appraisal Report (URAR) was agreed to by all interested parties. This form was then revised, and beginning on January 1, 1993, this revised URAR was required by the Federal National Mortgage Association, the Federal Home Loan Mortgage Corporation, the Federal Housing Administration, the Veterans Administration, and the Farmers Home Administration.

In 1986, the various appraisal organizations also developed a set of professional practice standards that govern appraisers in preparing the Uniform Residential Appraisal Report. These standards represented an important step forward for the profession, since they are the first uniform standards ever adopted by the appraisal industry as a whole. These standards are called the Uniform Standards for Professional Appraisal Practice, or USPAP.

Attesting to the increased use of personal computers in real estate, the new appraisal report form is designed to be used with various computer appraisal software programs. Use of this form allows appraisers to produce professional reports that are self-contained and logically support the final value estimate given.

UNIFORM STANDARDS OF PROFESSIONAL APPRAISAL PRACTICE

The Financial Institution Reform, Recovery, and Enforcement Act (FIRREA) also addressed the issue of appraisals as a part of the real estate lending process and formally adopted the Uniform Standards of Professional Appraisal Practice as developed by the various appraisal organizations. This process was facilitated by the appraisal industry through the nonprofit body known as the Appraisal Foundation. The FIRREA legislation also required that beginning on January 1, 1993, all real estate transactions needing an appraisal must include one performed by either a state licensed or certified appraiser. A licensed appraiser is one who possesses a basic level of skills and education in real estate appraising sufficient to prepare a "noncomplex" residential assignment. A certified residential appraiser is one whose experience and education level is such that they are qualified to handle all residential properties, in particular those deemed complex or above a certain transaction level, currently $1 million.

PRINCIPLES OF REAL ESTATE VALUE

An appraisal may be required to provide an estimate of value at almost any stage of a real estate transaction or activity. For example, at any given moment an appraisal of real estate may be needed to estimate:

- market value for mortgage lending purposes,
- assessed value for taxation purposes,
- insurance value,
- market value for sale or exchange purposes,
- compensation for condemnation/municipal acquisition,
- investment value for rental income purposes.

The value determined for the same piece of real estate can vary according to the ultimate purpose of the appraisal assignment; the estimated value for insurance purposes could be much different than the value estimated for condemnation purposes. In this discussion, the value to be estimated for mortgage lending purposes must always be "market value," since most mortgage lenders are regulated by law to lend according to a certain percentage of market value.

Market Value

Market value is defined by the Appraisal Foundation and the Uniform Standards of Professional Appraisal Practice as "the most probable price which a property should bring in a competitive and open market under all conditions requisite to a fair sale, the buyer and seller, each acting prudently and knowledgeably, and assuming the price is not affected by undue stimulus." Implicit in this definition is the consummation of sale as of a specific date and the passing of title from seller to buyer under conditions whereby:

1. buyer and seller are typically motivated,
2. both parties are well informed and well advised and acting in what they consider their best interests,

3. a reasonable time is allowed for exposure in the open market,
4. payment is in terms of cash in U.S. dollars or in terms of financial arrangements comparable thereto,
5. the price represents the normal consideration for the property sold unaffected by special or creative financing or sales concessions granted by anyone associated with the sale.

Market Price

The market price is that price for which the real estate actually sells. In theory, market value and price should be the same, but they rarely are. For example, a seller may decide to accept less (market price) than asked (presumed market value) in order to facilitate the sale if the seller believes time is more valuable than the difference in money.

Changes to Value

The value of a particular piece of real estate does not remain constant. It changes over time, due to economics and due to the changing tastes of consumers. Value does not constantly go up, as mortgage lenders in the Southwest learned during the early 1980s and in New England during the late 1980s. For example, during 1986–87 it was not uncommon in some areas of Texas, notably Houston, for real estate values to drop 30 to 40 percent a year. In general, the value of a piece of real estate can change because of:

- population growth or decline,
- economic developments
  —micro or local changes,
  —macro or national changes,
- financial factors, such as
  —the rate of inflation,
  —cost of financing,
  —type of financing available,
- shifts in consumer preference,
- governmental regulations, such as
  —zoning,
  —building codes,
  —taxation,
- shifts in traffic patterns or public transportation,
- physical forces, such as
  —water supply,
  —soil contamination,
  —location on an earthquake fault.

If these factors remain constant, the market value assigned to a given piece of real estate may still change as a result of even more basic value determinants. The most basic is supply and demand. Real estate is similar to all other marketable commodities in that its value is increased or decreased by supply of that commodity and the demand for it. Supply conditions result from the number of housing units available in the market at any given time—the number of new units being constructed and the number of building permits issued, as well as the number of units lost or destroyed. Demand conditions depend on the level of employment, level of income, inflation rates, family size, and saving rates, along with other economic factors of this type.

Market value of real estate is influenced to a great extent by whether the real estate is put to its highest and best use. This use is defined as the use that creates the highest present value. The Uniform Standards state, "Two separate highest and best uses exist for each property site: one for the site as though it were vacant, and one for the site as though it were improved. The first looks through the existing building as though it did not exist and estimates the best use of the site as if it were vacant. The second estimates the best use of the site and building(s) with all improvements together."

All of this must be determined following four important considerations. In order for a particular use to be the highest and the best, it must be:

- physically possible,
- legally permissible,
- appropriate for the neighborhood,
- produce the highest present value.

The principle of diminishing returns recognizes that continuing additions to the whole will not continue to increase the value of the whole by the value of the additions after a certain point. For example, if we add a second bathroom to a house the value of the property might increase by an amount equal to the cost of the new bathroom. But if we add a third bathroom, the value will increase by an amount greatly less than the cost of the additional bathroom.

Finally, the principle of substitution demonstrates that the upper range of value for a piece of property tends to be established by the cost of acquiring an equally desirable substitute property, or the cost of building a similar structure.

THE APPRAISAL PROCESS

The first step in the appraisal process is to plan the appraisal. Since the appraisal is intended to solve a problem, that is to estimate value, it must be clearly stated as to what type of value is being sought. The process required to produce this estimate of value necessitates identification of the following:

- the real estate to be appraised,
- the type of value being sought,
- the effective date of the appraisal,
- the character of the property,
- property rights,
- the character of the market in which the property is located.

The next step in the appraisal process is to identify the data that the appraiser will need. The data required by the appraiser can be found in the public records, from mortgage lenders, from other appraisers, or from real estate agents. Other sources could include the local chamber of commerce, planning

THE APPRAISAL PROCESS

Definition of the Problem

Identify real estate	Identify rights	Date of value	Objective of appraisal	Definition of value

↓

Preliminary Survey and Appraisal Plan

Data needed	Data sources	Personnel needed	Time schedule	Completion flowchart

↓

Data Collection and Analysis

General Data		*Specific Data*	
Locational	*Economic*	*Subject Property*	*Comparative*
Region	Market	Title	Costs
City	Analysis	Site	Sales
Neighborhood	Financial	Physical	Rentals
etc.	Economic base	Highest and best use	Expenses
	Trends		

↓

Application of the Three Approaches

Cost   Market data   Income

↓

Reconciliation of Value Indications

↓

Final Estimate of Defined Value

and zoning authorities, and even local home builders. Finally, the appraiser has the professional dual responsibilities of keeping this data current and relying only on accurate data.

Alternative Approaches to Value

In developing a real estate appraisal, an appraiser is required to use three very specific appraisal techniques. Each of these "approaches" or techniques is most appropriate under certain circumstances, and the combination of the three is intended to provide the most complete solution to the appraisal problem. For most mortgage loans the method that best addresses the problem of determining the value of a residential property is the direct sales comparison approach.

Direct Sales Comparison Approach

This approach relies on the concept or principle that an informed and rational purchaser will pay no more for a property than the price or cost of a substitute property with the same characteristics and utility. As a result, this approach works on the ability to locate similar or "comparable" properties that have recently sold in that neighborhood. Recognizing that no two properties are identical, through an appropriate adjustment process, the two homes can be compared and an adjusted price can be developed. The principle of substitution is evident with this approach since the value of a property similar to the subject property should closely approximate the value of the subject property.

An appraiser uses as many recent sales of similar or comparable properties as possible; the more used, the more accurate is the estimate. The URAR requires the use of at least three comparable sales. The market prices of the comparables are adjusted for whatever physical differences exist between the comparable and the subject property. The rule of thumb used by appraisers is that comparables are always "adjusted to" the subject property. If the subject has a feature and the comparable does not, a positive adjustment is made to the comparable. If the subject lacks a feature present in the comparable, a negative adjustment is made to the comparable. The basic formula is as follows:

Sales Price of the Comparable + or − the Adjustment = Value of the Subject

---

Example: If House A with a finished basement worth $15,000 currently sells for $115,000 and is otherwise comparable to House B, except for the finished basement, then the estimate of value for House B would be $100,000: House A value of $115,000 − $15,000 for the finished basement = House B value of $100,000.

Financing Concessions

A complicating factor in using this approach is that the sales price of any property may have been established because of certain financing concessions. The seller, for example, may have paid all of the buyer's closing costs, paid to buy down the interest rate, or paid some other concession to facilitate the sale. This is done to increase the speed of selling the property or to increase the number of buyers capable of buying the property. The net result of these actions is that the sales price is raised to cover the cost of providing these concessions. The appraiser must take these items into consideration when preparing an appraisal that relies on comparables with these characteristics. This is important to a mortgage lender because the mortgage should be secured by real estate alone and not by real estate plus some concession. To assist the appraiser with this type of problem, a mortgage lender is required to provide the appraiser with as much information on the sale as possible. This includes providing a copy of the sales contract. In fact, the Uniform Standards require the appraiser to request a copy of the sales contract during the information-gathering phase of the appraisal.

Cost Approach

This approach is the second most important method used for estimating the market value for residential real estate. It involves an estimate of the current cost of production, which is defined as the reproduction cost, or the cost to build an exact replica of the improvements. This approach can also be stated as cost less accrued depreciation, plus the value of the land. When figuring costs, both direct costs (such as supplies, labor, and profits) and indirect costs (such as fees, taxes, and financing costs) are taken into consideration. In addition, an appraiser considers that the subject property will not be the same as a reproduced structure because of depreciation. Therefore, adjustments must be made to the reproduction cost to reflect any existing depreciation. This includes:

- Physical deterioration. A loss in value from the cost of a new structure is equal to the loss of economic life in the subject property caused by wear and tear. This physical deterioration may or may not be curable.
- Functional obsolescence. A loss in value resulting from structural components, such as bathrooms, or in the overall design or layout of the structure that is outmoded or inefficient, as judged by current standards.
- Economic obsolescence. A loss in value resulting from changes external to the property such as changes in zoning classifications, traffic patterns, or environmental hazards.

The cost approach can be explained using the formula:

$$\text{Cost of Reproduction} - \text{Depreciation} + \text{Land Value} = \text{Value of the Subject Property}$$

Example: Assume the appraisal assignment is to estimate the value of a 10-year-old Cape Cod that has depreciated 15 percent. The cost of building a comparable structure is $185,000. The estimate of value is made in this way: cost of reproduction is $185,000 − $27,750 (15 percent)= $157,250 + land value = value of the subject property.

Income Approach

The income approach to estimating market value uses the net operating income of the property. Although the sales comparison approach and the cost approach seem more applicable to residential real estate, the income approach seems better suited for income-producing properties, such as offices or apartment buildings. The value of this method for residential real estate is valid in that it does reflect the choice that the buyer has in the marketplace. The concept is that there is a relationship between the rental income a property earns and the price someone would prudently pay for that property. From the buyer's standpoint, why should the buyer pay more for a property when he or she can rent a similar property for less? The income approach allows the appraiser to compare rents with market prices.

Obviously, this approach makes the most sense for those properties that have or can produce rental income. But a special technique called the gross rent multiplier (GRM) can be used to either estimate value for a single-family residence or serve as a check against the other approaches. The theory behind the GRM is that the same economic influences affect both sales prices and rents. This relationship can be expressed as a ratio:

$$\frac{\text{Sales Price}}{\text{Gross Monthly Rental Income}} = \text{GRM}$$

Example: If a house recently sold for $125,000 and was rented for $750 per month, the GRM would be:

$$\frac{\$115,000}{\$750} = 153.33, \text{ say } 153$$

Thus, if the appraisal assignment is to estimate the value of another similar property that is being rented for $675 per month, the result would be: $675 × 153 = $103,275, say $103,000 (value of the subject house using the income approach).

Reconciliation and Final Value Estimate

Although most appraisal problems call for a single final estimate of market value, the Uniform Standards require that the appraiser consider all three approaches on the way toward the final estimate of value. While each method can serve as a check against the other approaches, it is true that certain types of properties lend themselves more to one method than the others. For example, the cost approach would lend itself to a property currently under construction, and the income approach would apply best to a duplex rental property.

In most situations, the estimates of value using all three approaches should be fairly similar. If the estimates are widely divergent, the data-gathering method and analysis for each approach should be carefully reviewed. If the estimates remain far apart, the appraiser must consider the purpose of the appraisal. If the appraisal is to estimate market value for mortgage lending purposes, the sales comparison approach is most important. For insurance claim purposes, the cost approach may be most important. If on the other hand the subject property is a residential rental property, then the income approach is the most applicable.

It is in the correlation of value that an appraiser's skill and experience comes to the forefront and the problem of estimating market value is resolved. This reconciliation process and final value estimate is not simply a mathematical exercise. It is, however, a process of judgment, analysis, and reason that will result in a professional, logical, and supportable estimate of market value.

Required Forms

The residential appraisal report must be submitted to a mortgage lender on the current appraisal forms. These include:

- single-family property—URAR (FNMA Form 1004/FHLMC Form 70),
- two- to four-family property—Small Residential Income Property Form (FNMA Form 1025/FHLMC Form 72),
- condominium or cooperatives—Individual Condominium Form (FNMA Form 1073/FHLMC Form 465),
- PUD properties—URAR Form or Individual Condominium Form.

The following attachments must be a part of each appraisal report:

- original photos of the subject property (front, rear, and street),
- original photos of the comparable sales (front),
- location map showing the subject and the comparable sales,
- exterior sketch of the subject dwelling, with measurements,
- Certification and Statement of Limiting Conditions (FNMA Form 1004B),
- addendum warranting compliance with all pertinent FIRREA requirements.

Age of Appraisal Report

The appraisal report must be signed and dated within 120 days of the date the mortgage loan was closed. If an appraisal is older than that (up to 180 days), it can be updated by the original appraiser certifying that the value has not declined since the original appraisal was prepared. (FNMA and FHLMC allow the appraisal to be no more than 180 days old from the date the loan closes if the property is considered new construction.) If the appraisal report is older than one year, a new appraisal is required.

CLOSING THE RESIDENTIAL LOAN ═══ *13*

After a decision to grant a residential mortgage loan is made (either by an authorized individual or a loan committee), the mortgage lending process proceeds to closing the mortgage loan. Before the actual closing can occur, a number of other events must happen. For example, the title to the real estate that will secure the loan must be examined to determine if the seller actually owns the property and if any other liens or encumbrances exist. The result of this examination of the seller's title is a title insurance policy protecting the lender. Mortgagors can also purchase title insurance protecting their interest. Depending on state law, a survey may also be needed (in some states, the title insurance policy contains a clause covering survey matters and thus a separate survey is generally not required).

MORTGAGE CLOSING

A mortgage transaction is closed by the delivery of the mortgage (or deed of trust) and note to the mortgage lender and the disbursement of the mortgage funds to the mortgagor or pursuant to the mortgagor's direction. The term *loan closing* as used in residential mortgage lending refers to the process of:

- formulating, executing, and delivering all documents required to create an obligation to repay a debt and to create a valid security instrument,
- disbursing the mortgage funds,
- protecting the security interest of the lender or investor (e.g., recording).

A clear distinction should be drawn between this type of closing and a real estate sales closing in which a different set of documents is required, such as a purchase agreement, deed, sales contract, and a closing statement, among

213

others. Of course, as is typical, when the sale of real estate also involves financing, both sets of documents or a combination of the two are usually required.

Most of the steps necessary to close a mortgage loan and create a valid security interest in the real estate are governed by state law. As a result, this text cannot establish the *exact* requirements for closing any residential mortgage loan. Mortgage lenders must be careful to understand the requirements of their state, and the best way to understand these requirements is to have a competent closing agent.

As previously mentioned, RESPA must be followed when closing "federally related mortgage loans." Practically all residential mortgage loans today are federally related. Thus, the act requires:

- "good faith" estimate of likely settlement service charges within three business days of application,
- lender to provide the HUD booklet, "Settlement Cost and You,"
- use of a HUD settlement sheet,
- limits on escrow (or impounds) accounts.

Process of Loan Closing

The process of loan closing actually begins with the mortgage application and the issuance of a commitment letter and concludes in the exchange of documents and funds and the recording of all pertinent instruments. It is important to realize that a loan closing is not the end of the mortgage lending cycle, which continues through servicing until the loan is finally repaid or refinanced.

Commitment Letter

Although most residential mortgage lenders use a commitment letter to inform an applicant that the application has been approved and what the conditions of the loan are, some lenders do not. Lenders that don't use a commitment letter should review that policy with a view toward using one. The commitment letter serves as the lender's acceptance of the mortgagor's application as submitted. If the lender makes a counteroffer then that offer must be accepted by the applicant. The commitment letter is what creates the contractual right of the borrower to receive a mortgage loan.

Besides the legal implications of a commitment letter, lenders should look at the marketing or public relations benefit of using a commitment letter. The letter can start off by congratulating the applicant on the approval of the mortgage loan. The letter can then spell out the specifics of the loan for which the applicant has been approved by listing the amount of the loan, term of the loan, interest rate, etc. This letter can also tell the applicant that he or she must

MORTGAGE LOAN COMMITMENT

Staten Island Savings Bank
15 Beach Street, Staten Island, N.Y. 10304
(718) 447-7900

L E N D E R

TO: John Smith and Susan Smith
40 Lynn Court
Oceanview, New York 10001

DATE: April 1, 1989
PREMISES: 59 Silver Lane
Staten Island, New York 10315

It is a pleasure to notify you that your application for a first/second mortgage loan has been approved subject to the following matters set forth below and on the reverse side hereof.

AMOUNT, TERMS AND FEES

Amount of Loan ....$ 80,000.00	Contract Interest Rate........ 10.50 %
* Loan Origination Fee ....$ 800.00	Annual Percentage Rate .... 10.7727 %
Loan Discount Fee ....$ n/a	Appraisal Fee ....$ 225.00 Pd.
Lenders Inspection Fee ....$ n/a	Credit Report Fee ....$ 37.00 Pd.
PMI Initial Premium..........$ n/a	Non-Refundable Stand-by Fee ..$ 800.00
Application Fee ....$ 100.00 Pd.	(Please Remit)
..........................$	Total amount to be paid: $1,600.00

*Non-refundable fee

REPAYMENT TERMS

☒ **Standard Fixed Payment Mortgage** Purchase – 30 Year Fixed Rate
To be repaid in __160__ equal monthly installments of $ 731.80 (principal and interest) with the first monthly installment due approximately 30 days after date of settlement, plus 1/12th of the annual tax and water and/or sewer charges, hazard and mortgage insurance premiums. All payments will be due on the first of each month.

☐ **Adjustable Rate Mortgage**
To be repaid in equal monthly installments of $_____ (principal and interest) for the initial adjustment period of _____ year(s), plus 1/12th of the annual tax and water and/or sewer charges, hazard and mortgage insurance premiums. All payments will be due on the first of each month. The above stated Contract Interest Rate shall be considered the "Initial Interest Rate" only, and can increase or decrease subject to the limitations in the Disclosure you received following application date.

EVIDENCE OF TITLE

Counsel for the Lender will order and examine title and prepare the note and mortgage and all related documents. The costs of these services together with disbursements are to be paid by you at the time of closing or upon demand. Title shall be subject to the approval of Lender's Counsel.

ADDITIONAL REQUIRED ITEMS OR CONDITIONS

All Items Checked ☒ Below Apply:
☐ Signed Sales Contract — required
☐ Plat of survey, acceptable to Lender, showing the improvements to be properly within the lot lines and no encroachments on other properties — required.
☐ Copy of present Evidence of Title showing Legal Description needed.
☐ The attached list of repairs is to be completed prior to settlement or an escrow in the amount of $_____ will be held until the work is satisfactorily completed.
☐ We will pay out on the Loan upon completion of the building, subject to a satisfactory Compliance Inspection Report by our Appraiser and a Certificate of Occupancy from the Governing Municipality.
☐ A Contractors Statement and Supporting Waivers of Lien are to be provided.
☐ Flood Insurance Mandatory, see reverse
☐ Notice of Recission, see attached
☒ Fire Insurance required in the amount of $ 80,000.00 , see reverse
☐ Private Mortgage Insurance is required. A certified or bank check in the amount of $_____ made payable to _____ must be presented at closing.
☐ _____

SEE REVERSE

The Continuation of Commitment Conditions is on the reverse and is made a part of this Commitment.

INSTRUCTIONS

This commitment will not become effective until the signed Disclosure Statement (if applicable) is received by the Lender together with your signed acceptance and your check to our order in the amount of $ 1,600.00 . This offer will be withdrawn unless accepted by you within TEN (10) DAYS, and further, the mortgage loan must close on or before __May 31, 1989__ or the commitment will be cancelled.

I (WE) hereby accept the terms and Conditions of this Commitment.

_____ John Smith _____ 4/6/89
Borrower   Date

_____ Susan Smith _____ 4/6/89
Borrower   Date

_____   _____
Borrower   Date

_____   _____
Borrower   Date

"LENDER FILE COPY"

COMMITMENT ISSUED BY: tmt

_____ Barry W. White _____
Authorized Signature

---

have a hazard insurance policy or binder at closing and how the mortgagee payable clause should read. In addition, a lender can inform the applicant of a need for flood insurance, what the closing fees will be, the date of closing, and other items. The issuance of a commitment letter should be a policy for all residential mortgage lenders.

Essential documents that should be contained in a complete residential mortgage file vary by state as well as by the type of loan—conventional or FHA/VA. A lender's peculiar requirements can also add to the list. As in any discussion involving legal documents, a review of the requirements of each state's law is required. When establishing a loan closing process, competent counsel should be consulted on state law concerning any of the documents discussed.

The Handling of the Loan Closing

The loan closing, depending on the law or custom in the jurisdiction, can be handled by any of the following:

- outside attorney for either the seller or buyer,
- escrow agent,
- title insurance company,
- staff of the mortgage lender.

Insured Closings

In most situations an insured closing is required. Today, most investors require insured closings. An insured closing agent can be anyone, such as an attorney, who has been approved and accepted by a title company. The title company is, in effect, insuring that the loan was closed according to the lender's directions as well as the title company's requirements and that they are insuring against any fraud or dishonesty on the part of the loan closer.

At one time, most closings were handled by an outside attorney, and many still are, but more and more mortgage lenders have staff members who are qualified loan closers. They have the competency to prepare and analyze all necessary closing documents and as a general rule, they can do it cheaper than an outside attorney. Care must be taken, though, to ascertain whether state law requires a licensed attorney to close a loan.

Whichever method is used, the purpose of the loan closing is to ensure that the loan is closed according to all laws of that state. The expected result, of course, is to provide the mortgage lender with a first lien on the property.

There are many types of loan closings including the closing of construction loans, loans to be warehoused, and loans with permanent investors. This chapter is concerned primarily with the closing of a permanent residential mortgage loan.

Steps in Closing a Residential Mortgage Loan

When the underwriter has indicated that the loan application is acceptable, certain steps should be taken to close the loan. These steps include the following:

1. advise applicant of loan acceptance by a commitment letter (and, if applicable, set rate, terms, etc.),
2. order final title report (and survey if separate) and any other documents or verifications still outstanding,
3. schedule closing and prepare closing documents,
4. conduct closing, obtain all required signatures, and disburse funds,
5. return all closing documents to mortgage lender for inclusion in loan file,
6. record mortgage.

DOCUMENTS REQUIRED

The following documents are discussed relative to the closing of a residential mortgage loan. The process of gathering, producing, and preparing the necessary documents and the careful checking of all forms is often referred to as a preclosing procedure. The documents normally required in a closed residential mortgage loan file appear following. Mortgage lenders should realize that in some states, additional documents may be required by state law or custom. Mortgage loan documents need not appear in any particular order in a loan file. However, some secondary mortgage market transactions may require the documents in a specified order.

Lenders may want to have printed on the inside cover of their loan files the documents that should be in that file. In that way, lenders can double-check that all required documents are in the file.

The following documents are listed in alphabetical order with a discussion of the reason for the required document. A few examples of these documents are found as exhibits in this chapter; others are found in the case study in Chapter 16.

Adjustable rate rider. If the mortgage is an adjustable-rate mortgage, a statement signed by the borrower acknowledging that he or she understands that the interest rate could increase should be in the loan file.

ARM disclosure. A separate disclosure explaining each ARM loan with 13 specific disclosures, plus the booklet "Consumer Handbook on ARMs," must be given to ARM applicants.

Application. Both the original and the typed final application are required for a closed loan. Be sure all lines are completed and all required signatures appear.

 **NFCU MORTGAGE LOAN REQUIREMENTS FORM**

The following information is provided to members who are applying for mortgage financing from NFCU and is intended to assist you in understanding what is required to complete processing of your loan. Your loan processor will notify you of any additional requirements applicable to your mortgage transaction.

Selection of Settlement Agent: You may select your own settlement agent to close your loan transaction or one recommended by NFCU. All settlement agents must meet NFCU requirements; If the one you select has not previously been approved by NFCU, the agent must provide NFCU with a Standard Closing Protection Letter at least one week prior to settlement, issued by the title insurance company which will insure the title to the property you are purchasing.

Title Insurance: You will be obligated to purchase a lender's title insurance policy, protecting NFCU's interest as mortgagee in the property, with coverage for at least the amount of your loan. Your settlement agent normally will obtain this insurance in your behalf.

Survey: The survey shows the location and dimensions of the property you are purchasing (land and structure) including all easements, rights of way, encroachments, and flood zone certification. The settlement agent will normally assist you in obtaining a current survey.

Hazard Insurance: This provides insurance protection to a dwelling and its contents in the case of fire or wind damage, theft, liability for property damage, and personal liability. You will be required to obtain a hazard insurance policy with the mortgagee clause reading as follows:

Navy Federal Credit Union, its successors and assigns
Security Place
P. O. Box 3303
Merrifield, VA 22119-3303

This policy must provide coverage for the amount of your loan or the replacement cost of the dwelling, whichever is less with a deductible amount not exceeding $500. The original policy (an insurance binder is acceptable for this requirement for properties in the state of Maryland) and a paid receipt for the first year's premium must be in NFCU's possession five days prior to settlement.

Escrow Account: NFCU requires that an escrow account be established for the payment of hazard insurance premiums; private mortgage and/or flood insurance premiums, if applicable; property taxes; special assessments and ground rent, if any. Your settlement agent will notify you of the initial deposits required to establish your escrow account. Dividends will be paid on this acocunt at the same rate and conditions as share savings accounts.

Termite/Soil Treatment Guarantee: A termite certificate from a licensed termite/pest exterminator guaranteeing that the property is free of infestation must be submitted to NFCU prior to settlement. If the property is new construction, a 5 year soil treatment guarantee is required in lieu of a termite guarantee.

Well/Septic Inspection: If the property you are purchasing has a well and/or septic sewer system, written evidence must be provided showing that the system(s) has/have been inspected and approved within the past 60 days by the local health authority.

Property Inspection: If a final inspection of the property is required to verify that construction or repairs are complete, NFCU must receive a satisfactory final inspection report *prior to settlement*. In the case of a VA or FHA loan, the final inspection must be countersigned by the local VA/FHA office.

Residential Use or Use and Occupancy Permit: (Required for newly constructed residences only.) This permit, issued by the applicable local government authority, certifies that all required preliminary inspections have been completed and approved and that the residence is habitable.

Residency Requirement: NFCU is legally prohibited from funding a mortgage loan if the secured property will not be occupied as your principal residence (unless your loan is classified as a future principal residence). You must occupy the premises as your principal residence (as opposed to rental or vacation property) within 90 days after settlement.

Membership Requirement: All mortgage loan applicants must be members of NFCU. If a borrower or co-borrower is not currently a member but is eligible for membership, we will gladly send a membership application upon receipt of your mortgage loan application.

Please acknowledge receipt of this Mortgage Loan Requirements Form by signing below and returning a copy in the stamped, self-addressed envelope provided. Give the second copy to your sales agent in this transaction.

_____
Signature of Member

_____6-28-92_____
Date

06011992

NFCU 851M (8-88)

Appraisal. An appraisal is required for all real estate loans. If the loan is a single-family detached conventional mortgage, the Uniform Residential Appraisal Report should be used. If another type of residential real estate, care should be exercised that the correct appraisal form is used.

Assignment of mortgage. If the mortgage is being purchased from a mortgage lender who originated it for later sale, an instrument assigning the mortgage to a permanent investor and an estoppel certificate should be included in the loan file.

Building restrictions. Any local building restrictions that affect the mortgaged premises should be contained in the loan file with a statement as to whether this property meets local building restrictions. This may be contained in a lawyer's opinion.

Canceled mortgage. If the loan being closed is for the purpose of refinancing a previous loan, the original mortgage and note should appear in the file and be canceled with the satisfaction of that mortgage recorded.

Certificate of occupancy. In all new construction and refurbishing that requires it, a certificate issued by the local authorities should appear declaring that the building is habitable.

Chattel lien. If personal property is serving as a security in addition to the real estate, a financing statement or other document creating the lien is required.

Closing instructions. These instructions to the closing agent informing him or her of what to do, and how, should be retained to help establish whether the closing was held correctly.

Closing statement. The closing statement for a mortgage closing (like a closing statement for a real estate sale) determines how the proceeds are to be apportioned to the parties. A receipt signed by the mortgagor is required, indicating that loan proceeds have been disbursed according to instructions.

Commitment letter. A commitment letter should be examined closely since it establishes the contractual rights and obligations between the lender and the borrower. Comparison should be made between this commitment letter and the application for the loan to determine if the applicant is receiving everything required. If the mortgage is to be insured, guaranteed, or sold to a third party, those commitment letters should also appear.

Contract of sale. If a loan is requested for the purchase of an existing property, the contract of sale should be in the loan file to verify an actual sale and to assist later in verifying the appraisal of the property.

Credit report. A credit report on the borrower is required on all mortgage loans. The correct credit report for a mortgage loan is a Residential Mortgage Credit Report provided by a local credit bureau with a tie-in to a national repository of credit information.

Deed. If a loan is to purchase real estate or refinance an existing mortgage, a copy of the deed should be included in the loan file along with instructions to record.

Disbursement papers. Instructions are required on how funds are to be delivered to the mortgagor or other involved parties.

Disclosures, federally mandated. In addition to federally mandated disclosures already listed, others needed include notice of right to copy of appraisal, disclosure of whether servicing will be transferred and what percentage had been transferred within past three years, and disclosure of business relationship if a particular provider of services is required.

Escrow. If the transaction involved has been closed in escrow, a copy of the escrow agreement should be in the loan file. When the term *escrow* or *im-*

DECLARATIONS -

METROPOLITAN

POLICY NUMBER	EFFECTIVE DATE	TYPE OF TRANSACTION	SALES REP. CODE	STATE CD	BILL	INSURED	MORT.	OTHER
123-45-6789	3/16/89	SAMPLE	145-023-1	17	TO		XXXX	

POLICY TERM	FROM 6/15/87 TO THE EFFECTIVE DATE OF CANCELLATION, 12 NOON STANDARD TIME AT THE LOCATION OF THE PROPERTY INSURED AS STATED IN THE POLICY.	**DIAL-A-SERVICE**—SEE SERVICE DIRECTORY **DIAL-A-CLAIM SERVICE**—SEE CLAIM DIRECTORY OR WRITE TO: METROPOLITAN PROPERTY AND LIABILITY INSURANCE COMPANY PO BOX 48020 DAYTON, OHIO 45448
PREMIUM PAYMENT SCHEDULE	PREMIUMS ARE PAYABLE IN ACCORDANCE WITH PAYMENT PLAN 1 AND UPON NOTICE OF SUBSEQUENT INTERIM AMENDMENTS AS MADE BOTH OF WHICH ARE INCORPORATED ON THE REVERSE SIDE OF THESE DECLARATIONS.	
NAMED INSURED AND MAILING ADDRESS	DAVID PRESTON WALTERS & DORIS MITCHELL WALTERS 127 MONET PLACE KENNER, LA 70065	VOID

THE DESCRIBED RESIDENCE PREMISES COVERED HEREUNDER IS LOCATED AT THE NAMED INSURED'S MAILING ADDRESS UNLESS OTHERWISE STATED HEREIN.

COVERAGES AND LIMITS OF LIABILITY	SECTION I					SECTION II		
	A. DWELLING	B. PRIVATE STRUCTURES	C. PERSONAL PROPERTY	D. ADDITIONAL EXPENSES	E. CREDIT CARD	F. PERSONAL LIAB. EA. OCCURRENCE	G. MEDICAL PAYMENTS EA. PERS.	EA. ACC.
	58,500.	5,850.	29,250.	14,625.	1,000.	100,000.	1,000.	25,000.

OTHER COVERAGES

REPLACEMENT PLUS

PREMIUM	BASIC POLICY PREMIUM	ADDITIONAL PREMIUM FOR OPTIONAL COVERAGES	SCHEDULED PERSONAL PROPERTY	TOTAL PREMIUM	PREVIOUS TOTAL PREMIUM	PRO-RATA CHANGE IN PREMIUM FOR THIS TRANSACTION
	$ 285.00	$	$	$ 285.00	$	

DEDUCTIBLE SECTION I OF THIS POLICY IS SUBJECT TO THE DEDUCTIBLE SHOWN BELOW:
$250.00 LOSS DEDUCTIBLE CLAUSE

FORMS AND ENDTS.
VIP PLUS MPL 7062-000
H-819, H-817, H-418, H-531-A

RATING	YEAR CONSTRUCTED	CONSTRUCTION	PROTECTION CLASS	TERRITORY	PREMIUM GROUP	FEET FROM FIRE HYDRANT
	1970	BRICK	2	52	16	1,000

MILES FROM FIRE DEPARTMENT	NUMBER OF FAMILIES	RENTERS AND CONDOMINIUM FIRE AND E.C. RATE	NO. APTS IN BLDG.	CONDOMINIUM RENTED OR SUBLET
3	1			

SECTION II — ADDITIONAL RESIDENCE PREMISES, IF ANY, LOCATED: (NO., STREET, TOWN OR CITY, COUNTY, STATE, ZIP CODE)

ADDITIONAL INSURED: THE DEFINITION OF THE INSURED IS AMENDED TO INCLUDE THE PERSON OR ORGANIZATION SHOWN BELOW WITH RESPECT TO COVERAGES A, B, F AND G, BUT ONLY WITH RESPECT TO THE PREMISES DESIGNATED ABOVE

MORTGAGEE(S)

1ST MORTGAGEE	LOAN NO. 582971	2ND MORTGAGEE	LOAN NO.
MELLON FINANCIAL SERVICES CORP #7 PO BOX 53334 NEW ORLEANS, LA 70153			

THIS POLICY, INCLUDING ALL ENDORSEMENTS, IS HEREBY COUNTERSIGNED BY _Antoinette Tansley_ DATE 3/16/89

ORIGINAL

MPL 1711-000 Printed in U.S.A. 0384

TICOR TITLE GUARANTEE   TICOR TITLE INSURANCE

This Certificate of Title has been prepared by TICOR TITLE GUARANTEE COMPANY, a New York Corporation, and TICOR TITLE INSURANCE COMPANY, a California Corporation, together herein called "The Company".

Certificate of Title

Prepared For:

JOHN G. HALL, ESQ.
57 Beach Street
Staten Island, New York 10304

Title No. TAA 87-00450
Appl. File No. 6527/87

Nature of Transaction: Mortgage

Amount of Insurance: $80,000.00

Proposed Insured: Staten Island Savings Bank

Seller or Borrower: JOHN SMITH and SUSAN SMITH, his wife

Seller/s or Borrower/s Atty: None

Premises (See Schedule "A"): 59 Silver Lane, Staten Island, N.Y. 10315

County: Richmond   Town/City: Inc. Village:
Tax Map Designation: :

Section: 15   Block: 3617   Lot/s: 12

The Certificate of Title has been prepared in accordance with the information and instructions received. If any changes or additions are desired, please notify The Company promptly.

Questions concerning the within certificate should be directed to:

LAND ABSTRACT STATEN ISLAND CORP.
57 Beach Street
Staten Island, N.Y. 10304

TICOR TITLE GUARANTEE COMPANY
and
TICOR TITLE INSURANCE COMPANY

Dated: April 1, 1989
Certified by: LAND ABSTRACT STATEN ISLAND CORP.
Authorized Signature
Redated:
By:
Julia M. Hall, Pres.
Authorized Signature

701

pounded is used to describe the way monthly payments of taxes and insurance are made, this agreement should also be in the loan file.

FHA/VA. All documents required by an FHA-insured or VA-guaranteed loan (e.g., credit report, verification of employment, building certificate, certificate of occupancy, flood insurance, etc.) should be in the loan file.

Flood insurance. A statement that the property is or is not in a flood area is required and, if in a flood area, whether flood insurance is available and provided.

Good faith estimate of closing costs. Lender must provide a loan applicant with a written estimate of charges payable at settlement within three business days of application. A signed, dated receipt of this Good Faith Estimate should be in the file. This estimate may also be combined with the Truth-in-Lending loan cost and APR disclosure. In addition, the HUD booklet "Settlement Costs and You" must be given out within the three business days.

Homeowners' association agreement. If the property is a condominium, the association agreement binding all homeowners is required in the file.

Insurance (hazard) policies. In a residential file the required insurance policy (probably a homeowners) covering losses for fire, liability, and any other hazard should exist with a mortgagee loss payable clause.

Mortgage or deed of trust. A mortgage or deed of trust creating the security interest must appear in the loan file. Any chattel liens on personal property or any financing statements should also appear. Recording instructions are required to protect all parties.

Mortgagor's affidavit. A mortgagor should be required to sign certain affidavits attesting to any current position regarding divorce proceedings, judgments, or liens or any recent improvement on the real estate or other pertinent facts that would affect the mortgage loan.

Note. It is essential to include a properly executed promissory note. This note creates the obligation to repay the debt that is secured by the mortgage; it should state the amount of the loan, the term, the interest rate, and any other pertinent conditions.

Perc test. If the property has or will need a septic tank, the result of a percolating test must be in the loan file.

Photographs. Photographs of good, clear quality are required of the front, rear, and street scene for the appraisal to adequately show the mortgaged real estate.

Private mortgage insurance documents. All documents required by a mortgage insurance company to issue their insurance, as well as a copy of their commitment, should appear in the loan file.

Right to cancel notice. Whenever a mortgagor puts up their primary residence as security, the notice of a three-day right of rescission is required. Not required for a purchase money mortgage.

Survey. Since the real estate is the loan security, it is in the mortgagee's interest that a survey be made to identify the property correctly and determine if any encroachments exist. In some states a separate survey is not required since the title insurance covers this area also.

Tax, real estate. In some states a form showing that all past due taxes have been paid is required. In other states this form is used to establish adequate reserve for taxes.

ALL NUMERICAL DISCLOSURES EXCEPT THE LATE PAYMENT DISCLOSURE
ARE ESTIMATES. NOTICE TO BORROWER(S) REQUIRED BY FEDERAL LAW AND
FEDERAL RESERVE BOARD.
REAL PROPERTY TRANSACTION SECURED BY A FIRST LIEN ON DWELLING.

LOAN:

LENDER:	DATE: 121792
DOMINION BANKSHARES MORTGAGE CORP.	TYPE: CONVENTIONAL
6110 Executive Boulvard	BORROWER: Theodore A. Miller
Rockville, MD 20852	CO-BORROWER: Vicki L. Miller
	ADDRESS: 2024 GEORGIAN PARK PL., #3
	CITY STATE/ZIP: WHEATON, MD 20902
	PROPERTY: 4463 LOVEDAY STREET
	CITY STATE/ZIP: SILVER SPRING, MD 20902
	EST SETTLEMENT DATE: 010192

ANNAUL PERCENTAGE RATE The cost of your credit as a yearly rate.	FINANCE CHARGE The dollar amount the credit will cost you.	AMOUNT FINANCED The amount of credit provided to you or on your behalf.	TOTAL OF PAYMENTS The amount you will have paid after you have made all payments as scheduled.
9.877%e	$342,935.38e	$164,571.86e	$507,507.14e

PAYMENT SCHEDULE:

NUMBER OF PAYMENTS	AMOUNTS OF PAYMENTS	WHEN PAYMENTS ARE DUE	NUMBER OF PAYMENTS	AMOUNTS OF PAYMENTS	WHEN PAYMENTS ARE DUE
106	1,454.02	03/01/93	360		
253	1,391.32	01/01/02			
1	1,377.06	02/02/23			

You should refer to the contract documents for information about nonpayment default,
lender's right to accelerate the debt, prepayment, and assumption.

( ) This loan contains a variable rate feature. Variable rate disclosures have been provided
earlier.

DEMAND FEATURE: (X) This loan does not have a Demand Feature.
                    ( ) This loan has a Demand Feature as follows:

VARIABLE RATE FEATURE: (X) This loan does not have a Variable Rate Feature.
                        ( ) This loan is an Adjustable Rate Loan.

SECURITY: (X) You are giving a security interest in the real property located at
4463 LOVEDAY STREET, SILVER SPRING, MD 20902

ASSUMPTION: Someone buying this property
            (X) cannot assume the remaining balance due under current loan
                 terms.
            ( ) may assume subject to lender's conditions the remaining balance
                 due under current loan terms.

FILING / RECORDING FEES: $50.00

PROPERTY INSURANCE: (X) Property hazard insurance in the amount of $1710
with a loss payable clause to the lender is a required condition of this loan. The Borrower can
purchase this insurance from any insurance company acceptable to the lender.

LATE CHARGES: If your payment is not received within 15 days, a late charge 5.00% of the
overdue amount will be added.

PREPAYMENT PENALTY: You will not be charged a penalty to prepay this loan in full
or in part. You may be entitled to a refund of part of the
finance charge.
(If your loan is an FHA loan and you prepay on other than
a regular installment date, you may be assessed interest
charges until the end of the month.)

THIS DOCUMENT HAS BEEN CHECKED FOR ACCURACY BY _____

I / We hereby acknowledge reading and receiving a complete copy of this disclosure along with copies of documents referred to in this disclosure.

_____ BORROWER/DATE   _____ BORROWER/DATE
_____ BORROWER/DATE   _____ BORROWER/DATE

224

Application No. _____ Name MILLER, THEODORE A. AND VICKI L.
                      4463 Loveday Street   Silver Spring, MD
Property _____

As required by the Real Estate Settlement Procedures Act of 1974 you are being furnished a "Good Faith
Estimate" of settlement charges applicable to your loan request on the above referenced property. These
figures are estimates only; and the items "#" may obviously vary. **"YOU MAY BE REQUIRED TO PAY
ADDITIONAL AMOUNTS AT SETTLEMENT. YOU MAY WISH TO INQUIRE AS TO THE
AMOUNTS OF SUCH OTHER ITEMS."**

Loan Application			Monthly Payment		
Amount	$	171,000	Principal & Interest	$	1422.29
Term	360	Mos	Tax escrow	$	128.00
Interest rate	9.375	%	Fire insurance	$	25.00
Annual percentage rate (APR)		%	PMI	$	48.00
			Other	$	
			Total	$	1575.29

Loan closing cost			Prepaid items				
Origination fee	$	1710.00 *	1st year fire ins. Premium		$	250.00 #
Construction fee Discount Points	$	3420.00 *	Escrow:				
Title insurance	$	600.00 #	Taxes	7 Mos @ $ 143.00 =	$	1001.00 #
Recording fees	$	2850.00 #	F. Ins.	2 Mos @ $ 21.00 =	$	42.00 #
Pest Inspection	$	35.00 #	PMI	2 Mo @ $ 64.00 =	$	128.00 #
Survey	$	125.00 *	Interest Maximum 30 days				
PMI premium	$	684.00 *		1 Days @ $ 43.00 day =	$	43.00 #
Inspection Fee	$				$	
Attorney fee	$	250.00 #			$	
Application fee (Includes credit report & Appr. Fee)	$	225.00			$	
Total	$	9899.00	Total		$	1464.00

* Included in Prepaid Finance Charges for Regulation Z Disclosure

Sales price	$	190,000.00
Less: Earnest money	$	9,000.00
Application fee	$	300.00
Loan Amount	$	171,000.00
Seller's share taxes	$	(2,000.00)
	$	
Plus: Estimated closing costs	$	9,899.00
	$	1,464.00
Prepaid items	$	incl.
Buyer's share taxes	$	
	$	
ESTIMATED AMOUNT NEEDED AT CLOSING	$	210,663.00

I am indicating below my preference of Attorney. Insurance agent. Surveyor. Title insurance company. and. if applicable. Private
mortgage insurance company:

Attorney	TO BE DETERMINED
Fire insurance agent	TO BE DETERMINED
Surveyor	TO BE DETERMINED
Title insurance company	TO BE DETERMINED
Private mortgage insurance company	GENERAL ELECTRIC MORTGAGE INSURANCE COMPANY

All of the above have been clearly explained to me and by acknowledging receipt of this statement I understand the following:

- I have been advised that I have the right to file a written loan application
- I have been advised that I have the right to a copy of Raleigh Federal's written underwriting standards.
- This loan may be called. if there is any change in ownership. or recorded agreement to sell. and that my transfer of this loan is sub-
  ject to the approval and consent of the lender.
- This loan may be paid in full at any time. without penalty. except current month's interest. Any other lump sum payments may be
  made in conformance with the amortization schedule.
- I have received the required HUD Guide Booklet.

Date: _13 /11/4±_____   _____
        _____   Applicant
                    Loan Officer   _____
                                                             Applicant

FORM # ML-0017 (REV. 1-87)

Termite certificate. Many lenders require a certificate from a reputable company stating that the property has no active termites.

Title insurance or examination. In all cases, it is essential that title be examined or that an approved American Land Title Association (ALTA) title insurance policy or binder be included. This requirement establishes who has right to the real estate and, therefore, who must execute the mortgage to encumber it. The title examination should also disclose any prior encumbrances, tax liens, or other interests. (In some states, a Torrens certificate is used.)

Truth-in-Lending. The loan file must contain a Loan Cost Disclosure Statement, which discloses both the annual percentage rate (APR) and the total finance charge. This may be combined with the Good Faith Estimate of Closing Costs.

Uniform Settlement Statement (HUD-1). This statement is required at loan closings by the Real Estate Settlement Procedures Act of 1974 (RESPA). The statement offers the borrower and seller a full disclosure of known or estimated settlement costs.

Verification reports. The mortgage lender should verify all relevant statements made on the loan application by obtaining verifying documentation. The most commonly used verification forms are those for employment and deposits.

FINAL REQUIREMENTS

Because most residential mortgage lenders understand the necessity of creating conforming mortgage loans, they must be aware of general requirements of the secondary mortgage market in regard to closing documentation. As mentioned previously, the secondary mortgage market has these requirements because of its desire to combat fraud when loans are sold to them.

The note and mortgage are the most important documents in the first mortgage package. As such they require special attention and care in completion. Some of these requirements include:

- all blanks on Uniform Instruments must be completed,
- all corrections on forms must be initialed by the borrowers,
- no liquid paper or correction fluid can be used on the documents,
- documents should contain original signatures,
- names of signers must be consistent through all documents and signatures should be the same as name,
- legal description and property address should be consistent throughout and agree with title policy,
- note and security instrument should be signed on same date,
- signatures should be notarized according to state requirements.

MORTGAGE LOAN ADMINISTRATION ——— *14*

After the closing of a mortgage loan, the next step in the residential lending process involves *loan administration*, or as it is sometimes known, *servicing*. All residential mortgage loans, whether retained in portfolio or sold, require servicing. The question is, who is responsible for servicing the loan? As a general rule, the mortgage originator services the loan, except those originators that sell the loan before it closes or, after closing the loan, sell the loan servicing released or enter into a subservicing arrangement.

Loan administration can be the most difficult of all the steps to perform in the residential lending process for any mortgage lender; on the other hand, it can also be the most profitable. The difficulty in performing this function stems from the myriad of problems that can develop when dealing with computers, servicing systems, people, and their problems. These problems are discussed in greater detail in the following sections. If these problems are handled correctly and sufficient servicing volume exists, this function can produce a meaningful source of revenue for those mortgage lenders that sell the loan but retain servicing. This servicing revenue may be the reason the lender is in residential mortgage lending since it allows that lender to offset other lending-related losses and still make a profit.

SERVICING: WHY SOME LENDERS ARE IN RESIDENTIAL LENDING

For some mortgage lenders such as mortgage bankers, servicing profits are the primary reason for being engaged in mortgage lending. Other mortgage lenders that were almost exclusively portfolio lenders in the past (such as thrifts or credit unions) are now selling a major portion of their originations and are placing a greater emphasis on loan administration. This shift in emphasis is a result of the servicing requirements of the secondary market and because these institutions now recognize the profit potential of servicing.

Servicing has also played a major role in the recent emergence of the so-called nontraditional mortgage lenders. Many of these players, such as General Motors Acceptance Corporation (GMAC), have entered the residential mortgage lending competition by buying large servicing portfolios. These large servicing portfolios give these new entrants immediate economies of scale and thus enhance profit potential. GMAC entered residential mortgage lending by buying servicing portfolios from two mortgage bankers, totaling nearly $19 billion. Overnight, this servicing portfolio made GMAC one of the largest servicers of mortgage debt in the world.

LOAN ADMINISTRATION DEFINED

Residential loan administration can be defined as the total effort required to perform both the day-to-day management of an entire servicing portfolio and the individual servicing of a residential loan. Thus, if performed correctly, loan administration should result in the following:

- rendering of all required services to the mortgagor,
- protecting the security interest of the mortgagee (or an investor),
- producing a profit for the servicer.

The Federal Home Loan Mortgage Corporation (Freddie Mac) defines servicing as "the performance of applicable obligations described in the purchase documents, including tasks necessary to maintain mortgages sold to Freddie Mac in a manner that protects Freddie Mac's interest." Freddie Mac defines a servicer as "an institution approved to service mortgages purchased by Freddie Mac. Any institution that fits a description applicable to a Seller . . . may become an approved Freddie Mac Servicer by satisfying the Servicer eligibility requirements." Other secondary market players have similar definitions.

Servicing: Required of All Mortgage Lenders

Servicing is a required function for all mortgage lenders whether all or some of the mortgages originated are sold to other investors. Some mortgage lenders that are only involved in the origination phase of mortgage lending, such as mortgage brokers, transfer the responsibility for servicing the mortgages they originate to mortgage investors. In most situations, but not all, the broker earns a fee from the investor to whom they have transferred servicing. This fee, called a servicing release fee or premium, is in recognition of the fact that something of value is being transferred. Depending on a number of variables (e.g., type of loan, expected life of the loan, and the volume of loans transferred), the broker could receive as much as 75 to 150 basis points from the investor for the servicing transferred. If the volume of loans is very low, the broker may receive less or nothing at all. This servicing strategy is discussed in greater detail later in this chapter.

_____ *SERVICING INCOME*

In addition to interest rate spread, origination fees and possible warehousing and marketing profits, the fee a mortgage lender receives from an investor for servicing a mortgage provides practically all of the mortgage lender's revenue. Servicing income is generated by a servicer retaining a previously agreed-upon fraction of 1 percent of the outstanding principal balance collected monthly. The servicing fee is earned only if the payment is collected. After receiving the monthly payment of principal and interest, a servicer forwards that amount less the servicing fee to the investor. The amount of the servicing fee has changed over the years, but today it ranges from 2/8 to 4/8 of 1 percent of the outstanding balance of the loan. The amount varies depending on volume of loans serviced and also by the type of mortgage (e.g., an ARM could require a servicing fee as high as 50 basis points). The average for all residential mortgage loans today is probably closer to 25 basis points.

LARGEST SERVICERS OF RESIDENTIAL MORTGAGE DEBT IN 1993
(dollars in billions)

Servicer	1993 Servicing Volume	1992 Servicing Volume
1. Countrywide Funding	$80.0	$50.0
2. Fleet Mortgage	70.0	63.0
3. Prudential Home Mortgage	68.0	43.0
4. General Electric Capital	64.0	36.0
5. Citibank	47.0	55.0

Source: American Banker.

In the current mortgage market, many mortgage lenders are unable to generate a profit from the origination function. These mortgage lenders must look to servicing income to offset origination losses, and sometimes marketing losses, to produce a net profit from mortgage lending.

Concerns About Servicing Profitability

The early 1980s experienced a period of such high inflation that the wisdom of servicing profitability came into serious question. This question is centered around the fact that while the servicing income from a mortgage loan continues to decrease each year over the life of the loan (because the servicing fee is based on the outstanding balance of the loan) servicing expenses can be expected to increase each year.

A Profitability Squeeze with the Refinancing Wave of the 1990s

The early 1990s presented an entirely different problem that called into question the profitability assumptions about servicing. The problem was that so many mortgagors refinanced their mortgages that lenders were unable to service the old loans long enough to make a profit on servicing. Regrettably from the servicer's viewpoint, when mortgagors refiananced their mortgages, most of them refinanced with other lenders; thus the servicing was lost to the other lender. For those lenders that counted on the servicing income to offset other lending expenses, the impact of the lost servicing income was painful. This loss of servicing income was an especially tough problem for those servicers that purchased servicing rights from other lenders. These servicers not only didn't make a profit on the servicing they purchased, they may not have even recouped their purchase price.

On loans serviced for others, the servicing function also provides an opportunity for the lender to benefit from *float*. Float exists with loans sold to some investors because of the unequal timing between loan payment collections and *remittance* of those payments to the investors. This float can be for as much as four to six weeks in some cases and potentially involve millions of dollars. The float depends upon the date a payment is received by a mortgage lender. Other remittance plans, such as FNMA's actual/actual option, require remittance whenever the servicer has collected $2,500.

OTHER INCOME

Often overlooked by institutions just getting into servicing is the importance of other fee income that can be generated by the loan administration department. These fees include, among others:

- late charges,
- processing an assumption or novation,
- preparation of discharge and release,
- reinstatement after default (if different from late fees),
- substitution of hazard insurance policies other than on the renewal or annual premium rate,
- insurance commissions from accident, health, mortgage life, and other casualty policies,

- prepayment penalty fees,
- bad check fees, and other misc. fees.

_____ *ESCROWS*

Another important function that positively impacts mortgage lending prof-itability is the value of funds that have been escrowed for the payment of real estate taxes and hazard insurance. (In certain parts of the country, these monthly payments are called *impounds*.) Many, but not all, mortgage lenders require that their mortgagors escrow one-twelfth of the annual real estate taxes and hazard insurance each month while paying their mortgage principal and interest. (If a mortgage has a loan-to-value ratio over 80 percent, the sec-ondary mortgage market requires escrows.) This action is justifiable for a lender because if real estate taxes are not paid, the local government could have a superior claim or position in the real estate that secures the mortgage debt. If the taxes remain unpaid, the local government could sell the real estate for the back taxes. It is for this reason that some lenders advance funds to pay real estate taxes even if the amount of the taxes was not collected from the mortgagor. This amount is recovered by increasing the escrow payments for the next year or by adding that amount onto the principal. This same risk ex-ists if the federal government places a tax lien on the real estate securing the mortgage for failure to pay income or other federal taxes. In the same vein, if the insurance premium is not paid and a loss occurs, the lender could suffer because its security, the real estate, will not be worth as much. For this reason, mortgage investors, such as Fannie Mae and Freddie Mac, require that loans sold to them carry hazard insurance.

Limits on Escrows

Many lenders believe that escrows actually help lower the number of delinquencies and foreclosures because when funds are due for taxes and in-surance on the mortgagor's home, those funds are already collected. Even though most consumers like the idea of escrows because it allows them to budget their insurance and tax payments, abuses have occurred with some lenders requiring too much money in the escrow account. RESPA now allows lenders to escrow only payments that have accrued from the last payment to the date of closing plus two months' cushion. Further, a servicer is required to send an analysis of the escrows collected over the past year to mortgagors within 30 days of the conclusion of each escrow account year. The servicer is also required to make payments for taxes and insurance from the escrow ac-count in a timely manner.

INITIAL ESCROW ACCOUNT STATEMENT

Required by Section 10(c)(1) of the Real Estate Settlement Procedures Act (RESPA)

Date _____

Mortgagor(s) _____ Loan Number: _____

Property Address _____ Zip _____

Mailing Address _____ Zip _____

> The terms of your loan require you to have an escrow account to assure that certain obligations relating to the mortgaged property, such as taxes, insurance premiums and other charges are paid. The amount specified below will be collected, along with your mortgage principal and interest payments, during the first 12 months after your account is opened to pay these anticipated expenses:

Escrow Account

Beginning Date: _____

Your escrow account payment will be $_____ per _____.

(month or other period)

Payee	Purpose	Anticipated Date Due	Estimated Amount
_____	_____	_____	$_____
_____	_____	_____	$_____
_____	_____	_____	$_____
_____	_____	_____	$_____
_____	_____	_____	$_____
_____	_____	_____	$_____
		Annual total due.	$_____

If you have any questions about this Initial Escrow Account Statement, please contact:

_____
NAME

_____
TITLE

_____
TELEPHONE NUMBER

44504 Initial Escrow Account Statement 4/91

BORROWER

ANNUAL ESCROW ACCOUNT STATEMENT

Date Jan. 5, 1996

Mortgagor(s) Michael and Audrey Robertson   **Loan Number:** 45678

Property Address 122 North Main St.   **Zip**

Mailing Address Madison, WI   **Zip** 12345

Computation Period: Jan. 1 - Dec. 31, 1995

Amount of your current monthly payment, including principal and interest..............$ 956.78

Portion of your current monthly payment placed in your escrow account...............$ 203.78

Total amount paid into the escrow account during the computation period............$ 2,445.36

Total amount paid out of the escrow account for each separately identified escrow item:

Real Estate Taxes.................................$ 1999.90

Hazard Insurance.................................$ 445.46

_____ ....$ _____

_____ ....$ _____

_____ ....$ _____

_____ ....$ _____

TOTAL PAID OUT....$ 2,445.36

Balance in escrow account at the end of the period:

Excess $ -0-

Shortage (See instructions below for removing escrow shortage) $ -0-

_____

_____

_____

Obligations for the next computation period:	Annual	Monthly
Real Estate Taxes.................................$	2233.56	$ 186.13
Hazard Insurance.................................$	490.60	$ 40.88
_____ ....$		$
_____ ....$		$
_____ ....$		$
_____ ....$		$
Shortage ....$		$

NEW MONTHLY ESCROW PAYMENT $ 227.01

PRINCIPAL AND INTEREST PORTION $ 956.78

NEW TOTAL MONTHLY PAYMENT AMOUNT $ 1,183.79

Effective Feb. 1, 1996

Date

If you have any questions about this Escrow Account Statement, please contact:

Kathy Brace

NAME

Utah Mortgage Company

TITLE

908-987-6543

TELEPHONE NUMBER

44507 Escrow Account Statement 4/91

© 1991 SAF Systems and Forms, Inc.

Chicago, IL • 1-800-323-3000

BORROWER

Use of Escrow Funds

These escrows are also important to many mortgage lenders because they can serve, if needed, as the compensating balance required for a line of credit from a commercial bank. The existence of these funds not only allows for this line of credit but also keeps the interest rate on that line lower than it would have been without the compensating balances. Mortgagors benefit from this arrangement because a lender is then able to offer lower mortgage rates. In addition to the use of these funds for compensating balances, mortgage lenders benefit from these funds because they are collected monthly but are only disbursed semi-annually or annually. As a result, the mortgage lender can use these funds during the interim for its own purposes. This can be a meaningful source of low or no-cost funds to the lender, the benefit of which can be passed on to borrowers by lower rates on their mortgages.

During the 1980s many states passed laws requiring lenders to pay interest on escrows. The federal government has also considered whether a federal law is needed that would require all lenders to pay interest on escrowed funds. The amount of interest that must be paid varies from state to state. Currently, in those states where interest is required, the minimum rates generally fall between 2 and 4 percent per annum while a few require interest as high as 5½ percent. Even when lenders must pay interest on escrow, these funds are still low-cost funds and can have a positive impact on profitability. A few lenders, usually thrifts, have decided not to escrow funds for taxes and insurance because they do not believe they benefit enough from these funds when the cost of collecting and disbursing the funds are calculated. This would appear to be the case only when the servicing volume is low.

When viewed from the mortgagor's side, many prefer the convenience of budgeting these expenses on a monthly basis. The additional income, like any income, received from the interest paid on escrows is nice but generally is not all that important, especially since mortgagors must pay income taxes on the interest paid on escrows.

ORGANIZATION OF A LOAN ADMINISTRATION DEPARTMENT

The organization of the loan administration department can vary from mortgage lender to mortgage lender. Most departments are organized using either the function system or the unit system. If the *function system* is used, each employee is assigned a specific servicing function such as real estate taxes or assumptions. This system allows for specialization and, if done correctly, speed of operation. The main drawback is if that person becomes sick or leaves the organization, that function will not get performed for a period of time. The *unit system* utilizes small teams of employees to perform all of the tasks related to a group of loans. The benefit is all employees have the capability to perform all of the functions and can cover for each other during vacations or sick leave. Of course, this also means no one will be an expert on any one function.

It appears that most large servicers of residential loans use the function system because speed and accuracy are critical to their economies of scale. Smaller lenders are more apt to use the unit system so as to have more coverage of all functions at all times.

SERVICING RESPONSIBILITIES

Setting Up the Loan File

The first step in loan administration is to establish a servicing file. Some lenders use this step as a type of quality control. As the servicing file is set up, the list of required documents is compared with the list of documents actually in the loan file. If any documents or signatures are missing, this is probably the last convenient time a lender will have to cure any defects.

Welcoming Letter

The next step is to mail a welcoming letter and a notification of first payment to the borrower. This welcoming letter mailed soon after the loan is closed can be a very important step in establishing a correct relationship with a borrower. It should also ensure that a borrower understands what is expected of him or her with a mortgage loan and realizes how important it is to make the monthly payments on time.

Method of Monthly Mortgage Payment

The methods of payment vary according to the lender, but the most common are:

- Coupons—provided in one-year supply; mortgagor submits one with each payment. The coupon has on it the loan number, due date, and payment amount.
- Monthly billing—a bill is mailed to the borrower each month. Its main advantage is as a reminder that the payment is due, but the cost of mailing is a drawback. This drawback can be offset by including advertising for other services or bills for other services rendered.
- Preauthorized automatic payment—mortgage payment is automatically deducted from the mortgagor's checking, share draft, or NOW account. This method ensures prompt payments on the due date. This is a requirement for biweekly mortgages.

This notification of first payment might well be the only correspondence with a mortgagor until:

- an annual escrow statement,
- an increase in taxes or insurance,
- a notice of increased monthly payment because of a change in an index for a variable-rate mortgage, or
- a late notice.

Servicing Contract

If mortgages to be serviced have been sold to another lender or mortgage investor such as Fannie Mae or Freddie Mac, the servicing relationship is established by a servicing contract. This contractual relationship should continue for the life of the mortgage loan sold to that investor, but it can be terminated. Termination can be either for cause (some failure to perform on the part of the servicer) or in some cases, without cause. If servicing is withdrawn without cause, then it is common for an investor to pay a fee, typically 1 or 2 percent of the amount serviced, as compensation.

The responsibilities of a servicer are usually described in detail in the servicing contract or in a servicing manual supplied by an investor. These responsibilities typically include:

- monthly collection and allocation of principal and interest,
- disbursement of funds to the investor,
- collection and periodic payment of real estate taxes and insurance premiums,
- handling of assumption, partial release, and modification of lien requests,
- annual review of loans involving, among other tasks, ARM adjustments, current insurance policy, taxes paid, and escrow analysis,
- any other activity necessary to protect the investor's security interest, including, if necessary, collection activity and foreclosure proceedings.

Servicing Functions

To fulfill these responsibilities successfully, a servicer of a mortgage loan needs either well-trained people or separate departments to perform five essential functions.

1. The *Cashier Department* is responsible for receiving payments, depositing these payments, and transmitting this information to loan accounting.

2. The *Loan Accounting Department* is responsible for notifying investors that a deposit has been made to their account and for drawing a check (payable to the investor) that distributes principal and interest less the servicing fee. Some investors also require that excess reserves be deposited with them and not in the custodial account.

3. The *Collection Department's* function is to collect those payments that are past due. In many ways this is the most difficult function, but it is also the most essential for a successful servicing operation. Those involved in this function must be familiar with the Fair Debt Collection Practices Act, which prohibits certain collection practices. Further, the Housing and Community Development Act of 1987 requires lenders to notify delinquent mortgagors (whose primary residence is serving as the security) within 45 days of delinquency that they have a right to receive counseling. If collection is impossible, then this function is also responsible for initiating foreclosure proceedings.

4. The *Insurance Department* ensures the protection of the investor's security interest by determining that adequate hazard insurance exists and is current with a mortgagee-payable clause. This department also has the responsibility of inspecting repaired property (if the claim was large and affects the actual structure of the security) before releasing the insurance claim payment to the mortgagor.

5. The *Real Estate Tax Department* protects an investor's security interest by ensuring that the real estate taxes are collected and paid to the local government.

Other departments that may be required, depending on the size of the servicing portfolio, are a Real Estate Owned (REO) Department to handle foreclosed property and a Customer Services Department to handle inquires relating to assumptions, payoffs, modifications, etc.

MANAGING DELINQUENCIES AND FORECLOSURES

Delinquencies

Of all of the functions that must be performed by the loan administration department, none can be any more important than managing delinquencies (defaults). A mortgagor who breaches any of the covenants in a mortgage is considered to be in default. A default is normally caused by a nonpayment of principal and interest but also could result from a failure to pay taxes, provide hazard insurance, or maintain the premises. A residential mortgage loan is generally classified as delinquent if it is 30 days past due. Technically, a residential loan is delinquent after the first of the month since that is when the payment is due. Uniform instruments allow for the mortgage payment to be received up to the fifteenth of the month with no late fee added and, of course, no additional interest due. If the payment is received on the sixteenth or later, the lender may impose a late fee of up to 5 percent of the payment due.

The successful performance of this delinquency management function can keep servicing expenses under control and therefore enhance servicing profits. Many of the steps available to servicers in managing delinquencies, especially when a loan is seriously delinquent, are dictated by a servicing contract if the loan has been sold.

Mortgagee options A mortgage instrument is usually worded in such a manner that the mortgagee has certain options in the event of a default. One option provided by the mortgage instrument is to immediately accelerate all future payments, but seldom does the instrument require immediate acceleration. Accelerating the entire debt may not be the best choice for a mortgagee and is certainly not the best alternative for a mortgagor. In practically all situations, a mortgagee does not want to proceed to foreclosure if it can be prevented. Accelerating the entire debt and suing for the total probably will lead to foreclosure. Although the average consumer may not believe it, mortgagees not only dislike foreclosure but generally lose money if they must foreclose. After all, most mortgagees are in the business of lending money, not owning or managing real property. Other options the mortgagee has depend on the reasons for the default and "work-out" possibilities.

Reasons for default There are many reasons why a mortgagor defaults on mortgage obligations. Some are purely honest mistakes on the part of a mortgagor. People do occasionally miss a mortgage payment because of vacation, forgetfulness, or some other logical reason. On the other hand, the more common reasons for residential mortgage defaults read like a list of personal tragedies:

- financial problems,
- loss of employment,
- strike,
- death of a wage earner,
- credit overextension or bankruptcy,
- illness of a wage earner or mounting family medical expenses,
- marital problems.

Collection procedures The collection activity should be aimed at bringing the delinquent mortgage current as quickly as possible for the benefit of both the mortgagor and mortgagee. Before this can successfully occur, a lender's accounting system must be able to identify a loan as delinquent before much time has expired. Time is of the essence when dealing with delinquent borrowers. The sooner they are contacted, the sooner the problem can be resolved.

The first step is usually a payment reminder notice sent out 7 to 10 days after the loan is overdue. This notice simply reminds the mortgagor that the payment was due on the first and that if not paid by the fifteenth a late fee will be assessed. If the mortgage payment is not received by the sixteenth, a letter informing the mortgagor that a late fee is now due in addition to the scheduled payment is sent. Some coupons may already have this information printed on the form.

Telephone contact   The telephone is a very effective and inexpensive instrument for contacting delinquent mortgagors. Some lenders use it if a habitually delinquent borrower has not paid by the seventh or tenth day after the due date. Other lenders use the telephone to contact a mortgagor if the scheduled payment and late fee are not received by the 20th of the first month. Of course, if a lender perfers, a personalized letter sent around the 20th of the first month can be a very effective way of explaining the difficult situation a mortgagor is in by not bringing the loan current.

Two months delinquent   When a mortgage loan reaches the point where two mortgage payments are past due, it is reaching a critical point. If the delinquency is not cured during this month, the chances of the loan going to foreclosure increase dramatically. Shortly after the 1st of the second month past due, the lender should send a strongly worded letter informing the mortgagor that unless the loan is brought current, the mortgagor may be seriously jeopardizing his or her credit rating. Lenders must be careful to advise delinqent borrowers within 45 days of the loan becoming past due that the borrower can seek counseling.

Once a loan has become 60 days past due, the lender should insist on a face-to-face interview with the mortgagor. This meeting should clearly establish the reason for delinquency and what the mortgagor intends to do about it. Based upon the reason or reasons for the default, the lender may be able to suggest ways to cure the default.

Mortgage lenders should report delinquent mortgagors to credit bureaus. They are required to report all 90-day delinqencies by the secondary market players. Many lenders report 30- and 60-day delinquencies also.

Curing delinquencies   The important concept for all collection people to realize is that most mortgage delinquencies are cured. Only a small percentage of delinquent mortgages ever reach foreclosure. Together, a mortgagee and mortgagor are often able to handle any problems that may have led to the delinquency. In assessing a delinquency, a lender should determine why the loan became delinquent, whether the delinquency reflects a temporary or permanent situation, and the mortgagor's attitude toward the mortgage debt.

Some of the options available to mortgage lenders for handling delinqencies include:

- accepting partial payments,
- collecting just a portion of the past due amount immediately,
- making a second mortgage to bring the loan current,
- extending the term,
- providing temporary indulgence,
- looking to other solutions tailored to the needs of both parties that will rectify the problem.

Before a lender agrees to one of the options mentioned, that lender may need to get the approval of an investor if the loan had been sold.

Foreclosure

After all attempts to cure a default fail, a mortgagee must move to foreclose and protect its investment. It is important for lenders to realize that when it forecloses a defaulted mortgage, it is only fulfilling its fiduciary responsibility to protect the funds loaned, which are actually the savings of individuals, whether in the form of passbook savings or life insurance.

Equitable right of redemption   Any time before a foreclosure sale or other disposition, a mortgagor or anyone claiming through the mortgagor, such as a spouse or junior lienholders, may exercise the *equitable right of redemption.* This right is exercised by paying the mortgagee the outstanding balance plus interest and costs.

The first judicial method of cutting off a mortgagor's equity of redemption was known as strict foreclosure. If not redeemed within a set time, a court decree transferred the mortgagor's interest in the real estate to the mortgagee irrespective of any equity of the mortgagor in the property. This result was grossly unfair to the mortgagor. Therefore, a more balanced approach followed that provided for selling the property to secure the debt. The proceeds of the sale went first to satisfy the mortgagee, then to other lienholders, and then to the mortgagor.

Methods of foreclosure   The four modern methods of foreclosure, depending on the law of a state, are:

- judicial proceeding,
- power of sale,
- strict foreclosure,
- entry and possession.

Judicial proceeding   Most states provide for mortgage foreclosure through a court proceeding. This method best protects the interests of the various parties. The action is much like any other civil suit in that the case must be brought in a court with jurisdiction, either a circuit or district court of the state, where the real estate is located. This procedure requires a complaint naming the borrower, who now is the defendant, alleging that a mortgage was executed by the defendant using specifically described real estate as security for a loan and that a default has occurred whereby the mortgagee has had to accelerate. The complaint will request foreclosure.

The defendant always has an opportunity to answer the allegations with any defenses available. For example, the defendant may attempt to prove that:

- no mortgage existed,
- the mortgage was satisfied,
- no default occurred,
- the interest rate was usurious.

If the decision of the court is in favor of a mortgagee, the decree of foreclosure terminates the equitable right of redemption at the time of sale. A mortgagor loses all rights to the real property except the right to any excess proceeds from the sale after secured parties are paid. The exception is if a state has a statutory right of redemption. The court decree orders a sale and the manner for its execution. Many courts include an *upset price* in the decree, which is the acceptable minimum bid at the sale. The court usually designates the officer, such as a sheriff or referee, who will conduct the sale after giving the statutory notice of the sale. To encourage purchasers, a successful bidder acquires title to the property unencumbered by any interest except that of the mortgagor's statutory right of redemption, if allowed.

With one possible exception, anyone who can enter into a contract can purchase property at a foreclosure sale. Some states prevent a defaulting mortgagor from purchasing the real estate since the unencumbered title would cut off the rights of junior lienholders. Other states allow a mortgagor to repurchase at a foreclosure sale, but if they do repurchase the property, all liens on the real estate prior to foreclosure reattach.

The key element in this form of foreclosure is that the sale must be accepted or confirmed by the court retaining jurisdiction. This requirement is for the protection of both the mortgagor and junior lienholders since a court will not approve a price that is unconscionably low.

Power of sale   This method is sometimes called foreclosure by advertisement, since the clause creating a power of sale calls for an advertisement to give notice of the sale. This method is used primarily with deeds of trust, but it can be used with mortgages. The power to use this method rather than the more cumbersome judicial proceeding comes from a clause that is part of the securing instrument. The clause specifically explains how the sale will be carried out. This foreclosure method does not preclude a mortgagor's statutory right of redemption if it exists. Some states do not allow the right of redemption if the instrument is a deed of trust.

Foreclosure by advertisement requires procedures that vary among the states. Therefore, extreme care should be taken to ensure that proper notice is given and that other requirements are fulfilled. The proceeds from the sale are distributed in the same way as those in a judicial proceeding.

Strict foreclosure   As mentioned earlier, this was the original method of foreclosure. It is still used in some states that classify themselves as title theory states. The action involves a court of equity and requests a decree giving a mortgagor a period of time to exercise the equitable right of redemption or lose all rights to the property, with title vesting irrevocably in the mortgagee. When requesting this type of relief, a mortgagee must be able to prove all allegations just as it must in judicial proceedings.

Entry and possession   Entry and possession is used only in Maine, Massachusetts, New Hampshire, and Rhode Island. After default, a mortgagee gives the mortgagor notice that possession will be taken. If the mortgagor does not agree peacefully to relinquish possession, the mortgagee uses a judicial method. This "peaceful possession" needs to be witnessed and recorded. If the mortgagor does not redeem in the statutory period, title vests with the mortgagee.

DEED IN LIEU

An alternative to foreclosure, which can be of benefit to both the mortgagor and mortgagee, would be the execution of a deed transferring the secured real estate to the mortgagee in lieu of foreclosure. The benefits to a mortgagor would include not being subject to the embarrassment of a foreclosure suit or possibly being liable for a deficiency judgment. A mortgagee would benefit by immediately acquiring title to the real estate for a quick sale.

For a deed in lieu to be effective in transferring title, the existing mortgage liability of the mortgagor must be extinguished. If not, the transaction and deed are considered as nothing more than a new security agreement.

The mortgagee must carefully consider the consequences of this alternative before it is used. If a mortgagee decides to take a deed in lieu of foreclosure, the rights of junior lienholders are not extinguished. On the other hand, if a mortgagee forecloses, junior lienholders' rights are extinguished if not satisfied by the proceeds of the sale, but the mortgagor has the right of redemption, which can be of serious consequence to a mortgagee.

REDEMPTION

In addition to the equity of redemption already discussed, 26 states provide another form of redemption right that begins to accrue to a mortgagor (or those claiming through the mortgagor) after foreclosure and sale. This is called the *statutory right of redemption* because it only exists if created by statute. This redemption period ranges from six months to two years depending on the state.

There are two reasons for a statutory right of redemption: (1) to provide a mortgagor with a chance to keep the real estate and (2) to encourage bidders at foreclosure sales to bid the market value. The first is more important in agricultural states, where a bad growing season can be followed by bumper crops. This right would provide a method for a mortgagor to keep the farm. This same reasoning applies in some income-property situations but rarely in a residential case. The second reason is equally important for all types of real estate since a bidder at a forced sale would more likely bid the true market value rather than chance later divestiture by the mortgagor.

The right of redemption currently has a limited impact on single-family transactions since most of these transactions are a trust deed rather than a mortgage. This makes a difference because many states do not allow the statutory right of redemption with a trust deed based on the concept that a grantor had conveyed all interest to the trustee at the creation of the transaction and consequently had nothing on which to base the redemption. Other states allow it, regardless of what the transaction is called, because if real estate secures a debt, then the transaction is a mortgage and all rights attach. Even if the redemption right exists for a mortgagor, it is seldom exercised by single-family mortgagors, who are more likely to sell their property before foreclosure if there is equity to protect.

SERVICING PORTFOLIOS

Cost of Servicing

It is generally assumed that a mortgage lender must be servicing $100 million of loans sold to an investor before the cost of servicing those loans is offset by the servicing income. The $100 million may vary somewhat for different lenders but as a general rule appears to be a sound assumption. For example, in 1993, the average annual cost of servicing a residential mortgage loan in a portfolio of $100 million (about 1,400 loans with an average balance of $72,000) was approximately $175. If the cost of servicing ($175) is multiplied by the number of loans (1,400), the cost of servicing $100 million is about 24 to 25 basis points (1,400 x $175 = $245,000 or 24.5 basis points).

With the average servicing fee of 25 basis points, the cost of servicing the $100 million is offset by the servicing revenue earned.

As the servicing portfolio of a mortgage lender increases, economies of scale probably will also develop. That average annual cost can drop to approximately $100 when the portfolio reaches $1 billion (or about 14,000 loans) and may get as low as $75 when the portfolio reaches $2 or $3 billion. Because of this evident economy of scale, some lenders with large servicing operations will purchase servicing from other lenders.

Purchasing Servicing

At certain points in the economic cycle, the purchase of servicing may be a cheaper way for some servicers to grow a servicing portfolio than increasing servicing by originations. During these periods of time, those lenders who are active in the servicing of residential loans will attempt to buy servicing from other mortgage lenders. These other lenders may be mortgage brokers, other originators, or other servicers. The price paid for servicing varies, but it has ranged from 100 to 250 basis points of the amount serviced. Thus, if one servicer desires to purchase $100 million of servicing from another, the price, depending on the market, could be in the $1.0 to $2.5 million range.

The price one servicer would pay for servicing purchased from another servicer can be better calculated by equating the purchase price to the actual cash flow being generated by the portfolio. For example, all other aspects being equal, a servicer would pay less for a cash flow generated by a 25-basis-point servicing fee than one generated by a 375-basis-point fee. In determining the price that a servicer will pay for another's servicing portfolio, the following items are reviewed:

- average loan balance,
- weighted average servicing fee,
- weighted average remaining maturity,
- weighted average coupon rate,
- type of loan
  —fixed rate or adjustable rate,
  —biweekly,
  —terms and caps of adjustable-rate mortgages,
- average escrow amounts,
- interest to be paid on reserves,
- delinquency and foreclosure experience,
- geographic make-up of the loans,
- investors (determines float),

- assumption and prepayment provisions,
- remaining life expectations,
- ancillary income and other miscellaneous items.

SELLING SERVICING

It has been estimated by the Mortgage Bankers Association of America that as much as $300 billion in mortgage servicing changes hands yearly. This number is higher some years than others, but servicing today is often viewed as a marketable asset by many mortgage lenders. If a mortgage lender wants to sell servicing, the selling servicer—called the transferor—must (according to RESPA) provide to the mortgagor at least 15 days before the effective date of the transfer a "Notice of Assignment, Sale, or Transfer of Servicing Rights." This notice from the transferor (sometimes called a "goodbye letter") informs the mortgagor of the effective date of the transfer and provides a toll-free or collect phone number of the transferee and the name of someone at the transferor who can answer questions. The purchasing servicer—called the transferee—must send a similar notice (a "hello letter") to the mortgagor within 15 days of the transfer. This notice states that no late fee will be charged for 60 days after the servicing is transferred, if the borrower sends the payment to the wrong servicer.

A mortgagor is advised at the time a residential mortgage application is submitted what the mortgagee's loan transferring practices have been based upon actual transfers over the past three years. This disclosure should be signed by all applicants and be retained in the loan file.

One of the key components in the decision to buy another lender's servicing portfolio is establishing the purchaser's cost of servicing. Many lenders have a difficult time establishing a figure for cost of servicing with which they are comfortable. When a mortgage lender calculates its cost of loan servicing the following expenses should be included:

- personnel expenses (including fringe benefits),
- occupancy,
- data processing,
- other direct operating expenses
  —equipment rentals
  —postage
  —telephone
  —office supplies
  —travel and entertainment
  —automobiles

      —advertising
      —legal and auditing fees
      —other operating expenses
- provision for loan losses.

ALTERNATIVES TO SERVICING RESIDENTIAL MORTGAGE LOANS

For various reasons, usually involving the issue of whether a lender can service profitably, many residential mortgage lenders have decided not to service the loans they originate. Other lenders realize that they simply don't have the talent to do servicing well. For these mortgage lenders, alternative strategies exist. They include selling the mortgage loans servicing released or entering into a subservicing arrangement.

Servicing Released

As has been mentioned, servicing residential loans sold to an investor has great value to some large servicers. The reason servicing has value to these large servicers is because these servicers can service the loan for less money than they receive as a servicing fee. For that reason, some of these servicers pay other lenders for the right to service loans the other lender originated. The large servicers acquire the servicing rights by purchasing a mortgage loan or loans for a premium and then selling (normally, but not always) the mortgage loans into the secondary mortgage market, retaining the servicing. The amount of servicing released premium servicers pay to originating lenders depends on a number of factors, including the volume of mortgages sold, where interest rates are, prepayment assumptions, etc. For example, if one lender can sell $5 million of mortgages a month, the acquiring lender may pay as much as 100 basis points as a premium for the servicing. The acquiring lender/servicer is simply buying the right to the future stream of income associated with servicing that loan for a number of years. If the loan prepays early, the servicer loses. This situation is exactly what happened to many purchasers of servicing in the early 1990s.

Subservicing

In order to make residential mortgage lending profitable as soon as possible, some new mortgage lenders, such as credit unions, have opted not to establish a servicing department for the mortgages they have sold into the secondary mortgage market. As a general rule, they make this decision because they don't have sufficient volume to perform the function profitably or don't have a qualified staff. In addition, there are some mortgage lenders that don't

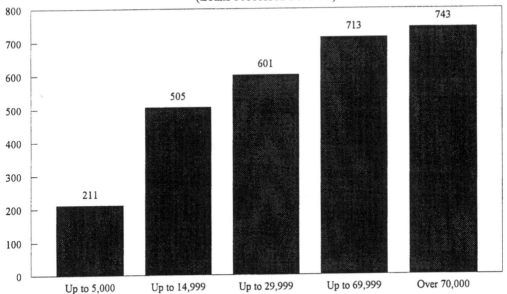

LOAN SERVICING PRODUCTIVITY
(Loans Processed Per FTE)

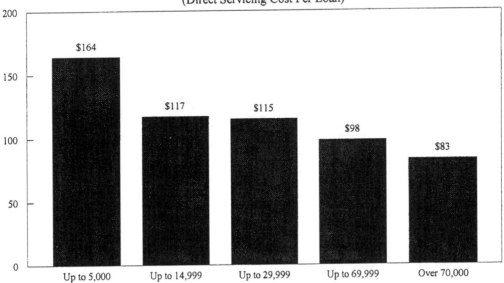

LOAN SERVICING COSTS
(Direct Servicing Cost Per Loan)

SOURCE: 1991 MBA Cost Study.

NOTICE OF ASSIGNMENT, SALE OR TRANSFER OF SERVICING RIGHTS

Mortgagor(s) Mr. and Mrs. Mort Gaston

Property Address 543 Faston St.

Mailing Address same

Date Jan. 15th, 1995

Loan Number: 8909

Zip 12345

Zip ___

You are hereby notified* that the servicing of your mortgage loan, that is, the right to collect payments from you, is being assigned, sold or transferred from ___Lemmer Mortgage Company___ to ___Downtown Commercial Bank___ effective ___Feb. 1, 1995___.

(date)

The assignment, sale or transfer of the servicing of the mortgage loan does not affect any term or condition of the mortgage instruments, other than terms directly related to the servicing of your loan.

Except in limited circumstances, the law requires that your present servicer send you this notice at least 15 days before the effective date of transfer, or at closing. Your new servicer must also send you this notice no later than 15 days after this effective date or at closing. [In this case, all necessary information is combined in this one notice].

Your present servicer is ___Lemmer Mortgage Company   800-666-7890___

If you have any questions relating to the transfer of servicing from your present servicer call ___Sally Servicer___

(name of an individual or department)

between _9:00_ a.m. and _4:00_ p.m. on the following days ___Mon. - Friday___

This is a ☒ toll-free ☐ collect call number.

Your new servicer will be ___Downtown Commercial Bank___

The business address for your new servicer is: ___123 Main St., San Jose, Calif. 12345___

The ☒ toll-free ☐ collect call telephone number of your new servicer is ___800-999-6543___

If you have any questions relating to the transfer of servicing to your new servicer call ___Ann Lynn___

(name of individual or department)

at ___800-999-6543___ [☒ toll free ☐ collect call telephone number] between _9:00_ a.m. and _4:00_ p.m. on the following days ___Mon. - Friday___

The date that your present servicer will stop accepting payments from you is ___Jan. 31, 1995___

The date that your new servicer will start accepting payments from you is ___Feb. 1, 1995___

☐ If box is checked, note the following paragraph; otherwise omit.

The transfer of servicing rights may affect the terms of or the continued availability of mortgage life or disability insurance or any other type of optional insurance in the following manner: _____

_____

and you should take the following action to maintain coverage: _____

_____

_____

You should also be aware of the following information, which is set out in more detail in Section 6 of RESPA (12 U.S.C. 2605):

During the 60-day period following the effective date of the transfer of the loan servicing, a loan payment received by your old servicer before its due date may not be treated by the new loan servicer as late, and a late fee may not be imposed on you.

Section 6 of RESPA (12 U.S.C. 2605) gives you certain consumer rights. If you send a "qualified written request" to your loan servicer concerning the servicing of your loan, your servicer must provide you with a written acknowledgement within 20 Business Days of receipt of your request. A "qualified written request" is a written correspondence, other than notice on a payment coupon or other payment medium supplied by the servicer, which includes your name and account number, and your reasons for the request. Not later than 60 Business Days after receiving your request, your servicer must make any appropriate corrections to your account, and must provide you with a written clarification regarding any dispute. During the 60-Business Day period, your servicer may not provide information to a consumer reporting agency concerning any overdue payment related to such period or qualified written request.

A Business Day is any day, excluding legal public holidays (State or Federal), Saturday and Sunday.

Section 6 of RESPA also provides for damages and costs for individuals or classes of individuals in circumstances where servicers are shown to have violated the requirements of that Section. You should seek legal advice if you believe your rights have been violated.

- - - - - - - - - - - - - -

* This notification is a requirement of Section 6 of the Real Estate Settlement Procedures Act (RESPA) (12 U.S.C. 2605).

44512 Servicing Rights Notice (5/91)
(Present and New Servicers)

© 1991 SAF Systems and Forms, Inc. • Chicago, IL • 1-800-323-3000

MORTGAGE APPLICANT

want to sell loans servicing released (as described previously) because they don't want another financial institution in contact with their customers. Instead, these mortgage lenders contract with another mortgage lender or servicing company to conduct all of the servicing responsibilities for them. These lenders pay the subservicer a servicing fee (usually between $100 to $125 per loan) based on the total dollars serviced. The originating lender is still responsible to investors for the loans being serviced properly, but by using another qualified servicer, the originating lender can have the servicing function performed profitably. For example, if one of these lenders sells a $100,000 mortgage to Fannie Mae and receives a 25-basis-point servicing fee ($250 a year), it can contract with a subservicer to service the loan for, say, $125. The difference between the two fees is profit to the originating lender.

Many of these originating lenders put into the servicing contract with the subservicer the right to pull servicing when sufficient volume is reached to make the function profitable.

REAL ESTATE LAW AND SECURITY INSTRUMENTS ————— *15*

This chapter is divided into two parts. The first part deals with real estate and mortgage law and how it developed under the common law and, finally, in America. This part of the chapter provides reference material for the other chapters of the book. In addition, the first part of the chapter is designed to be a fundamental survey of the basic principles of American real estate and mortgage law. The second part of the chapter deals with the various forms of security instruments common to residential mortgage lending. These instruments are reviewed in order to better understand the purpose of each instrument, how they are constructed, and what legal rights and duties the various clauses contained therein create.

Possibly no other segment of the U.S. socioeconomic system is more involved with law than real estate and mortgage lending. Whether as a homeowner, a developer, or a financier, those involved with real estate and mortgage lending must understand the legal framework upon which real estate is defined and the interests therein protected.

Law and real estate have been inseparable since the early days of the development of Anglo-American jurisprudence. This close relationship continues because of custom and the perception that real estate is normally an owner's most precious possession. However, this also has hindered the changes in real estate and mortgage lending concepts needed in an evolving society.

A fundamental review of how this relationship between law and real estate developed and a discussion of the interests a person can have in real estate appear in the following sections. Nonlegal terminology is used as often as possible where the meaning or concept is not altered or affected in any way.

In light of broad differences in state law, this review covers only the general principles of real estate law with no discussion of the unique features of any one state's law. In those situations where there is a basic conflict in the general principles, the majority position is reviewed. Nevertheless, the laws of individual jurisdictions should be carefully determined. This is best accomplished by consulting a competent local attorney.

PART ONE: REAL ESTATE LAW

ENGLISH COMMON LAW

Real estate law throughout the U.S., with few exceptions, is based almost entirely on the English common law as it existed at the time of the American Revolutionary War. This common background has been modified as each jurisdiction legislated changes or as courts interpreted the law differently. Developments in real estate finance since 1776 have required new indigenous laws, but the fact still remains that most of our real estate law is derived from the common law. As a result, the chief problem facing contemporary American real estate law is the existence of 51 jurisdictions (including the District of Columbia) with separate real estate laws based on an archaic system of law. This problem is compounded by the fact that this archaic system uses language hundreds of years old and is based on a socio-economic environment entirely different from that of modern-day America. A short review of the development of the common law is vital to an understanding of current real estate law.

Feudal System of Land Tenure

Before the Norman invasion of England in 1066, there was no well-developed system of land ownership in England. Land was owned by the family unit rather than the individual, and when the head of the household died, the new head of the household would represent the ownership of the family in a particular piece of land. In 1066, when William the Conquerer invaded England, he imposed a European concept of land ownership upon the English called the *feudal system of land tenure*, an economic, military, and political system of government that held that the king exclusively owned all land. The most valuable and important commodity in such a society was land. Land represented wealth, and all wealth came from the land. Money hardly existed and barter was the means of exchange. Since the king owned all land, he had complete control over the country and the economy.

A king, of course, needed arms for protection of the realm. For this he depended on the loyalty, fidelity, and allegiance of the lords. In return for their allegiance and military service, the king allowed the lords to *use* the land, although no ownership was being conveyed. The lords, in turn, allowed lesser lords to use a portion of this land in return for a share of the profits and for swearing allegiance to them. Finally, these lesser lords allowed serfs, who were nothing more than slaves indentured to the land, to use the land in return for a promise of military service. In this pyramid of military allegiance, the serfs owed military service to the lesser lords, who in turn owed service to the lords, who swore allegiance to the king.

The right to own land didn't exist for many years, but one of the incidents of ownership, the ability to pass the use of land to heirs, produced a confrontation with King John in 1215. The result was the Magna Carta, which provided greater rights for the lords, including the right to pass the use of the land on to their sons. Land was passed on to sons only as a result of the doctrine of primogeniture, which dictated that the oldest male child had the right to inherit the land. This was desirable at the time, since it prevented estates from being broken up into smaller tracts and allowed for the development of a landed gentry, which eventually developed the English society. Out of this society evolved the common law and, eventually, English real estate law. Although modified over the years, the feudal system survived until 1660, when it was abolished by law.

Allodial System

As contrasted with the feudal system, the allodial system recognizes that an owner of real estate has title irrespective of the sovereign and thus owes no duty, such as rent or the rendering of military service, to the sovereign. This system developed throughout the world with the exception of Western Europe and certain other areas where the feudal system remained.

The feudal system was an early part of the American land ownership system in a few locations such as New York and Maryland. With those exceptions, the allodial system was paramount in America based on either conquest, discovery, or purchase.

PRINCIPLES OF REAL ESTATE LAW

The first step in understanding the principles of real estate law is to define terms. *Real property* is land and everything permanently attached to it. Under the common law, and as a general rule today, this included ownership from the center of the earth, the surface, and up to the heavens. All other property is *personal property.* Real estate denotes both real property and the business of real estate, including financing.

Property can change from one classification to another fairly rapidly. For example, a tree standing in a forest is real property. When it is felled, it becomes personal property and, finally, after being made into lumber and becoming part of a house, it is real property again. The term *fixture* is used to describe a piece of personal property that has been attached in such a manner that it is now considered real property. This distinction is important, since title to real property is normally transferred by a deed, while personal property is transferred by a bill of sale.

Estate

Today, when people talk about their ownership of land, they are legally talking about the type of estate they have in real estate. This is as true in America as it was in England 500 years ago. An *estate* is defined as an interest in real property that is measured by its potential duration. There are two recognized classifications of estate in real property: freehold and leasehold, sometimes referred to as nonfreehold. The classification *freehold estate* is the highest form of interest possible in real property, as it involves all the rights in real property including use, passing the property to one's heirs, or selecting who is going to take it in a transfer. It is an estate of infinite duration, in that the chain of title could theoretically last forever. An example of a freehold estate would be a fee simple absolute.

On the other hand, the classification *leasehold estate* is an inferior interest in real property, because the owner of a leasehold interest only has the right of possession for a period of time. The owner of this interest does not have seisin, which is defined as the ability to pass title to one's heirs or assigns. An example of a leasehold estate would be a tenant's interest in leased property.

Fee Simple Absolute

There has never been nor will there ever be complete ownership of land. Examples of the restraints or limitations on ownership of land include, among others, eminent domain, adverse possession, and easements. The greatest interest a person can have in real property is known as a *fee simple absolute*. Any owner of real property, whether it be a large corporation or John Doe, has a fee simple absolute if all possible rights to that piece of real property are possessed.

In order to explain a fee simple absolute, legal pedagogues use the *bundle of rights* concept. For example, assume that all rights (such as the right to sell, mortgage, and build on a piece of real property) are represented by "sticks" and are contained in this bundle of rights. If all of the "sticks" are present and the owner has all possible rights to the real property, then the bundle of rights is complete and is called a fee simple absolute. If a "stick" is missing, such as the right to use the property the way one wants, then the interest is less than a fee simple absolute.

Defeasible or Conditional Fee

A freehold estate, which is similar to a fee simple absolute but minus a "stick" (or a right) from the bundle of rights, is the defeasible fee simple. This is a freehold estate that could but will not necessarily last forever. An example of a defeasible fee simple occurs when conditions are placed on how the property may be used. Grantors of land may put any restrictions they desire on how the land is to be used after it has been conveyed. There are, of course, a few exceptions, such as those that are racially oriented. Grantors can always give less than the full interests they own in conveying land, but never more. They can give possession for any desired period of time, or for any specific use—only as a church, for example. If so conveyed, a defeasible fee simple is created that could last forever, but it could also be terminated.

An example of a *defeasible fee simple* that would automatically end if a certain event occurs is when A grants land to B church on condition that the premises are used only for church purposes. The church has a defeasible fee simple that could last forever but will automatically end if the property ceases to be used for church purposes. When that happens, the title automatically reverts to A or A's heirs. This interest is classified as a fee simple since it could last forever if the property is always used for church purposes.

A distinction is made legally between two types of defeasible fee simple. They are a fee simple subject to a condition subsequent and a fee simple determinable. The typical person involved in real estate does not need to know the distinction, but counsel for that person should. An example of a fee simple subject to a condition subsequent would occur when A conveys property to B as long as liquor is never sold on the premises. In this situation, the grantee B (the person to whom the land has been conveyed) has a fee simple, but it is subject to a condition subsequent in that if liquor is ever sold on the premises the land will revert to the grantor (the one making the conveyances). The grantor must make an affirmative action for the property to revert, that is, reenter the property and sue to terminate the estate.

The fee simple determinable has been described. Most courts lump these together as being basically the same. If forced to distinguish, courts attempt to find a fee on a condition subsequent in order that the grantor must reenter to terminate rather than have the estate terminate automatically.

Fee Tail

This type of estate came into being from a desire in feudal England to keep land in whole parcels within the family. A fee tail is an estate of potentially infinite duration but is inheritable only by the grantee's lineal descendants, such as children or grandchildren. For a fee tail to be created under the common law it was necessary to state in the conveyance that the land was being transferred to A and "the heirs of his body." This differed from the wording of any other common law transfer, which required only "and his heirs" to be used.

There were various types of the fee tail. The fee tail general meant the property was inheritable by the issue of the grantee. A fee tail special meant the land was inheritable only by the issue of the grantee and a specifically named spouse. (A conveyance to A and the heirs of body, by his wife, Mary, would be an example.) A fee tail general could specify whether the issue need be male or female, and there also was the possibility of a fee tail special, male or female. Although the fee tail is still allowed in some New England states, the practical effect of it has been abolished in all states today.

Life Estates

A life estate is a freehold estate like the fee simple absolute and others already mentioned, but it is not inheritable. *Life estates* can be either conventional (created by the grantor) or legal (created by operation of law). The creation of a life estate is a tool often used in estate planning and is a fairly common interest in real estate. By the creation of a life estate the life tenant (the one granted the right) has the use of real estate for a period of time measured by a human life. The human life used to measure the duration of the life estate may be that of another human life, but it is most commonly measured by the life of the life tenant. An example is: A conveys a life estate to B for life, and as long as B is alive, B has the right to use the real estate, with certain exceptions, as if he or she owned it. The only incident of ownership that B lacks is the power to pass a fee simple absolute. The right to sell or mortgage the interest is not expressly given, but a person could acquire only that which B had, which was the use of the land for a period measured by a life.

When A created this life estate, only a part of the complete interest was transferred. In other words, someone else was allowed to use the land for a period of time. However, at the expiration of that period of time, the remaining rights to the real estate are with the grantor. In the example given, where A conveyed land to B for the duration of B's life, the land will revert to A (the grantor) or A's heirs upon the death of B (the life tenant) since no other conveyance was made.

When A created the life estate in B, the remainder could have been transferred in this way: A to B for life, and then to C. In this situation, C is the vested remainderman, because the grantor has transferred the remaining interest to C. The rights of C are vested irrespective of whether C survives the life tenant or not. If a vested remainderman does die before a life tenant, then the vested remainderman's heirs would inherit the fee interest.

On the other hand, a life estate could be created this way: A to B for B's life, and then to C if C is alive, in which case C must survive B to acquire any rights to the land. If C dies before B, the land reverts to the original owner. If it is impossible to determine at the time of the creation of the life estate who definitely will take the fee simple after the death of the life tenant, the remainderman is referred to as a contingent remainderman.

Another common example of this situation would be: A to B for life, and then to B's children. B may not have any children; therefore, their interest is contingent upon their being born. To complicate it even further, the conveyance could read A to B for B's life, and then to B's surviving children. The children, if any, must survive B before they can acquire any interest.

In summary, a conventional life estate is an interest that an individual has in real estate providing most of the incidences of ownership, with the exception of the ability to pass a fee simple absolute. The person who takes possession after the life tenant dies could be either the grantor, if the grantor did not convey the remainder, or it could be a third person who would be classified as either a contingent or a vested remainderman, depending on whether the identity can be determined precisely at the time of the creation of the life estate.

Legal Life Estates

In contrast with the conventional life estate, created intentionally by the grantor, a legal life estate is created by operation of the law. An example of a legal life estate is the right of dower. Dower was originally conceived to prevent a widow from being penniless during a period of English history when life insurance, welfare, and Social Security were unknown. Dower is a common law right of a widow still present in many jurisdictions. The equivalent right of the husband is *curtesy*, which has either been abolished or merged with dower in nearly all states.

Basically, the right of dower gives a wife, at her husband's death, a life estate in one-third of the real estate owned by her husband during marriage. Generally, the widow has a choice of which real estate will be subject to her dower right, and this right is applicable to all real estate owned by the husband during the marriage, even if he had transferred it before death. In those states where this right exists, a wife's potential dower interest is extinguished if she executes a deed with her husband transferring the land to another.

Currently, in some states, the right of dower has been abolished as unnecessary. This is probably because the need for a right such as dower has been eliminated in most states by the creation of a statutory right of each spouse to a minimum one-third share of the decedent's estate and because of life insurance, Social Security, and other benefits.

LEASEHOLD ESTATES (NONFREEHOLD ESTATES)

As mentioned earlier, this estate gives the owner the right to possession of real estate for a period of time. The actual duration may or may not be ascertainable at the beginning, but it does not carry with it the ability to pass title to the real estate. The owner of the land (the fee) has given up possession for a period of time but retains the legal title to the real estate, and the owner (or heirs or assigns) will eventually retake possession. The legal term to describe the missing element in a leasehold estate is seisin.

Although the use of leases can be traced to the beginning of written history, the leasehold estate in England was originally used to circumvent the prohibition against lending money for interest since any interest was usury under early church law. The person borrowing money would allow the lender to use some or all of the land for a period of time in lieu of interest. Therefore, under the common law, a leasehold was considered personal property but now is considered an estate in real estate. A lease, which creates the leasehold estate, is a peculiar instrument in that it is both a conveyance giving the tenant possession for a period of time and a contract establishing rights and duties for the parties. The essential elements for a lease are:

- name of landlord and tenant,
- agreement to lease,
- description of leased property,
- duration of lease,
- rental agreement,
- rights and duties of the parties,
- signature.

A lease for a year or less may be verbal or in writing, but one for more than a year must be in writing. For the safety of both the landlord and tenant, all leases should be in writing. Most states have a 99-year limitation on a lease, although the vast majority of leases is for fewer than 10 years. The degree of complexity in leases increases from the relatively simple residential lease to the very complex shopping center lease. The type of tenancy acquired from a lease depends on whether or not the term is renewable and whether notice to terminate must be given by either party.

Additional Interests in Real Estate

In addition to the freehold and leasehold estates in real estate, there are certain other limited interests or rights to real estate. These include easements, profits, and covenants. The effect of these interests is to create a limited right to the real estate of another, although the fact that a piece of real property is subject to an easement, for instance, does not prevent it from being owned in fee simple absolute.

Easements

An easement is a nonpossessory interest in the real estate of another, giving the holder the right to a limited use of real estate. An example is the right to drive across the real estate of another to reach a highway. An easement is either in gross (a personal right) or appurtenant (belonging to whoever owns the benefited real estate). Although most easements are expressed in writing, they can be simply implied. The right of a gas company to install a gas line on a back property line is an example of an expressed easement appurtenant.

Covenant

Like the previous interests discussed, this interest is in the real estate of another. The difference between a *covenant* or a promise to do or not to do something and other interests is that the former restricts or limits how the owner can use the real estate. An example of a covenant is the requirement a farmer may put on the part of a farm being sold that the grantee use the real estate only for residential purposes. This interest is of benefit to the grantor because it allows control of the use of the real estate. Therefore, it is an interest in the real estate of another. This interest can be either in gross or appurtenant, although the term often used with covenants is *running with the land*. This interest should not be confused with a defeasible fee simple since title cannot be lost if a covenant is breached—only damages or an injunction can be sought.

JOINT OR CONCURRENT OWNERSHIP

Joint Tenancy

Ownership in land can be and usually is held by more than one person. The most common type of joint or concurrent ownership is joint tenancy, which can exist between any two or more persons. Although joint tenants share a single title to the real estate, each owns an equal share of the whole. Joint tenancies are quite common, but a few states have abolished or limited them for reasons that are discussed later. Most states allow the creation of a joint tenancy by simply referring to A and B as joint tenants. But other jurisdictions require reference to A and B as joint tenants with the right of survivorship. This interest can be created only by affirmative action of the grantor, not by operation of law.

The right of survivorship is the key concept of a joint tenancy. Upon the death of one of the joint tenants, all the decedent's interests in the real property terminate and the ownership in the land is retained by the surviving joint tenant or tenants. In other words, a joint tenancy is not an inheritable estate. Therefore, it does not pass through the estate of the decedent and does not pass to the heirs. Instead, it passes to or is possessed automatically by the surviving joint tenants. For this reason, some states have abolished joint tenancy, and most courts disfavor joint tenancy because it automatically prevents property from flowing through the estate of an individual to the heirs. Therefore, if one wishes to create a joint tenancy, it is mandatory to follow the strict statutory requirements of the respective state. To avoid the possibility that a court could misunderstand a grantor's intention, a joint tenancy should be created by using this phrase: to A and B, as joint tenants with right of survivorship and not as tenants in common.

During the time a joint tenancy is in existence, the portion of the whole belonging to any one of the joint tenants usually may be attached to satisfy that individual's legal debts. But the portion belonging to the other joint tenant(s) may not. Some states have laws that modify this approach if the joint tenants are husband and wife and the property in question is their home.

Although any joint tenant may sell or mortgage his or her interest (with some exceptions for married joint tenants), the effect is a termination of the joint tenancy by either a voluntary or involuntary transfer. It is also terminated by the death of one of two joint tenants, but not by the death of one of more than two. The survivors in that case still have a joint tenancy among themselves.

Under the common law, if both parties did not acquire ownership to real estate at the same time, a joint tenancy could not exist. Consequently, a husband who owned property before marriage could not create a joint tenancy with his wife. One method devised to circumvent this requirement was the usage of a "straw man." For instance, the husband would convey title to his real estate to a friend or relative (the so-called straw man) who would then transfer the title back to the husband and wife as joint tenants, and the unit of time requirement would be satisfied.

Tenancy by the Entirety

A form of concurrent ownership much like joint tenancy is tenancy by the entirety, which is allowed in about 20 states. The reason for its existence is because of a vestige from the common law of some technical requirement for a joint tenancy, such as the unity of time or because the state had abolished joint tenancy. The primary difference between this form of ownership and the joint tenancy is that a tenancy by the entirety can exist only between a legally married husband and wife, while a joint tenancy can exist between any two or more persons.

Another important feature of a tenancy by the entirety is that the interest of one of the parties cannot be attached for the legal debts of that person. Only if the debts are of both parties can an attachment be made. For this reason, both a husband and wife in some states will be asked to sign the mortgage note if the form of ownership of the real estate is to be as tenants by the entirety, even if only one has income. Many states allowing tenancy by the entirety presume that a conveyance to a husband and wife, silent as to the type of ownership, will be a tenancy by the entirety.

The surviving tenant becomes the sole owner like the surviving joint tenant, but this survivorship right stems from the concept that the husband and wife were one, so ownership was already with the survivor. Divorce or annulment terminates this tenancy.

Tenants in Common

Tenancy in common is a concurrent estate with no right of survivorship. Therefore, when a person dies, the interest held in the real property passes through the estate. This interest can exist between any two or more individuals and, in effect, jointly gives them the rights and duties of a sole owner. Each of the co-tenants is considered an owner of an undivided interest (not necessarily equal) in the whole property, and each has separate legal title, unlike joint tenants who share a single title. Courts of law look with favor on a tenancy in common, because a co-tenant's share of ownership passes upon death to the heirs and is not forfeited. As contrasted with a joint tenancy or a tenancy by the entirety, a tenancy in common can arise by operation of law; for example, when a person dies intestate (without a will), heirs automatically inherit as tenants in common.

Any tenant in common can sell his or her interest, mortgage it, or have it attached for debts without destroying the joint interest. A grantee of a tenancy in common acquires only the percentage of the whole owned by the grantor. A tenancy in common is terminated by agreement between the parties or upon a petition to a court.

Community Property

Another form of concurrent ownership is community property, which is the law primarily in those states located in the western part of the U.S. Basically, the concept is that half of all property, personal and real, created during marriage belongs to each spouse. The underlying theory of this concept is that both have contributed to the creation of the family's wealth, even though only one was gainfully employed. There are three exceptions to this rule:

1. property acquired from separate funds, such as a trust account,
2. property acquired individually before the marriage,
3. property inherited from another's estate.

With these exceptions, if the necessity of terminating the marriage occurs each should receive a one-half share. Since each has equal interests, both must sign a mortgage note and security agreement.

Tenancy in Partnership

The last form of concurrent ownership is tenancy in partnership. Under the common law, a partnership could not own real estate in its partnership name. Therefore, one of the partners had to own the real estate in his or her own name. This presented the possibility of fraud. The Uniform Partnership

Act, as adopted by many states, provides that a partnership can own real property in its firm's name. Upon the death of a partner in a partnership, the surviving partners are vested with the share of the decedent or a percentage ownership of all property owned by the partnership. One partner's share of ownership may not necessarily be equal to that of another. It is quite common for partnerships to provide for a means of compensation for a deceased partner's estate, usually by insurance or a buy-sell agreement.

TRANSFER OF LAND

All title to real estate in America can be traced to one of three origins: conquest, discovery, or purchase. Today, title to real property can be transferred either voluntarily or involuntarily.

Voluntary Transfers

Most transfers of land are voluntary in that a grantor usually intends to transfer title to land to a grantee by the use of a deed or possibly a will. A deed is a legal instrument that purports to transfer a grantor's interest. If a grantor had no actual interest in a particular piece of real estate, an executed deed would transfer nothing. In addition, a properly executed deed from a grantor who did have title but lacked legal capacity (the grantor was legally insane, for example) would also transfer nothing. The validity of the title of the grantor can be determined by abstracting or checking the chain of title for defects.

All states have a law known as a statute of frauds requiring written transfers of real estate. Today, technical words are not needed in a deed, since any words that clearly show the grantor's intention to transfer are sufficient.

There are eight essential elements of a modern deed:

- grantor's name,
- grantee's name,
- description of real estate to be conveyed,
- consideration (does not have to be actual amount paid),
- words of conveyance,
- signature of grantor,
- delivery and acceptances,
- proper execution.

Three basic types of deeds are used, each having a specific purpose and function to perform. The least complicated is a *quit claim deed,* which is used to clear title to real estate. A person signing this deed makes no title guarantee. Instead, a grantor is simply transferring whatever interest is owned, if any. This deed can be used to clear a cloud on the title caused by a widow having a potential right of dower. She would be requested to execute the deed, possibly for a fee, whereby she transferred whatever interest she had (in this case dower), thus clearing the title.

A *general warranty deed* is the most common deed used to transfer interest in real estate. With this deed a grantor guarantees to a grantee that the title transferred is good against the whole world. This guarantee extends past the grantor to those in the chain of title. If a grantor refuses to use this deed, it may be an indication that the title is defective.

The *special warranty deed* is a relatively rare deed used in situations where a grantor wants to limit the guarantee. This instrument would be used by an executor of an estate to convey real estate to those specified in a will. By this deed the grantor only guarantees that nothing was done to interfere with the title to the real estate while under the grantor's control and makes no guarantee about a decedent's claim to the real estate.

Real estate that passes according to a will is also a voluntary conveyance, since it passes as the testator or the one making the will intended.

Involuntary Transfers

An involuntary conveyance occurs when a legal owner of real estate loses title contrary to the owner's intention. An example of this would be eminent domain. Any sovereign in the U.S. (federal, state, city, or county) and some quasi-public entities (such as the telephone company or gas line company) can exercise the right of eminent domain. This right is inherent in a sovereign and is not granted by a constitution, although it is limited by it. The key elements are that it must be exercised for a valid public purpose or use and that it requires compensation to be paid the legal owner.

Another example of involuntary transfer of title is *adverse possession.* The public policy behind the doctrine of adverse possession is the encouragement of the usage of land, in addition to settling old claims to real property. Normally, a person possessing the real property of another holds that real estate for the legal owner's benefit. But if certain requirements are satisfied, the one occupying the real property could acquire legal title.

To claim title to real property by adverse possession, in most states the one occupying the real property must prove:

- actual possession,
- hostile intent,
- notorious and open possession,
- exclusive and continuous possession,
- possession for a statutory period (which ranges from 5 to 20 years).

Some states also require that the party claiming title by adverse possession base the claim on some written instrument—even if the instrument is not valid. Other states require the claimant to pay real estate taxes for the statutory period.

Other examples of the possibility of involuntary transfer would include foreclosure and subsequent sale if an owner of real estate does not pay the mortgage, real estate tax, or other encumbrances.

When a person dies intestate the title to real property along with the personal property passes, not according to the dictates of the owner, but according to the statutes of that particular state. If the individual had no discernible heirs, the property would escheat (pass) to the state.

Recording

Any time an interest in real estate is being created, transferred, or encumbered, that transaction should be recorded. As in England centuries ago, the reason for recording is to prevent fraud. For example, situations existed where the owner of land would sell, possibly inadvertently, the same real estate to two or more innocent purchasers. Therefore, it was necessary to develop a system by which fraudulent transactions could be prevented. This was accomplished by devising a system of recording transactions affecting real estate. In order to protect a buyer's interest, recording statutes require purchasers of real estate to record the instrument by which they acquired the interest. If recorded, any subsequent purchaser will have either actual knowledge of the prior interest (because he or she checked the record), or constructive notice (because if he or she did check the interest would be discovered).

If the party (the prior purchaser, for instance) who could have prevented a subsequent fraud by recording does not record, then that party suffers the loss. An individual who wants to purchase real property has an obligation to check the record, usually in a county courthouse, to determine if there have been any transactions involving that particular real estate. Recording gives constructive notice to the whole world that a party has acquired an interest in a particular real property. Therefore, any subsequent purchaser could not acquire the same interest. If no transaction appears, an innocent purchaser acquiring an interest will be protected against the whole world, even against a prior purchaser.

In summary, a prior purchaser is protected if a record is made, whether a subsequent purchaser checks the record or not. The same is true if there is actual notice. If A sold land to B, and B failed to record, and C, knowing of that transaction, buys the same land and records, B will be protected since C had actual notice of the transaction between A and B. If C did not have actual notice and recorded before B, C would be protected in any dispute between B and C.

All states have a "race statute," which dictates that the first of two innocent parties to record are protected.

PART TWO: SECURITY INSTRUMENTS

In all segments of our economy a lender normally requires some security or collateral to protect itself against nonperformance of a borrower. This protection may take the form of a conditional sales contract, an installment sales contract, or some other form. In real estate transactions it takes the form of either a mortgage or a deed of trust.

A mortgage and a deed of trust (sometimes called a trust deed or trust indenture) are alternate forms of real estate finance security instruments used throughout the U.S. The purpose of each is to provide an instrument whereby a mortgage lender can obtain a security interest in the real estate that is securing a debt. As used in the U.S. today, the mortgage is unique in many features, but its fundamentals are based on the common law as it has developed in England over the past 900 years.

HISTORICAL DEVELOPMENT

The classic common law mortgage, which developed in England after the Norman invasion in 1066, was well developed and established by 1400. Basically it was an actual conveyance—a title transfer—of real estate serving as security for a debt. For a conveyance to be effective under the common law, possession of that real estate actually had to pass, putting the mortgagee in possession of the real estate.

The instrument conveying the real estate title to the mortgagee contained a defeasance clause whereby the mortgagee's title was defeated if payment was made on the due date, called the law day. Originally, when title and possession were in the hands of the mortgagee, all rents and profits generated by the land could be retained by the mortgagee. This practice was established because a mortgagee could not charge interest on a loan; any interest was usury, which was illegal at this time. After this law changed and interest could be charged, the mortgagee was forced to credit all rents and profits to the mortgagor.

Early common law mortgages did not require any action on behalf of mortgagees to protect their rights if a mortgagor failed to perform. Since a conveyance had already been made, the mortgagee had title and possession and thus the only effect of the mortgagor's nonperformance was the termination of the possibility of reversion through the defeasance clause.

Equity of Redemption

The harsh result of a mortgagor not performing after the due date, even when not personally at fault, led mortgagors to petition the king for redress from an inequitable practice. Eventually, the courts of equity gave relief to mortgagors by allowing them to redeem their real estate through payment with interest of past due debts. This was called the equity of redemption. By 1625, this practice had become so widespread that mortgagees were reluctant to lend money with real estate as security since they never knew when a mortgagor might elect to redeem the real estate. Mortgagees attempted to change this by inserting a clause in mortgages whereby the mortgagor agreed not to seek this redress. But courts of equity refused to allow the practice and would not enforce the clause. In order to restore an equitable balance, the courts began to decree that a mortgagor had a certain amount of time after default, usually six months, in which to redeem the real estate. If this were not done, the mortgagor's equity of redemption would be canceled or foreclosed. This action soon became known as a foreclosure suit and is still used in some states today.

AMERICAN MORTGAGE LAW

In American law, the most important change from the common law relates to the concept of who actually owns the real estate that is serving as security for the performance of an obligation. The common law held that the mortgagee was the legal owner of the real estate while it served as security. This was called the title theory: the mortgagee held title. Shortly after the Revolutionary War, a New Jersey court held that a mortgagor did not lose title to real estate serving as security. The court's reasoning was that since the law already recognized the right of a mortgagor to redeem the real estate after default, the law had to accept a continuing ownership interest in the mortgagor. The court held that a mortgage created only a security interest for the mortgagee and that title should therefore remain with the mortgagor. This is the law in 28 states today and is called the lien theory. Although 23 states still classify themselves as either intermediate or title theory states, all states recognize the mortgagor as the legal owner of the real estate. The principal difference between these two theories is in the manner of foreclosure. Currently, mortgagors are able to do as they please with mortgaged real estate as long as the activity does not interfere with the security interest of a mortgagee.

According to current law, any interest in real estate that can be sold can be mortgaged, including a fee simple, a life estate, or a lease. The determining factor is whether a mortgagee can be found willing to lend money with that particular interest as security.

THE SECURITY INTEREST

The Note: Mortgage Debt

The debt secured by a mortgage is evidenced by either a promissory note or a bond. The note is the promise to pay. Normally, the mortgage and the note are separate documents, but in some jurisdictions they are combined. The note should be negotiable so that the originating mortgagee can assign it. This is the normal practice today for most mortgage lenders. Both Fannie Mae and Freddie Mac use the same uniform note, which meets all legal requirements for each of the states. These uniform notes are the ones that all mortgage lenders should use since they contain well-conceived and tested language that protects the rights of both the borrower and lender.

The mortgage instrument, discussed following, must in one way or another acknowledge and identify the debt it secures. When the entire debt is paid (satisfied), the note and the mortgage that secures the debt lose their effectiveness and no longer create a valid lien. A notice of satisfaction, or notice of full payment of a note and mortgage, should be recorded when the debt is paid. This recording is done to clear the cloud on the title created by the mortgage.

Provisions of the Note

As mentioned, the uniform note provides protection for the various parties and also establishes important provisions such as what the interest rate is, how repayment will be made, etc. For example, the note should state that the first payment is due on the first of the month following a full month after closing (if a loan closed on May 15, the first payment would be due on July 1st).

Other items that are important include the following:

- original signatures of the borrowers,
- all blanks must be filled and any corrections must be initialed (no white-outs),
- interest rate, payment schedule, and due dates must be clear,
- date of note and mortgage must match,
- appropriate uniform note used for each loan type.

The Mortgage Instrument

The mortgage instrument, which creates the security interest in the real estate for the lender, does not have to appear in any particular legal form. There are no set requirements except that a mortgage instrument be in writing.

NOTE

.........May 3,................................, 19 89...   **Staten Island**, ...**New York**.........
                                              [City]   [State]

59 Silver Lane...   Staten Island, New York 103 15
                                              [Property Address]

1. BORROWER'S PROMISE TO PAY

In return for a loan that I have received, I promise to pay U.S. $ 80,000.00 .... (this amount is called "principal"), plus interest, to the order of the Lender. The Lender is ....**Staten Island Savings Bank**,................
81 Water Street, Staten Island, New York 10304
.... I understand that the Lender may transfer this Note. The Lender or anyone who takes this Note by transfer and who is entitled to receive payments under this Note is called the "Note Holder."

2. INTEREST

Interest will be charged on unpaid principal until the full amount of principal has been paid. I will pay interest at a yearly rate of ....10.50........%.

The interest rate required by this Section 2 is the rate I will pay both before and after any default described in Section 6(B) of this Note.

3. PAYMENTS

(A) Time and Place of Payments

I will pay principal and interest by making payments every month.

I will make my monthly payments on the ....1st.... day of each month beginning on ....July 1,...............................
19 89.... I will make these payments every month until I have paid all of the principal and interest and any other charges described below that I may owe under this Note. My monthly payments will be applied to interest before principal. If, on June 1, 2019.........................., ..., I still owe amounts under this Note, I will pay those amounts in full on that date, which is called the "maturity date."

I will make my monthly payments at ....**81 Water Street, Staten Island**................
New York 10304... or at a different place if required by the Note Holder.

(B) Amount of Monthly Payments

My monthly payment will be in the amount of U.S. $....731.80.....................

4. BORROWER'S RIGHT TO PREPAY

I have the right to make payments of principal at any time before they are due. A payment of principal only is known as a "prepayment." When I make a prepayment, I will tell the Note Holder in writing that I am doing so.

I may make a full prepayment or partial prepayments without paying any prepayment charge. The Note Holder will use all of my prepayments to reduce the amount of principal that I owe under this Note. If I make a partial prepayment, there will be no changes in the due date or in the amount of my monthly payment unless the Note Holder agrees in writing to those changes.

5. LOAN CHARGES

If a law, which applies to this loan and which sets maximum loan charges, is finally interpreted so that the interest or other loan charges collected or to be collected in connection with this loan exceed the permitted limits, then: (i) any such loan charge shall be reduced by the amount necessary to reduce the charge to the permitted limit; and (ii) any sums already collected from me which exceeded permitted limits will be refunded to me. The Note Holder may choose to make this refund by reducing the principal I owe under this Note or by making a direct payment to me. If a refund reduces principal, the reduction will be treated as a partial prepayment.

6. BORROWER'S FAILURE TO PAY AS REQUIRED

(A) Late Charge for Overdue Payments

If the Note Holder has not received the full amount of any monthly payment by the end of ....15.............. calendar days after the date it is due, I will pay a late charge to the Note Holder. The amount of the charge will be ..2...% of my overdue payment of principal and interest. I will pay this late charge promptly but only once on each late payment.

(B) Default

If I do not pay the full amount of each monthly payment on the date it is due, I will be in default.

(C) Notice of Default

If I am in default, the Note Holder may send me a written notice telling me that if I do not pay the overdue amount by a certain date, the Note Holder may require me to pay immediately the full amount of principal which has not been paid and all the interest that I owe on that amount. That date must be at least 30 days after the date on which the notice is delivered or mailed to me.

(D) No Waiver By Note Holder

Even if, at a time when I am in default, the Note Holder does not require me to pay immediately in full as described above, the Note Holder will still have the right to do so if I am in default at a later time.

(E) Payment of Note Holder's Costs and Expenses

If the Note Holder has required me to pay immediately in full as described above, the Note Holder will have the right to be paid back by me for all of its costs and expenses in enforcing this Note to the extent not prohibited by applicable law. Those expenses include, for example, reasonable attorneys' fees.

7. GIVING OF NOTICES

Unless applicable law requires a different method, any notice that must be given to me under this Note will be given by delivering it or by mailing it by first class mail to me at the Property Address above or at a different address if I give the Note Holder a notice of my different address.

Any notice that must be given to the Note Holder under this Note will be given by mailing it by first class mail to the Note Holder at the address stated in Section 3(A) above or at a different address if I am given a notice of that different address.

MULTISTATE FIXED RATE NOTE—Single Family—FNMA/FHLMC UNIFORM INSTRUMENT   Form 3200 12/83

8. OBLIGATIONS OF PERSONS UNDER THIS NOTE

If more than one person signs this Note, each person is fully and personally obligated to keep all of the promises made in this Note, including the promise to pay the full amount owed. Any person who is a guarantor, surety or endorser of this Note is also obligated to do these things. Any person who takes over these obligations, including the obligations of a guarantor, surety or endorser of this Note, is also obligated to keep all of the promises made in this Note. The Note Holder may enforce its rights under this Note against each person individually or against all of us together. This means that any one of us may be required to pay all of the amounts owed under this Note.

9. WAIVERS

I and any other person who has obligations under this Note waive the rights of presentment and notice of dishonor. "Presentment" means the right to require the Note Holder to demand payment of amounts due. "Notice of dishonor" means the right to require the Note Holder to give notice to other persons that amounts due have not been paid.

10. UNIFORM SECURED NOTE

This Note is a uniform instrument with limited variations in some jurisdictions. In addition to the protections given to the Note Holder under this Note, a Mortgage, Deed of Trust or Security Deed (the "Security Instrument"), dated the same date as this Note, protects the Note Holder from possible losses which might result if I do not keep the promises which I make in this Note. That Security Instrument describes how and under what conditions I may be required to make immediate payment in full of all amounts I owe under this Note. Some of those conditions are described as follows:

Transfer of the Property or a Beneficial Interest in Borrower. If all or any part of the Property or any interest in it is sold or transferred (or if a beneficial interest in Borrower is sold or transferred and Borrower is not a natural person) without Lender's prior written consent, Lender may, at its option, require immediate payment in full of all sums secured by this Security Instrument. However, this option shall not be exercised by Lender if exercise is prohibited by federal law as of the date of this Security Instrument.

If Lender exercises this option, Lender shall give Borrower notice of acceleration. The notice shall provide a period of not less than 30 days from the date the notice is delivered or mailed within which Borrower must pay all sums secured by this Security Instrument. If Borrower fails to pay these sums prior to the expiration of this period, Lender may invoke any remedies permitted by this Security Instrument without further notice or demand on Borrower.

WITNESS THE HAND(S) AND SEAL(S) OF THE UNDERSIGNED.

....(Seal)
John Smith   -Borrower

....(Seal)
Susan Smith   -Borrower

WITNESS: ....(Seal)
                                                        -Borrower

Maria Puglia

                            [Sign Original Only]

Any wording that clearly indicates the purpose of the instrument, which is to create a security interest in described real estate for the benefit of a mortgagee, is sufficient. Today, most mortgage lenders have adopted the Fannie Mae and Freddie Mac uniform mortgage instrument used in their particular state.

What Is and Isn't a Mortgage

If a conveyance is made to a mortgagee that appears to be a deed absolute but is actually intended to be a conveyance as security for a debt, all state courts have uniformly held that transaction to be a mortgage even if the defeasance clause is missing. On the other hand, if the parties agree in writing that money will be advanced, with the debt for those funds secured by a later mortgage, and a mortgage is not executed, the law holds that a creditor has a security interest in the real estate. This interest is called an equitable mortgage.

A valid mortgage instrument should include:

- names of the mortgagor and mortgagee,
- words of conveyance or a mortgaging clause,
- amount of the debt,
- interest rate and terms of payment,
- a repeat of the provisions of the promissory note or bond in some jurisdictions,
- description of the real estate securing the debt,
- clauses to protect the rights of the parties,
- date (same date as note),
- signature of the mortgagor (and notarized, if required),
- any requirements particular to that jurisdiction.

Clauses to Protect the Rights of the Parties

The elements mentioned are the framework upon which a complete mortgage instrument is built. A mortgage instrument, such as the Fannie Mae and Freddie Mac uniform mortgage or deed of trust, contains clauses to solve all foreseeable problems. Of course there are many types of mortgage clauses, but the most typical and important ones are the acceleration clause, the prepayment clause, and the payment clause.

Acceleration clause   The acceleration clause is the most important clause in the entire mortgage for the protection of the mortgagee. This clause is generally found in both the mortgage and the instrument that evidences the debt. It states that the entire amount of the debt can be accelerated at the mortgagee's election if the mortgagor defaults or breaches any stated covenant. (In some states, automatic acceleration clauses are allowed, but these should be avoided if possible because other options for curing defaults or breaches are available to the mortgagee and may be more beneficial.)

The most common defaults or breaches of covenants by a mortgagor that could trigger acceleration are:

- failure to pay principal and interest when due,
- failure to pay taxes or insurance when due,
- failure to maintain the property,
- committing waste (destructive use of property).

Recently, some mortgagees have inserted clauses providing for acceleration if a mortgagor either further mortgages the secured real estate or sells the real estate with the mortgage still attached. This clause ostensibly protects the mortgagee from a change in risk.

Prepayment clause   Since 1979, residential mortgage loans sold to Fannie Mae or Freddie Mac may not have a prepayment penalty. Before that date, these clauses existed and were enforceable.

Payment clause   The most obvious clause in a mortgage is the one by which a mortgagor agrees to pay the obligation in an agreed-upon manner. Reference usually is made to the note or bond whereby a mortgagor was obligated to pay a certain amount of money. A separate clause may stipulate a covenant to pay taxes and hazard insurance (with a mortgage-payable clause) as they become due. However, this often is a part of the payment clause. A mortgagee may require taxes and insurance to be placed in escrow and collected monthly as part of the mortgage payment.

Deeds of Trust

Before deeds of trust can be used in any state, special enabling legislation must be enacted. This is required since the deed of trust was not known in the common law. One of the basic legal differences between a mortgage and a deed of trust is that a mortgage is a two-party instrument between a mortgagor and a mortgagee, while a deed of trust is a three-party instrument between a borrower, a lender, and a third party, called a trustee. If a deed of trust is used, a borrower conveys title to a trustee who holds it until the obligation is satisfied, at which time title is conveyed back to the borrower. The title is held for the benefit of the lender.

Another theoretical difference is the necessity of a mortgagee foreclosing on a mortgage if there has been a default. On the other hand, in most states there is no requirement for a foreclosure, with its time-consuming court proceedings, if a deed of trust is used. Instead, the trustee has the power of sale to satisfy the debt. Some states, however, require a foreclosure even if the financing vehicle is a deed of trust. Regardless of the situation, there is always a requirement for a public notice of sale.

In using a deed of trust there is generally no statutory right of redemption, as there is with a mortgage. This is one of the more important reasons why a mortgagee would use a deed of trust rather than a mortgage. In many jurisdictions, a mortgagor has a period of time to redeem the property after default and foreclosure. If the right to redeem exists, this period varies from six months to two years, depending on state law. To a mortgagor, the advantage of a deed of trust is that a mortgagee does not have the right to a deficiency judgment. A deficiency judgment is the result of a lawsuit to make up the difference between the amount obtained at a foreclosure sale and the mortgage obligation.

TRANSFERS OF MORTGAGED REAL ESTATE _____

In all jurisdictions, whether the title or lien theory is followed, the mortgagor has the ability to transfer real estate that is serving as security for a debt and has options on the method of transfer.

Free and Clear

The grantor (the one transferring) could transfer the land free and clear. This would occur if a mortgagor satisfied the obligation secured by the real estate and presumes that the mortgage could be prepaid. In such an event, a prepayment penalty might be required. Much mortgaged real estate sold today is transferred in this manner, with the new owner obtaining new financing. The reason for this is inflation, which has produced increased equity in real estate. The value of this equity is more than a purchaser would want to buy for cash. Therefore, a new purchaser normally would rather finance the purchase price than assume the mortgage and pay cash for the equity. During periods of exceedingly high interest rates, purchasers may desire to assume an existing lower interest rate mortgage and pay cash or use another financing technique for the equity.

Subject to the Mortgage

The grantor could transfer the real estate subject to the mortgage, with the grantee (the one to whom the property is transferred) paying the grantor for any equity. If this occurs, the original mortgage remains effective and the personal liability of the original mortgagor to pay the mortgage continues, although the mortgage payment will probably be made by the grantee from that point on. The grantee becomes the legal owner of the real estate after the sale, although it continues to serve as security for the original mortgage. The grantee assumes no personal liability for the original mortgage payment and could decide to abandon the real estate with no danger of contingent liability. If the grantee stops the mortgage payment and the mortgagee forecloses, the grantee loses only equity in the real estate while the original mortgagor is liable for any amount of the obligation not satisfied by the sale of the mortgaged real estate.

Assumption of the Mortgage

The real estate could be transferred to the grantee, who would buy the grantor's equity and assume the mortgage. This is the most common manner in which real estate is transferred in those cases where the existing mortgage remains intact. In this situation, the grantee assumes personal liability for satisfying the mortgage debt, while the original mortgagor retains only secondary liability.

Recently, some mortgagees have inserted clauses into conventional mortgages to either prohibit the transfer of the mortgage or make the transfer conditional on the approval of the mortgagee. Other mortgagees, especially savings and loan institutions, have inserted due-on-sale clauses in conventional mortgages, which accelerate the entire debt if the real estate is sold with the mortgage still intact. The stated rationale for such a clause is to protect the mortgagee's security interest by forcing the new mortgagor to meet the mortgagee's underwriting requirements. Often, however, the real reason is to force the grantee to assume an increase in the interest rate from the rate on the assumed mortgage to the higher current rate. The validity of these clauses evolved to the point where many courts enforced the mortgagee's right to accelerate. In 1982, a provision of the Garn–St. Germain bill preempted state laws and limited the enforceability of due-on-sale clauses until October 1985. After that date, states may allow enforcement again.

Many mortgagors, after selling the real estate to the grantee who assumes the mortgage, have requested that the mortgagee sign a novation contract that would end any secondary liability on the part of the original mortgagor. Many mortgagees have agreed to sign, but normally they require that the assuming grantee agree to an increase in the interest rate to the level of the prevailing rate.

Assignment Of Mortgages

Many originators of mortgage loans, such as mortgage bankers, originate loans for sale to other investors. Any mortgage lender has the right to assign a mortgage even if the mortgagor is unaware of the assignment.

The instrument by which mortgages are assigned should be in writing and the assignment should be recorded immediately to protect the investor from another assignment. At the time of assignment, the mortgagor may be required to sign an estoppel certificate. This is a statement by a mortgagor that there is a binding obligation not yet satisfied and that the mortgagor has no defenses against the mortgagee. An assigned mortgage has full effect and the mortgage payments may be made directly to the assignee or through the original mortgagee.

STATE-BY-STATE COMPARISON OF SELECTED ASPECTS OF FORECLOSURE

State	Nature of Mortgage	Customary Security Instrument	Predominant Method of Foreclosure	Redemption Period (months)	Possession During Redemption (if customary security instrument used)	Deficiency Judgment Allowed?
Alabama	Title	Mortgage	Power of sale	12	Purchaser	Yes
Alaska	Lien	Trust deed	Power of sale	None	—	No
Arizona	Lien	Trust deed	Judicial	None	—	Yes
Arkansas	Intermediate	Mortgage	Power of sale	12	Purchaser	Yes
California	Lien	Trust deed	Power of sale	None	—	No
Colorado	Lien	Trust deed	Power of sale	2½	Mortgagor	Yes
Connecticut	Intermediate	Mortgage	Strict foreclosure	None	—	No
Delaware	Intermediate	Mortgage	Judicial	None	—	No
Dist. of Columbia	Intermediate	Trust deed	Power of sale	None	—	Yes
Florida	Lien	Mortgage	Judicial	None	—	Yes
Georgia	Title	Security deed	Power of sale	None	—	Yes
Hawaii	Title	Trust deed	Power of sale	None	—	Yes
Idaho	Lien	Trust deed	Power of sale	None	—	Yes
Illinois	Intermediate	Mortgage	Judicial	12	Mortgagor	No
Indiana	Lien	Mortgage	Judicial	3	Mortgagor	Yes
Iowa	Lien	Mortgage	Judicial	6	Mortgagor	No
Kansas	Lien	Mortgage	Judicial	12	Mortgagor	Yes
Kentucky	Lien	Mortgage	Judicial	None	—	Yes

State	Theory	Security instrument	Foreclosure	Redemption (months)	Possession during redemption	Deficiency
Louisiana	—	Mortgage	—	—	—	Yes
Maine	Title	Trust deed	Entry and possession	12	—	—
Maryland	Title	Mortgage	Power of sale	None	Mortgagor	Yes
Massachusetts	Intermediate	Mortgage	Power of sale	None	—	Yes
Michigan	Lien	Mortgage	Power of sale	6	—	Yes
Minnesota	Lien	Trust deed	Power of sale	12	Mortgagor	Yes
Mississippi	Intermediate	Trust deed	Power of sale	None	Mortgagor	Yes
Missouri	Intermediate	Trust deed	Power of sale	12	—	Yes
Montana	Lien	Mortgage	Judicial	12	Mortgagor	Yes
Nebraska	Lien	Mortgage	Judicial	None	Mortgagor	No
Nevada	Lien	Mortgage	Power of sale	None	—	Yes
New Hampshire	Title	Mortgage	Power of sale	None	—	Yes
New Jersey	Intermediate	Mortgage	Judicial	None	—	No
New Mexico	Lien	Mortgage	Judicial	1	Purchaser	Yes
New York	Lien	Mortgage	Judicial	None	—	Yes
North Carolina	Intermediate	Trust deed	Power of sale	None	—	No

STATE-BY-STATE COMPARISON OF SELECTED ASPECTS OF FORECLOSURE (continued)

State	Nature of Mortgage	Customary Security Instrument	Predominant Method of Foreclosure	Redemption Period (months)	Possession During Redemption (if customary security instrument used)	Deficiency Judgment Allowed?
North Dakota	Lien	Mortgage	Judicial	12	Mortgagor	Yes
Ohio	Intermediate	Mortgage	Judicial	None	—	Yes
Oklahoma	Lien	Mortgage	Judicial	None	—	Yes
Oregon	Lien	Trust deed	Power of sale	None	—	Yes
Pennsylvania	Title	Mortgage	Judicial	None	—	Yes
Rhode Island	Title	Mortgage	Power of sale	None	—	No
South Carolina	Lien	Mortgage	Judicial	None	—	Yes
South Dakota	Lien	Mortgage	Power of sale	12	Mortgagor	Yes
Tennessee	Title	Trust deed	Power of sale	None	—	No
Texas	Lien	Trust deed	Power of sale	None	—	Yes
Utah	Lien	Mortgage	Judicial	6	Mortgagor	Yes
Vermont	Intermediate	Mortgage	Strict foreclosure	6	Mortgagor	Yes
Virginia	Intermediate	Trust deed	Power of sale	None	—	Yes
Washington	Lien	Mortgage	Judicial	12	Purchaser	Yes
West Virginia	Intermediate	Trust deed	Power of sale	None	—	Yes
Wisconsin	Lien	Mortgage	Power of sale	None	—	Yes
Wyoming	Lien	Mortgage	Power of sale	6	Mortgagor	Yes

CAVEAT This chart only lists the customary form of security instrument used in each state and not all the forms that could be used. Therefore, the method of foreclosure and period of redemption (if allowed) will be listed only for the customary form and not for all possible security instruments. The reader is further cautioned that many states have extensive qualifications and limitations on the period of redemption and for obtaining a delinquency judgment. *Consult a local attorney for details.*

RESIDENTIAL MORTGAGE LOAN CASE STUDY — *16*

Both the practitioner and the student of residential mortgage lending should understand which loan documents are essential for a well-processed residential mortgage loan and usually found in a closed loan file. Uniform documents (Fannnie Mae/Freddie Mac) are used since this lender (similar to most) wants the loan to be salable in the secondary mortgage market. Some of the documents used are critical for establishing a valid lien on the real estate in this particular state thereby creating a security interest for the lender. Other states may have different requirements for creating a valid lien. Further, other states may have consumer compliance requirements that are unique to their states and not found in this loan file.

The case selected represents the most common residential mortgage loan in the U.S. today:

- conventional mortgage,
- no private mortgage insurance,
- single-family detached dwelling,
- made to a husband and wife.

This is a fictionalized case study containing the complete loan file for a residential mortgage loan for one of the co-authors of this textbook, Michael J. Robertson.

AnchorBank, S.S.B.   Uniform Residential Loan Application

This application is designed to be completed by the applicant(s) with the Lender's assistance. Applicants should complete this form as "Borrower" or "Co-Borrower", as applicable. Co-Borrower information must also be provided (and the appropriate box checked) when [X] the income or assets of a person other than the "Borrower" (including the Borrower's spouse) will be used as a basis for loan qualification or [ ] the income or assets of the Borrower's spouse will not be used as a basis for loan qualification, but his or her liabilites must be considered because the Borrower resides in a community property state, the security property is located in a community property state, or the Borrower is relying on other property located in a community property state as a basis for repayment of the loan.

I. TYPE OF MORTGAGE AND TERMS OF LOAN

Mortgage Applied for:	[ ] VA [ ] FHA [X] Conventional [ ] FmHA [ ] Other:		Agency Case Number	Lender Case No. 0015149

Amount	Interest Rate	No. of Months	Amortization Type:	
$ 65,000.00	6.570 %	360	[X] Fixed Rate [ ] GPM	[ ] Other (explain): [ ] ARM (type):

II. PROPERTY INFORMATION AND PURPOSE OF LOAN

Subject Property Street Address	City	County	State	Zip	No. of Units
5806 SUFFOLK ROAD	MADISON	DANE	WI	53711	1

Legal Description of Subject Property (attach description if necessary)	Year Built 1973

Purpose of Loan	[ ] Purchase [ ] Construction [ ] Other (explain): [X] Refinance [ ] Construction-Permanent	Property will be: [X] Primary Residence [ ] Secondary Residence [ ] Investment

Complete this line if construction or construction-permanent loan.

Year Lot Acquired	Original Cost	Amount Existing Liens	(a) Present Value of Lot	(b) Cost of Improvements	Total (a + b)
	$ 0.00	$ 0.00	$ .00	$ 0.00	$ 0.00

Complete this line if this is a refinance loan.

Year Acquired	Original Cost	Amount Existing Liens	Purpose of Refinance	Describe Improvements [ ] made [ ] to be made
	$ 0.00	$ 0.00		Cost: $ 0.00

Title will be held in what Name(s)	Manner in which Title will be held	Estate will be held in: [X] Fee Simple
Source of Down Payment, Settlement Charges and/or Subordinate Financing (explain)		[ ] Leasehold (show expiration date)

III. BORROWER INFORMATION

Borrower	Co-Borrower

Borrower's Name (include Jr. or Sr. if applicable)	Co-Borrower's Name (include Jr. or Sr. if applicable)
MICHAEL J. ROBERTSON	AUDREY F. ROBERTSON

Social Security Number	Home Phone (incl. area code)	Age	Yrs. School	Social Security Number	Home Phone (incl. area code)	Age	Yrs. School
	(608) 274-5040	36	17		(608) 274-5040	32	16

[X] Married [ ] Unmarried (include single, divorced, widowed) [ ] Separated	Dependents (not listed by Co-Borrower) no. ages	[X] Married [ ] Unmarried (include single, divorced, widowed) [ ] Separated	Dependents (not listed by Borrower) no. ages

Present Address (street, city, state, zip code) [X] Own [ ] Rent 7 No. Yrs. 5806 SUFFOLK RD. MADISON, WIS. 53711 Landlord:	Present Address (street, city, state, zip code) [X] Own [ ] Rent 7 No. Yrs. 5806 SUFFOLK RD. MADISON, WIS. 53711 Landlord:

If residing at present address for less than two years, complete the following:

Former Address (street, city, state, zip code) [ ] Own [ ] Rent No. Yrs. Landlord:	Former Address (street, city, state, zip code) [ ] Own [ ] Rent No. Yrs. Landlord:
Former Address (street, city, state, zip code) [ ] Own [ ] Rent No. Yrs. Landlord:	Former Address (street, city, state, zip code) [ ] Own [ ] Rent No. Yrs. Landlord:

IV. EMPLOYMENT INFORMATION

Borrower	Co-Borrower

Name & Address of Employer [ ] Self Employed PROMACS 5806 SUFFOLK RD MADISON WI 53711	Yrs. on this job 2 / Yrs. employed in this line of work/profession 10	Name & Address of Employer [ ] Self Employed CUNA MUTUAL INS GROUP 5910 MINERAL PT RD MADISON WI 53701	Yrs. on this job 6 / Yrs. employed in this line of work/profession 6

Position/Title/Type of Business MORTGAGE CONSULTING	Business Phone (incl. area code) (608) 277-8870	Position/Title/Type of Business UNDERWRITER	Business Phone (incl. area code) (608) 231-7118

If employed in current position for less than two years or if currently employed in more than one position, complete the following:

Name & Address of Employer [ ] Self Employed	Dates (from - to)	Name & Address of Employer [ ] Self Employed	Dates (from - to)
	Monthly Income $ 0.00		Monthly Income $ 0.00
Position/Title/Type of Business	Business Phone (incl. area code) ( )	Position/Title/Type of Business	Business Phone (incl. area code) ( )

Name & address of Employer [ ] Self Employed	Dates (from - to)	Name & address of Employer [ ] Self Employed	Dates (from - to)
	Monthly Income $ 0.00		Monthly Income $ 0.00
Position/Title/Type of Business	Business Phone (incl. area code) ( )	Position/Title/Type of Business	Business Phone (incl. area code) ( )

MICHAEL J. ROBERTSON AND AUDREY F. ROBERTSON

V. MONTHLY INCOME AND COMBINED HOUSING EXPENSE INFORMATION

Gross Monthly Income	Borrower	Co-Borrower	Total	Combined Monthly Housing Expense	Present	Proposed
Base Empl. Income *	$ 4,500.00	$ 2,520.00	$ 7,020.00	Rent	$ 0.00	
Overtime	0.00	0.00	0.00	First Mortgage (P&I)	471.21	$ 413.85
Bonuses	0.00	0.00	0.00	Other Financing (P&I)	0.00	0.00
Commissions	0.00	0.00	0.00	Hazard Insurance	0.00	0.00
Dividends/Interest	0.00	0.00	0.00	Real Estate Taxes	0.00	0.00
Net Rental Income	0.00	0.00	0.00	Mortgage Insurance	0.00	0.00
Other (Before completing, see the notice in "Describe Other Income," below)	0.00	0.00	0.00	Homeowner Assn. Dues	0.00	0.00
				Other:	0.00	0.00
Total	$ 4,500.00	$ 2,520.00	$ 7,020.00	Total	$ 471.21	$ 413.85

* Self Employed Borrower(s) may be required to provide additional documentation such as tax returns and financial statements.

Describe Other Income *Notice:* Alimony, child support, or separate maintenance income need not be revealed if the Borrower (B) or Co-Borrower (C) does not choose to have it considered for repaying this loan.

B/C		Monthly Amount
B		$ 0.00
C		0.00

VI. ASSETS AND LIABILITIES

This Statement and any applicable supporting schedules may be completed jointly by both married and unmarried Co-Borrowers if their assets and liabilities are sufficiently joined so that the Statement can be meaningfully and fairly presented on a combined basis; otherwise separate Statements and Schedules are required. If the Co-Borrower section was completed about a spouse, this Statement and supporting schedules must be completed about that spouse also.   Completed ☐ Jointly ☐ Not Jointly

ASSETS Description	Cash or Market Value	Liabilities and Pledged Assets. List the creditor's name, address and account number for all outstanding debts, including automobile loans, revolving charge accounts, real estate loans, alimony, child support, stock pledges, etc. Use continuation sheet, if necessary. Indicate by (*) those liabilities which will be satisfied upon sale of real estate owned or upon refinancing of the subject property.	Monthly Payt. & Mos. Left to Pay	Unpaid Balance
Cash deposit toward purchase held by:	$ 0.00	**Credit Cards** CUNA CU	0.00 /	$ 0.00
List checking and savings accounts below		CUNA CU	0.00 /	$ 0.00
Name and address of Bank, S&L, or Credit Union		AMERICAN EXPRESS	0.00 /	$ 0.00
CUNA CREDIT UNION 401 S YELLOWSTONE DR MADIOSN WI 53719		AT & T UNIV CARD	0.00 /	$ 0.00
Acct. no. 59104000	$ 18,766.79		0.00 /	$ 0.00
Name and address of Bank, S&L, or Credit Union		Name and address of Company - Mortgage ANCHORBANK 25 W MAIN ST MADISON WI 53703	$ Payt./Mos.	$
Acct. no.	$ 0.00			
Name and address of Bank, S&L, or Credit Union		Acct. no. 41-15102284	471.21	66,114.00
		Name and address of Company - Mortgage	$ Payt./Mos.	$
Acct. no.	$ 0.00			
Name and address of Bank, S&L, or Credit Union		Acct. no.	0.00	0.00
		Name and address of Company - Other Loan	$ Payt./Mos.	$
Acct. no.	$ 0.00			
Stocks & Bonds (Company name/number & description) AIM FUN AMERICAN FUND PHOENIX WALL ST DISCNT	$ 0.00 0.00 0.00 4,306.00	Acct. no. Name and address of Company - Other Loan	$ Payt./Mos.	0.00 / $ 0.00
Life insurance net cash value Face amount: $ 0.00	$ 0.00	Acct. no. Name and address of Company - Other Loan	$ Payt./Mos.	0.00 / $ 0.00
Subtotal Liquid Assets	$ 23,072.79			
Real estate owned (enter market value from schedule of real estate owned)	$ 110,000.00			
Vested interest in retirement fund	$ 0.00			
Net worth of business(es) owned (attach financial statement)	$ 0.00	Acct. no. Alimony/Child Support/Separate Maintenance Payments Owed to:	$	0.00 / 0.00
Automobiles owned (make and year) VW 1986 JEEP 1992	$ 3,500.00 18,000.00 0.00	Job Related Expenses (child care, union dues, etc.) CHILDCARE	$ 0.00 0.00	0.00 / 0.00 /
Other Assets (itemize)	$ 0.00 0.00 0.00	Total Monthly Payments	$ 471.21	
Total Assets a.	$ 154,572.79	Net Worth (a minus b) $ 88,458.79	Total Liabilities b.	$ 66,114.00

Freddie Mac Form 65/Rev. 10/92   Page 2 of 4   Borrower's Initial(s) MR AR   Fannie Mae Form 1003/Rev. 10/92
Form URLA2

0015149

VI. ASSETS AND LIABILITIES (cont.)

Schedule of Real Estate Owned (If additional properties are owned, use continuation sheet.)

Property address (enter S if sold, PS if pending sale or R if rental being held for income)	Type of Property	Present Market Value	Amount of Mortgages & Liens	Gross Rental Income	Mortgage Payments	Insurance, Maintenance, Taxes & Misc.	Net Rental Income
5806 SUFFOLK RD	RES	$110,000.00	$ 66,114.00	$ 0.00	$ 471.21	$ 0.00	$ 471.21-
			0.00	0.00	0.00	0.00	0.00
			0.00	0.00	0.00	0.00	0.00
Totals		$110,000.00	$ 66,114.00	$ 0.00	$ 471.21	$ 0.00	$ 471.21-

List any additional names under which credit has previously been received and indicate appropriate creditor name(s) and account number(s):

Alternate Name	Creditor Name	Account Number

VII. DETAILS OF TRANSACTION

a. Purchase price	$	0.00
b. Alterations, improvements, repairs		0.00
c. Land (if acquired separately)		0.00
d. Refinance (incl. debts to be paid off)		0.00
e. Estimated prepaid items		0.00
f. Estimated closing costs		871.00
g. PMI, MIP, Funding Fee		0.00
h. Discount (if Borrower will pay)		0.00
i. Total costs (add items a through h)		871.00
j. Subordinate financing		0.00
k. Borrower's closing costs paid by Seller		0.00
l. Other Credits (explain)		0.00
Application Fee		900.00
Earnest Money Deposit		0.00
m. Loan amount (exclude PMI, MIP, Funding Fee financed)		65,000.00
n. PMI, MIP, Funding Fee financed		0.00
o. Loan amount (add m & n)		65,000.00
p. Cash from/to Borrower (subtract j, k, l, and o from i)		-65,029.00

VIII. DECLARATIONS

If you answer "yes" to any questions a through i, please use continuation sheet for explanation

	Borrower		Co-Borrower	
	Yes	No	Yes	No
a. Are there any outstanding judgments against you?	☐	☒	☐	☒
b. Have you been declared bankrupt within the past 7 years?	☐	☒	☐	☒
c. Have you had property foreclosed upon or given title or deed in lieu thereof in the last 7 years?	☐	☒	☐	☒
d. Are you a party to a law suit?	☐	☒	☐	☒
e. Have you directly or indirectly been obligated on any loan which resulted in foreclosure, transfer of title in lieu of foreclosure, or judgment? (This would include such loans as home mortgage loans, SBA loans, home improvement loans, educational loans, manufactured (mobile) home loans, any mortgage, financial obligation, bond, or loan guarantee. If "Yes", provide details, including date, name and address of Lender, FHA or VA case number, if any, and reasons for the action.)	☐	☒	☐	☒
f. Are you presently delinquent or in default on any Federal debt or any other loan, mortgage, financial obligation, bond, or loan guarantee? If "Yes," give details as described in the preceding question.	☐	☒	☐	☒
g. Are you obligated to pay alimony, child support, or separate maintenance?	☐	☒	☐	☒
h. Is any part of the down payment borrowed?	☐	☒	☐	☒
i. Are you a co-maker or endorser on a note?	☐	☒	☐	☒
j. Are you a U.S. citizen?	☒	☐	☒	☐
k. Are you a permanent resident alien?	☐	☒	☐	☒
l. Do you intend to occupy the property as your primary residence? If "Yes," complete question m below.	☒	☐	☒	☐
m. Have you had an ownership interest in a property in the last three years?	☒	☐	☒	☐
(1) What type of property did you own-principal residence (PR), second home (SH), or investment property (IP)?	PR		PR	
(2) How did you hold title to the home–solely by yourself (S), jointly with your spouse (SP), or jointly with another person (O)?	SP		SP	

IX. ACKNOWLEDGMENT AND AGREEMENT

The undersigned specifically acknowledge(s) and agree(s) that: (1) the loan requested by this application will be secured by a first mortgage or deed of trust on the property described herein; (2) the property will not be used for any illegal or prohibited purpose or use; (3) all statements made in this application are made for the purpose of obtaining the loan indicated herein; (4) occupation of the property will be as indicated above; (5) verification or reverification of any information contained in the application may be made at any time by the Lender, its agents, successors and assigns, either directly or through a credit reporting agency, from any source named in this application, and the original copy of this application will be retained by the Lender, even if the loan is not approved; (6) the Lender, its agents, successors and assigns will rely on the information contained in the application and I/we have a continuing obligation to amend and/or supplement the information provided in this application if any of the material facts which I/we have represented herein should change prior to closing; (7) in the event my/our payments on the loan indicated in this application become delinquent, the Lender, its agents, successors and assigns, may, in addition to all their other rights and remedies, report my/our name(s) and account information to a credit reporting agency; (8) ownership of the loan may be transferred to successor or assign of the Lender without notice to me and/or the administration of the loan account may be transferred to an agent, successor or assign of the Lender with prior notice to me; (9) the Lender, its agents, successors and assigns make no representations or warranties, express or implied, to the Borrower(s) regarding the property, the condition of the property, or the value of the property. **Certification:** I/We certify that the information provided in this application is true and correct as of the date set forth opposite my/our signature(s) on this application and acknowledge my/our understanding that any intentional or negligent misrepresentation(s) of the information contained in this application may result in civil liability and/or criminal penalties including, but not limited to, fine or imprisonment or both under the provisions of Title 18, United States Code, Section 1001, et seq. and liability for monetary damages to the Lender, its agents, successors and assigns, insurers and any other person who may suffer any loss due to reliance upon any misrepresentation which I/we have made on this application.

I/we understand that completion of this application does not constitute a complete application until submitted with required documentation.

I/we understand regular loan payments are made utilizing AnchorBank's Automatic payment method.

This information may be shared by AnchorBank and its subsidiaries for the purposes of providing financial services.

Borrower's Signature	Date	Co-Borrower's Signature	Date
X	8-13-93	X	8-13-93

X. INFORMATION FOR GOVERNMENT MONITORING PURPOSES

The following information is requested by the Federal Government for certain types of loans related to a dwelling, in order to monitor the Lender's compliance with equal credit opportunity, fair housing and home mortgage disclosure laws. You are not required to furnish this information, but are encouraged to do so. The law provides that a Lender may neither discriminate on the basis of this information, nor on whether you choose to furnish it. However, if you choose not to furnish it, under Federal regulations this Lender is required to note race and sex on the basis of visual observation or surname. If you do not wish to furnish the above information, please check the box below. (Lender must review the above material to assure that the disclosures satisfy all requirements to which the Lender is subject under applicable state law for the particular type of loan applied for.)

BORROWER

☐ I do not wish to furnish this information

Race/National Origin:
☐ American Indian or Alaskan Native ☐ Asian or Pacific Islander
☐ Black, not of Hispanic origin ☐ Hispanic ☒ White, not of Hispanic origin
☐ Other (specify) _____

Sex: ☐ Female ☒ Male

CO-BORROWER

☐ I do not wish to furnish this information

Race/National Origin:
☐ American Indian or Alaskan Native ☐ Asian or Pacific Islander
☐ Black, not of Hispanic origin ☐ Hispanic ☒ White, not of Hispanic origin
☐ Other (specify) _____

Sex: ☒ Female ☐ Male

To be Completed by Interviewer	Interviewer's Name (print or type)	Name and Address of Interviewer's Employer
This application was taken by: ☒ face-to-face interview ☐ by mail ☐ by telephone	ROY WHITE	
	Interviewer's Signature Roy White Date 8-13-93	
	Interviewer's Phone Number (incl. area code)	

Freddie Mac Form 65/Rev. 10/92

0015149

Page 3 of 4

Fannie Mae Form 1003/Rev. 10/92
Form URLA3

Date JANUARY 28, 1994

Account Number 0015149

ANCHORBANK, S.S.B.

AUDREY F. ROBERTSON
MICHAEL J. ROBERTSON

Borrower

25 W. Main Street

Address

5806 SUFFOLK RD.

Address

Madison, WI 53703

City   State   Zip Code

MADISON, WIS. 53711

City   State   Zip Code

FEDERAL TRUTH-IN-LENDING DISCLOSURES

ANNUAL PERCENTAGE RATE	FINANCE CHARGE	AMOUNT FINANCED	TOTAL OF PAYMENTS
The cost of your credit as a yearly rate.	The dollar amount the credit will cost you.	The amount of credit provided to you or on your behalf.	This amount you will have paid after you have made all payments as scheduled.
6.598 %	$ 28,853.48	$ 64,747.90	$ 93,601.38

You have the right to receive an itemization of the Amount Financed   ☐ I want an itemization.   ☐ I do not want an itemization.
Your payment schedule will be:

Number of Payments	Amount of Payments	Payments Are Due	Number of Payments	Amount of Payments	Payments Are Due
83	413.85	OCTOBER 1, 1993			
1	59,251.83	SEPTEMBER 1, 2000			

Security : **Security for this loan is**
☐ a mortgage on the property being purchased.
☒ a mortgage on the property located at   5806 SUFFOLK ROAD, MADISON, WISCONSIN 53711
☐

Filing Fees: $ 38.00

Late Charge: ☐ If a payment is more than 15 days late, you will be charged four% of the unpaid amount of the payment.
☒ If a payment is more than 15 days late, you will be charged five% of the unpaid amount of the payment.

Prepayment: If you pay the loan off early, you
☐ may   ☒ will not   ☒ have to pay a penalty.
☐ may   ☒ will not   ☒ be entitled to a refund of part of the finance charge.

Insurance: Credit Life Insurance and Credit Disability Insurance are not required to obtain credit, and will not be provided unless you sign and agree to pay the additional cost, after approval by the insurance company. The premium stated below is for a one year term.

Type	Premium	Signature(s)
Credit Life/ Single Coverage		I want credit life insurance _____ Signature
Credit Life/ Joint Coverage		We want credit life insurance _____ Signature _____ Signature
Credit Disability		I want credit disability insurance _____ Signature

You may obtain property insurance from anyone you want that is acceptable to Anchor. If you get the insurance from Anchor, you will pay $___N/A___ for a ___N/A___ month term.

Assumption: Unless Anchor gives prior written consent and certain conditions are met, someone buying the property will not be allowed to assume the remainder of the mortgage on its original terms and conditions.

Variable Rate: If checked, ☐ this loan has a variable rate feature. Disclosures about the variable rate feature have been provided to you earlier.

ADDENDUM: ☒ See Attached Special Features Addendum.

See your contract documents for any additional information about non-payment, transfer of this property, termination or occupancy by owner, default, any required repayment in full before the scheduled date, and prepayment refunds and penalties.

I have received a copy of this Disclosure.

*e means estimate

Michael J. Robertson
MICHAEL J. ROBERTSON

Audrey F. Robertson
AUDREY F. ROBERTSON

LTIL General

24

PAA

Anchor Form LTIL2

ANCHORBANK, S.S.B.

Good Faith Estimate of Settlement Charges and Costs
Loan Program Disclosures
(This is not a commitment for a mortgage loan.)

The Good Faith Estimate of Settlement Charges is made pursuant to the requirements of the Real Estate
Settlement Procedures Act (RESPA). These figures are only estimates and the actual charges may be different.

LOAN PROGRAM

Type of Loan: CONVENTIONAL
Kind of Loan: BALLOON FIXED
Purpose: Refinance - Anchor Holds Underlying

Price:	$	0.00
Down Payment	$	65,000.00–
VA Funding Fee Financed	($	0.00)
Financed MI	($	0.00)
Proposed Mortgage	$	65,000.00

SETTLEMENT CHARGES

0.000 % Origination Fee	$	0.00
Appraisal Fee	$	250.00
Credit Report	$	40.00
Private Mtg. Insurance/MIP Prepaid	$	0.00
Title Insurance	$	318.00
Recording Fees	$	38.00
Survey	$	0.00
Closing Fee	$	125.00
VA Funding Fee Prepaid	$	0.00
VA/FHA Discount Points	$	0.00
Property/Energy Inspection	$	0.00
Processing Fee	$	100.00
	$	0.00
	$	0.00
	$	
Estimated Interest	$	152.10
Costs Paid by Seller/Other	($	0.00)
TOTAL	$	923.10

TERMS QUOTED

Interest Rate:	6.570
Term:	360

ADJUSTABLE RATE MORTGAGES

Current Index:	0.000
Margin:	0.000
Annual Cap:	0.000
Lifetime Cap:	0.000

MONTHLY HOUSING EXPENSE

Principal & Interest	$	413.85
Hazard Insurance	$	0.00
Real Estate Taxes	$	0.00
PMI/FHA MIP	$	0.00
	$	0.00
TOTAL	$	413.85

ESTIMATED ESCROWS

Hazard Insurance				
Mos. @	0.00	$		0.00
Real Estate Taxes				
Mos. @	0.00	$		0.00
PMI/FHA MIP				
Mos. @	0.00	$		0.00
Mos. @	0.00	$		0.00

Total Escrows $	0.00

HOMEOWNERS CHECKING

When your loan is approved and closed, you will become eligible for a service charge free Homeowners Checking account. Also you
will receive 50 Antique style checks with this account. Your account will remain free of monthly service charges as long as you
have a mortgage with Anchor.

PAYMENT METHOD

If your loan is approved, monthly payments will be made by an "Automatic Payment" plan. Your payments will be scheduled to occur
on the _____ day of each month. Payments are due on the first day of each month, payable by the 15th. All extra payments will
be applied to principal.
Transfers will be drawn from your checking account # _____

Name of Financial Institution _____   City, State _____

Yes! I/we accept and agree to this payment method.

By: _____   By: _____

Borrower Name: **MICHAEL J. ROBERTSON**   Borrower Name: **AUDREY F. ROBERTSON**

Loan Officer: **Ron Steinhofer**

APPLICATION FEE

Each application must be accompanied by a $ _____ 900.00 _____ non-refundable application fee. If this application results in a
closed loan, the full amount of the application fee will be credited toward your closing costs. All loans must close within 120 days of the
date of the application or all fees and deposits are forfeited, and the application shall be deemed to be withdrawn by the applicant(s).

The undersigned hereby acknowledges receipt of this form, the HUD Booklet "Settlement Costs and You", and if an ARM loan, the ARM
Program Disclosures and the ARM Booklet.

_____   _____
Signature   Date   Signature   Date
                                                                                                      GFE2

ANCHORBANK, S.S.B.

OTHER LOAN DISCLOSURES

FOR ONE TO FOUR FAMILY OWNER-OCCUPIED PROPERTIES

1. Your loan contract does contain a due on sale clause; if you sell this property or transfer ownership, the lender has the option of calling the loan due and payable in full.

2. Your loan contract does contain a late charge provision; if your payment is received more than 15 days after the due date, there will be a charge of 5% of the past due principal and interest payment. For example: a past due principal and interest payment of $500 would have a late charge due of $25, for a total due that month of $525. This applies to conventional loans. Various government programs may have a different late charge.

3. Your loan contract does contain a provision requiring escrow payments for the timely payment of real estate taxes, home owners insurance, and if applicable, private mortgage insurance. The monthly payments equal one twelfth of the annual amounts due for the escrowed items. As the items are paid you will be notified at least once per year of the status of your escrow account. If there is a shortage, the shortage may be corrected in one lump payment, or over the balance of the escrow year. If there is a surplus, you may request reimbursement or leave the funds in your account. Wisconsin statutes provide for the payment of interest on escrow accounts for owner-occupied one to four family dwellings.

   If you do not make the monthly payments for escrow as required by the lender, this is a default under the mortgage contract, and the lender may take legal action including but not limited to a foreclosure action.

4. This loan may be pre-paid in full or in part at any time without penalty.

LOAN SERVICING TRANSFER PRACTICES DISCLOSURE

AnchorBank, S.S.B. has, in the past three years (1991, 1992 and 1993), retained the servicing of all (100%) home loans except for Federal VA and FHA loans. Servicing of all (100%) Federal VA and FHA loans have been transferred to another lender/servicer on or about the date of closing and we expect this practice to continue.

WISCONSIN ESCROW DISCLOSURE

Funds held in escrow for payment of property taxes are disbursed to you once a year. A check is issued made jointly payable to you and your local taxing authority. You have the option of receiving the check in December or January. Unless directed otherwise we will schedule the disbursement for December.

This form does not cover all the items you will be required to pay in cash at Settlement; attorney's fees (if any), your homeowners insurance, etc. You may wish to inquire as to the amounts of such items, as you may be required to pay other additional amounts at Settlement. AnchorBank makes no representations as to the deductability of interest or costs. For tax advice consult your own attorney or tax preparer.

I/(WE) ACKNOWLEDGE RECEIPT OF A COPY OF THIS FORM.

Signature(s)

Signature(s)

GFEA

DISCLOSURE STATEMENT

NOTICE TO MORTGAGE LOAN APPLICANTS: THE RIGHT TO COLLECT YOUR MORTGAGE LOAN PAYMENTS MAY BE TRANSFERRED. FEDERAL LAW GIVES YOU CERTAIN RIGHTS. READ THIS STATEMENT AND SIGN IT ONLY IF YOU UNDERSTAND ITS CONTENTS.

Because you are applying for a mortgage loan covered by the Real Estate Settlement Procedures Act (RESPA) (12 U.S.C. s2601 et seq.) you have certain rights under that Federal law. This statement tells you about those rights. It also tells you what the chances are that the servicing for this loan may be transferred to a different loan servicer. "Servicing" refers to collecting your principal, interest and escrow account payments. If your loan servicer changes, there are certain procedures that must be followed. This statement generally explains those procedures.

Transfer practices and requirements

If the servicing of your loan is assigned, sold, or transferred to a new servicer, you must be given written notice of that transfer. The present loan servicer must send you notice in writing of the assignment, sale or transfer of the servicing not less than 15 days before the date of transfer. The new loan servicer must also send you notice within 15 days after the date of the transfer. Also, a notice of prospective transfer may be provided to you at settlement (when title to your new property is transferred to you) to satisfy these requirements. The law allows a delay in the time (not more than 30 days after a transfer) for servicers to notify you under certain limited circumstances, when your servicer is changed abruptly. This exception applies only if your servicer is fired for cause, is in bankruptcy proceedings, or is involved in a conservatorship or receivership initiated by a Federal agency.

Notices must contain information. They must contain the effective date of the transfer of the servicing of your loan to the new servicer, the name, address, and toll-free or collect call telephone number of the new servicer, and toll-free or collect call telephone numbers of a person or department for both your present servicer and your new servicer to answer your questions about the transfer of servicing. During the 60-day period following the effective date of the transfer of the loan servicing, a loan payment received by your old servicer before its due date may not be treated by the new loan servicer as late, and a late fee may not be imposed on you.

Complaint Resolution

Section 6 of RESPA (12 U.S.C. s2605) gives you certain consumer rights, whether or not your loan servicing is transferred. If you send a "qualified written request" to your loan servicer concerning the servicing of your loan, your servicer must provide you with a written acknowledgment within 20 business days of receipt of your request. A "qualified written request" is a written correspondence, other than notice on a payment coupon or other payment medium supplied by the servicer, which includes your name and account number, and your reasons for the request. Not later than 60 business days after receiving your request, your servicer must make any appropriate corrections to your account, and must provide you with a written clarification regarding any dispute. During this 60-day period, your servicer may not provide information to a consumer reporting agency concerning any overdue payment related to such period or qualified written request.

Damages and Cost

Section 6 of RESPA also provides for damages and costs for individuals or classes of individuals in circumstances where servicers are shown to have violated the requirements of that Section.

Servicing Transfer Estimates by Original Lender

The following is the best estimate of what will happen to the servicing of your mortgage loan:

1. _____ We do not service mortgage loans. We intend to assign, sell, or transfer the servicing of your loan to another party. You will be notified at settlement regarding the servicer.

LF-136 #4 1/94

OR

2. _____ We are able to service this loan and presently intend to do so. However, that may change in the future. For all the loans that we make in the 12-month period after your loan is funded, we estimate that the chances that we will transfer the servicing of those loans is between:

    X   0 to 25%

    _____ 26 to 50%

    _____ 51 to 75%

    _____ 76 to 100%

This is only our best estimate and it is not binding. Business conditions or other circumstances may affect our future transferring decisions.

3. This is our record of transferring the servicing of the loans we have made in the past:

Year	Percent of Loans Transferred	(Rounded to nearest quartile -- 0%, 25%, 50%, 75% or 100%)
19 __93__	__0 - 25__ %	
19 __92__	__0 - 25__ %	
19 __91__	__0 - 25__ %	

The estimates in 2. and 3. above do not include transfers to affiliates or subsidiaries. If the servicing of your loan is transferred to an affiliate or subsidiary in the future, you will be notified in accordance with RESPA.

_____
LENDER (Signature Not Mandatory)

_____
DATE

INSTRUCTIONS TO PREPARER: For applications received in calendar year 1991 after the effective date of this Notice, the information in 3. above will be for calendar year 1990 only; for applications received in 1992, this information will be for calendar years 1990 and 1991; and for applications received in 1993 and thereafter, this information will be for the previous three calendar years.

ACKNOWLEDGMENT OF MORTGAGE LOAN APPLICANT

I/we have read this disclosure form, and understand its contents, as evidenced by my/our signature(s) below.

_____
APPLICANT'S SIGNATURE

_____
CO-APPLICANT'S SIGNATURE

__8-13-93_____
DATE

ANCHORBANK, s.s.s.
25 West Main Street, Madison, Wisconsin 53703

Date 08/13/93

Loan No.   0115220208

NOTICE OF RIGHT TO CANCEL
(For Refinancing of Security Interest in Consumer's Principal Dwelling)

Your Right To Cancel

You are entering into a new transaction to increase the amount of credit provided to you. Anchor (hereinafter "We") acquired a mortgage, lien or other security interest on your home under the original transaction and will retain that mortgage, lien or security interest in the new transaction. You have a legal right under Federal law to cancel the new transaction, without cost, within three business days from whichever of the following events occurs last:

(1) The date of the new transaction, which is **AUGUST 13, 1993** ; or

(2) The date you received your new Truth in Lending disclosures; or

(3) The date you received this notice of your right to cancel.

If you cancel the new transaction, your cancellation will apply only to the increase in the amount of credit. It will not affect the amount that you presently owe on the mortgage, lien or security interest we already have on your home. If you cancel, the mortgage, lien or security interest as it applies to the increased amount is also cancelled. Within 20 calendar days after we receive your notice of cancellation of the new transaction, we must take the steps necessary to reflect the fact that our mortgage, lien or security interest on your home no longer applies to the increase of credit. We must also return any money you have given to us or anyone else in connection with the new transaction.

You may keep any money we have given you in the new transaction until we have done the things mentioned above, but you must then offer to return the money at the address below. If we do not take possession of the money within 20 calendar days of your offer, you may keep it without further obligation.

How to Cancel

If you decide to cancel the new transaction, you may do so by notifying us in writing, at: **AnchorBank**

_____25 W. Main Street_____   Madison, WI 53703
                                             Address

You may use any written statement that is signed and dated by you and states your intention to cancel, or you may use this notice by dating and signing below. Keep one copy of this notice because it contains important information about your rights.

If you cancel by mail or telegram, you must send the notice no later than midnight of **AUGUST 18, 1993**
(or midnight of the third business day following the latest of the three events listed above). If you send or deliver your written notice to cancel some other way, it must be delivered to the above address no later than that time.

I WISH TO CANCEL

_____
CONSUMER'S SIGNATURE   DATE

RECEIPT

Each of the undersigned acknowledges receipt of two (2) copies of this Notice and warrants that the undersigned include all the persons whose ownership interest will be subject to the security interest in the dwelling.

Dated this **13TH** day of **AUGUST**   **1993**

CONFIRMATION

More than 3 business days have elapsed since the undersigned received this Notice and Truth in Lending disclosures with regard to this transaction. The undersigned certify that the transaction has not been rescinded.

Dated this _19th_ day of _August_ _1993_

refi in

0015149

LF154

ANCHORBANK, s.s.b.
25 West Main Street, Madison, Wisconsin 53703

Date 08/13/93

Loan No.   0115220208

NOTICE OF RIGHT TO CANCEL
(For Refinancing of Security Interest in Consumer's Principal Dwelling)

Your Right To Cancel

You are entering into a new transaction to increase the amount of credit provided to you. Anchor (hereinafter "We") acquired a mortgage, lien or other security interest on your home under the original transaction and will retain that mortgage, lien or security interest in the new transaction. You have a legal right under Federal law to cancel the new transaction, without cost, within three business days from whichever of the following events occurs last:

(1) The date of the new transaction, which is   AUGUST 13, 1993   ; or

(2) The date you received your new Truth in Lending disclosures; or

(3) The date you received this notice of your right to cancel.

If you cancel the new transaction, your cancellation will apply only to the increase in the amount of credit. It will not affect the amount that you presently owe on the mortgage, lien or security interest we already have on your home. If you cancel, the mortgage, lien or security interest as it applies to the increased amount is also cancelled. Within 20 calendar days after we receive your notice of cancellation of the new transaction, we must take the steps necessary to reflect the fact that our mortgage, lien or security interest on your home no longer applies to the increase of credit. We must also return any money you have given to us or anyone else in connection with the new transaction.

You may keep any money we have given you in the new transaction until we have done the things mentioned above, but you must then offer to return the money at the address below. If we do not take possession of the money within 20 calendar days of your offer, you may keep it without further obligation.

How to Cancel

If you decide to cancel the new transaction, you may do so by notifying us in writing, at: **AnchorBank**

  25 W. Main Street   Madison, WI 53703
                                                      Address

You may use any written statement that is signed and dated by you and states your intention to cancel, or you may use this notice by dating and signing below. Keep one copy of this notice because it contains important information about your rights.

If you cancel by mail or telegram, you must send the notice no later than midnight of   AUGUST 18, 1993
(or midnight of the third business day following the latest of the three events listed above). If you send or deliver your written notice to cancel some other way, it must be delivered to the above address no later than that time.

I WISH TO CANCEL

_____   _____
CONSUMER'S SIGNATURE   DATE

RECEIPT

Each of the undersigned acknowledges receipt of two (2) copies of this Notice and warrants that the undersigned include all the persons whose ownership interest will be subject to the security interest in the dwelling.

Dated this 13TH day of   AUGUST   1993

Ahy F. R.t.

CONFIRMATION

More than 3 business days have elapsed since the undersigned received this Notice and Truth in Lending disclosures with regard to this transaction. The undersigned certify that the transaction has not been rescinded.

Dated this 19th day of August   1993

Ahy F. R.t.

LF154

refi in

0015149

FannieMae

Request for Verification of Employment

Privacy Act Notice: This information is to be used by the agency collecting it or its assignees whether you qualify as a prospective mortgagor under its program. It will not be disclosed outside the agency except as required and permitted by law. You do not have to provide this information, but if you do not your application for approval as a prospective mortgagor or borrower may be delayed or rejected. The information requested in this form is authorized by Title 38, USC, Chapter 37 (if VA); by 12 USC, Section 1701 et.seq. (if HUD/FHA); by 42 USC, Section 1452b (if HUD/CPD); and Title 42 USC, 1471 et.seq., or 7 USC, 1921 et.seq. (if USDA/FmHA).

Instructions: Lender – Complete items 1 through 7. Have applicant complete item 8. Forward directly to employer named in item 1.
Employer – Please complete either Part II or Part III as applicable. Complete Part IV and return directly to lender named in item 2.
The form is to be transmitted directly to the lender and is not to be transmitted through the applicant or any other party.

Part I -- Request

1. To (Name and address of employer)	2. From (Name and address of lender)
PROMACS **5806 SUFFOLK RD** **MADISON WI 53711**	**AnchorBank, s.s.b.** **25 W. Main Street** **Madison, WI 53703**

I certify that this verification has been sent directly to the employer and has not passed through the hands of the applicant or any other interested party.

3. Signature of Lender	4. Title **Pamela A. Allen** **LN PROCESSING SPECIALIST** **(608) 252-8993**	5. Date **01/28/94**	6. Lender's Number (Optional)

I have applied for a mortgage loan and stated that I am now or was formerly employed by you. My signature below authorizes verification of this information.

7. Name and Address of Applicant (include employee or badge number) **MICHAEL J. ROBERTSON** **5806 SUFFOLK RD.** **MADISON, WIS. 53711**	8. Signature of Applicant **SEE ATTACHED**

Part II -- Verification of Present Employment

9. Applicant's Date of Employment **5-17-91**	10. Present Position **President / COO**	11. Probability of Continued Employment **Excellent**

12A. Current Gross Base Pay (Enter Amount and Check Period)

[X] Annual [ ] Hourly [ ] Monthly [ ] Other (Specify) [ ] Weekly

$ **54,500**

13. For Military Personnel Only

Pay Grade		
Type	Monthly Amount	

14. If Overtime or Bonus is Applicable, Is Its Continuance Likely?
Overtime [ ] Yes [X] No
Bonus [ ] Yes [X] No

15. If paid hourly -- average hours per week

12B. Gross Earnings

Type	Year To Date	Past Year 19 ___	Past Year 19 ___			
	Thru ___ 19 ___			Rations	$	
Base Pay	$ 31,500	$ 58,000	$ 28,650	Flight or Hazard	$	16. Date of applicant's next pay increase **Unknown**
Overtime	$	$	$	Clothing	$	
				Quarters	$	17. Projected amount of next pay increase
Commissions	$	$	$	Pro Pay	$	**Unknown**
Bonus	$	$	$	Overseas or Combat	$	18. Date of applicant's last pay increase
Total	$ 31,500	$ 58,000	$ 28,650	Variable Housing Allowance	$	19. Amount of last pay increase

20. Remarks (If employee was off work for any length of time, please indicate time period and reason)

Part III - Verification of Previous Employment

21. Date Hired	23. Salary/Wage at Termination Per (Year) (Month) (Week)
22. Date Terminated	Base _____ Overtime _____ Commissions _____ Bonus _____
24. Reason for Leaving	25. Position Held

Part IV - Authorized Signature

Federal statutes provide severe penalties for any fraud, intentional misrepresentation, or criminal connivance or conspiracy purposed to influence the issuance of any guaranty or insurance by the VA Secretary, the U.S.D.A., FmHA/FHA Commissioner, or the HUD/CPD Assistant Secretary.

26. Signature of Employer	27. Title (Please print or type) **Owner**	28. Date
29. Print or type name signed in item 26 **C. R. Hemingway**	30. Phone No. **277-8870**	**7-25-93**

0015149 24 PAA   Anchor Form LF104   Fannie Mae Form 1005 Mar. 90   LF104

Request for Verification of Employment

Privacy Act Notice: This information is to be used by the agency collecting it or its assignees whether you qualify as a prospective mortgagor under its program. It will not be disclosed outside the agency except as required and permitted by law. You do not have to provide this information, but if you do not your application for approval as a prospective mortgagor or borrower may be delayed or rejected. The information requested in this form is authorized by Title 38, USC, Chapter 37 (if VA); by 12 USC, Section 1701 et.seq. (if HUD/FHA); by 42 USC, Section 1452b (if HUD/CPD); and Title 42 USC, 1471 et.seq., or 7 USC, 1921 et.seq. (if USDA/FmHA).

Instructions: Lender - Complete items 1 through 7. Have applicant complete item 8. Forward directly to employer named in item 1.
Employer - Please complete either Part II or Part III as applicable. Complete Part IV and return directly to lender named in item 2.
The form is to be transmitted directly to the lender and is not to be transmitted through the applicant or any other party.

Part I -- Request

1. To (Name and address of employer)	2. From (Name and address of lender)
CUNA MUTUAL INS GROUP **5910 MINERAL PT RD** **MADISON WI 53701**	**AnchorBank, s.s.b.** **25 W. Main Street** **Madison, WI 53703**

I certify that this verification has been sent directly to the employer and has not passed through the hands of the applicant or any other interested party.

3. Signature of Lender	4. Title **Pamela A. Allen** **LN PROCESSING SPECIALIST** **(608) 252-8993**	5. Date **01/28/94**	6. Lender's Number (Optional)
Pam Allen			

I have applied for a mortgage loan and stated that I am now or was formerly employed by you. My signature below authorizes verification of this information.

7. Name and Address of Applicant (include employee or badge number) **AUDREY F. ROBERTSON** **5806 SUFFOLK RD.** **MADISON, WIS. 53711**	8. Signature of Applicant **SEE ATTACHED**

Part II -- Verification of Present Employment

9. Applicant's Date of Employment **11-22-86**	10. Present Position Underwriter Consultant	11. Probability of Continued Employment Company Policy Prohibits Response

12A. Current Gross Base Pay (Enter Amount and Check Period)

[X] Annual [ ] Hourly [ ] Monthly [ ] Other (Specify) [ ] Weekly

$ 30,250

13. For Military Personnel Only		14. If Overtime or Bonus is Applicable, Is Its Continuance Likely?
Pay Grade		Overtime [ ] Yes [X] No
Type	Monthly Amount	Bonus [X] Yes [ ] No
Base Pay	$	15. If paid hourly -- average hours per week

12B. Gross Earnings

Type	Year To Date	Past Year 19 ___	Past Year 19 ___			
	Thru ___ 19 ___			Rations	$	16. Date of applicant's next pay increase
Base Pay	$ 17,640	$ 28,750	$ 27,500	Flight or Hazard	$	
Overtime	$	$	$	Clothing	$	17. Projected amount of next pay increase
Commissions	$	$	$	Quarters	$	
				Pro Pay	$	18. Date of applicant's last pay increase
Bonus	$ 350	$ 350	$ 150	Overseas or Combat	$	
Total	$ 17,990	$ 29,100	$ 27,650	Variable Housing Allowance	$	19. Amount of last pay increase

20. Remarks (If employee was off work for any length of time, please indicate time period and reason)

Part III - Verification of Previous Employment

21. Date Hired	23. Salary/Wage at Termination Per (Year) (Month) (Week)
22. Date Terminated	Base ____ Overtime ____ Commissions ____ Bonus ____
24. Reason for Leaving	25. Position Held

Part IV - Authorized Signature
Federal statutes provide severe penalties for any fraud, intentional misrepresentation, or criminal connivance or conspiracy purposed to influence the issuance of any guaranty or insurance by the VA Secretary, the U.S.D.A., FmHA/FHA Commissioner, or the HUD/CPD Assistant Secretary.

26. Signature of Employer	27. Title (Please print or type) Human Resource Mgr.	28. Date
29. Print or type name signed in item 26 Jeanette Newhouse	30. Phone No. 238-0045	7-22-93

0015149   24   PAA

Form LF10A   Fannie Mae Form 1005 Mar. 90   LF104

REQUEST FOR VERIFICATION OF DEPOSIT

Privacy Act Notice: This information is to be used by the agency collecting it or its assignees in determining whether you qualify as a prospective mortgagor under its program. It will not be disclosed outside the agency except as required and permitted by law. You do not have to provide this information, but if you do not your application for approval as a prospective mortgagor or borrower may be delayed or rejected. The information requested in this form is authorized by Title 38, USC, Chapter 37 (If VA); by 12 USC, Section 1701 et.seq. (If HUD/FHA); by 42 USC, Section 1452b (If HUD/CPD); and Title 42 USC, 1471 et.seq. or 7 USC, 1921 et.seq. (If USDA/FmHA).

Instructions: Lender - Complete Items 1 through 8. Have applicant(s) complete Item 9. Forward directly to depository named in Item 1.
Depository - Please complete Items 10 through 18 and return DIRECTLY to lender named in Item 2.
The form is to be transmitted directly to the lender and is not to be transmitted through the applicant(s) or any other party.

Part I - Request

1. To (Name and address of depository)	2. From (Name and address of lender)
CUNA CREDIT UNION **401 S YELLOWSTONE DR** **MADIOSN WI 53719**	**AnchorBank, S.S.B.** **25 W. Main Street** **Madison, WI 53703**

I certify that this verification has been sent directly to the bank or depository and has not passed through the hands of the applicant or any other party.

3. Signature of lender	4. Title	5. Date	6. Lender's No. (optional)
Pam Allen	**Pamela A. Allen** **LN PROCESSING SPECIALIST** (608) 252-8993	01/28/94	

7. Information To Be Verified

Type of Account	Account in Name of	Account Number	Balance
SAV	MICHAEL J OR AUDREY F ROBERTSON	59104000	12,273.70
CHKG	MICHAEL J OR AUDREY F ROBERTSON	59104000	2,924.87
SAVG	MICHAEL J OR AUDREY F ROBERTSON	80472004	2,553.49
CHKG	MICHAEL J OR AUDREY F ROBERTSON	80472004	1,014.73

TO DEPOSITORY: I/We have applied for a mortgage loan and stated in my financial statement that the balance on deposit with you is as shown above. You are authorized to verify this information and to supply the lender identified above with the information requested in Items 10 through 13. Your response is solely a matter of courtesy for which no responsibility is attached to your institution or any of your officers.

8. Name and Address of Applicant(s)	9. Signature of Applicant(s)
MICHAEL J OR AUDREY F ROBERTSON **5806 SUFFOLK RD.** **MADISON, WIS. 53711**	**SEE ATTACHED**

To Be Completed by Depository
Part II - Verification of Depository

10. Deposit Accounts of Applicant(s)

Type of Account	Account Number	Current Balance	Average Balance For Previous Two Months	Date Opened
Sav	59104000	12,273	10,565	6-15-85
Chk	59104000	2,924	2,345	6-15-85
Sav	80472004	2,553	2,085	8-10-87

11. Loans Outstanding To Applicant(s)

Loan Number	Date of Loan	Original Amount	Current Balance	(Monthly/Quarterly)	Secured By	Late Payments
All Paid						

12. Please include any additional information which may be of assistance in determination of credit worthiness. (Please include information on loans paid-in-full in Item 11 above.)

13. If the name(s) on the account(s) differ from those listed in Item 7, please supply the name(s) on the account(s) as reflected by your records.

Part III - Authorized Signature - Federal statutes provide severe penalties for any fraud, intentional misrepresentation, or criminal connivance or conspiracy purposed to influence the issuance of any guaranty or insurance by the VA Secretary, the U.S.D.A., FmHA/FHA Commissioner, or the HUD/CPD Assistant Secretary.

14. Signature of Depository Representative	15. Title (Please print or type)	16. Date
Mary Jackson		
17. Please print or type name signed in item 14 Mary Jackson	18. Phone No. 277-5590	7-19-93

0015149   24   PAA   Form LF1A1   Fannie Mae Form 1006 Mar.90 * LF107

 **FannieMae**

REQUEST FOR VERIFICATION OF DEPOSIT

Privacy Act Notice: This information is to be used by the agency collecting it or its assignees in determining whether you qualify as a prospective mortgagor under its program. It will not be disclosed outside the agency except as required and permitted by law. You do not have to provide this information, but if you do not your application for approval as a prospective mortgagor or borrower may be delayed or rejected. The information requested in this form is authorized by Title 38, USC, Chapter 37 (If VA); by 12 USC, Section 1701 et.seq. (If HUD/FHA); by 42 USC, Section 1452b (If HUD/CPD); and Title 42 USC, 1471 et.seq. or 7 USC, 1921 et.seq. (if USDA/FmHA).

Instructions: Lender - Complete Items 1 through 8. Have applicant(s) complete Item 9. Forward directly to depository named in Item 1.
Depository - Please complete Items 10 through 18 and return DIRECTLY to lender named in Item 2.
The form is to be transmitted directly to the lender and is not to be transmitted through the applicant(s) or any other party.

Part I - Request

1. To (Name and address of depository)	2. From (Name and address of lender)
CUNA CREDIT UNION **401 S YELLOWSTONE DR** **MADIOSN WI 53719**	**AnchorBank, s.s.b.** **25 W. Main Street** **Madison, WI 53703**

I certify that this verification has been sent directly to the bank or depository and has not passed through the hands of the applicant or any other party.

3. Signature of lender	4. Title	5. Date	6. Lender's No. (optional)
Pam Allen	**Pamela A. Allen** **LN PROCESSING SPECIALIST** **(608) 252-8993**	**01/28/94**	

7. Information To Be Verified

Type of Account	Account in Name of	Account Number	Balance
SAV	MICHAEL J OR AUDREY F ROBERTSON	59104000	12,273.70
CHKG	MICHAEL J OR AUDREY F ROBERTSON	59104000	2,924.87
SAVG	MICHAEL J OR AUDREY F ROBERTSON	80472004	2,553.49
CHKG	MICHAEL J OR AUDREY F ROBERTSON	80472004	1,014.73

TO DEPOSITORY: I/We have applied for a mortgage loan and stated in my financial statement that the balance on deposit with you is as shown above. You are authorized to verify this information and to supply the lender identified above with the information requested in Items 10 through 13. Your response is solely a matter of courtesy for which no responsibility is attached to your institution or any of your officers.

8. Name and Address of Applicant(s)	9. Signature of Applicant(s)
MICHAEL J OR AUDREY F ROBERTSON **5806 SUFFOLK RD.** **MADISON, WIS. 53711**	**SEE ATTACHED**

To Be Completed by Depository
Part II - Verification of Depository

10. Deposit Accounts of Applicant(s)

Type of Account	Account Number	Current Balance	Average Balance For Previous Two Months	Date Opened

11. Loans Outstanding To Applicant(s)

Loan Number	Date of Loan	Original Amount	Current Balance	(Monthly/Quarterly)	Secured By	Late Payments

12. Please include any additional information which may be of assistance in determination of credit worthiness. (Please include information on loans paid-in-full in Item 11 above.)

13. If the name(s) on the account(s) differ from those listed in Item 7, please supply the name(s) on the account(s) as reflected by your records.

Part III - Authorized Signature - Federal statutes provide severe penalties for any fraud, intentional misrepresentation, or criminal connivance or conspiracy purposed to influence the issuance of any guaranty or insurance by the VA Secretary, the U.S.D.A., FmHA/FHA Commissioner, or the HUD/CPD Assistant Secretary.

14. Signature of Depository Representative	15. Title (Please print or type)	16. Date
SAM SPADE		*2-3-94*
17. Please print or type name signed in Item 14 *Sam Spade*	18. Phone No.	

| 0015149 24 PAA | Form LF1A1 | Fannie Mae Form 1006 Mar.90 | LF107 |

TRW REAL ESTATE LOAN SVC
1400 E. Washington Ave. Suite 233
Madison, WI 53703
800 - 256 - 0259

Residential Mortgage Credit Report

AnchorBank, S.S.B.
25 West Main Street
Madison, WI 53703

Customer #: 9050592 (R)
Ordered By: Debbie

Report #: 03-4913
Price: SUPP
Ordered: 7-6-93
Released: 7-9-93
Loan Type: CONV

Property: **5806 Suffolk Road   Madison, WI**

Applicant:	**Robertson, Michael J.**
Co-Applicant:	**Robertson, Audrey F.**
Street Address:	**5806 Suffolk Road**
City, State, Zip:	**Madison, WI 53711**
Length of Time:	**7 Years**
AKA:	
Previous Address:	

Social Security#:	
Social Security #:	
Marital Status:	**Married**
Housing Status:	**Own**
Repositories:	**TRW / TU**

Creditor Account Number	Reported Date	Open Date	Type	Amount	Terms	Balance	Mos. Rev.	Times Past Due 30 / 60 / 90+
A FCNB PRF CHG 2500300517	09-89	01-79	CC	$900	REV	$0	84	0 0 0
A GE CAPITAL 5530049555072987	10-85	05-85	CC	$1300	REV	$0	05	0 0 0
A MACYS 31849089472	04-91	10YR	CC	$1700	REV	$0	84	0 0 0
A AMWAY CHICAGO 8000042668345111	03-91	07-85	CC	$0	OPEN	$0	68	0 0 0
A AMERICAN EXP 3728093984711	02-91	11-74	CC	$1400	OPEN	$0	84	0 0 0
A CITIBANK MASTERCH 54241007543	01-91	10YR	CC	$0	REV	$0	84	0 0 0
A CITIBANK MASTERCH 54241002017533	01-91	07-84	CC	$5900	REV	$0	74	0 0 0
A CITIBANK PRF VISA 4271382345680	02-91	07-84	CC	$6000	M158	$0	79	0 0 0
A ATT Universal VISA 412842257	12-90	07-83	CC	$4000	REV	$0	75	0 0 0

A	DISCOVER 60119943340	03-91	04-87 CC	$2600	M13	$0	58	0 0 0
A	SEARS 4500836886421	03-91	10YR CC	$200	REV	$0	84	0 0 0
C	CUNA Credit Union 4163672449	02-87	10YR CC	$500	REV	$0	84	0 0 0
A	AnchorBank S.S.B. 52174115102284	03-86	01-87 R/E	$71000	M471	$66K	84	0 0 0

DELINQUENT PAYMENT HISTORY

C	GECAP MARC HENRY 30790482875859	05-87	10-86 AUT$7000 LATES PRIOR TO 5-87		$0	10	2 0 0
C	J C PENNY 70456318890	04-90	06-88 CC $500	REV	$0 LAST PAST DUE: 03-86	84	1 0 0
A	SEARS 450054870325	03-91	10-81 CC $4400	REV	$0 LAST PAST DUE: 02-89	07	1 0 0

INQUIRIES

NO INQUIRIES IN THE PAST 90 DAYS

TRW certifies that this report meets the standards for the format and research procedures prescribed by

FNMA, FHLMC, FHA, VA, and FmHA.

------------ END (my)

PAGE 2 OF OMB No. 2502-0265

L. SETTLEMENT CHARGES

700. TOTAL SALES/BROKER'S COMMISSION Based on amount	$.00 @ .000% =	FILE: 93070608	
Division of commission (line 700) as follows:		PAID FROM BORROWER'S FUNDS AT SETTLEMENT	PAID FROM SELLERS FUNDS AT SETTLEMENT
701.			
702.			
703. Commission paid at settlement			
704.			
800. ITEMS PAYABLE IN CONNECTION WITH LOAN.			
801. Loan Origination Fee			
802. Loan Discount			
803. Appraisal Fee	to BENCHMARK APPRAISAL SERVICES	250.00	
804. Credit Report	to ANCHORBANK SSB	40.00	
805. Lender's Inspection Fee			
806. Mortgage Insurance application Fee			
807. Assumption Fee			
808.			
809. PROCESSING FEE	to ANCHORBANK SSB	100.00	
810.			
811.			
812.			
900. ITEM REQUIRED BY LENDER TO BE PAID IN ADVANCE.			
901. Interest from 08/19/93 to 09/01/93 @	$11.7000/Day	152.10	
902. Mortgage insurance premium for			
903. Hazard insurance premium for			
904.			
905.			
1000. RESERVES DEPOSITED WITH LENDER			
1001. Hazard insurance			
1002. Mortgage insurance			
1003. City property taxes			
1004. County property taxes			
1005. Annual assessments (Maint.)			
1006.			
1007.			
1008.			
1009.			
1100. TITLE CHARGES:			
1101. Settlement or closing fee	to BADGER ABSTRACT & TITLE	125.00	
1102. Abstract or title search			
1103. Title examination			
1104. Title insurance binder			
1105. Document preparation			
1106. Notary fees			
1107. Attorney' fees to			
(includes above items No. :)			
1108. Title insurance	to BADGER ABSTRACT & TITLE	340.00	
(includes above items No.:)			
1109. Lender's coverage $65,000.00	$340.00		
1110. Owner's coverage			
1111.			
1112. BALOON ENDORSEMENT	to BADGER ABSTRACT & TITLE	60.00	
1113.			
1114.			
1200. GOVERNMENT RECORDING AND TRANSFER CHARGES:			
1201. Recording fees: Mortgage: 20.00 Releases: 10.00		30.00	
1202. City/county tax/stamps:			
1203. State tax/stamps:			
1204.			
1205.			
1206.			
1300. ADDITIONAL SETTLEMENT CHARGES:			
1301. Survey			
1302. Pest inspection			
1303.			
1304.			
1305.			
1400. TOTAL SETTLEMENT CHARGES (entered on lines 103, Section J and 502, Section K)		1,097.10	

CERTIFICATION

The HUD-1 Settlement Statement which I have prepared is a true and accurate account of this transaction. I have caused or will cause the funds to be disbursed in accordance with this statement.

Paula Fraser _8/13/93_
Settlement Agent   Date

WARNING: It is a crime to knowingly make false statements to the United States on this or any other similar form. Penalties upon conviction can include a fine and imprisonment. For details see: Title 18: U.S. Code Section 1001 and Section 1010.

8/12/93 11:49:58

(Exp. 12-31-86)
OMB No. 2502-0265

A.	U.S. DEPARTMENT OF HOUSING AND URBAN DEVELOPMENT	B. TYPE OF LOAN:

8/12/93
11:49:54

BADGER ABSTRACT & TITLE CORPORATION

SETTLEMENT STATEMENT

B. TYPE OF LOAN: X
1. ☐ FHA   2. ☐ FMHA   3. ☐ CONV. UNINS.
4. ☐ VA   5. ☐ CONV. INS.
6. FILE NUMBER   93070608   7. LOAN NUMBER   0115220208
8. MORTGAGE INSURANCE CASE NO.

C. NOTE: This form is furnished to give you a statement of actual settlement costs. Amounts paid to and by the settlement agent are shown. Items marked "(p.o.c.)" were paid outside the closing; they are shown here for informational purposes and are not included in the totals.

D. NAME AND ADDRESS OF BORROWER:	E. NAME AND ADDRESS OF SELLER:	F. NAME AND ADDRESS OF LENDER:
MICHAEL J. ROBERTSON AUDREY F.. ROBERTSON	REFINANCE	ANCHORBANK SB 25 WEST MAIN STREET MADISON, WI 53703

G. PROPERTY LOCATION:	H. SETTLEMENT AGENT: 4800 BADGER ABSTRACT & TITLE	I. SETTLEMENT DATE:
5806 SUFFOLK ROAD MADISON, WI 53711	PLACE OF SETTLEMENT: 900 JOHN NOLEN DR. MADISON, WI 53713	8/13/93 Disbursement Date: 8/19/93

J. SUMMARY OF BORROWER'S TRANSACTION		K. SUMMARY OF SELLER'S TRANSACTION	
100. GROSS AMOUNT DUE FROM BORROWER:		**400. GROSS AMOUNT DUE TO SELLER:**	
101. Contract sales price		401. Contract sales price	
102. Personal property		402. Personal property	
103. Settlement charges to borrower (line 1400)	1,097.10	403.	
104. PAYOFF ANCHORBANK	66,137.64	404.	
105.		405.	
Adjustments for items paid by seller in advance:		Adjustments for items paid by seller in advance:	
106. City/town taxes		406. City/town taxes	
107. County taxes		407. County taxes	
108. Assessments		408. Assessments	
109.		409.	
110.		410.	
111.		411.	
112.		412.	
120. GROSS AMOUNT DUE FROM BORROWER:	67,234.74	**420. GROSS AMOUNT DUE TO SELLER:**	
200. AMOUNTS PAID BY OR IN BEHALF OF BORROWER:		**500. REDUCTIONS IN AMOUNT DUE TO SELLER:**	
201. Deposit or earnest money		501. Excess deposit (see instructions)	
202. Principal amount of new loan(s)	65,000.00	502. Settlement charges to seller (line 1400)	
203. Existing loan(s) taken subject to		503. Existing loan(s) taken subject to	
204. APPLICATION FEE CREDIT	900.00	504. Payoff of first mortgage loan	
205.		505. Payoff of second mortgage loan	
206.		506.	
207.		507.	
208.		508.	
209.		509.	
Adjustment for items unpaid by seller:		Adjustment for items unpaid by seller:	
210. City/town taxes		510. City/town taxes	
211. County taxes		511. County taxes	
212. Assessments		512. Assessments	
213.		513.	
214.		514.	
215.		515.	
216.		516.	
217.		517.	
218.		518.	
219.		519.	
220. TOTAL PAID BY/FOR BORROWER:	65,900.00	**520. TOTAL REDUCTIONS IN AMOUNT DUE SELLER:**	
300. CASH AT SETTLEMENT FROM/TO BORROWER:		**600. CASH AT SETTLEMENT TO/FROM SELLER:**	
301. Gross amount due from borrower (line 120)	67,234.74	601. Gross amount due to seller (line 420)	
302. Less amounts paid by/for borrower (line 220)	65,900.00	602. Less total reductions in amount due seller (line 520)	
303. CASH (☐ FROM) (☐ TO) BORROWER:	1,334.74	**603. CASH (☐ TO) (☐ FROM) SELLER:**	.00

CERTIFICATION

I have carefully reviewed the HUD-1 Settlement Statement and to the best of my knowledge and belief, it is a true and accurate statement of all receipts and disbursements made on my account or by me in this transaction. I further certify that I have received a copy of the HUD-1 Settlement Statement.. I/we hereby approve this closing statement and agree to adjust any errors or omissions that may be discovered, including any variations in tax amounts unless expressly set forth herein to the contrary.

_____   _____
Borrowers   Sellers

HUD-1 (Rev. 9-88)
RESPA, HB 4305.2

ORT Form 3125 Rev. 1/88

VI. Additional Delivery Data   (Completion of this section is optional; however, the data must be transmitted on the applicable Fannie Mae or Freddie Mac delivery from when the mortgage is delivered for sale.) (See FNMA 1008A/FHLMC 1077A for a list of valid codes.)

A. All Mortgages

Loan Information	Fannie Mae Only	Freddie Mac Only
First P&I Payment Date __10/01/93__	Assumable ☐ Yes ☐ No	Reduced Documentation ☐ Yes ☐ No
Current UPB $ __64,640.75__	Interest Only ☐ Yes ☐ No	Loan Feature code _____
	Interest Only end Date _____	Interest Paid-To-Date __09/01/93__
	FHA/VA Section of Act _____	Note Maturity Date __0900__
	Original Term (in months) __84__	
	Amortization Term (in months) _____	
	Maximum Term (in months) _____	
	Due Date of Last Paid Installment __09/01/93__	

B. Adjustable Rate Mortgages (ARMs)

Loan Information	Fannie Mae Only	Freddie Mac Only
Current Interest Rate __6.570__ %	First Payment Change Date _____	Next Rate Adjustment Date _____
Current P&I Payment $ __413.85__	Original Index Value _____ %	Next Payment Adjustment Date _____
First Rate Change Date _____	Lookback (in days) _____	Is ARM Convertible? ☐ Yes ☐ No
Mortgage Margin __0.000__ %	Rounding Feature Code	Net Negative Amortization $ _____
Maximum Interest Rate __0.000__ %	☐ 027 (1/8%)	Periodic Interest Rate Cap ☐ Yes ☐ No
Minimum Interest Rate __0.000__ %	☐ _____ (negotiated commitment code)	Rate Cap Percent _____ %
		Payment Cap ☐ Yes ☐ No
		Payment Cap ☐ Opt ☐ Man
		Payment Cap Percent _____ %
		Rate Rounded ☐ Yes ☐ No
		Percent Rounded By _____ %

C. Other Mortgage Programs

Fannie Mae Only

For Growing Equity Mortgages (GEMs):   *For Balloon Mortgages:*

Percent of Increase _____ %   Balloon Call Date _____

. . . .

Fannie Mac Only

For Graduated-Payment Mortgages (GPMs):   *For EQUALᴛᴍ and Tiered-Payment Mortgages (TPMs):*

Yearly Payment Increase _____ %   Borrower's First Payment Change Date _____
                                             Borrower's Initial P&I Payment $ _____
                                             Yearly Payment Increase _____ %

For Affordable Housing Initiatives Program Mortgages

Down Payment Source Codes	Amounts	Closing Costs	Amounts	Secondary Fiancing Source Codes	Amounts
_____	$ _____	_____	$ _____	_____	$ _____
_____	$ _____	_____	$ _____	_____	$ _____
_____	$ _____	_____	$ _____		
_____	$ _____	_____	$ _____	**Borrower Education Counseling Codes**	
				Administrator Codes	Format Codes
				_____	_____
				_____	_____

VII. Additional Underwriter Comments

_____
_____
_____
_____
_____
_____
_____
_____
_____

VIII. For Seller Use

Uniform Underwriting and Transmittal Summary

I. Borrower and Property Information

Borrower Name **MICHAEL J. ROBERTSON**   SSN: _____

Co-Borrower Name **AUDREY F. ROBERTSON**   SSN: _____

Property Address **5806 SUFFOLK ROAD, MADISON, WISCONSIN   53711**

Property Type
- [X] Detached Housing
- [ ] Attached Housing
- [ ] Condominium
- [ ] PUD   [ ] CO-OP

Project Classification
- [ ] A/III Condo   [ ] E PUD   [ ] 1 CO-OP
- [ ] B/II Condo   [ ] F PUD   [ ] 2 CO-OP
- [ ] C/I Condo   [ ] III PUD
- Project Name

Occupancy Status
- [X] Primary Residence
- [ ] Second Home
- [ ] Investment Property

Number of Units __1__
Sales Price $ __0.00__
Appraised Value $ __108,000.00__

II. Mortgage Information

Loan Type
- [X] Conventional
- [ ] FHA
- [ ] VA
- [ ] FmHA

Amortization Type
- [ ] Fixed Rate - Monthly Payments
- [ ] Fixed Rate - Bi-Weekly Payments
- [X] Balloon
- [ ] ARM (type)
- [ ] Other (specify)

Loan Purpose Type
- [ ] Purchase
- [ ] Cash-Out Refinance
- [X] No Cash-Out Refinance
- Purpose of Refinance:

Lien Position
- [X] First Mortgage
- [ ] Second Mortgage

Amount of Subordinate Financing $ __0.00__

Note Information

Original Loan Amount $ __65,000.00__
Initial P&I Payment $ __0.00__
Initial Note Rate __6.570__ %
Note Date __08/13/93__
Term (in months) __84__

Mortgage Originator
- [X] Seller
- [ ] Third Party
Third Party Name:

Buydown
- [ ] Yes
- [X] No

If Second Mortgage
Owner of First Mortgage
- [ ] Fannie Mae   [ ] Freddie Mac
- [ ] Seller/Other
Original Loan Amount of First Mortgage
$ __0.00__

III. Underwriting Information

Underwriter's Name

Appraiser's Name/License # **Greunisen, Gary/55**

Appraisal Company Name **Benchmark Appraisal Serv. Ltd.**

Stable Monthly Income

	Borrower	Co-Borrower	Total
Base Income	$ 3,738.58	$ 2,144.08	$ 5,882.66
Other Income	$ 0.00	$ 0.00	$ 0.00
Positive Cash Flow (Subject Property)	$ 0.00	$	$ 0.00
Total Income	$ 3,738.58	$ 2,144.08	$ 5,882.66

Qualifying Ratios
Primary Housing Expense/Income __12__ %
Total Obligations/Income __15__ %

Loan-to-Value Ratios
LTV __61__ %
Total LTV __61__ %

Qualifying Rate
- [ ] Note Rate __0.000__ %
- [ ] __0.000__ % Above Note Rate __0.000__ %
- [ ] __0.000__ % Below Note Rate __0.000__ %
- [ ] Bought Down Rate __0.000__ %
- [ ] Other __0.000__ %

Proposed Monthly Payments

Borrower's Primary Residence:
First Mortgage P&I	$ 413.85
Second Mortgage P&I	$ 0.00
Hazard Insurance	$ 20.00
Taxes	$ 251.15
Mortgage Insurance	$ 0.00
Homeowners Association Fees	$ 0.00
Lease/Ground Rent	$ 0.00
Other	$ 0.00
Total Primary Housing Expense	$ 685.00
Other Obligations:	
Negative Cash Flow (subject property)	$ 0.00
All Other Monthly Payments	$ 183.00
Total All Monthly Payments	$ 868.00

Underwriting Comments (If more space is needed, use page two)

IV. Seller, Contract, and Contact Information

Seller Name **ANCHORBANK, S.S.B.**
Seller Address **25 WEST MAIN STREET**
MADISON, WI 53703
Seller No. _____   Investor Loan No. _____
Seller Loan No. **0115220208**
Master Commitment No. _____
Contract No. _____

Contact Name **DEBORAH SHUTVET**
Contact Title **MANAGER OF CONTRACTS AND SALES**
Contact's Phone Number **608/252-1818** ext. _____
Contact's Signature _____
Date _____
Date of Commitment   [ ] Standard   [ ] Negotiated

V. Delivery Data

Borrower Information

Number of Borrowers	2
Borrower Age	36
Co-Borrower Age	32
Are any of the occupant borrowers first-time homebuyers?	[ ] Yes [X] No

Property Information

Number of Bedrooms	
Unit 1	
Unit 2	
Unit 3	
Unit 4	

Gross Monthly Rents
Unit 1 $ _____
Unit 2 $ _____
Unit 3 $ _____
Unit 4 $ _____

Year Built __1973__

Information for Government Monitoring Purposes Only

Borrower Race Code __5__   Borrower Gender Code __1__   Co-Borrower Race Code __5__   Co-Borrower Gender Code __2__

Mortgage Insurance
Mortgage Insurer (MI) Code _____   Percentage of Coverage ____ %
Certificate Number _____   Adjustor Coverage [ ] Yes [X] No

Special Feature/Characteristics Codes
Code 1 __018__   Code 3 ____   Code 5 ____
Code 2 __007__   Code 4 ____   Code 6 ____

Freddie Mac Form 1077 11/92
Fannie Mae Form 1008 11/92
Form UTS

0015149

APPRAISER'S CERTIFICATION: The Appraiser certifies and agrees that:

1. I have taken into consideration the factors that have an impact on value in my development of the estimate of market value in the appraisal report. I have not knowingly withheld any significant information from the appraisal report and I believe, to the best of my knowledge, that all statements and information in the appraisal report are true and correct.

2. I stated in the appraisal report only my own personal, unbiased, and professional analysis, opinions, and conclusions, which are subject only to the contingent and limiting conditions specified in this form.

3. I have no present or prospective interest in the property that is the subject to this report, and I have no present or prospective personal interest or bias with respect to the participants in the sale. I did not base, either partially or completely, my analysis and/or the estimate of market value in the appraisal report on the race, color, or national origin of either the prospective owners or occupants of the subject property or of the present owners or occupants of the properties in the vicinity of the subject property.

4. I have no present or contemplated future interest in the subject property, and neither my current or future employment nor my compensation for performing this appraisal is contingent on the appraised value of the property.

5. I was not required to report a predetermined value or direction in value that favors the cause of the client or any related party, the amount of the value estimate, the attainment of a specific result, or the occurrence of a subsequent event in order to receive my compensation and/or employment for performing the appraisal. I did not base the appraisal report on a requested minimum valuation, a specific valuation, or the need to approve a specific mortgage loan.

6. I performed this appraisal in conformity with the Uniform Standards of Professional Appraisal Practice that were approved and published by the Appraisal Standards Board of The Appraisal Foundation as of December 31, 1990, with the exception of the departure provision of those Standards, which does not apply. I acknowledge that an estimate of a reasonable time for exposure in the open market is a condition in the definition of market value and the estimate I developed is consistent with the marketing time noted in the neighborhood section of this report, unless I have otherwise stated in the reconciliation section.

7. I have personally inspected the interior and exterior areas of the subject property and the exterior of all properties listed as comparables in the appraisal report. I further certify that I have noted any apparent or known adverse conditions in the subject improvements, on the subject site, or on any site within the immediate vicinity of the subject property of which I am aware and have made adjustments for these adverse conditions in my analysis of the property value to the extent that I had market evidence to support them. I have also commented about the effect of the adverse conditions on the marketability of the subject property.

8. I personally prepared all conclusions and opinions about the real estate that were set forth in the appraisal report. If I relied on significant professional assistance from any individual or individuals in the performance of the appraisal or the preparation of the appraisal report, I have named such individual(s) and disclosed the specific tasks performed by them in the reconciliation section of this appraisal report. I certify that any individual so named is qualified to perform the tasks. I have not authorized anyone to make a change to any item in the report; therefore, if an unauthorized change is made to the appraisal report, I will take no responsibility for it.

SUPERVISORY APPRAISER'S CERTIFICATION: If a supervisory appraiser signed the appraiser report, he or she certifies and agrees that: I directly supervise the appraiser who prepared the appraisal report, have reviewed the appraisal report, agree with the statements and conclusions of the appraiser, and am taking full responsibility for the appraisal and the appraisal report.

Address of Property Appraised: 5806 Suffolk Road, Madison, WI   53711

APPRAISER:	**SUPERVISORY APPRAISER** (if applicable)
Signature: _John Smith_	Signature: _____
Name: _John Smith_	Name: _____
State Certification/License #: __999__	State Certification/License # _____
State: _Wisconsin_	State: _____
Expiration Date: __12/31/93__	Expiration Date: _____
Date Signed: __7/28/93__	Date Signed: _____

DEFINITION OF MARKET VALUE: The most probable price which a property should bring in a competitive and open market under all conditions requisite to a fair sale, the buyer and seller, each acting prudently, knowledgeably and assuming the price is not affected by undue stimulus. Implicit in this definition is the consummation of a sale as of a specified date and the passing of title from seller to buyer under conditions whereby: (1) buyer and seller are typically motivated; (2) both parties are well informed or well advised, and each acting in what he considers his own best interest; (3) a reasonable time is allowed for exposure in the open market; (4) payment is made in terms of cash in U. S. dollars or in terms of financial arrangements comparable thereto; and (5) the price represents the normal consideration for the property sold unaffected by special or creative financing or sales concessions* granted by anyone associated with the sale.

*Adjustments to the comparables must be made for special or creative financing or sales concessions. No adjustments are necessary for those costs which are normally paid by sellers as a result of tradition or law in a market area; these costs are readily identifiable since the seller pays these costs in virtually all sales transactions. .Special or creative financing adjustments can be made to the comparable property by comparisons to financing terms offered by a third party institutional lender that is not already involved in the property or transaction. Any adjustment should not be calculated on a mechanical dollar for dollar cost of the financing or concession but the dollar amount of any adjustment should approximate the market's reaction to the financing or concessions based on the appraiser's judgment.

STATEMENT OF LIMITING CONDITIONS AND APPRAISER'S CERTIFICATION

CONTINGENT AND LIMITING CONDITIONS: The appraiser's certification that appears in the appraisal report is subject to the following conditions:

1. The appraiser will not be responsible for matters of a legal nature that affect either the property being appraised or the title to it. The appraiser assumes that the title is good and marketable and, therefore, will not render any opinions about the title. The property is appraised on the basis of it being under responsible ownership.

2. The appraiser has provided a sketch in the appraisal report to show approximate dimensions of the improvements and the sketch is included only to assist the reader of the report in visualizing the property and understanding the appraiser's determination of its size.

3. The appraiser will not give testimony or appear in court because he or she made an appraisal of the property in question, unless specific arrangements to do so have been made beforehand.

4. The appraiser has distributed the value of the property between the land and the improvements in the cost approach to value on the basis of the existing use of the property. These separate valuations must not be used in conjunction with any other appraisal and are invalid if they are so used.

5. The appraiser has noted in the appraisal report any adverse conditions (such as, but not limited to, hazardous wastes, toxic substances, etc.) observed during the inspection of the subject property or that he or she became aware of during the normal research involved in performing the appraisal. Unless otherwise stated in the appraisal report, the appraiser has no knowledge of any hidden or unapparent conditions of the property or adverse environmental conditions (including the presence of hazardous wastes, toxic substances, etc.) that would make the property more or less valuable, and has assumed that there are no such conditions and makes no guarantees or warranties, express or implied, regarding the condition of the property. The appraiser will not be responsible for any such conditions that do exist or for any engineering or testing that might be required to discover whether such conditions exist. Because the appraiser is not an expert in the field of environmental hazards, the appraisal report must not be considered as an environmental assessment of the property.

6. The appraiser obtained the information, estimates, and opinions that were expressed in the appraisal report from sources that he or she considers to be reliable and believes them to be true and correct. The appraiser does not assume responsibility for the accuracy of such items that were furnished by other parties.

7. The appraiser will not disclose the contents of the appraisal report except as provided for in the Uniform Standards of Professional Appraisal Practice.

8. The appraiser has based his or her appraisal report and valuation conclusion for an appraisal that is subject to satisfactory completion, repairs, or alterations on the assumption that completion of the improvements will be performed in a workmanlike manner.

9. The appraiser must provide his or her prior written consent before all (or any part) of the content of the appraisal report (including conclusions about the property value, the appraiser's identity and professional designations, and references to any professional appraisal organizations or the firm with which the appraiser is associated) can be used for any purposes by anyone except: the client specified in the report; the borrower if he or she paid the appraisal fee; the mortgagee or its successors and assigns; the mortgage insurer; consultants; professional appraisal organizations; any state or federally approved financial institution; or any department, agency, or instrumentality of the United States or any state or the District of Columbia. The appraiser's written consent and approval must also be obtained before the appraisal (or any part of it) can be conveyed by anyone to the public through advertising, public relations, news, sales, or other media.

UNIFORM RESIDENTIAL APPRAISAL REPORT File No. _____

Valuation Section

COST APPROACH

ESTIMATED SITE VALUE........................... = $ 36,000

ESTIMATED REPRODUCTION COST-NEW OF IMPROVEMENTS:

Dwelling 1240 Sq. Ft @ $ 52.00 = $ 64,480

Bsmt 1240 Sq. Ft @ $ 12.75 = 15,810

Porch 140 SF = 2,000

Garage/Carport 420 Sq. Ft @ $ 12.00 = 5,040

Total Estimated Cost-New.................... = $ 87,330

Less   Physical | Functional | External
Depreciation 17,466 | 0 | 0   = $ 17,466

Depreciated Value of Improvements............... = $ 69,864

"As-is" Value of Site Improvements............... = $ 3,500

INDICATED VALUE BY COST APPROACH........... = $ 109,364

Comments on Cost Approach (such as, source of cost estimate, site value, square foot calculation and, for HUD, VA and FmHA, the estimated remaining economic life of the property): No functional or external obsolescence. Basement at $9.00/SF, basement finish at $7.50/SF. SOURCE: Marshall & Swift Cost Manual.

SALES COMPARISON ANALYSIS

ITEM	SUBJECT	COMPARABLE NO. 1	+ (-) $ Adjustment	COMPARABLE NO. 2	+ (-) $ Adjustment	COMPARABLE NO. 3	+ (-) $ Adjustment
Address	5806 Suffolk Madison	5800 Tolman Terrace Madison		5414 Fenton Place Madison		5902 Piping Rock Road Madison	
Proximity to Subject		4 Blocks South		1/2 Mile SE		2 Blocks West	
Sales Price	$ Refi	$ 105,900		$ 98,900		$ 114,000	
Price/Gross Liv. Area	$ N/A	$ 95.23		$ 75.15		$ 88.51	
Data and/or Verification Sources	Inspection	Madison MLS		Madison MLS/Realtor		Madison MLS	
VALUE ADJUSTMENTS	DESCRIPTION	DESCRIPTION		DESCRIPTION		DESCRIPTION	
Sales or Financing Concessions		Cash to Seller	-0-	Cash to Seller	-0-	Cash to Seller	-0-
Date of Sale/Time		6/93	-0-	4/93	-0-	5/93	-0-
Location	Green Tree	Green Tree	-0-	Orchard Ridge	-0-	Green Tree	-0-
Leasehold/Fee Simple	Fee	Fee	-0-	Fee	-0-	Fee	-0-
Site	11,050 SF	15,000 SF	-0-	15,750 SF	-0-	11,968 SF	-0-
View	Residential	Residential	-0-	Residential	-0-	Residential	-0-
Design and Appeal	R.Ranch/Good	Ranch/Good	-0-	Ranch/Good	-0-	R.Ranch/Good	-0-
Quality of Construction	Average	Average	-0-	Average	-0-	Average	-0-
Age	30	35	-0-	36	-0-	32	-0-
Condition	Good	Good	-0-	Average	+5,000	Good	-0-
Above Grade Room Count	Total 5 / Bdrms 3 / Baths 1.5	Total 5 / Bdrms 3 / Baths 1.0	+1,500	Total 6 / Bdrms 3 / Baths 1.5	-0-	Total 5 / Bdrms 3 / Baths 1.5	-0-
Gross Living Area	1,240 Sq. Ft.	1,112 Sq. Ft.	+2,600	1,316 Sq. Ft.	-1,500	1,288 Sq. Ft.	-1,000
Basement & Finished Rooms Below Grade	100% / 50% Family Room	100% / 50% FR, BR	-1,500	100% / 60% 2 Rooms,Bath	-800	100% / 60% Rec.Rm. Bath	-800
Functional Utility	Average	Average	-0-	Average	-0-	Average	-0-
Heating/Cooling	Gas FWA/O	FWA/CAC	-1,500	FWA/CAC	-1,500	FWA/CAC	-1,500
Energy Efficient Items	None	None	-0-	None	-0-	None	-0-
Garage/Carport	2-Attached	2-Attached	-0-	1-Attached	+3,000	1-Attached	+3,000
Porch, Patio, Deck, etc.	Covered Porch	Deck	-0-	None	-0-	Patio, Deck	-1,000
Fireplace(s), etc.	1 FP	0 FP	+1,500	0 FP	+1,500	1 FP	-0-
Fence, Pool, etc.	None	None	-0-	None	-0-	None	-0-
Net Adj. (total)		X + □ -	$ 2,600	X + □ -	$ 5,700	□ + X -	$ 1,300
Adjusted Sales Price of Comparable			$ 108,500		$ 104,600		$ 112,700

Comments on Sales Comparison (including the subject property's compatibility to the neighborhood, etc.): Comparables are generally similar to subject in location, age, size, and amenities. Subject and comparables are representative of the smaller homes in this neighborhood. Sale 2 adjusted for condition based on realtor report of older furnace and kitchen.

ITEM	SUBJECT	COMPARABLE NO. 1	COMPARABLE NO. 2	COMPARABLE NO. 3
Date, Price and Data Source for prior sales within year of appraisal	N/A	N/A	N/A	N/A

Analysis of any current agreement of sale, option, or listing of the subject property and analysis of any prior sales of subject and comparables within one year of the date of appraisal: Subject purchased 1986, not recently listed. List prices of comparables were $108,900; $105,900; $114,900.

INDICATED VALUE BY SALES COMPARISON APPROACH.................................... $ 108,000

INDICATED VALUE BY INCOME APPROACH (If Applicable) Estimated Market Rent $ N/A /Mo. x Gross Rent Multiplier _____ = $ N/A

This appraisal is made [X] "as is" □ subject to the repairs, alterations, inspections, or conditions listed below □ subject to completion per plans and specifications.

Conditions of Appraisal: Subject to standard assumptions and limiting conditions attached.

RECONCILIATION

Final Reconciliation: Income Approach not applicable; SFR properties like subject not traded based on income. Cost Approach sets upper limit of value. Most weight to Sales Comparison based on closely similar comparables in active market.

The purpose of this appraisal is to estimate the market value of the real property that is the subject of this report, based on the above conditions and the certification, contingent and limiting conditions, and market value definition that are stated in the attached Freddie Mac Form 439/Fannie Mae Form 1004B (Revised 6-93).

I (WE) ESTIMATE THE MARKET VALUE, AS DEFINED, OF THE REAL PROPERTY THAT IS THE SUBJECT OF THIS REPORT, AS OF 7/21/93 (WHICH IS THE DATE OF INSPECTION AND THE EFFECTIVE DATE OF THIS REPORT) TO BE $ 108,000

APPRAISER: SUPERVISORY APPRAISER (ONLY IF REQUIRED):

Signature _John Smith_   Signature _____   □ Did □ Did Not

Name John Smith   Name _____   Inspect Property

Date Report Signed 7/28/93   Date Report Signed _____

State Certification # 999   State WI   State Certification # _____   State _____

Or State License # _____   State   Or State License # _____   State _____

Freddie Mac Form 70   6-93   10 CH   PAGE 2 OF 2   Fannie Mae Form 1004   6-93

X X
Property Description

UNIFORM RESIDENTIAL APPRAISAL REPORT   File No.

Property Address	5806 Suffolk Road	City Madison State WI Zip Code 53711
Legal Description	Lot 54, Green Tree Estates	County Dane
Assessor's Parcel No. 0709-312-0206-7		Tax Year 1992 R.E. Taxes $ 3,005.67 Special Assessments $ 0

SUBJECT

Borrower Robertson   Current Owner Same   Occupant [X] Owner [ ] Tenant [ ] Vacant
Property rights appraised [X] Fee Simple [ ] Leasehold   Project Type [ ] PUD [ ] Condominium (HUD/VA only) HOA$ ____ /Mo.
Neighborhood or Project Name Green Tree / Orchard Ridge   Map Reference ____   Census Tract 5.98
Sales Price $ Refinance   Date of Sale 7/93   Description and $ amount of loan charges/concessions to be paid by seller
Lender/Client AnchorBank S.S.B.   Address 25 W. Main St., Madison, WI 53703
Appraiser John Smith   Address 101 Nob Hill Road, Madison, WI 53713

NEIGHBORHOOD

Location	[X] Urban	[ ] Suburban	[ ] Rural	Predominant occupancy	Single family housing		Present land use %	Land use change
					PRICE $ (000)	AGE (yrs)		
Built up	[X] Over 75%	[ ] 25-75%	[ ] Under 25%				One family 85	[X] Not likely [ ] Likely
Growth rate	[ ] Rapid	[X] Stable	[ ] Slow	[X] Owner	95 Low 7		2-4 family	[ ] In process
Property values	[X] Increasing	[ ] Stable	[ ] Declining	[ ] Tenant	200 High 35		Multi-family 10	To: ____
Demand/supply	[ ] Shortage	[X] In balance	[ ] Over supply	[X] Vacant (0-5%)	Predominant		Commercial 5	
Marketing time	[X] Under 3 mos.	[ ] 3-6 mos.	[ ] Over 6 mos.	[ ] Vacant (over 5%)	135 25		( )	

Note: Race and the racial composition of the neighborhood are not appraisal factors.

Neighborhood boundaries and characteristics: Located on Madison's southwest side bounded by W. Beltline, Verona Road, Raymond Rd., Salsaa Rd. Mainly single family developed 1960-75, middle price range

Factors that affect the marketability of the properties in the neighborhood (proximity to employment and amenities, employment stability, appeal to market, etc.):
Established neighborhood with good amenities, parks, schools, neighborhood shopping. Good access to employment centers. Homogenous housing stock of average quality and condition, with good appeal to middle-income owner occupants.

Market conditions in the subject neighborhood (including support for the above conclusions related to the trend of property values, demand/supply, and marketing time -- such as data on competitive properties for sale in the neighborhood, description of the prevalence of sales and financing concessions, etc.):
Average city assessment increase 1992-93 = 8% for neighborhood. Of 17 listings on MLS 1/93 - 6/93, 13 (75%) sold within 90 days.

PUD

Project Information for PUDs (If applicable) -- Is the developer/builder in control of the Home Owners' Association (HOA)? [ ] Yes [ ] No
Approximate total number of units in the subject project ____ . Approximate total number of units for sale in the subject project ____
Describe common elements and recreational facilities:

SITE

Dimensions 85 x 130			Topography	Slight grade
Site area 11,050 SF	Corner Lot [ ] Yes [X] No		Size	Typical for area
Specific zoning classification and description R-1 Single Family			Shape	Rectangular
Zoning compliance [X] Legal [ ] Legal nonconforming (Grandfathered use) [ ] Illegal [ ] No zoning			Drainage	Adequate
Highest & best use as improved [X] Present use [ ] Other use (explain)			View	Residential

Utilities	Public	Other	Off-site Improvements	Type	Public	Private	Landscaping	Typical for area
Electricity	[X]		Street	Asphalt	[X]		Driveway Surface	Asphalt
Gas	[X]		Curb/gutter	Concrete	[X]		Apparent easements	None Observed
Water	[X]		Sidewalk	Concrete	[X]		FEMA Special Flood Hazard Area [ ] Yes [X] No	
Sanitary sewer	[X]		Street lights	Yes	[X]		FEMA Zone C Map Date 9/86	
Storm sewer	[X]		Alley	No			FEMA Map No. 550083 005D	

Comments (apparent adverse easements, encroachments, special assessments, slide areas, illegal or legal nonconforming zoning use, etc.): Subject site is a typical lot for neighborhood. Nearby properties are compatible. No adverse conditions observed.

DESCRIPTION OF IMPROVEMENTS

GENERAL DESCRIPTION		EXTERIOR DESCRIPTION		FOUNDATION		BASEMENT		INSULATION	
No. of Units	1	Foundation	Poured Conc	Slab		Area Sq. Ft. 1240		Roof	
No. of Stories	1	Exterior Walls	Wood	Crawl Space		% Finished 50		Ceiling Avg. [X]	
Type (Det./Att.)	Detached	Roof Surface	Asph.Shing	Basement	100%	Ceiling Drywall		Walls Avg. [X]	
Design (Style)	R.Ranch	Gutters & Dwnspts.	Aluminum	Sump Pump		Walls Pine Pan.		Floor	
Existing/Proposed	No	Window Type	Double Hung	Dampness	None Noted	Floor Carpet		None	
Age (Yrs.)	30	Storm/Screens	Comb.	Settlement	None Noted	Outside Entry Yes		Unknown	
Effective Age (Yrs.)	20	Manufactured House	No	Infestation	None Noted				

ROOMS	Foyer	Living	Dining	Kitchen	Den	Family Rm.	Rec. Rm.	Bedrooms	# Baths	Laundry	Other	Area Sq. Ft.
Basement						X						620
Level 1	X	X		X				3	1.5			1240
Level 2												

Finished area above grade contains: 5 Rooms;   3 Bedroom(s);   1.5 Bath(s);   1240 Square Feet of Gross Living Area

IMPROVEMENTS

INTERIOR	Materials/Condition	HEATING		KITCHEN EQUIP.		ATTIC		AMENITIES		CAR STORAGE:	
Floors	Wood & SV	Type	FWA	Refrigerator		None		Fireplace(s) # 1 [X]		None	
Walls	Drywall	Fuel	Gas	Range/Oven		Stairs		Patio Fieldstone [X]		Garage 2 # of cars	
Trim/Finish	Varnished Wd.	Condition	Good	Disposal	[X]	Drop Stair		Deck		Attached X	
Bath Floor	Sheet Vinyl	COOLING		Dishwasher	[X]	Scuttle	[X]	Porch Covered [X]		Detached	
Bath Wainscot	Ceramic Tile	Central	None	Fan/Hood	[X]	Floor		Fence		Built-In	
Doors	Varnished Wd.	Other		Microwave		Heated		Pool		Carport	
		Condition		Washer/Dryer		Finished				Driveway	

COMMENTS

Additional features (special energy efficient items, etc.): 100 Amp electric service, 50 gallon gas water heater, 20 x 7 covered porch at rear. Fieldstone sidewalk and patio.

Condition of the improvements, depreciation (physical, functional, and external), repairs needed, quality of construction, remodeling/additions, etc.: Good overall condition. average quality construction typical of neighborhood, newer gas furnace and new carpeting in lower-level family room.

Adverse environmental conditions (such as, but not limited to, hazardous wastes, toxic substances, etc.) present in the improvements, on the site, or in the immediate vicinity of the subject property: None observed.

Freddie Mac Form 70 6-93   10 CH   PAGE 1 OF 2   Fannie Mae Form 1004 6-93

100   DECLARATIONS   48-PW4605-01

WISCONSIN HOMEOWNERS POLICY - SPECIAL DELUXE FORM (ED 10.84) WI

NON-ASSESSABLE POLICY ISSUED BY AMERICAN FAMILY MUTUAL INSURANCE COMPANY
A MEMBER OF THE AMERICAN FAMILY INSURANCE GROUP MADISON. WI.

PLEASE READ YOUR POLICY

POLICY NUMBER 48-PW4605-01

MORTGAGEE

ANCHORBANK SSB AND/OR ITS ASSIGNS
LOAN SERVICES DEPARTMENT
PO BOX 7933
MADISON WI 53707-7933

NAMED INSURED

ROBERTSON, MICHAEL J & AUDREY F
5806 SUFFOLK RD
MADISON WI   53711-2533

EFFECTIVE
FROM 07-03-93 **TO** 10-09-93

COVERAGES AND LIMITS PROVIDED

```
        001 FAMILY FRAME DWELLING IN TOWN CLASS 3
SECTION I                                       LIMITS
    DWELLING                            $  94,000
    PERSONAL PROPERTY ON  PREMISES      $  70,500
    PERSONAL PROPERTY OFF PREMISES 100% SUBJECT TO POLICY LIMITATION
    LOSS OF USE - ACTUAL LOSS SUSTAINED WITHIN 12 MONTHS OF THE LOSS
    DEDUCTIBLE AMOUNT - ALL PERIL       $     250
SECTION II
    PERSONAL LIABILITY                  $ 300,000
    MEDICAL EXPENSE                     $   1,000
ADDITIONAL PROTECTION/ENDORSEMENTS
    AMENDATORY HOMEOWNERS ENDORSEMENT (END. 473 EDITION 4/89)
    SCHEDULED PERSONAL PROPERTY (END. 457 EDITION 10/84)
    OPTION 2 - EXTENDED COVERAGE ON JEWELRY, WATCHES AND FURS
```

THIS POLICY INCLUDES THE GUARANTEED BUILDING REPLACEMENT
AND PERSONAL PROPERTY REPLACEMENT COST COVERAGES.

TOTAL PREMIUM DUE $10.10

LATEST BUILDING COST INDEX FROM AMERICAN APPRAISAL COMPANY IS 400

Declarations effective on the date shown above. These declarations form a part of this policy and replace all other
declarations which may have been issued previously for this policy. If this declarations is accompanied by a new
policy, the policy replaces any which may have been issued before with the same policy number.

AUTHORIZED
REPRESENTATIVE   *Dale F. Mathwich*   *Ben T. Newberg*
                         President   Secretary

AGENT 094-026

J PATRICK NEWBERRY
PO BOX 44361
MADISON WI   53711

OPID   1QQ
TC   38
ENTRY DATE   07-21-93

Form No. HO-47C

Stock No. 11339 ERev.

BALLOON RIDER
(CONDITIONAL MODIFICATION AND EXTENSION OF LOAN TERMS)

THIS BALLOON RIDER is made this ___13th___ day of ___August___, 19 _93_, and is incorporated into and shall be deemed to amend and supplement the Mortgage, Deed of Trust or Deed to Secure Debt (the "Security Instrument") of the same date given by the undersigned (the "Borrower") to secure the Borrower's Note to ___AnchorBank, s.s.b.___ (the "Lender") of the same date and covering the property described in the Security Instrument and located at:

___5806 SUFFOLK ROAD, MADISON, WISCONSIN___   ___53711___
[Property Address]

The interest rate stated on the Note is called the "Note Rate." The date of the Note is called the "Note Date." I understand the Lender may transfer the Note, Security Instrument and this Rider. The Lender or anyone who takes the Note, the Security Instrument and this Rider by transfer and who is entitled to receive payments under the Note is called the "Note Holder."

ADDITIONAL COVENANTS. In addition to the covenants and agreements in the Security Instrument, Borrower and Lender further covenant and agree as follows (despite anything to the contrary contained in the Security Instrument or the Note):

1. CONDITIONAL MODIFICATION AND EXTENSION OF LOAN TERMS

At the maturity date of the Note and Security Instrument (the "Note Maturity Date"), I will be able to extend the Note Maturity Date to ___SEPTEMBER 1, 2023___, (the "Extended Maturity Date") and modify the Note Rate to the "Modified Note Rate" determined in accordance with Section 3 below if all the conditions provided in Sections 2 and 5 below are met (the "Conditional Modification and Extension Option"). If those conditions are not met, I understand that the Note Holder is under no obligation to refinance the Note or to modify the Note, reset the Note Rate or extend the Note Maturity Date, and that I will have to repay the Note from my own resources or find a lender willing to lend me the money to repay the Note.

2. CONDITIONS TO OPTION

If I want to exercise the Conditional Modification and Extension Option, certain conditions must be met as of the Note Maturity Date. These conditions are: (1) I must still be the owner and occupant of the property subject to the Security Instrument (the "Property"); (2) I must be current in my monthly payments and cannot have been more than 30 days late on any of the 12 scheduled monthly payments immediately preceding the Note Maturity Date; (3) there are no liens, defects, or encumbrances against the Property, or other adverse matters affecting title to the Property (except for taxes and special assessments not yet due and payable) arising after the Security Instrument was recorded; (4) the Modified Note Rate cannot be more than 5 percentage points above the Note Rate; and (5) I must make a written request to the Note Holder as provided in Section 5 below.

3. CALCULATING THE MODIFIED NOTE RATE

The Modified Note Rate will be a fixed rate of interest equal to the Federal Home Loan Mortgage Corporation's required net yield for 30-year fixed rate mortgages subject to a 60-day mandatory delivery commitment, plus one-half of one percent (0.5%), rounded to the nearest one-eighth of one percent (0.125%)(the "Modified Note Rate"). The required net yield shall be the applicable net yield in effect on the date and time of day that I notify the Note Holder of my election to exercise the Conditional Modification and Extension Option. If this required net yield is not available, the Note Holder will determine the Modified Note Rate by using comparable information.

4. CALCULATING THE NEW PAYMENT AMOUNT

Provided the Modified Note Rate as calculated in Section 3 above is not greater than 5 percentage points above the Note Rate and all other conditions required in Section 2 above are satisfied, the Note Holder will determine the amount of the monthly payment that will be sufficient to repay in full (a) the unpaid principal, plus (b) accrued but unpaid interest, plus (c) all other sums I will owe under the Note and Security Instrument on the Note Maturity Date (assuming my monthly payments then are current, as required under Section 2 above), over the remaining extended term at the Modified Note Rate in equal monthly payments. The result of this calculation will be the new amount of my principal and interest payment every month until the Note is fully paid.

5. EXERCISING THE CONDITIONAL MODIFICATION AND EXTENSION OPTION

The Note Holder will notify me at least 60 calendar days in advance of the Note Maturity Date and advise me of the principal, accrued but unpaid interest, and all other sums I am expected to owe on the Note Maturity Date. The Note Holder also will advise me that I may exercise the Conditional Modification and Extension Option if the conditions in Section 2 above are met. The Note Holder will provide my payment record information, together with the name, title and address of the person representing the Note Holder that I must notify in order to exercise the Conditional Modification and Extension Option. If I meet the conditions of Section 2 above, I may exercise the Conditional Modification and Extension Option by notifying the Note Holder no earlier than 60 calendar days and no later than 45 calendar days prior to the Note Maturity Date. The Note Holder will calculate the fixed Modified Note Rate based upon the Federal Home Loan Mortgage Corporation's applicable published required net yield in effect on the date and time of day notification is received by the Note Holder and as calculated in Section 3 above. I will then have 30 calendar days to provide the Note Holder with acceptable proof of my required ownership, occupancy and property lien status. Before the Note Maturity Date the Note Holder will advise me of the New interest rate (the Modified Note Rate), new monthly payment amount and a date, time and place at which I must appear to sign any documents required to complete the required Note Rate modification and Note Maturity Date extension. I understand the Note Holder will charge me a $250 processing fee and the costs associated with the exercise of the Conditional Modification and Extension Option, including but not limited to the cost of updating the title insurance policy.

BY SIGNING BELOW, BORROWER accepts and agrees to the terms and covenants contained in this Balloon Rider.

_____(Seal)
MICHAEL J. ROBERTSON   Borrower

_____(Seal)
AUDREY F. ROBERTSON   Borrower

_____(Seal)
                                   Borrower

_____(Seal)
                                   Borrower
[Sign Original Only]

MULTISTATE BALLOON RIDER (MODIFICATION AND EXTENSION)–Single Family–Freddie Mac UNIFORM INSTRUMENT   Form M3190 (10/90)
0015149

B A D G E R   A B S T R A C T   &   T I T L E   C O R P O R A T I O N

900 John Nolen Drive, Suite 200 * P.O. Box 1805   D 93070608 D
Madison, Wisconsin 53701
608-251-7700

ABSTRACTS * TITLE INSURANCE * CLOSING SERVICES

STATE OF WISCONSIN	}	
COUNTY OF DANE	}	OWNER'S Affidavit as to Liens and Possession

The undersigned being first duly sworn on oath deposed and says:

The affiant is owner of certain premises located at 5806 Suffolk Road, Madison, DANE County, described as follows:

Lot Fifty-four (54), Green Tree Estates, in the City of Madison, Dane County, Wisconsin.

That all bills or obligations incurred in connection with said improvements including the construction or repair thereof, have been paid in full, and in cash (as distinguised from any method requiring any payment in the future), and that there are not claims for labor, services or material furnished in connection with said improvements which remain unpaid, except: (if any unpaid claimants and amount due each)   *none*

That there is no person in actual possession or having a right to possession of said property or any part thereof, other than said owner(s), except: *none*

That as of the date hereof no mortgage, judgment, mechanics' lien, old age assisstance lien, repair bill, state or federal tax lien has been filed and is unpaid affected said real estate;

That there are no unpaid bills for, conditional bills of sale or other liens affecting any fixtures used in connection with the improvements upon said property;

That this affidavit is made for the purpose of inducing the BADGER ABSTRACT AND TITLE CORPORATION AND/OR OLD REPUBLIC NATIONAL TITLE INSURANCE COMPANY to insure the title to said property without exception to possible claims of mechanics, materialmen and laborers and the Michael J. Robertson and Audrey F. Robertson hereby expressly agree(s) to indemnify and save harmless BADGER ABSTRACT AND TITLE CORPORATION AND/OR OLD REPUBLIC NATIONAL TITLE INSURANCE COMPANY from any and all loss arising from claims for labor or material furnished.

x _____

Subscribed and sworn to before me this 13th day of August , 1993.

_____
Notary Public ___Dane___ County,
State of Wisconsin
My commission expires 3/24/96

OLD REPUBLIC NATIONAL TITLE INSURANCE COMPANY

BALLOON NOTE
(FIXED RATE)

THIS LOAN IS PAYABLE IN FULL AT MATURITY. YOU MUST REPAY THE ENTIRE PRINCIPAL BALANCE OF THE LOAN AND UNPAID INTEREST THEN DUE. THE LENDER IS UNDER NO OBLIGATION TO REFINANCE THE LOAN AT THAT TIME. YOU WILL, THEREFORE, BE REQUIRED TO MAKE PAYMENT OUT OF OTHER ASSETS THAT YOU MAY OWN, OR YOU WILL HAVE TO FIND A LENDER, WHICH MAY BE THE LENDER YOU HAVE THIS LOAN WITH, WILLING TO LEND YOU THE MONEY. IF YOU REFINANCE THIS LOAN AT MATURITY, YOU MAY HAVE TO PAY SOME OR ALL OF THE CLOSING COSTS NORMALLY ASSOCIATED WITH A NEW LOAN EVEN IF YOU OBTAIN REFINANCING FROM THE SAME LENDER.

August 13 , 19 93   Madison _____ ,   Wisconsin _____
                          [City]   [State]

5806 SUFFOLK ROAD, MADISON, WISCONSIN 53711 _____
                          [Property Address]

1. BORROWER'S PROMISE TO PAY

In return for a loan that I have received, I promise to pay U.S. $ __65,000.00__ (this amount is called "principal"), plus interest, to the order of the Lender. The Lender is __AnchorBank, s.s.b.__ . I understand that the Lender may transfer this Note. The Lender or anyone who takes this Note by transfer and who is entitled to receive payments under this Note is called the "Note Holder."

2. INTEREST

Interest will be charged on unpaid principal until the full amount of principal has been paid. I will pay interest at a yearly rate of __6.570__ %.

The interest rate required by Section 2 is the rate I will pay both before and after any default described in Section 6(b) of this Note.

3. PAYMENTS

(A) Time and Place of Payments

I will pay principal and interest by making payments every month.

I will make my monthly payments on the __1ST__ day of each month beginning on __OCTOBER__ __01__ __1993__ . I will make these payments every month until I have paid all of the principal and interest and any other charges described below that I may owe under this Note. My monthly payments will be applied to interest before principal. If, on __SEPTEMBER 1, 2000__ , I still owe amounts under this Note, I will pay those amounts in full on that date, which is called the "maturity date."

I will make my monthly payments at __25 W. Main Street, Madison, WI 53703__ or at a different place if required by the Note Holder.

(B) Amount of Monthly Payments

My monthly payment will be in the amount of U.S. $ __413.85__

4. BORROWER'S RIGHT TO PREPAY

I have the right to make payments of principal at any time before they are due. A payment of principal only is known as a "prepayment." When I make a prepayment, I will tell the Note Holder in writing that I am doing so.

I may make a full prepayment or partial prepayments without paying any prepayment charge. The Note Holder will use all of my prepayments to reduce the amount of principal that I owe under this Note. If I make a partial prepayment, there will be no changes in the due date or in the amount of my monthly payment unless the Note Holder agrees in writing to those changes.

5. LOAN CHARGES

If a law, which applies to this loan and which sets maximum loan charges, is finally interpreted so that the interest or other loan charges collected or to be collected in connection with this loan exceed the permitted limits, then: (i) any such loan charge shall be reduced by the amount necessary to reduce the charge to the permitted limit; and (ii) any sum already collected from me which exceeded permitted limits will be refunded to me. The Note Holder may choose to make this refund by reducing the principal I owe under this Note or by making a direct payment to me. If a refund reduces principal, the reduction will be treated as a partial prepayment.

6. BORROWER'S FAILURE TO PAY AS REQUIRED

(A) Late Charges for Overdue Payments

If the Note Holder has not received the full amount of any monthly payments by the end of __15__ calendar days after the date it is due, I will pay a late charge to the Note Holder. The amount of the charge will be __5__ % of my overdue payment of principal and interest. I will pay this late charge promptly but only once on each late payment.

(B) Default

If I do not pay the full amount of each monthly payment on the date it is due, I will be in default..

(C) Notice of Default

If I am in default, the Note Holder may send me a written notice telling me that if I do not pay the overdue amount by a certain date, the Note Holder may require me to pay immediately the full amount of principal which has not been paid and all the interest that I owe on that amount. That date must be at least 30 days after the date on which the notice is delivered or mailed to me.

MULTISTATE BALLOON NOTE (FIXED RATE)—Single Family—Freddie Mac UNIFORM INSTRUMENT Form 3290A (6/90)

015149

(D) No Waiver By Note Holder

Even if, at a time when I am in default, the Note Holder does not require me to pay immediately in full as described above, the Note Holder will still have the right to do so if I am in default at a later time.

(E) Payment of Note Holder's Costs and Expenses

If the Note Holder has required me to pay immediately in full as described above, the Note Holder will have the right to be paid back by me for all of its costs and expenses in enforcing this Note to the extent not prohibited by applicable law. Those expenses include, for example, reasonable attorney's fees.

7. GIVING OF NOTICES

Unless applicable law requires a different method, any notice that must be given to me under this Note will be given by delivering it or by mailing it by first class mail to me at the Property Address above or at a different address if I give the Note Holder a notice of my different address.

Any notice that must be given to the Note Holder under this Note will be given by mailing it by first class mail to the Note Holder at the address stated in Section 3(A) above or at a different address if I am given a notice of that different address.

8. OBLIGATIONS OF PERSONS UNDER THIS NOTE

If more than one person signs this Note, each person is fully and personally obligated to keep all of the promises made in this Note, including the promise to pay the full amount owed. Any person who is a guarantor, surety or endorser of this Note is also obligated to do these things. Any person who takes over these obligations, including the obligations of a guarantor, surety or endorser of the Note, is also obligated to keep all of the promises made in this Note. The Note Holder may enforce its rights under this Note against each person individually or against all of us together. This means that any one of us may be required to pay all of the amounts owed under this Note.

9. WAIVERS

I and any other person who has obligations under this Note waive the rights of presentment and notice of dishonor. "Presentment" means the rights to require the Note Holder to demand payment of amounts due. "Notice of dishonor" means the right to require the Note Holder to give notice to other persons that amounts due have not been paid.

10. UNIFORM SECURED NOTE

This Note is a uniform instrument with limited variations in some jurisdictions. In addition to the protections given to the Note Holder under this Note, a Mortgage, Deed of Trust or Security Deed (the "Security Instrument"), dated the same date as this Note, protects the Note Holder from possible losses which might result if I do not keep the promises which I make in this Note. That Security Instrument describes how and under what conditions I may be required to make immediate payment in full of all amounts I owe under the Note. Some of those conditions are described as follows:

Transfer of the Property or a Beneficial Interest in Borrower. If all or any part of the Property or any interest in it is sold or transferred (or if a beneficial interest in Borrower is sold or transferred and Borrower is not a natural person) without Lender's prior written consent, Lender may, at its option, require immediate payment in full of all sums secured by this Security Instrument. However, this option shall not be exercised by Lender if exercise is prohibited by federal law as of the date of this Security Instrument.

If Lender exercises this option, Lender shall give Borrower notice of acceleration. The notice shall provide a period of not less than 30 days from the date the notice is delivered or mailed within which Borrower must pay all sums secured by this Security Instrument. If Borrower fails to pay these sums prior to the expiration of this period, Lender may invoke any remedies permitted by this Security Instrument without further notice or demand on Borrower.

WITNESS THE HAND(S) AND SEAL(S) OF THE UNDERSIGNED.

_____ ____(Seal)
MICHAEL J. ROBERTSON   Borrower

_____ ____(Seal)
AUDREY F. ROBERTSON   Borrower

_____ ____(Seal)
                                           Borrower

_____ ____(Seal)
                                           Borrower

[Sign Original Only]

0015149

Form 3290B

93070608

—————[Space Above This Line For Recording Data]—————

MORTGAGE

THIS MORTGAGE ("Security Instrument") is given on   August 13   19 93   The mortgagor is

MICHAEL J. ROBERTSON, AND AUDREY F. ROBERTSON, AS HUSBAND AND WIFE

("Borrower"). This Security Instrument is given to **AnchorBank, s.s.s.**

which is organized and existing under the laws of the **STATE OF WISCONSIN**, and whose address is **25 West Main Street, Madison, Wisconsin 53703 ("Lender").** Borrower owes Lender the principal sum of   **SIXTY FIVE THOUSAND AND NO/100**

Dollars (U.S. $ **65,000.00**   ). This debt is evidenced by Borrower's note dated the same date as this Security Instrument ("Note"), which provides for monthly payments, with the full debt, if not paid earlier, due and payable on   **SEPTEMBER 1, 2000**   . This Security Instrument secures to Lender: (a) the repayment of the debt evidenced by the Note, with interest, and all renewals, extensions and modifications of the Note; (b) the payment of all other sums, with interest, advanced under paragraph 7 to protect the security of this Security Instrument; and (c) the performance of Borrower's covenants and agreements under this Security Instrument and the Note. For this purpose, Borrower does hereby mortgage, grant and convey to Lender, with power of sale, the following described property located in   **DANE**   County, Wisconsin:

Lot Fifty-four (54), Green Tree Estates, in the City of Madison, Dane County, Wisconsin.

This is homestead property.

which has the address of   **5806 SUFFOLK ROAD**   **MADISON**   ,
                                                [Street]   [City]
Wisconsin   **53711**   ("Property Address");
                    [Zip Code]

TOGETHER WITH all the improvements now or hereafter erected on the property, and all easements, appurtenances, and fixtures now or hereafter a part of the property. All replacements and additions shall also be covered by this Security Instrument. All of the foregoing is referred to in this Security Instrument as the "Property."

BORROWER COVENANTS that Borrower is lawfully seised of the estate hereby conveyed and has the right to mortgage, grant and convey the Property and that the Property is unencumbered, except for encumbrances of record. Borrower warrants and will defend generally the title to the Property against all claims and demands, subject to any encumbrances of record.

THIS SECURITY INSTRUMENT combines uniform covenants for national use and non-uniform covenants with limited variations by jurisdiction to constitute a uniform security instrument covering real property.

WISCONSIN --Single Family--Fannie Mae/Freddie Mac UNIFORM INSTRUMENT   Form 3050   9/90   Page 1 of 5   30501

UNIFORM COVENANTS. Borrower and Lender covenant and agree as follows:

1. Payment of Principal and Interest; Prepayment and Late Charges. Borrower shall promptly pay when due the principal of and interest on the debt evidenced by the Note and any prepayment and late charges due under the Note.

2. Funds for Taxes and Insurance. Subject to applicable law or to a written waiver by Lender, Borrower shall pay to Lender on the day monthly payments are due under the Note, until the Note is paid in full, a sum ("Funds") for: (a) yearly taxes and assessments which may attain priority over this Security Instrument as a lien on the Property; (b) yearly leasehold payments or ground rents on the Property, if any; (c) yearly hazard or property insurance premiums; and (d) yearly flood insurance premiums, if any; (e) yearly mortgage insurance premiums, if any; and (f) any sums payable by Borrower to Lender, in accordance with the provisions of paragraph 8, in lieu of the payment of mortgage insurance premimums. These items are called "Escrow Items." Lender may, at any time, collect and hold Funds in an amount not to exceed the maximum amount a lender for a federally related mortgage loan may require for Borrower's escrow account under the federal Real Estate Settlement Procedures Act of 1974 as amended from time to time, 12 U.S.C. 2601 *et seq.* ("RESPA"), unless another law that applies to the Funds sets a lesser amount. If so, Lender may, at any time, collect and hold Funds in an amount not to exceed the lesser amount. Lender may estimate the amount of Funds due on the basis of current data and reasonable estimates of expenditures of future Escrow Items or otherwise in accordance with applicable law.

The Funds shall be held in an institution whose deposits are insured by a federal agency, instrumentality, or entity (including Lender, if Lender is such an institution) or in any Federal Home Loan Bank. Lender shall apply the Funds to pay the Escrow Items. Lender may not charge Borrower for holding and applying the Funds, annually analyzing the escrow account, or verifying the Escrow Items, unless Lender pays Borrower interest on the Funds and applicable law permits Lender to make such a charge. However, Lender may require Borrower to pay a one-time charge for an independent real estate tax reporting service used by Lender in connection with this loan, unless applicable law provides otherwise. Unless an agreement is made or applicable law requires interest to be paid, Lender shall not be required to pay Borrower any interest or earnings on the Funds. Borrower and Lender may agree in writing, however, that interest shall be paid on the Funds. Lender shall give to Borrower, without charge, an annual accounting of the Funds, showing credits and debits to the Funds and the purpose for which each debit to the Funds was made. The Funds are pledged as additional security for all sums secured by this Security Instrument.

If the Funds held by Lender exceed the amounts permitted to be held by applicable law, Lender shall account to Borrower for the excess Funds in accordance withthe requirements of applicable law. If the amount of the Funds held by Lender at any time is not sufficient to pay the Escrow Items when due, Lender may so notify Borrower in writing, and, in such case Borrower shall pay to Lender the amount necessary to make up the deficiency. Borrower shall make up the deficiency in no more than twelve monthly payments, at Lender's sole discretion.

Upon payment in full of all sums secured by this Security Instrument, Lender shall promptly refund to Borrower any funds held by Lender. If, under paragraph 21, Lender shall acquire or sell the Property, Lender, prior to the acquisition or sale of the Property, shall apply any Funds held by Lender at the time of acquisition or sale as a credit against the sums secured by this Security Instrument.

3. Application of Payments. Unless applicable law provides otherwise, all payments received by Lender under paragraphs 1 and 2 shall be applied: first, to any prepayment charges due under the Note; second, to amounts payable under paragraph 2; third, to interest due; fourth, to principal due; and last, to any late charges due under the Note.

4. Charges; Liens. Borrower shall pay all taxes, assessments, charges, fines and impositions attributable to the Property which may attain priority over this Security Instrument, and leasehold payments or ground rents, if any. Borrower shall pay these obligations in the manner provided in paragraph 2, or if not paid in that manner, Borrower shall pay them on time directly to the person owed payment. Borrower shall promptly furnish to Lender all notices of amounts to be paid under this paragraph. If Borrower makes these payments directly, Borrower shall promptly furnish to Lender receipts evidencing the payments.

Borrower shall promptly discharge any lien which has priority over this Security Instrument unless Borrower: (a) agrees in writing to the payment of the obligation secured by the lien in a manner acceptable to Lender; (b) contests in good faith the lien by, or defends against enforcement of the lien in, legal proceedings which in the Lender's opinion operate to prevent the enforcement of the lien; or (c) secures from the holder of the lien an agreement satisfactory to Lender subordinating the lien to this Security Instrument. If Lender determines that any part of the Property is subject to a lien which may attain priority over this Security Instrument, Lender may give Borrower a notice identifying the lien. Borrower shall satisfy the lien or take one or more of the actions set forth above within 10 days of the giving of notice.

5. Hazard or Property Insurance. Borrower shall keep the improvements now existing or hereafter erected on the Property insured against loss by fire, hazards included within the term "extended coverage" and any other hazards, including floods or flooding, for which Lender requires insurance. This insurance shall be maintained in the amounts and for the periods that Lender requires. The insurance carrier providing the insurance shall be chosen by Borrower subject to Lender's approval which shall not be unreasonably withheld. If Borrower fails to maintain coverage described above, Lender may, at Lender's option, obtain coverage to protect Lender's rights in the Property in accordance with paragraph 7.

All insurance policies and renewals shall be acceptable to Lender and shall include a standard mortgage clause. Lender shall have the right to hold the policies and renewals. If Lender requires, Borrower shall promptly give to Lender all receipts of paid premiums and renewal notices. In the event of loss, Borrower shall give prompt notice to the insurance carrier and Lender. Lender may make proof of loss if not made promptly by Borrower.

Unless Lender and Borrower otherwise agree in writing, insurance proceeds shall be applied to restoration or repair of the Property damaged, if the restoration or repair is economically feasible and Lender's security is not lessened. If the restoration or repair is not economically feasible or Lender's security would be lessened, the insurance proceeds shall be applied to the sums secured by this Security Instrument, whether or not then due, with any excess paid to Borrower. If Borrower abandons the Property, or does not answer within 30 days a notice from Lender that the insurance carrier has offered to settle a claim, then Lender may collect the insurance proceeds. Lender may use the proceeds to repair or restore the Property or to pay sums secured by this Security Instrument, whether or not then due. The 30-day period will begin when the notice is given.

Unless Lender and Borrower otherwise agree in writing, any application of proceeds to principal shall not extend or postpone the due date of the monthly payments referred to in paragraphs 1 and 2 or change the amount of the payments. If under paragraph 21 the Property is acquired by Lender, Borrower's right to any insurance policies and proceeds resulting from damage to the Property prior to the acquisition shall pass to Lender to the extent of the sums secured by this Security Instrument immediately prior to the acquisition.

WISCONSIN –Single Family–Fannie Mae/Freddie Mac UNIFORM INSTRUMENT   Form 3050   Page 2 of 5   9/90   30502

6. Occupancy, Preservation, Maintenance and Protection of the Property; Borrower's Loan Application; Leaseholds. Borrower shall occupy, establish, and use the Property as Borrower's principal residence within sixty days after the execution of this Security Instrument and shall continue to occupy the Property as Borrower's principal residence for at least one year after the date of occupancy, unless Lender otherwise agrees in writing, which consent shall not be unreasonably withheld, or unless extenuating circumstances exist which are beyond Borrower's control. Borrower shall not be destroy, damage or impair the Property, allow the Property to deteriorate, or commit waste on the Property. Borrower shall be in default if any forfeiture action or proceeding, whether civil or criminal, is begun that in Lender's good faith judgment could result in forfeiture of the Property or otherwise materially impair the lien created by this Security Instrument or Lender's security interest. Borrower may cure such a default and reinstate, as provided in paragraph 18, by causing the action or proceeding to be dismissed with a ruling that, in Lender's good faith determination, precludes forfeiture of the Borrower's interest in the Property or other material impairment of the lien created by this Security Instrument or Lender's security interest. Borrower shall also be in default if Borrower, during the loan application process, gave materially false or inaccurate information or statements to Lender (or failed to provide Lender with any material information) in connection with the loan evidenced by the Note, including, but not limited to, representations concerning Borrower's occupancy of the Property as a principal residence. If this Security Instrument is on a leasehold, Borrower shall comply with all the provisions of the lease. If Borrower acquires fee title to the Property, the leasehold and the fee title shall not merge unless Lender agrees to the merger in writing.

7. Protection of Lender's Rights in the Property. If Borrower fails to perform the covenants and agreements contained in this Security Instrument, or there is a legal proceeding that may significantly affect Lender's rights in the Property (such as a proceeding in bankruptcy, probate, for condemnation or forfeiture or to enforce laws or regulations), then Lender may do and pay for whatever is necessary to protect the value of the Property and Lender's rights in the Property. Lender's actions may include paying any sums secured by a lien which has priority over this Security Instrument, appearing in court, paying reasonable attorneys' fees and entering on the Property to make repairs. Although Lender may take action under this paragraph 7, Lender does not have to do so.

Any amounts disbursed by Lender under this paragraph 7 shall become additional debt of Borrower secured by this Security Instrument. Unless Borrower and Lender agree to other terms of payment, these amounts shall bear interest from the date of disbursement at the Note rate and shall be payable, with interest, upon notice from Lender to Borrower requesting payment.

8. Mortgage Insurance. If Lender required mortgage insurance as a condition of making the loan secured by this Security Instrument, Borrower shall pay the premiums required to maintain the mortgage insurance in effect. If, for any reason, the mortgage insurance coverage required by Lender lapses or ceases to be in effect, Borrower shall pay the premiums required to obtain coverage substantially equivalent to the mortgage insurance previously in effect, at a cost substantially equivalent to the cost to Borrower of the mortgage insurance previously in effect, from an alternate mortgage insurer approved by Lender. If substantially equivalent mortgage insurance coverage is not available, Borrower shall pay to Lender each month a sum equal to one-twelfth of the yearly mortgage insurance premium being paid by Borrower when the insurance coverage lapsed or ceased to be in effect. Lender will accept, use and retain these payments as a loss reserve in lieu of mortgage insurance. Loss reserve payments may no longer be required, at the option of Lender, if mortgage insurance coverage (in the amount and for the period that Lender requires) provided by an insurer approved by Lender again becomes available and is obtained. Borrower shall pay the premiums required to maintain mortgage insurance in effect, or to provide a loss reserve, until the requirement for mortgage insurance ends in accordance with any written agreement between Borrower and Lender or applicable law.

9. Inspection. Lender or its agent may make reasonable entries upon and inspections of the Property. Lender shall give Borrower notice at the time of or prior to an inspection specifying reasonable cause for the inspection.

10. Condemnation. The proceeds of any award or claim for damages, direct or consequential, in connection with any condemnation or other taking of any part of the Property, or for conveyance in lieu of condemnation, are hereby assigned and shall be paid to Lender.

In the event of a total taking of the Property, the proceeds shall be applied to the sums secured by this Security Instrument, whether or not then due, with any excess paid to Borrower. In the event of a partial taking of the Property in which the fair market value of the Property immediately before the taking is equal to or greater than the amount of the sums secured by this Security Instrument immediately before the taking, unless Borrower and Lender otherwise agree in writing, the sums secured by this Security Instrument shall be reduced by the amount of the proceeds multiplied by the following fraction: (a) the total amount of the sums secured immediately before the taking, divided by (b) the fair market value of the Property immediately before the taking. Any balance shall be paid to Borrower. In the event of a partial taking of the Property in which the fair market value of the Property immediately before the taking is less than the amount of the sums secured immediately before the taking, unless Borrower and Lender otherwise agree in writing or unless applicable law otherwise provides, the proceeds shall be applied to the sums secured by this Security Instrument whether or not the sums are then due.

If the Property is abandoned by Borrower, or if, after notice by Lender to Borrower that the condemnor offers to make an award or settle a claim for damages, Borrower fails to respond to Lender within 30 days after the date the notice is given, Lender is authorized to collect and apply the proceeds, at its option, either to restoration or repair of the Property or to the sums secured by this Security Instrument, whether or not then due.

Unless Lender and Borrower otherwise agree in writing, any application of proceeds to principal shall not extend or postpone the due date of the monthly payments referred to in paragraphs 1 and 2 or change the amount of such payments.

11. Borrower Not Released; Forbearance by Lender Not a Waiver. Extension of the time for payment or modification of amortization of the sums secured by this Security Instrument granted by Lender to any successor in interest of Borrower shall not operate to release the liability of the original Borrower or Borrower's successors in interest. Lender shall not be required to commence proceedings against any successor in interest or refuse to extend time for payment or otherwise modify amortization of the sums secured by this Security Instrument by reason of any demand made by the original Borrower or Borrower's successors in interest. Any forbearance by Lender in exercising any right or remedy shall not be a waiver of or preclude the exercise of any right or remedy.

12. Successors and Assigns Bound; Joint and Several Liability; Co-signers. The covenants and agreements of this Security Instrument shall bind and benefit the successors and assigns of Lender and Borrower, subject to the provisions of paragraph 17. Borrower's covenants and agreements shall be joint and several. Any Borrower who co-signs this Security Instrument but does not execute the Note: (a) is co-signing this Security Instrument only to mortgage, grant and convey that Borrower's interest in the Property under the terms of this Security Instrument; (b) is not personally obligated to pay the sums secured by this Security Instrument; and (c) agrees that Lender and any other Borrower may agree to extend, modify, forbear or make any accommodations with regard to the terms of this Security Instrument or the Note without that Borrower's consent.

13. Loan Charges. If the loan secured by this Security Instrument is subject to a law which sets maximum loan charges, and that law is finally interpreted so that the interest or other loan charges collected or to be collected in connection with the loan exceed the permitted limits, then: (a) any such loan charge shall be reduced by the amount necessary to reduce the charge to the permitted limit; and (b) any sums already collected from Borrower which exceeded permitted limits will be refunded to Borrower. Lender may choose to make this refund by reducing the principal owed under the Note or by making a direct payment to Borrower. If a refund reduces principal, the reduction will be treated as a partial prepayment without any prepayment charge under the Note.

14. Notices. Any notice to Borrower provided for in this Security Instrument shall be given by delivering it or by mailing it by first class mail unless applicable law requires use of another method. The notice shall be directed to the Property Address or any other address Borrower designates by notice to Lender. Any notice to Lender shall be given by first class mail to Lender's address stated herein or any other address Lender designates by notice to Borrower. Any notice provided for in this Security Instrument shall be deemed to have been given to Borrower or Lender when given as provided in this paragraph.

15. Governing Law; Severability. This Security Instrument shall be governed by federal law and the law of the jurisdiction in which the Property is located. In the event that any provision or clause of this Security Instrument or the Note conflicts with applicable law, such conflict shall not affect other provisions of this Security Instrument or the Note which can be given effect without the conflicting provision. To this end the provisions of this Security Instrument and the Note are declared to be severable.

16. Borrower's Copy. Borrower shall be given one conformed copy of the Note and of this Security Instrument.

17. Transfer of the Property or a Beneficial Interest in Borrower. If all or any part of the Property or any interest in it is sold or transferred (or if a beneficial interest in Borrower is sold or transferred and Borrower is not a natural person) without Lender's prior written consent, Lender may, at its option, require immediate payment in full of all sums secured by this Security Instrument. However, this option shall not be exercised by Lender if exercise is prohibited by federal law as of the date of this Security Instrument.

If Lender exercises this option, Lender shall give Borrower notice of acceleration. The notice shall provide a period of not less than 30 days from the date the notice is delivered or mailed within which Borrower must pay all sums secured by this Security Instrument. If Borrower fails to pay these sums prior to the expiration of this period, Lender may invoke any remedies permitted by this Security Instrument without further notice or demand on Borrower.

18. Borrower's Right to Reinstate. If Borrower meets certain conditions, Borrower shall have the right to have enforcement of this Security Instrument discontinued at any time prior to the earlier of: (a) 5 days (or such other period as applicable law may specify for reinstatement) before sale of the Property pursuant to any power of sale contained in this Security Instrument; or (b) entry of a judgment enforcing this Security Instrument. Those conditions are that Borrower: (a) pays Lender all sums which then would be due under this Security Instrument and the Note as if no acceleration had occurred; (b) cures any default of any other covenants or agreements; (c) pays all expenses incurred in enforcing this Security Instrument, including, but not limited to, reasonable attorneys' fees; and (d) takes such action as Lender may reasonably require to assure that the lien of this Security Instrument, Lender's rights in the Property and Borrower's obligation to pay the sums secured by this Security Instrument shall continue unchanged. Upon reinstatement by Borrower, this Security Instrument and the obligations secured hereby shall remain fully effective as if no acceleration had occurred. However, this right to reinstate shall not apply in the case of acceleration under paragraph 17.

19. Sale of Note; Change of Loan Servicer. The Note or a partial interest in the Note (together with this Security Instrument) may be sold one or more times without prior notice to Borrower. A sale may result in a change in the entity (known as the "Loan Servicer") that collects monthly payments due under the Note and this Security Instrument. There also may be one or more changes of the Loan Servicer unrelated to a sale of the Note. If there is a change of the Loan Servicer, Borrower will be given written notice of the change in accordance with paragraph 14 above and applicable law. The notice will state the name and address of the new Loan Servicer and the address to which payments should be made. The notice will also contain any other information required by applicable law.

20. Hazardous Substances. Borrower shall not cause or permit the presence, use, disposal, storage, or release of any Hazardous Substances on or in the Property. Borrower shall not do, nor allow anyone else to do, anything affecting the Property that is in violation of any Environmental Law. The preceding two sentences shall not apply to the presence, use, or storage on the Property of small quantities of Hazardous Substances that are generally recognized to be appropriate to normal residential uses and to maintenance of the Property.

Borrower shall promptly give Lender written notice of any investigation, claim, demand, lawsuit or other action by any governmental or regulatory agency or private party involving the Property and any Hazardous Substance or Environmental Law of which Borrower has actual knowledge. If Borrower learns, or is notified by any governmental or regulatory authority, that any removal or other remediation of any Hazardous Substance affecting the Property is necessary, Borrower shall promptly take all necessary remedial actions in accordance with Environmental Law.

As used in this paragraph 20, "Hazardous Substances" are those substances defined as toxic or hazardous substances by Environmental Law and the following substances: gasoline, kerosene, other flammable or toxic petroleum products, toxic pesticides and herbicides, volatile solvents, materials containing asbestos or formaldehyde, and radioactive materials. As used in this paragraph 20, "Environmental Law" means federal laws and laws of the jurisdiction where the Property is located that relate to health, safety or environmental protection.

NON-UNIFORM COVENANTS. Borrower and Lender further covenant and agree as follows:

21. Acceleration; Remedies. Lender shall give notice to Borrower prior to acceleration following Borrower's breach of any covenant or agreement in this Security Instrument (but not prior to acceleration under paragraph 17 unless applicable law provides otherwise). The notice shall specify: (a) the default; (b) the action required to cure the default; (c) a date, not less than 30 days from the date the notice is given to Borrower, by which the default must be cured; and (d) that failure to cure the default on or before the date specified in the notice may result in acceleration of the sums secured by this Security Instrument and sale of the Property. The notice shall further inform Borrower of the right to reinstate after acceleration and the right to bring a court action to assert the non-existence of a default or any other defense of Borrower to acceleration and sale. If the default is not cured on or before the date specified in the notice, Lender at its option may require immediate payment in full of all sums secured by this Security Instrument without further demand and may invoke the power of sale and any other remedies permitted by applicable law. Lender shall be entitled to collect all expenses incurred in pursuing the remedies provided in this paragraph 21, including, but not limited to, reasonable attorneys' fees and costs of title evidence.

WISCONSIN –Single Family–Fannie Mae/Freddie Mac UNIFORM INSTRUMENT   Form 3050   Page 4 of 5   9/90   30504

If Lender invokes the power of sale, Lender shall give notice of sale in the manner prescribed by applicable law to Borrower and to the other persons prescribed by applicable law. Lender shall publish the notice of sale, and the Property shall be sold in the manner prescribed by applicable law. Lender or its designee may purchase the Property at any sale. The proceeds of the sale shall be applied in the following order: (a) to all expenses of the sale, including, but not limited to, reasonable attorneys' fees; (b) to all sums secured by this Security Instrument; and (c) any excess to the clerk of the circuit court of the county in which the sale is held.

22. Release. Upon payment of all sums secured by this Security Instrument, Lender shall release this Security Instrument without charge to Borrower. Borrower shall pay any recordation costs.

23. Accelerated Redemption Periods. If (a) the Property is 20 acres or less in size, (b) Lender in an action to foreclose this Security Instrument waives all right to a judgment for deficiency and (c) Lender consents to Borrower's remaining in possession of the Property, then the sale of the Property may be 6 months from the date the judgment is entered if the Property is owner-occupied at the time of the commencement of the foreclosure action. If conditions (b) and (c) above are met and the Propety is not owner-occupied at the time of the commencement of the foreclosure action, then the sale of the Property may be 3 months from the date the judgment is entered. In any event, if the Property has been abandoned, then the sale of the Property may be 2 months from the date the judgment is entered.

24. Attorneys' Fees. If this Security Instrument is subject to Chapter 428 of the Wisconsin Statutes, "reasonable attorneys' fees" shall mean only those attorneys' fees allowed by that Chapter.

25. Riders to this Security Instrument. If one or more riders are executed by Borrower and recorded together with this Security Instrument, the covenants and agreements of each such rider shall be incorporated into and shall amend and supplement the covenants and agreements of this Security Instrument as if the rider(s) were a part of this Security Instrument. [Check applicable box(es)]

☐ Adjustable Rate Rider	☐ Condominium Rider	☐ 1-4 Family Rider
☐ Graduated Payment Rider	☐ Planned Unit Development Rider	☐ Biweekly Payment Rider
☒ Balloon Rider	☐ Rate Improvement Rider	☐ Second Home Rider
☐ Other(s) [specify]		

BY SIGNING BELOW, Borrower accepts and agrees to the terms and covenants contained in this Security Instrument and in any rider(s) executed by Borrower and recorded with it.

_____ (Seal)   _____ (Seal)
                        --Borrower   MICHAEL J. ROBERTSON   --Borrower

_____ (Seal)   _____ (Seal)
                        --Borrower   AUDREY F. ROBERTSON   --Borrower

———————————————— [Space Below This Line For Acknowledgement] ————————————————

STATE OF __WISCONSIN__   )
) ss
COUNTY OF ___DANE___   )

The foregoing instrument was acknowledged before me this _____   August 13, 1993
                                                                                  (date)

by __MICHAEL J. ROBERTSON AND AUDREY F. ROBERTSON__
                        (person(s) acknowledging)

                                                                    (SEAL)
                                        Notary Public

                                        My Commission Expires: ____3/54/96____

This instrument was prepared by ___Ron Steinhofer___

WISCONSIN --Single Family--Fannie Mae/Freddie Mac UNIFORM INSTRUMENT   Form 3050   Page 5 of 5   9/90   30505

0015149

GLOSSARY ─────────────────────────

Abstract of title   A written history of the title transaction or conditions bearing on the title to designated real estate. An abstract of title covers the period from the original source of title to the present and summarizes all subsequent instruments of public record by setting forth their material parts.

Acceleration clause   A common provision of a mortgage, trust deed, and note providing that the entire principal shall become immediately due and payable in the event of default.

Accrued interest   The interest earned for the period of time that has elapsed since interest was last paid.

Acknowledgment   A formal declaration, attached to or a part of an instrument, made before a duly authorized officer (usually a notary public) by the person who has executed the instrument, declaring the execution to be a free act and deed and that the signature is genuine.

Acquisition cost   The FHA-appraised value or purchase price (whichever is less) plus some closing costs.

Acre   A measure of land, 43,560 square feet.

Action to quit title   A court action to remove any interest or claim to the title to real property, taken to remove a cloud on the title.

Actual/actual (A/A)   A type of remittance requiring the lender to remit to Fannie Mae only principal and interest payments actually collected from borrowers. Compare with *Scheduled/actual* and *Scheduled/scheduled.*

Adjustable rate mortgage loan (ARM)   A type of alternative mortgage instrument in which the interest rate adjusts periodically according to a predetermined index and margin. This adjustment results in the mortgage payment either increasing or decreasing. In some situations, the adjustment is made to the outstanding principal.

Adjustment date   The date for periodic interest rate adjustments for an adjustable rate mortgage loan.

Adjustment period   The length of time between interest or payment rate change on an ARM.

Administrator   A person appointed by a probate court to administer the estate of a person who died intestate (without a will).

Ad valorem   "According to the value," used in connection with taxation.

Advance commitment   A written promise to make an investment at some time in the future if specified conditions are met.

Adverse possession   The right by which someone occupying a piece of land might acquire title against the real owner, if the occupant's possession has been actual, continuous, hostile, visible, and distinct for a statutory period of time.

Affidavit   A sworn statement in writing before a proper official, usually a notary. See *Acknowledgment*.

After-acquired property   Property acquired after the execution of a security agreement and that will serve as additional security for the underlying debt.

Agent   One who legally represents another, called a principal, from whom authority has been derived.

Agreement for sale   A written document in which the purchaser agrees to buy certain real estate (or personal property) and the seller agrees to sell under stated terms and conditions. Also called sales contract, binder, or earnest money contract.

Air rights   The ownership of the right to use, control, or occupy the air space over designated real estate.

Alienation   Transference of real property from one person to another.

Alternative mortgage instrument   Any one of the various new mortgage loans that is different from a traditional mortgage because the monthly payment, interest rate, term, or other provisions are changed in an agreed-upon manner.

Amenity   An aspect of a property that enhances its value. Examples are off-street reserved parking within a condominium community, the nearness of good public transportation, tennis courts, or a swimming pool.

American Land Title Association (ALTA)   A national association of title insurance companies, abstractors, and attorneys specializing in real property law. The association speaks for the title insurance and abstracting industry and establishes standard procedures and title policy forms.

Amortization   Repayment of a debt in equal installments of principal and interest, rather than interest-only payments.

Amortization schedule   A table showing the amounts of principal and interest due at regular intervals and the unpaid balance of the loan after each payment is made.

Annual percentage rate (APR)   A rate that represents the relationship of the total finance charge (interest, loan fees, points) to the amount of the loan.

Annual statement   An annual statement sent to mortgagors detailing all activity in their mortgage loan account, including all escrow activity.

Application   A form used to apply for a mortgage loan and to record pertinent information concerning a prospective mortgagor and the proposed security.

Appraisal   A report by a qualified person setting forth an opinion or estimate of value. Also, the process by which this estimate is obtained.

Appraised value   An opinion of value reached by an appraiser based upon knowledge, experience, and a study of pertinent data.

Appraiser   A person qualified by education, training, and experience to estimate the value of real and personal property.

Appreciation   An increase in value; the opposite of depreciation.

Appurtenance   Anything attached to the land and thus part of the property, such as a barn, garage, or an easement.

ARM margin   The spread (or difference) between the index rate and the interest rate of an adjustable-rate mortgage.

Assessed valuation   The value that a taxing authority places upon real or personal property for the purpose of taxation.

Assessment   The process of placing a value on property for the strict purpose of taxation. May also refer to a levy against property for a special purpose, such as a sewer assessment.

Assignee   The person to whom property or a right is assigned or transferred.

Assignment of mortgage   A document that evidences a transfer of ownership of a mortgage from one party to another.

Assignment of rents   An agreement between property owner and mortgagee specifically fixing the rights and obligations of each regarding rent transferred to a mortgagee if a mortgagor defaults.

Assignor   A person who transfers or assigns a right or property.

Assumption   A written agreement by one party to pay an obligation originally incurred by another.

Assumption fee   The fee paid to a lender (usually by the purchaser of real property) resulting from the assumption of an existing mortgage.

Assumption of mortgage   Agreement by a buyer to assume the liability under an existing note secured by a mortgage or deed of trust. The lender usually must approve the new debtor in order to release the existing debtor (usually the seller) from liability.

Attachment   A seizure of defendant's property by court order as security for any judgment a plaintiff may recover in a legal action.

Automatic guarantee   An approved mortgage lender can make a VA-guaranteed mortgage loan without any prior approval from the VA.

Balance sheet   A financial statement showing assets, liabilities, and the net worth as of a specific date.

Balloon mortgage   A mortgage with periodic installments of principal and interest that does not fully amortize the loan. The balance of the mortgage is due in a lump sum at the end of the term.

Balloon payment   The unpaid principal amount of a mortgage or other long-term loan due at a certain date in the future, usually the amount that must be paid in a lump sum at the end of the term.

Bankrupt   A person, firm, or corporation who, through a court proceeding, is relieved from the payment of all debts after the surrender of all assets to a court-appointed trustee.

Basis point   A basis point is 1/100 of 1 percent interest; thus, 50 basis points equals ½ of 1 percent.

Basis risk   The risk that the price of a hedge tool will not move as expected relative to the market value of a hedged loan.

Basket provision   A provision contained in the regulatory acts governing the investments of insurance companies, savings and loan associations, and mutual savings banks. It allows for a certain small percentage of total assets to be placed in investments not otherwise permitted by the regulatory acts.

Beneficiary   The person designated to receive the income from a trust estate or trust deed.

Bequeath   To transfer personal property by will.

Bill of sale   A document in writing that transfers title to personal property.

Binder, insurance   A written evidence of temporary hazard or title coverage that only runs for a limited time and must be replaced by a permanent policy.

Biweekly mortgage   A mortgage with payments due every two weeks totaling 26 payments a year.

Blanket mortgage   A lien on more than one parcel or unit of land frequently incurred by subdividers or developers who have purchased a single tract of land for the purpose of dividing it into smaller parcels for sale or development.

Blue Sky laws   State laws to regulate the sale of securities to avoid investments in fraudulent companies or high-risk investments without disclosure of the risks to the investor.

Bona fide   In good faith, without fraud.

Borrower   One who receives funds with the expressed or implied intention of repaying the loan in full.

Breach   Violation of a legal obligation.

Break-even point   In residential or commercial property, the figure at which occupancy income is equal to all required expenses and debt service.

Broker   The person who, for a commission or a fee, brings parties together and assists in negotiating contracts between them.

Building codes   Local regulations that control design, construction, and materials used in construction. Building codes are based on safety and health standards.

Bundle of rights   The total rights or interests a person has in property, for example, the exclusive right of an individual to own, possess, use, enjoy, and dispose of real property.

Buy-back   See *Pair-off*.

Buy-down mortgage   A mortgage made by a lender with a below-market interest rate in return for an interest rate subsidy in the form of money received from a builder, seller, or in some situations a home buyer.

Call provision   A clause in the mortgage or deed of trust giving the mortgagee or beneficiary the right to accelerate payment of the mortgage debt in full on a certain date or on the occurrence of specified conditions.

Cap   A limitation on the interest rate increase of either the periodic or lifetime rate or both for an adjustable-rate mortgage.

Capitalization   The process of converting into present value a series of anticipated future installments of net income by discounting them into a present worth using a specific desired rate of earnings.

Capitalization rate   The rate that is believed to represent the proper relationship between real property and the net income it produces.

Capital markets   Markets (including informal markets as well as organized markets and exchanges) where long-term loanable funds in the form of mortgages, stocks, and bonds are bought and sold.

Capital market security   Financial instrument, including both debt and equity securities, with maturities greater than one year. Those instruments with maturities of less than a year are traded in the money markets.

Cash delivery   The submission of a whole mortgage or a participation to an investor in exchange for cash rather than a mortgage-backed security.

Cash flow The income from an investment after gross income is subtracted from all operating expenses, loan payments, and the allowance for the income tax attributed to the income.

Certificate of eligibility A document used by the VA to certify a veteran's eligibility for a VA loan.

Certificate of occupancy Written authorization given by a local municipality that allows a newly completed or substantially completed structure to be inhabited.

Certificate of reasonable value (CRV) A document issued by the VA establishing maximum value and loan amount for a VA-guaranteed mortgage.

Certificate of title A statement furnished by an abstract or title company or an attorney to a client stating that the title to real estate is legally vested in the present owner.

Certified mortgage banker (CMB) A professional designation of the mortgage banking industry.

Chain of title The history of all the documents transferring title to a parcel of real property starting with the earliest existing document and ending with the most recent.

Chattel real All estates in real property less than fee estates, such as a lease.

Closing The conclusion or consummation of a transaction. In real estate closing includes the delivery of a deed, financial adjustments, the signing of notes, and the disbursement of funds necessary to the sale or loan transaction.

Closing costs Expenses incidental to a sale of real estate, such as loan fees, title fees, appraisal fees, and others.

Closing statement A financial disclosure accounting for all funds received and expected at the closing, including the escrow deposits for taxes, hazard insurance, and mortgage insurance for the escrow account.

Cloud on title Any conditions revealed by a title search that adversely affect the title to real estate. Usually they cannot be removed except by a quit claim deed, release, or court action.

Co-insurance A sharing of insurance risk between insurer and insured depending on the relation of the amount of the policy and a specified percentage of the actual value of the property insured at the time of loss.

Collateral   Any property pledged as security for a debt.

Collateralized mortgage obligation (CMO)   Issuer guarantees that a minimum repayment schedule will be met.

Collection   Procedure followed to bring the mortgage account current and to file the necessary notices to proceed with foreclosure when necessary.

Commercial loan   A mortgage loan on property that produces income.

Commercial paper   Short-term unsecured promissory notes of large firms sold to meet short-term capital needs.

Commission   An agent's fee for negotiating a real estate or loan transaction.

Commitment   A written promise to make or insure a loan for a specified amount and on specified terms.

Commitment fee   Any fee paid by a borrower to a lender for the lender's promise to lend money at a specified date in the future. The lender may or may not expect to fund the commitment.

Common law   An unwritten body of law based on general custom in England and used to an extent in the U.S.

Community property   In some western and southwestern states, a form of ownership under which property acquired during a marriage is presumed to be owned jointly unless acquired in such manner as to be legally considered as separate property of either spouse.

Comparables   Also "comps," an abbreviation for comparable properties used for comparative purposes in the appraisal process; facilities of approximately the same size and location with similar amenities; properties that have been recently sold, that have characteristics similar to property under consideration, thereby indicating the approximate fair market value of the subject property.

Compensating balance   A demand deposit usually required by a commercial bank as a condition for extending a line of credit or a bank loan.

Compound interest   Interest paid on original principal and on the accrued and unpaid interest that has accumulated.

Condemnation   The court proceedings for taking private property under the right of eminent domain for public use with just compensation to the owner.

Condominium   A form of ownership of real property. The owner receives title to a particular unit and a proportionate interest in certain common areas. A condominium generally defines each unit as a separately owned space to the interior surfaces of the perimeter walls, floor, and ceilings.

Conduit   An entity that issues mortgage-backed securities backed by mortgages that were originated by another, probably one or more of the traditional originators.

Constant   The percentage of the original loan paid in equal annual payments that provides for interest and principal reduction over the life of the loan.

Construction contract   An agreement between a general contractor and an owner-developer stating the specific duties the general contractor will perform according to blueprints and specifications at a stipulated price and terms of payment.

Construction loan   A short-term, interim loan for financing the cost of construction. The lender makes payments to the builder at periodic intervals as the work progresses.

Construction loan agreement   A written agreement between a lender and a builder or borrower in which the specific terms and conditions of a construction loan, including the schedule of payments, are spelled out.

Construction loan draw   The partial disbursement of the construction loan, based on the schedule of payments in the loan agreement. Also called *take-down*.

Contract   An oral or written agreement to do or not to do a certain thing.

Conventional loan   A mortgage loan neither insured by FHA nor guaranteed by VA.

Convertible mortgage   An adjustable-rate mortgage whereby the mortgagor can convert the mortgage to a fixed-rate mortgage during a predetermined time period.

Cooperative   A form of multiple ownership of real estate in which a corporation or business trust entity holds title to a property and grants the occupancy rights to particular apartments or units to shareholders by means of proprietary leases or similar arrangements.

Corporation   An artificial person created by law with certain rights, privileges, and duties of natural persons.

Correspondent   A mortgage banker who services mortgage loans as a representative or agent for the owner of the mortgage or investor. Also applies to the mortgage banker's role as originator of mortgage loans for an investor.

Co-signer   A person who signs a legal instrument and therefore becomes individually and jointly liable for repayment or performance of an obligation.

Cost approach   An appraisal technique used to establish value by estimating the cost to reproduce the improvement, allowing for depreciation, then adding in the fair market value of the land.

Cost of funds index   An index that is used to determine interest rate changes for some ARMs. It represents the weighted average cost of savings, borrowings, and advances of members of the 11th District of the Federal Home Loan Bank of San Francisco.

Coupon rate   The annual interest rate on a debt instrument. In mortgage lending, the term is used to describe the contract interest rate on the face of the note or bond. The interest rate of a security that will be less than the rate of the underlying mortgages. GNMA MBSs have a coupon which is 50 basis points less than the single-family mortgages in the pool.

Covenant   A legally enforceable promise or restriction in a mortgage. For example, the borrower may covenant to keep the property in good repair and adequately insured against fire and other casualties. The breach of a covenant in a mortgage usually creates a default as defined by the mortgage or deed of trust and can be the basis for foreclosure.

Credit report   A report to a prospective lender on the credit standing of a prospective borrower or tenant. Used to help determine creditworthiness.

Current-production loan   A newly originated loan. Compare with *Seasoned loan.*

Curtesy   The common law interest a husband had in the real estate owned by the wife at the time of her death.

Custodial account   A bank account that the servicer of a mortgage must establish to hold funds on behalf of the borrower and investor.

Custodian   Usually a commercial bank that holds for safekeeping mortgages and related documents backing an MBS. Custodian may be required to examine and certify documents.

Debenture   An unsecured debt instrument backed only by the general credit standing and earning capacity of the issuer.

Debt coverage ratio   The ratio of effective annual net income to annual debt service.

Debt service   The periodic payment of principal and interest earned on mortgage loans.

Deed   A written legal document that purports to transfer ownership of land from one party to another.

Deed in lieu   A deed given by a mortgagor to a mortgagee to satisfy a debt and avoid foreclosure.

Deed of reconveyance   The transfer of legal title from the trustee to the trustor (the borrower) after the trust deed debt is paid in full.

Deed restriction   A limitation placed in a deed limiting or restricting the use of real property.

Deed of trust   In some states it is the document used in place of a mortgage; a type of security instrument conveying title in trust to a third party covering a particular piece of property; used to secure the payment of a note; a conveyance of the title land to a trustee as collateral security for the payment of a debt with the condition that the trustee shall reconvey the title upon the payment of the debt, and with power of the trustee to sell the land and pay the debt in the event of a default on the part of the debtor.

Default   Breach or nonperformance of a clause in either a note or mortgage that, if not cured, could lead to foreclosure.

Default point   See *Break-even point.*

Defeasance clause   The clause in a mortgage that gives the mortgagor the right to redeem property upon the payment to the mortgagee of the obligation due.

Deficiency judgment   A court order to pay the balance owed on a loan if the proceeds from the sale of the security are insufficient to pay off the loan. Not allowed in all states.

Delinquency experience   The level of loans past due, expressed as a percentage of the total portfolio of loans. Most commonly, record keeping for delinquent loans is according to 30-, 60-, and 90-day intervals.

Delinquent   The status of a mortgage with a payment past due.

Delivery   The legal, final, and absolute transfer of a deed from seller to buyer in such a manner that it cannot be recalled by the seller; a necessary requisite to the transfer of title; in mortgage banking, the physical delivery of loan documents to an investor or agent in conformance with the commitment.

Demand note   A note that is due whenever the holder demands payment.

Department of Housing and Urban Development (HUD)   The department of the federal government that is responsible for administering government housing and urban development programs.

Deposit   A sum of money given to bind a sale of real estate, or a sum of money given to ensure payment, or an advance of funds in the processing of a loan. Also known as *earnest money*.

Depository Institutions Deregulation Committee (DIDC)   A committee established by the U.S. Congress in 1980 to oversee the orderly phasing out of interest rate ceilings in depository institutions.

Depreciation   A loss of value in real estate property brought about by age, physical deterioration, or functional or economic obsolescence. Broadly, a loss in value from any cause. The opposite of *appreciation*.

Developer   A person or entity who prepares raw land for building sites and sometimes builds on the sites.

Development loan   A loan made for the purpose of preparing raw land for the construction of one or more buildings. Development may include grading and installation of utilities and roadways. See *Construction loan.*

Direct reduction mortgage   An amortized mortgage with principal and interest paid at the same time and with interest calculated only on the remaining balance.

Disbursements   The payment of monies on a previously agreed-upon basis. Used to describe construction loan draws.

Discount   In loan obligations, a discount refers to an amount withheld from loan proceeds by a lender. In secondary market sales, a discount is the amount by which the sale price of a note is less than its face value. In both instances, the purpose of a discount is to adjust the yield upward, either in lieu of interest or in addition to interest. The rate or amount of discount depends on money market conditions, the credit of the borrower, and the rate and terms of the note.

Discount point   See *Point.*

Disintermediation   The flow of funds out of savings institutions into short-term investments in which interest rates are higher. This shift normally results in a net decrease in the amount of funds available for long-term real estate financing. Also, the market condition that exists when this shift occurs.

Dower   The rights of a widow to a life estate in the real property of her husband at his death. Not allowed in all states.

Down payment   Cash portion paid by a buyer from his own funds, as opposed to that portion of the purchase price that is financed.

Due-on-sale clause   A type of acceleration clause calling for a debt under a mortgage or deed of trust to be due in its entirety upon transfer of ownership of the secured property.

Earnest money   See *Deposit.*

Easement   Right or interest in the land of another entitling the holder to a specific limited use, privilege, or benefit such as laying a sewer, putting up electric power lines, or crossing the property.

Economic rent   The rent that a property would bring if offered in the open market at the fair rental value. Not necessarily the contract rent.

Economic value   The valuation of real property based on its earning capabilities.

Effective gross income (personal)   Normal annual income including overtime that is regular or guaranteed. It may be from more than one source. Salary is generally the principal source, but other income may qualify if it is significant and stable.

Effective rate   The actual rate of return to the investor. It may vary from the contract rate for a variety of reasons. Also called *yield.* See *Yield.*

Eminent domain   The right of a government to take private property for public use upon payment of its fair value. It is the basis for condemnation proceedings. See *Condemnation.*

Encroachment   An improvement that intrudes illegally upon another's property.

Encumbrance   Anything that affects or limits the fee simple title to property, such as mortgages, leases, easements, or restrictions.

Equal Credit Opportunity Act (ECOA)   ECOA is a federal law that requires lenders and other creditors to make credit equally available without discrimination based on race, color, religion, national origin, age, sex, marital status, receipt of income from public assistance programs or reliance on any consumer protection law. Also known as Regulation B.

Equity   In real estate, equity is the difference between fair market value and current indebtedness, usually referring to the owner's interest.

Equity participation   Partial ownership of income property, given by the owner to the lender as part of the consideration for making the loan.

Equity of redemption   The common law right to redeem property during the foreclosure period. In some states the mortgagor also has a statutory right to redeem property after a foreclosure sale.

Escalator clause   A clause providing for the upward or downward adjustment of rent payments to cover specified contingencies, such as the provision in a lease to provide for increases in property tax and operating expenses.

Escheat   The reversion of property to the state if the owner dies intestate and without heirs.

Escrow   A transaction in which a third party, acting as the agent for the buyer and the seller, carries out instructions of both and assumes the responsibilities of handling all the paperwork and disbursement of funds.

Escrow analysis   The periodic examination of escrow accounts to determine if current monthly deposits will provide sufficient funds to pay taxes, insurance, and other bills when due.

Escrow payment   That portion of a mortgagor's monthly payment held by the lender to pay for taxes, hazard insurance, mortgage insurance, lease payments, and other items as they become due. Known as impounds or reserves in some states.

Estate   The ownership interest of an individual in real property. The sum total of all the real and personal property owned by an individual at time of death.

Estoppel letter   A statement that in itself prevents its issuer from later asserting different facts.

Eviction   The lawful expulsion of an occupant from real property.

Exclusive listing   A written contract giving a licensed real estate agent the exclusive right to sell a property for a specified time but reserving the owner's right to sell the property alone without the payment of commission.

Exclusive right to sell   The same as exclusive listing, but the owner agrees to pay a full commission to the broker even though the owner may sell the property.

Executor   A person named in a will to administer an estate. The court will appoint an administrator if no executor is named. Executrix is the feminine form.

Face value   The value of notes, mortgages, etc., as stated on the face of the instrument and not considering any discounting.

Fair market value   The price at which property is transferred between a willing buyer and a willing seller, each of whom has a reasonable knowledge of all pertinent facts and neither of whom is under any compulsion to buy or sell.

Fallout   Loans that fail to close because the borrower decides not to take the loan (borrower fallout); also loans that fail to sell in the secondary market because an investor reneges on a commitment (investor fallout).

Fallout risk   The risk incurred by the lender that a borrower will not close on a loan after filing an application or that an investor will renege on a contract to purchase the loan.

Fannie Mae   See *Federal National Mortgage Association.*

Farmers Home Administration (FmHA)   An agency within the Department of Agriculture that operates principally under the Consolidated Farm and Rural Development Act of 1921 and Title V of the Housing Act of 1949. This agency provides financing to farmers and other qualified borrowers who are unable to obtain loans elsewhere. Funds are borrowed from the U.S. Treasury.

Federal Home Loan Mortgage Corporation (FHLMC)   A private corporation authorized by Congress to provide secondary mortgage market support for conventional mortgages. It also sells participation certificates secured by pools of conventional mortgage loans, their principal and interest guaranteed by the federal government through the FHLBB. Popularly known as Freddie Mac.

Federal Housing Administration (FHA)   A division of HUD. Its main activity is the insuring of residential mortgage loans made by private lenders. It sets standards for construction and underwriting. FHA does not lend money, or plan or construct housing.

Federal National Mortgage Association (FNMA)   A privately owned corporation created by Congress to support the secondary mortgage market. It purchases and sells residential mortgages insured by FHA or guaranteed by VA as well as conventional home mortgages; also issues mortgage-backed securities. Popularly known as Fannie Mae.

Fee option   An option allowing lenders to pay a one-time commitment fee in exchange for a reduction in Fannie Mae's required yield. Also called "fee/yield tradeoff."

Fee simple   An estate under which the owner is entitled to unrestricted powers to dispose of the property and that can be left by will or inherited; commonly, the greatest interest a person can have in real estate.

FHA mortgage   A mortgage that is insured by the Federal Housing Administration.

Fiduciary   A person in a position of trust and confidence for another.

Finance company   A limited-purpose financing entity organized and controlled by a builder for the purpose of facilitating the issuance of bonds.

Financial intermediary   A financial institution that acts as an intermediary between savers and borrowers by selling its own obligations or serving as a depository and in turn lending the accumulated funds to borrowers.

Financing package   The total of all financial interest in a project. It may include mortgages, partnerships, joint venture capital interests, stock ownership, or any financial arrangement used to carry a project to completion.

Financing statement   Under the Uniform Commercial Code this is a prescribed form filed by a lender with the registrar of deeds or secretary of state to perfect a security interest. It gives the name and address of the debtor and the secured party (lender) along with a description of the personal property securing the loan. It may show the amount of indebtedness.

Finder's fee   A fee or commission paid to a broker for obtaining a mortgage loan for a client or for referring a mortgage loan to a broker. It may also refer to a commission paid to a broker for locating a property.

Firm commitment   A lender's agreement to make a loan to a specific borrower of a specific property. An FHA or PMI agreement with a designated borrower to insure a loan on a specific property.

First mortgage   A mortgage having priority over all other voluntary liens against certain property.

Fixed-rate mortgage   A mortgage in which the interest rate does not change during the entire term of the loan.

Fixture   Personal property that becomes real property when attached in a permanent manner to real estate.

Float   The time between a lender's collection of payments from borrowers and the remittance of those funds to an investor.

FNMA   See *Federal National Mortgage Association.*

Forbearance   The act of refraining from taking legal action despite the fact that a mortgage is in arrears. It is usually granted only when a mortgagor makes a satisfactory arrangement by which the arrears will be paid at a future date.

Foreclosure   An authorized procedure taken by a mortgagee or lender under the terms of a mortgage or deed of trust for the purpose of having the property sold and the proceeds applied to the payment of a defaulted debt.

Forward delivery   The delivery of mortgages or mortgage-backed securities to satisfy cash or future market transactions of an earlier date.

Forward sale   An agreement in which a lender agrees to sell to an investor a specified amount of mortgages or securities at an agreed-upon price at a specified future date. A mandatory delivery commitment is a type of forward sale.

Freehold estate   An estate in real estate that could last forever.

Freddie Mac   See *Federal Home Loan Mortgage Corporation.*

Front-end money   Funds required to start a development and generally advanced by the developer or equity owner as a capital contribution to the project.

Funding   The disbursement of funds to complete a transaction. In mortgage finance, it occurs when the lender provides money to close a real estate sale and when an investor transfers funds to the lender to purchase a mortgage loan.

Futures contract   A contract purchased on an organized market (e.g., Chicago Board of Trade) either for the purchase of a GNMA certificate at a specified price on a specified future date or for the sale of the certificate at a specified future date.

Garnishment   A proceeding that applies specified monies, wages, or property to a debt or creditor by proper statutory process against a debtor.

GNMA-backed bond   A "mortgage-backed bond" using GNMA certificates as the collateral rather than the individual mortgages.

GNMA futures market   A regulated central market in which standardized contracts for the future delivery of GNMA securities are traded.

GNMA mortgage-backed securities   Securities guaranteed by GNMA that are issued by mortgage bankers, commercial banks, savings and loan associations, savings banks, and other institutions. The GNMA security holder is protected by the "full faith and credit of the U.S." GNMA securities are backed by FHA, VA, or FmHA mortgages.

GNMA II   Similar to GNMA certificates except that the mortgages within the pool may have interest rates that vary within 100 basis points.

Government National Mortgage Association (GNMA)   On September 1, 1968, Congress enacted legislation to partition FNMA into two continuing corporate entities. GNMA has assumed responsibility for the special assistance loan program and the management and liquidation function of the older FNMA. Also, GNMA administers the mortgage-backed securities program, which channels new sources of funds into residential financing through the sale of privately issued securities carrying a GNMA guaranty. Popularly known as Ginnie Mae.

Graduated-payment mortgage   Residential mortgage that has monthly mortgage payments that start at a low level and increase at a predetermined rate.

Grantee   The person to whom an interest in real property is conveyed.

Grantor   The person conveying an interest in real property.

Gross rent multiplier   A figure used to compare rental properties to determine value. It gives the relationship between the gross rental income and the sales price. Synonyms are gross multiplier and gross income multiplier.

Ground rent   The earnings of improved property allocated to the ground it-self after allowance is made for earnings of the improvement. Also, payment for the use of land in accordance with the terms of a ground lease.

Growing equity mortgage (GEM)   Residential mortgage that has monthly payments increasing according to an agreed-upon schedule. This increased payment reduces principal, allowing the loan to be paid off sooner than a traditional mortgage.

Guaranteed loan   A loan guaranteed by VA, FmHA, or any other interested party.

Guaranty fee   A guarantor's charge to lenders for guaranteeing to an investor the timely payment of principal and interest from all the mortgages underlying a Fannie Mae mortgage-backed security.

Hard money mortgage   A mortgage given in return for cash, rather than to secure a portion of the purchase price, as with a purchase money mortgage.

Hazard insurance   A contract whereby an insurer, for a premium, under-takes to compensate the insured for loss on a specific property due to certain hazards.

Hedging   In mortgage lending, the purchase or sale of mortgage futures con-tracts to offset cash market transactions to be made at a later date.

Highest and best use   The available present use or series of future uses that will produce the highest present property value and develop a site to its full economic potential.

Home Owners Loan Corporation (HOLC)   An agency formed in 1933 to help stabilize the economy. The HOLC issued government-guaranteed bonds to lenders for delinquent mortgages and then refinanced homeowner indebt-edness.

Homeowners policy   A multiple-peril policy commonly called a "package policy." It is available to owners of private dwellings and covers the dwelling and contents in the case of fire or wind damage, theft, liability for property damage, and personal liability.

Homestead estate   In some states, the home and property occupied by an owner are protected by law up to a certain amount from attachment and sale for the claims of creditors.

Housing expense-to-income ratio   The amount of a borrower's housing ex-penses expressed as a percentage of the borrower's income. One of the criteria used by lenders to calculate the risk involved in making a loan to a prospective borrower.

HUD   The Department of Housing and Urban Development. It is responsible for the implementation and administration of government housing and urban development programs. The broad range of programs includes community planning and development, housing production and mortgage credit (FHA), equal opportunity in housing, and research and technology.

Hypothecate   To give a thing as security without the necessity of giving up possession of it.

Impound   See *Escrow payment.*

Income approach to value   The appraisal technique used to estimate real property value by capitalizing net income. See *Capitalization.*

Income property   Real estate developed or improved to produce income.

Index   An economic measurement that is used to measure periodic interest rate adjustments for an adjustable-rate mortgage.

Installment   The regular periodic payment that a borrower agrees to make to the mortgagee.

Institutional lender   A financial institution that invests in mortgages carried in its own portfolio. Savings banks, life insurance companies, commercial banks, pension and trust funds, and savings and loan associations are examples.

Insurance   A contract for indemnification against loss.

Insured loan   A loan insured by FHA or a private mortgage insurance company.

Interest   Consideration in the form of money paid for the use of money, usually expressed as an annual percentage. Also, a right, share, or title in property.

Interest rate   The percentage of an amount of money that is paid for its use for a specified time. Usually expressed as an annual percentage.

Intermediate-term mortgage   A first mortgage with a term of less than 30 years.

Intestate   To die leaving no valid will.

Inventory The loans a lender has closed but has not yet delivered to an investor.

Investor The holder of a mortgage or the permanent lender for whom a mortgage lender services the loan. Any person or institution investing in mortgages.

Involuntary lien A lien imposed against property without consent of an owner. Examples include taxes, special assessments, federal income tax liens, mechanics liens, and materials liens.

Joint tenancy An equal undivided ownership of property by two or more persons whose survivors take the interest upon the death of any one of them.

Joint venture An association between two or more parties to own or develop real estate. It may take a variety of legal forms including partnership, tenancy in common, or a corporation. It is formed for a specific purpose and duration.

Judgment That which has been adjudicated, allowed, or decreed by a court.

Judgment lien A lien upon the property of a debtor resulting from the decree of a court.

Judicial foreclosure A type of foreclosure proceeding used in some states that is handled as a civil lawsuit and conducted entirely under auspices of a court.

Junior mortgage A lien subsequent to the claims of the holder of a prior (senior) mortgage.

Land contract A contract ordinarily used in connection with the sale of property in cases where the seller does not wish to convey title until all or a certain part of the purchase price is paid by the buyer. This financing vehicle is often used when property is sold on a small down payment.

Landlord Owner or lessor of real property.

LASER Fannie Mae's computerized delivery and reporting system for lenders.

Late charge An additional charge a borrower is required to pay as penalty for failure to pay a regular installment when due.

Lease   A written document containing the conditions under which the possession and use of real or personal property are given by the owner to another for a stated period and for a stated consideration.

Leaseback   See *Sale-leaseback*.

Leasehold   An interest in real property held by virtue of a lease.

Leasehold mortgage   A loan to a lessee secured by a leasehold interest in a property.

Legal description   A property description recognized by law that is sufficient to locate and identify the property without oral testimony.

Legal lists   A term describing investments that life insurance companies, mutual savings banks, or other regulated investors may make under a state charter or court order.

Lessee (tenant)   The person(s) holding rights of possession and use of property under terms of a lease.

Lessor (landlord)   The one leasing property to a lessee.

Leverage   The use of borrowed money to increase the return on a cash investment. For leverage to be profitable, the rate of return on the investment must be higher than the cost of the money borrowed (interest plus amortization).

Lien   A legal hold or claim of one person on the property of another as security for a debt or charge. The right given by law to satisfy a debt.

Limited partnership   A partnership that consists of one or more general partners who are fully liable and one or more limited partners who are liable only for the amount of their investment.

Line of credit   An agreement by a commercial bank or other financial institution to extend credit up to a certain amount for a certain time to a specific borrower.

Liquidating plan   A relief provision that allows borrowers to make additional payments to cure a delinquency.

Liquidity   Cash position based on assets that can readily be converted to cash.

Lis pendens A notice recorded in the official records of a county to indicate that there is a pending suit affecting the lands within that jurisdiction.

Loan A sum of money loaned at interest to be repaid.

Loan constant The yearly percentage of interest, which remains the same over the life of an amortized loan based on the monthly payment in relation to the principal originally loaned.

Loan submission A package of pertinent papers and documents regarding specific property or properties. It is delivered to a prospective lender for review and consideration for the purpose of making a mortgage loan.

Loan-to-value ratio (LTV) The relationship between the amount of the mortgage loan and the appraised value of the security expressed as a percentage of the appraised value.

Loss payable clause A clause in a fire insurance policy listing the priority of claims in the event of destruction of the property insured. Generally, a mortgagee, or beneficiary under a deed of trust, is the party appearing in the clause being paid the amount owed under the mortgage or deed of trust before the owner is paid.

MAI (Member, Appraisal Institute) The highest professional designation awarded by the American Institute of Real Estate Appraisers.

Mandatory delivery commitment An agreement that a lender will deliver loans or securities to an investor by a certain date at an agreed-upon price and yield. Compare with *Optional commitment.*

Margin The number of basis points a lender adds to an index to determine the interest rate of an adjustable-rate mortgage.

Marketable title A title that may not be completely clear but has only minor defects that a well-informed and prudent buyer of real estate would accept.

Market approach to value In appraising, the market value estimate is predicated upon actual prices paid in market transactions. It is a process of correlation and analysis of similar recently sold properties. The reliability of this technique is dependent upon the degree of comparability of each property with the subject property, the time of sale, the verification of the sale dates, the absence of unusual conditions affecting the sale, and the terms of the sale.

Market rent   The price a tenant pays a landlord for the use and occupancy of real property based upon current prices for comparable property.

Market value   The highest price that a buyer, willing but not compelled to buy, would pay, and the lowest a seller, willing but not compelled to sell, would accept.

Master agreement   A vehicle designed by an investor or insuror to help lenders deliver mortgages into standard and negotiated cash and MBS commitments. Also know as a "master commitment."

Master servicer   For MBSs, the master servicer is responsible for servicing and administering mortgage loans in a mortgage pool. This function may be contracted to the originator of each mortgage loan under the supervision of the master servicer.

Maturity   The terminating or due date of a note, time, draft, acceptance, bill of exchange, or bond. The date a time instrument or indebtedness becomes due and payable.

MBS   Mortgage-backed securities of all types.

Metes and bounds   A description in a deed of the land location in which the boundaries are defined by directions and distances.

Military indulgence   A relief provision that can be made available to a borrower who is in the military service.

Modification   The act of changing any of the terms of a mortgage.

Modified pass-through   A variation of the "pass-through security" that guarantees and pays the investor the scheduled monthly principal and interest payment, irrespective of what amounts are collected from the pool mortgages.

Moratorium   A period during which a borrower is granted the right to delay fulfillment of an obligation.

MORNET   Fannie Mae's communications network, which enables customers to use a data terminal, personal computer, or mainframe to send and receive documents and reports electronically.

Mortgage   A conveyance of an interest in real property given as security for the payment of a debt.

Mortgage-backed bonds   A "bond" or debt instrument that is backed by a pool of mortgages and for which the cash flow of the mortgages serves as the source of repayment.

Mortgage-backed securities   Bond-type investment securities representing an undivided interest in a pool of mortgages or trust deeds. Income from the underlying mortgage is used to pay off the securities. See *GNMA mortgage-backed securities.*

Mortgage banker   A firm or individual active in the field of mortgage banking. Mortgage bankers, as local representatives of regional or national institutional lenders, act as correspondents between lenders and borrowers. Mortgage bankers need to borrow the funds they lend out.

Mortgage banking   The packaging of mortgage loans secured by real property to be sold to a permanent investor with servicing retained for the life of the loan for a fee. The origination, sale, and servicing of mortgage loans by a firm or individual. The investor-correspondent system is the foundation of the mortgage banking industry.

Mortgage broker   A firm or individual bringing the borrower and lender together and receiving a commission. A mortgage broker does not retain servicing.

Mortgage company   A private corporation (sometimes called a mortgage banker) whose principal activity is the origination and servicing of mortgage loans that are sold to other financial institutions.

Mortgage discount   The difference between the principal amount of a mortgage and the amount for which it actually sells. Sometimes called points, loan brokerage fee, or new loan fee. The discount is computed on the amount of the loan, not the sale price.

Mortgagee   A person or firm to whom property is conveyed as security for a mortgage loan.

Mortgagee in possession   A mortgagee who, by virtue of a default under the terms of a mortgage, has obtained possession but not ownership of the property.

Mortgage insurance   The function of mortgage insurance (whether government or private) is to insure a mortgage lender against loss caused by a mortgagor's default. This insurance may cover a percentage of or virtually all of the mortgage loan depending on the type of mortgage insurance.

Mortgage insurance premium (MIP)   The consideration paid by a mortgagor for mortgage insurance either to FHA or a private mortgage insurance (PMI) company.

Mortgage life insurance   A type of term life insurance often bought by mortgagors. The amount of coverage decreases as the mortgage balance declines. In the event that the borrower dies while the policy is in force, the debt is automatically satisfied by insurance proceeds.

Mortgage note   A written promise to pay a sum of money at a stated interest rate during a specified term. It is secured by a mortgage.

Mortgage portfolio   The aggregate of mortgage loans held by an investor or serviced by a mortgage lender.

Mortgagor   One who borrows money, giving a mortgage or deed of trust on real property as security (a debtor).

Multifamily housing   Buildings with five or more residential units.

Mutual mortgage insurance fund   One of four FHA insurance funds into which all mortgage insurance premiums and other specified revenue of the FHA are paid and from which the losses are met.

Negative amortization   Also called deferred interest. A loan payment schedule that produces additions to principal, not a reduction, because the interest collected is insufficient to cover interest earned. The unpaid interest is added to the principal balance.

Negative cash flow   Cash expenditures of an income-producing property in excess of the cash receipts.

Negotiated transaction   A secondary market transaction in which the terms and conditions of a loan swap or sale are negotiated between the lender and an investor. Compare with *Standard commitment.*

Net income   The difference between effective gross income and expenses including taxes and insurance. The term is qualified as net income before depreciation and debt service.

Net worth   The value of all assets, including cash, less total liabilities. It is often used as an underwriting guideline to indicate an individual's creditworthiness and financial strength.

Net yield   The part of gross yield that remains after the deduction of all costs, such as servicing, and any reserves for losses.

Nondisturbance agreement   An agreement that permits a tenant under a lease to remain in possession despite any foreclosure.

Nonrecourse loan   A loan not allowing for a deficiency judgment. The lender's only recourse in the event of default is the security (property), and the borrower is not personally liable.

Nontraditional mortgage investors   Those investors, such as pension funds, traditionally had not invested in mortgages but instead looked to stocks and bonds.

Notice of default   A notice recorded after the occurrence of a default under a deed of trust or mortgage, or a notice required by an interested third party insuring or guaranteeing a loan.

Novation   The substitution of a new contract or obligation between the same or different parties. The substitution, by mutual agreement, of one debtor for another or one creditor for another whereby the existing debt is extinguished.

Obsolescence   The loss of value of a property occasioned by going out of style, by becoming less suitable for use, or by other economic influences.

Open-end mortgage   A mortgage with a provision that the outstanding loan amount may be increased upon mutual agreement of the lender and the borrower.

Option   A contract agreement granting a right to purchase, sell, or otherwise contract for the use of a property at a stated price during a stated period of time.

Optional commitment   A commitment that gives the lender the option to sell loans to an investor under specified terms. The lender pays a nonrefundable fee to obtain the commitment but, because delivery is not mandatory, suffers no penalty for not fulfilling the commitment. Compare with *Mandatory delivery commitment.*

Origination   The process of originating mortgages. Solicitation may be from individual borrowers, builders, or brokers.

Origination fee   A fee or charge for the work involved in the evaluation, preparation, and submission of a proposed mortgage loan.

Originator   A person who solicits builders, brokers, and others to obtain applications for mortgage loans. Origination is the process by which the mortgage lender brings into being a mortgage secured by real property.

Overcollateralization   Sufficient mortgages must be placed into a collateral pool so that their discounted value is sufficient to cover the bond, plus a reserve. Overcollateralization is usually defined as a percentage of the bond, such as 110 percent.

Package mortgage   A mortgage or deed of trust that includes items that are technically chattels, such as appliances, carpeting, and drapery.

Pair-off   A transaction whereby Fannie Mae allows a lender to "buy back" the mortgages it previously agreed to sell by means of a mandatory delivery commitment.

Par   The principal amount of a mortgage with no premium or discount.

Partially modified pass-through   A variation of the "pass-through security" that guarantees, to a certain extent, that monthly principal and interest payments will be made to the investor, even if not collected from the mortgage pool.

Partial payment   A payment that is less than the scheduled monthly mortgage payment.

Participation certificate (PC)   Mortgage-backed security issued by FHLMC that consists of mortgages purchased from eligible sellers. Called PC because seller retains some interest (5 or 10 percent) in the mortgages sold to FHLMC.

Participation loan   A mortgage made by one lender, known as the lead lender, in which one or more other lenders, known as participants, own a part interest, or a mortgage originated by two or more lenders.

Pass-through rate   The rate at which interest is paid to an investor for a mortgage. It is the lower of an investor's required yield or the mortgage interest rate after a minimum servicing fee has been deducted.

Pass-through security   A form of a "mortgage-backed bond" for which the monthly collections on the mortgage pool are "passed through" to the investor.

Pay-through security   A form of a "mortgage-backed bond" that is secured by a mortgage pool and for which the payment features closely resemble those of a "modified pass-through security." The bond is fully amortizing with scheduled principal and interest payments that closely track the scheduled collections on the collateral mortgage pool.

Personal property   Any property that is not real property.

Pipeline   The aggregate of loans in process for eventual sale in the secondary market. The term encompasses both loans that are in production and those that have been closed but have not yet been delivered to an investor.

PITI (principal, interest, taxes, and insurance)   The principal and interest payment on most loans is fixed for the term of the loan; the tax and insurance portion may be adjusted to reflect changes in taxes or insurance costs.

Planned-unit development (PUD)   A real estate project in which each unit owner has title to a residential lot and building and a nonexclusive easement on the common areas of the project.

Plans and specifications   Architectural and engineering drawings and specifications for construction of a building or project including a description of materials to be used and the manner in which they are to be applied.

Point   An amount equal to 1 percent of the principal amount of an investment or note. Loan discount points are a one-time charge assessed at closing by the lender to increase the yield on the mortgage loan to a competitive position with other types of investments.

Police power   That right by which the state or other government authority may take, condemn, destroy, impair the value, limit the use, or otherwise invade property rights. It must be affirmatively shown that the property was taken to protect the public health, public morals, public safety, or the general welfare.

Pool   A group of mortgages that back an issue of mortgage-backed securities. Also, the act of packaging loans with similar characteristics for sale in the secondary mortgage market.

Pool insurance   Pool insurance represents various forms of insurance that provide investors with additional safety by insuring against default by homeowners to a certain percent of initial principal amount.

Portfolio   Investments (including mortgages and mortgage securities) held by an individual or institution. In mortgage lending, the term variously refers to mortgages held by a lender prior to their sale in the secondary market, to

MBSs held by lenders for investment purposes, and to loans that a lender continues to service for investors.

Portfolio mortgage   A loan that an originator places in its portfolio or an investor purchases for cash and holds as an asset.

Preforeclosure sale   A procedure in which the borrower is allowed to sell a mortgaged property for an amount less than that which is owed on it in order to avoid a foreclosure.

Premium   The amount, often stated as a percentage, paid in addition to the face value of a note or bond.

Prepayment (recovery of principal)   Payment in full on a mortgage, due either to a sale of the property or to foreclosure and, in either case, before the loan has been fully amortized.

Prepayment assumption   A calculated guess of how a portfolio of single-family loans will perform over time, relative to the incidence of recoveries of principal. The assumption is expressed as a percentage of long-term FHA experience, or PSA.

Prepayment fee   A consideration paid to the mortgagee for the prepayment privilege. Also known as prepayment penalty or reinvestment fee.

Prepayment penalty   A fee charged a mortgagor who prepays a loan before it is due. Not allowed for FHA or VA loans.

Prepayment privilege   The right given a borrower to pay all or part of a debt prior to its maturity. The mortgagee cannot be compelled to accept any payment other than those originally agreed to.

Price risk   The risk that, because of a rise in the general level of interest rates, a loan will decrease in value between the time of commitment to originate and the time of commitment to sell.

Primary loan insurance   Type of insurance for loans with minimal down payments, usually less than 20 percent. Typically, provided by the Federal Housing Administration or private mortgage insurance companies.

Primary mortgage market   The market in which lenders originate mortgages by making direct loans to home buyers. See also *Secondary mortgage market.*

Principal   Amount of debt, not including interest. The face value of a note, mortgage, etc.

Principal balance   The outstanding balance of a mortgage, exclusive of interest and any other charges.

P&I (principal and interest)   That portion of a home buyer's monthly payments to the lender that composes the debt service on the mortgage. See also *T&I.*

Priority   As applied to claims against property, priority is the status of being prior or having precedence over other claims. Priority is usually established by filing or recordation in point of time but may be established by statute or agreement.

Private mortgage insurance (PMI)   Insurance written by a private company protecting the mortgage lender against loss occasioned by a mortgage default.

Processing   The steps taken to prepare a mortgage loan file for submission to an underwriter including ordering all verifications.

Product risk   The risk that the market value of a particular loan will not respond as expected to changes in the general level of interest rates.

Purchase money mortgage   A mortgage given by a mortgage lender to a purchaser of real property to finance the purchase of real estate.

Put option   A hedging tool that gives the lender the right, but not the obligation, to deliver a loan or security at a prearranged price.

Quality control   A system of safeguards to ensure that all loans are originated, processed, underwritten, closed, and serviced according to the lender's and an investor's standards.

Quit claim deed   A deed that transfers (with no warranty) only such interest, title, or right a grantor may have at the time the conveyance is executed.

Real Estate Investment Trust (REIT)   A financial intermediary that can own and hold mortgages on real estate and pass earnings from these assets on, free of income tax to the corporation, but taxable to shareholders.

Real Estate Mortgage Investment Conduit (REMIC).   A type of mortgage-backed security that allows for income to be taxed only to the holders of the instrument.

Real estate owned (REO) A term frequently used by lending institutions as applied to ownership of real property acquired for investment or as a result of foreclosure.

Real property Land appurtenances, including anything of a permanent nature such as structures, trees, minerals, and the interest, benefits, and inherent rights thereof.

Realtor A real estate broker or an associate holding active membership in a local real estate board affiliated with the National Association of Realtors.

Reconveyance The transfer of the title of land from one person to the immediately preceding owner. It is used when the performance of debt is satisfied under the terms of a deed of trust.

Record date The date that determines who is the holder of record entitled to receive payment of principal, interest, and any prepayment from the servicer or custodian.

Recorder The public official in a political subdivision who keeps records of transactions affecting real property in the area. Sometimes known as a registrar of deeds or county clerk.

Recording The noting in the registrar's office of the details of a properly executed legal document, such as a deed, mortgage, a satisfaction of mortgage, or an extension of mortgage, thereby making it a part of the public record.

Recourse The right of the holder of a note secured by a mortgage or deed of trust to look personally to the borrower or endorser for payment, not just to the property. In the secondary mortgage market, the forced repurchase of a defaulted mortgage by the seller.

Redemption period That period of time (in those states where it is allowed) in which a foreclosed mortgagor has to buy back his or her property by paying principal amount and interest and fees.

Redemption, right of The right allowed by law in some states whereby a mortgagor may buy back property by paying the amount owed on a foreclosed mortgage, including interest and fees.

Refinance (1) The renewing of an existing loan with the same borrower and lender; (2) a loan on the same property by either the same lender or borrower; (3) the selling of loans by the original lender.

Release of lien An instrument discharging secured property from a lien.

Relief provision   A formal arrangement designed to help a borrower resolve a *delinquency.*

Remainder   That part of an estate that remains after the termination of a prior estate.

Remittance options   See *Actual/actual, Scheduled/actual,* and *Scheduled/ scheduled.*

Rent   Consideration paid for use or occupancy of property, buildings, or dwelling units .

Reproduction cost   The money required to reproduce a building under current market conditions less an allowance for depreciation.

Required yield   An investor's required yield. It is quoted on a net basis— that is, it does not include the lender's servicing fee.

Rescission   The cancellation or annulment of a transaction or contract by the operation of law or by mutual consent.

Residence   A place where someone lives.

Residential balance provision   A provision that allows a lender to deliver an additional mortgage to Fannie Mae against a remaining balance of at least $1.00 on a mandatory delivery commitment.

Residential home mortgage   A mortgage covering a one- to four-family dwelling. Mortgages for larger residential buildings are classified as multi-family housing loans.

Residential Mortgage Credit Report   The more inclusive credit report required for mortgages sold into the secondary mortgage market. Verifies employment, address, and checks national repositories of credit.

RESPA   Real Estate Settlement Procedures Act.

Restrictive covenant   A clause in a deed limiting use of the property conveyed for a certain period of time.

Reverse price risk   Exposure to the risk of falling interest rates that occurs when a lender makes a commitment to sell a loan to an investor before making a loan commitment to the borrower. See also *Price risk.*

Reversion   A right to future possession retained by an owner at the time of a transfer of an owner's interest in real property.

Reversionary clause   A clause providing that any violations of restrictions will cause title to the property to revert to the party who imposed the restriction.

Right of survivorship   In joint tenancy, the right of survivors to acquire the interest of a deceased joint tenant.

Right-of-way   A privilege operating as an easement upon land, whereby a land owner, by grant or agreement, gives another the right to pass over land. See *Easement.*

Sale-leaseback   A technique in which a seller deeds property to a buyer for a consideration and the buyer simultaneously leases the property back to the seller, usually on a long-term basis.

Sales contract   Another name for a sales agreement, purchase agreement, etc. Not to be confused with a land contract, which is a conditional sales contract.

Satisfaction of mortgage   The recordable instrument given by the lender to evidence payment in full of the mortgage debt. Sometimes known as a release deed.

Savings and loan association   A mutual or stock association chartered and regulated by either the federal government or a state. S&Ls accept time deposits and lend funds primarily on residential real estate.

Scheduled/actual (S/A)   A type of remittance requiring the lender to remit to Fannie Mae the scheduled interest due (whether or not it is collected from borrowers) and the actual principal payments collected.

Scheduled/scheduled (S/S)   A type of remittance requiring the lender to remit to Fannie Mae the scheduled interest due and the scheduled principal due (whether or not payments are collected from borrowers).

Seasoned loan   A loan on which a borrower has made payments for more than one year, as compared to newly originated or current production loans. For some investors, a loan may require three years before it is considered "seasoned."

Secondary financing   Financing real estate with a loan or loans subordinate to a first mortgage or first trust deed.

Secondary mortgage market   A market where existing mortgages are bought and sold. It contrasts with the primary mortgage market, where mortgages are originated. See also *Primary mortgage market*.

Second mortgage   An additional mortgage placed on a property that has rights secondary to the first mortgage.

Secured party   The party holding a security interest or lien; on real estate referred to as the mortgagee.

Securities and Exchange Commission (SEC)   The federal agency that regulates securities and the securities business. It is involved in real estate and mortgage lending when MBSs are issued.

Securitization   The process of converting mortgages into mortgage-backed securities.

Security   The collateral given, deposited, or pledged to secure the fulfillment of an obligation or payment of a debt.

Security instrument   The mortgage or trust deed evidencing the pledge of real estate security as distinguished from the note or other credit instrument.

Security interest   According to the Uniform Commercial Code, security interest is a term designating the interest of the creditor in the property of the debtor in all types of credit transactions. It thus replaces such terms as chattel mortgage, pledge, trust receipt, chattel trust, equipment trust, conditional sale, and inventory lien. See *Financing statement*.

Seller/servicer   A term for an approved corporation that sells and services mortgages for either FNMA or FHLMC.

Servicing   The duties of the mortgage lender as a loan correspondent as specified in the servicing agreement for which a fee is received. The collection for an investor of payments, interest, principal, and trust items such as hazard insurance and taxes on a note by the borrower in accordance with the terms of the note. Servicing also consists of operational procedures covering accounting, bookkeeping, insurance, tax records, loan payment follow-up, delinquency loan follow-up, and loan analysis.

Servicing fee   The compensation a lender receives from an investor each month for servicing loans on its behalf.

Servicing released   Sale of the rights to service a loan when the loan is sold in the secondary market.

Servicing retained   Retention of the rights to service a loan when the loan is sold in the secondary market.

Settlement   See *Closing.*

Single-purpose issuer   An entity, such as a "finance company," whose single purpose is the accumulation of mortgages and the issuance and servicing of bonds.

Special hazard insurance   Special hazard insurance is a form of pool insurance that covers losses from such freaks of nature as earthquakes and floods. This insurance, typically 1 percent of the initial aggregate amount of the pool, is placed in a collateral pool as a whole.

Special limited obligation debt   Bonds issued by housing agency that are secured (as defined) only by the revenues and funds pledged in the specific indenture. Funds held by the agency for other programs or in general funds are not pledged for debt service.

Special warranty deed   A deed containing a covenant whereby the grantor agrees to protect the grantee against any claims arising during the grantor's period of ownership. Often used during probate.

Specific performance   A remedy in a court of equity compelling the defendant to carry out the terms of an agreement or contract.

Spread   The difference between the average rate at which money can be borrowed and the average rate at which it can be loaned.

Standard commitment   An agreement to sell or swap loans based on an investor's posted yields, rather than on negotiated terms.

Stand-by commitment   A commitment to purchase a loan or loans with specified terms; both parties understanding that delivery is not likely unless circumstances warrant. The commitment is issued for a fee with willingness to fund in the event that a permanent loan is not obtained. Such commitments are typically used to enable the borrower to obtain construction financing at a lower cost on the assumption that permanent financing of the project will be available on more favorable terms when the improvements are completed and the project is generating income.

Stand-by fee   The fee charged by an investor for a stand-by commitment. The fee is earned upon issuance and acceptance of the commitment.

State (moral obligation) pledge   A security device frequently used by state governments to enhance the marketability of revenue bond debt. The pledge requires that notification of a shortfall in a bond program's debt service (capital) reserve fund be sent formally to the governor of the state. It is intended that the shortfall be included in the governor's next budget message to the legislature. There are state-to-state variations in the use of the pledge; however, none except Idaho's are legally binding.

Statute of frauds   A state law requiring that certain contracts be in writing. In real estate, a contract for the sale of land must be in writing to be enforceable.

Statute of limitations   A law that limits the length of time in which a lawsuit must be commenced, or the right to sue is lost. It varies from state to state.

Straight bond   A form of a "mortgage-backed bond" that is required by a mortgage pool. The instrument is similar to corporate bonds, with scheduled periodic interest payments. Principal repayment is usually at the end of the bond term.

Subject to mortgage   When a purchaser buys subject to a mortgage but does not endorse the same or assume to pay the mortgage, a purchaser cannot be held for any deficiency if the mortgage is foreclosed and the property sold for an amount not sufficient to cover the note. See *Assumption of mortgage.*

Subordinate   To make subject to, or junior to.

Subordination   The act of a party acknowledging, by written recorded instrument, that a debt due is inferior to the interest of another in the same property. Subordination may apply not only to mortgages but to leases, real estate rights, and any other types of debt instruments.

Subrogation   The substitution of one person for another in reference to a debt claim or right.

Substitute sale   A hedging vehicle, such as a futures contract, in which a lender sells for future delivery something that the lender does not own.

Swap   The exchange of loans for mortgage-backed securities rather than cash.

Table funding   A financing technique that occurs when a broker closes a mortgage loan with funds belonging to an acquiring lender and immediately assigns the loan to that lender. This activity gives the mortgage broker the opportunity to say it is a direct lender since it can close loans with its own funds.

Takeout commitment A promise to make a loan at a future specified time. It is commonly used to designate a higher cost, shorter term, backup commitment as a support for construction financing until a suitable permanent loan can be secured.

Tax deed A deed on property purchased at public sale for nonpayment of taxes.

Tax lien A claim against property for the amount of its due and unpaid taxes.

Temporary indulgence A relief provision that allows the borrower additional time before more formal action is taken to cure a delinquency.

Tenancy A holding of real estate under any kind of right of title. Used alone, tenancy implies a holding under a lease.

Tenancy in common In law, the type of tenancy or estate created when real or personal property is granted, devised, or bequeathed to two or more persons in the absence of expressed words creating a joint tenancy. There is no right of survivorship. See *Joint tenancy*.

Tenancy by entirety The joint ownership of property by a husband and wife where both are viewed as one person under common law that provides for the right of survivorship.

Tenancy at will A holding of real estate that can be terminated at the will of either the lessor or the lessee, usually with notice.

Tenant One who is not the owner of, but occupies, real property under consent of the owner and in subordination to the owner's title. The tenant is entitled to exclusive possession, use, and enjoyment of the property, usually for a rent specified in the lease.

Term The period of time between the commencement date and termination date of a note, mortgage, legal document, or other contract.

Testate The estate or condition of leaving a will at death.

T & I (taxes and insurance) That portion of a home buyer's monthly payments to the lender that goes into an escrow fund to pay property taxes, the homeowner's insurance premiums, and mortgage insurance, if applicable.

Title   The evidence of the right to or ownership in property. In the case of real estate, the documentary evidence of ownership is the title deed, which specifies in whom the legal state is vested and the history of ownership and transfers. Title may be acquired through purchase, inheritance, devise, gift, eminent domain, adverse possession, or through foreclosure of a mortgage.

Title insurance policy   A contract by which the insurer, usually a title insurance company, agrees to pay the insured a specified amount for any loss caused by defects of title to real estate, wherein the insured has an interest as purchaser, mortgagee, or otherwise.

Total obligations-to-income ratio   The amount of a borrower's debt stated as a percentage of the borrower's total income. One of the criteria used by lenders to calculate the risk involved in making a loan to a prospective borrower.

Treasury index   An index that is commonly used to determine interest rate changes for ARM plans. The index is usually based on a yield adjusted to a constant maturity.

Trial balance   A report that gives the status of each mortgage in a servicer's portfolio.

Trust deed   The instrument given by a borrower (*trustor*) to a trustee vesting title to a property in the trustee as security for the borrower's fulfillment of an obligation. See *Deed of trust*.

Trustee   One who holds title to a real property under the terms of a deed of trust. With MBSs, the party responsible for determining whether all other parties are performing as contractually required to do.

Two-step mortgage   A type of ARM in which the interest rate can be adjusted only one time, usually after five or seven years, and then remains constant for the remaining term of the loan.

Underwriting   The analysis and matching of risk to an appropriate rate and term. The process of deciding whether to make a mortgage loan.

Unencumbered property   A property to which the title is free and clear.

Uniform Commercial Code (UCC)   A comprehensive law regulating commercial transactions. It has been adopted, with modification, by all states.

Usury   Charging more for the use of money than allowed by law.

Vacancy factor   A percentage rate expressing the loss from gross rental income due to vacancy and collection losses.

VA Certificate of Reasonable Value   The VA issues a Certificate of Reasonable Value at a specific figure, agreeing to guarantee a mortgage loan to an eligible qualified veteran buyer upon completion and sale of the house. The veteran must be aware of the VA's appraised value of the property.

Valuation   See *Appraisal.*

VA mortgage   A mortgage that is guaranteed by the Department of Veterans Affairs.

Variable-rate mortgage   A mortgage agreement that allows for adjustment of the interest rate in keeping with a fluctuating market and terms agreed upon in the note.

Vendee   The party to whom personal or real property is sold.

Veterans Affairs, Department of (VA)   The Servicemen's Readjustment Act of 1944 authorized this agency to administer a variety of benefit programs designed to facilitate the adjustment of returning veterans to civilian life. The VA home loan guaranty program is designed to encourage lenders to offer long-term, low down payment mortgages to eligible veterans by guaranteeing the lender against loss.

Warehousing   The holding of a mortgage on a short-term basis pending either a sale to an investor or other long-term financing. These mortgages may be used as collateral security with a bank to borrow additional funds. A builder "warehouses" mortgages when he or she takes back a mortgage from a home buyer and holds the mortgage for a time period.

Warranty deed   A deed in which the grantor or seller warrants or guarantees that good title is being conveyed, as opposed to a quit claim deed that contains no representation or warranty as to the quality of title being conveyed.

Waste   Damage to real estate by neglect or other cause.

Whole loan   The entire mortgage loan package representing 100 percent ownership and not individual ownership as in a mortgage pool.

Will   A written document providing for the distribution of property at death.

Yield   In real estate, the effective annual amount of income that is being accrued on an investment. Expressed as a percentage of the price originally paid.

Yield to maturity   A percent returned each year to the lender on actual funds borrowed considering that the loan will be paid in full at the end of maturity.

Zoning   The act of city or county authorities specifying the type of use to which property may be put in specific areas. See *Restrictive covenant.*

INDEX

A

B

N

O

P

Q

R

W